Fascist Modernism in Italy

Fascist Modernism in Italy

Arts and Regimes

Francesca Billiani

BLOOMSBURY ACADEMIC
LONDON • NEW YORK • OXFORD • NEW DELHI • SYDNEY

BLOOMSBURY ACADEMIC
Bloomsbury Publishing Plc
50 Bedford Square, London, WC1B 3DP, UK
1385 Broadway, New York, NY 10018, USA
29 Earlsfort Terrace, Dublin 2, Ireland

BLOOMSBURY, BLOOMSBURY ACADEMIC and the Diana logo
are trademarks of Bloomsbury Publishing Plc

First published in Great Britain 2021
This paperback edition published by Bloomsbury Academic in 2023

Cover design by Adriana Brioso

Cover image: Italian interior by architects C. E. Rava and S. Larco', 1930.
From The Studio Volume 99. (© Print Collector/Getty Images)

A catalogue record for this book is available from the British Library.

A catalog record for this book is available from the Library of Congress.

ISBN: HB: 978-1-7845-3523-0
PB: 978-0-7556-4207-6
ePDF: 978-1-7883-1759-7
ePub: 978-1-7883-1758-0

Typeset by Integra Software Services Pvt. Ltd.

To find out more about our authors and books visit
www.bloomsbury.com and sign up for our newsletters.

Per Γεώργιος
Per Harvey

Contents

Figures

Acknowledgements

Obvious as it might seem, I should like to state that this book has been in the making for much more time than I believed it was possible. Putting an end to it was more of a wilful decision than a deliberate act. Therefore, I would like to start by thanking Tomasz Hoskins and the editorial team at I.B. Tauris/Bloomsbury for their patience with me over the years as well as the anonymous readers of the proposal and manuscript.

I would also like to acknowledge the support of the Arts and Humanities Research Centre and that of the School of Arts, Languages and Cultures at the University of Manchester for allowing me the necessary time and space to complete the manuscript. Stephen Hutchings has taught me the importance of 'rigorous inventiveness', a notion I have subscribed to unequivocally. Many other recognitions are in order. To all my colleagues and friends who have read earlier drafts: Erica Baffelli, Ruth Chester, Chiara Costa, Roberta Mazza, Maddalena Mazzocut-Mis, Mila Milani, Laura Moure Cecchini, Monica Jansen, Laura Pennacchietti, Loredana Polezzi, Andrea Pollio, Katherine Powlesland, Philipp Rössner, Gerardo Serra, Alvise Sforza-Tarabochia, Gigliola Sulis. My gratefulness goes to many other friends and colleagues who have supported me in this project in Manchester and abroad; and it is not only a long list but a truly interdisciplinary one. I have many other intellectual debts, more than I will ever be able to pay off. But one in particular. The 2018 exhibition at the Fondazione Prada about the arts during the Fascist period, curated by Germano Celant, was a turning point in my journey because it showed how the arts function as intersecting fields, and thus provided reassurance about the direction my work had taken.

This is why I am especially grateful to those of you who were prepared to listen even when I did not make much sense at all. You have given me the strength to keep going even when I felt that this particular mountain was far too high to climb. Susanna De Gaudenzi and Fabio Detto have given me the opportunity of 'practising' research in one of the Milanese homes this book discusses. In a similar vein, I would also like to express my gratitude to my students. Over the years, they have patiently listened to my lectures when I have often formulated some of the points which are now part of the book. My second-year course on the aesthetics and politics of Fascism has truly been a constant source of inspiration and dialogue.

Chiara Berrani, Phil Bradbury, Silvia Colombo, Anna Lanfranchi, Gianmarco Mancosu, Louise Lever and Laura Pennacchietti have contributed to the creation of the website/database which stores much of the material discussed in this book. I should like to thank the staff at several institutions in Italy: Museo d'Arte Moderna e Contemporanea di Trento e Rovereto, MART; the Triennale in Milan; the Fondazione Prada; the Quadriennale in Rome. I have presented this project at various conferences and seminars in Italy, France, the UK and the USA, and thank all who have taken the trouble of organizing such events, and especially to my Milan-based contingency of friends and colleagues.

Adriana e Enrico, *grazie*. Vince made sure I finished this book – I am grateful. And thank you Georgios for your best efforts at not keeping me sane.

Prologue

Fascist Modernism in Italy explores the highly charged interactions between aesthetics and politics during a totalitarian regime, the Italian Fascist regime, which styled itself as modern and intended to modernize the public sphere. From literature to the visual arts, to photography, to advertising, to architecture – the latter possibly the regime's most powerful weapon in this regard – what was to be achieved was not simply a plurality of artistic expressions under the overarching concept of State art but rather a system of the arts: one that had the potential of becoming identical with the regimes of State art or that of the arts of the fascist era, or both.

Our central hypothesis is that the arts as a system proved foundational in shaping totalitarian practices, by producing a repertoire of images, designs, concepts and tropes – often displayed in public buildings (stadia, post offices, for example) – capable of formulating new expressions of modern and collective subjectivities within a modernized society and to develop utopian views about new civilizations, for example through urban developments.[1]

This book has two principal objectives. One is to claim that to make sense of the relationship between arts and politics it is imperative to engage with a view of 'the arts' as a series of diverse but interconnecting fields rather than discrete entities, and outside rigid taxonomies such as autonomy or heteronomy, modern and traditional, elitist or popular, pluralist or monistic, under the regime or within the regime. For we believe that the system of the arts should not be seen as an assemblage of separate parts operating simultaneously. Rather only by seeing the wavering fields of the arts as interrelated phenomena – as a system – can we try to understand how artistic production itself responded to the regime's will to use the arts in building a totalitarian State. Broadly speaking, within the changing conception of State art, the arts as a system converged towards aesthetic paradigms that were consistent with concepts of construction, rationalism and realism, whilst by means of patronage and of legislation the regime was creating a widespread State-supported structure of exhibitions – one that was sufficiently robust as to sustain dynamically artists and the circulation of their artworks.

The other is to demonstrate the crucial role that the arts as system played in representing the identity of the Italian totalitarian regime both by visualizing to

---

[1] For further examples, see Mabel Berezin, *Making the Fascist Self: The Political Culture of Interwar Italy* (Ithaca, NY, Cornell UP, 1997) and Simonetta Falasca-Zamponi, *Fascist Spectacle: The Aesthetics of Power in Mussolini's Italy* (Berkeley, CA, University of California Press, 2000). On this point, see the analysis in Monica Cioli, *Il fascismo e la 'sua' arte* (Florence, L. S. Olschki, 2011), 169–81; and Sileno Salvagnini, *Il sistema delle arti in Italia 1919–1943* (Bologna, Minerva Soluzioni Editoriali, 2011), 354–63.

varying degrees its myth-making machines and by contributing to the planning of its projects to modernize the country's infrastructures. The system of the arts in interwar Italy was a theoretical and practical way of making the arts converge towards State art, as we see in the debates in leading journals on State art (*Critica fascista*, as well as more specialized ones dedicated to the arts) or on new architecture or on the new modern national novel. The arts often assumed reactionary as well as progressive overtones, whilst acting in concert to give shape to the totalitarian project, as we can observe in mural paintings, in late State-sponsored competitions such as the Premio Bergamo and Cremona, or later architectural styles looking back at the Roman empire for inspiration.[2] In all, the system of the arts functioned like an incomplete jigsaw: a model that could, notwithstanding, find within itself the dialectical propulsive force to overcome the regime as repression and standardization – as we will discuss, for example, in the sections dedicated to the case of youth culture or in the late Corrente movement.

We have privileged a mode of analysis that rejected rigid chronological categories and rather explored shared conceptual markers in the artefacts under scrutiny. This book ranges widely, just like we were walking thought an art exhibition, in order both to give a comprehensive view of the arts as a system and to highlight the contradictions and paradoxes of such artistic regimes. Yet, to achieve its two main aims, it pauses on those artistic forms and cultural events that have most clearly evidenced interconnectivity, and on those artefacts or aesthetic theories that were more directly engaged in the dialectical struggle between arts and politics, and which thereby have clarified their contribution to State art.

Selecting the most illustrative artworks for this argument has been challenging. The book's corpus comprises of a set of modern novels by Corrado Alvaro, Alberto Moravia and Mario Soldati spanning different artistic styles but all united by the drive towards experimental realism; of artworks by Corrado Cagli and Mario Sironi especially conceived as Public art, and by a long list of futurists – Benedetta Cappa, Fortunato Depero, Fillìa, Vinicio Paladini, Enrico Prampolini, Pippo Rizzo and the aeropaniters because all these were expressions of how the avant-gardes attempted to become the official State art. Similarly, we analysed several architectural projects by Giuseppe de Finetti, Giovanni Muzio amongst the Novecentists, the Gruppo 7, Luigi Figini and Gino Pollini, Giuseppe Terragni, Alberto Sartoris within the modern and rationalist ranks and Angiolo Mazzoni for the futurists, all selected because over less than two decades they embodied different theoretical and practical applications of the art of building, which was deemed to be the art that could help the most the regime in modernizing the public sphere. And finally, we concentrate on sculptures by Bruno Munari, Mino Rosso, Thayaht, Adolfo Wildt and on photography by impresario Anton Giulio Bragaglia to illustrate some pivotal aesthetic shifts in the process of theorizing the arts' contribution to the cultural life of and under the regime.

---

[2] Matthew Affron and Mark Antliff (eds), 'Introduction', *Fascist Visions: Art and Ideology in France and Italy* (Princeton, NJ, Princeton UP, 1997), 3–24.

You, Readers. This is a political history of the arts and an artistic history of their politics. If interested in understanding how the arts have dialogued with the Fascist regime, you might read this book as a reflection on the contribution the aesthetic regimes made to the political ones; if interested in the political nature of the Fascist regime, you might find insights on the singular importance of the arts in shaping any given political project.

Parode

Autonomy and Heteronomy: Regimes

The 1920s and 1930s were decades notorious for intense artistic ferment as well as for political turmoil in Italy as elsewhere in Europe, and possibly in Germany and Russia above all.[1] Italy had its dictatorship, but what makes the 1920s and 1930s exceptional in Rome, as in Moscow and Berlin, is the way in which this period foregrounds a relationship of interconnectedness between aesthetics and politics, which called into question the relationship between autonomy and heteronomy of the artworks.

As Theodor Adorno suggested in posthumous *Aesthetic Theory* (1970) – his text that singled out abstracticism as the epitome of autonomous bourgeois art because of its detachment from its historical context – the aesthetic is implicated in the historical no less than in the political because 'Art is autonomous and it is not; without what is heterogeneous to it, its autonomy eludes it'.[2] Autonomy can be described as an independent, stand-alone practice that assumes a separation between two or more given spheres and which is characterized by a divide between art and the life-praxis of the bourgeoisie, or indeed between art and the structure of production of bourgeois society. Heteronomy, by contrast, is the condition according to which one is subject to an external law, and thus possesses no capacity nor suitable placement for acting independently, and therefore must refer to the rules of circulation and to the institutions that determine them. Art cannot be defined either in a discourse of simple self-identification, nor of autonomy, nor of heteronomy: the arts, their artefacts and their associated theorizations are formed and shaped in specific historical and cultural contexts – while seeking to make meaning beyond these boundaries. Still, in the framework of a cultural analysis of the arts under a totalitarian regime, Adorno's position might be fruitful but it cannot be exhaustive. We do not uphold the notion of an autonomous art that is distinct from a committed and heteronomous art: the avant-garde and realism are not in an oppositional dichotomy. Or, to return to Adorno's dialectics of negativity: the work of art is a field of tensions moving in

[1] Elena Pontiggia, 'Una stagione neo-romantica. Pittura e scultura a Milano negli anni Trenta', in Nicoletta Colombo and Elena Pontiggia (eds), *Milano anni trenta. L'arte e la città* (Milan, Mazzotta, 2005), 9.
[2] Adorno, *Aesthetic Theory*, Robert Hullot-Kentor (ed.) (London, Continuum, 2002), 8. Neil Lazarus, 'Modernism and Modernity: T. W. Adorno and White South African Literature', *Cultural Critique*, 5 (Winter 1986–7), 139.

different directions without producing any synthesis that can resolve a correlation between art and nature, or art and mimesis, since 'by its difference from empirical reality the artwork necessarily constitutes itself in relation to what it is not, and to what makes it an artwork in the first place'.[3] The artwork is defined by a negative dialectical relationship with reality, according to the German philosopher, whereby truth and untruth can be done and undone. By claiming the subjectivity of the aesthetics, Adorno does not renounce society; rather he disclaims that the artworks are monads because they act as forces which shape a field and as objective facts in themselves. The artworks are therefore linked to reality but not by a relationship of exclusivity. In this respect, Adorno quotes the example of romantic art which cannot 'simply ignore the compulsion towards objectivation. It degrades what objectively refuses synthesis to something that is disconnected'.[4] Similarly, Adorno's concept of the dialectics of aesthetics sees rationalization and mimesis as conflicting tendencies within the same artwork. In other words, Adorno does not advocate absolute forms of autonomy or heteronomy for the artworks but permutations of such negative dialectical relations.

To evade such a theoretical impasse, it is equally important to reflect on the interconnectedness between aesthetics and politics, as Jacques Rancière has explained in *Le Partage du sensible. Esthétique et politique* (2000).[5] The act of 'partage' is a process by which a system of self-evident facts reveals something in common between its parts as well as their delimitations. Such mapping is based on the distribution of spaces, times and forms of activity, and thus explains how these paradigms interest or create oppositions between each other. In other words, 'a history of aesthetic politics, understood in this sense, has to take into account the way in which these major forms stand in opposition to one another or intermingle'.[6] Naturally, aesthetic and political regimes can even clash or be out of synchronization with each other, since 'the important thing is that the question of the relationship between aesthetics and politics be raised at this level, the level of the sensible delimitation of what is common to the community, the forms of its visibility and of its organisation'.[7] The distribution therefore accounts for both forms of inclusion and exclusion in so far as they are all organized around a system of facts.

Consistent with Rancière and Adorno, our initial and guiding line of argument in this book is that the domains of politics and art are never autonomous or separate from one another but, to account for the complexities of cultural systems, one needs to take the argument further. Rancière uses the expression regime of art to illustrate how artworks are done or made, how they are rendered visible and conceptualized. A regime is not defined by its temporal dimension either: rather, a regime is a series of propositions, which map and organize the arts in relation to other practices. More specifically, in the aesthetic realm, there are three different forms of partition which

---

[3]   Adorno, *Aesthetic Theory*, 9 and 53–4.

[4]   Ibid., 252.

[5]   Jacques Rancière, *The Politics of Aesthetics: The Distribution of the Sensible* (London, Bloomsbury, 2013), 8–11 and passim.

[6]   Ibid., 12.

[7]   Ibid., 13.

correspond to doing, visualizing and conceptualizing: and in turn to the ethical regime of images, the representative regime of arts and the aesthetic regime of arts. The ethical regime is the reproduction of images to educate the public, the representative regime organizes the arts according to their forms, genres, subject matters, and the aesthetic regime isolates the arts from both the infrastructures that produce it and the axioms which classify it.

These three regimes working collectively allow us to speak of the arts as forms of production, ways of disclosing them to the public; as well as of their theoretical conceptualizations. In our study, however, these three regimes are in action throughout. For we explain the relationship between aesthetics and politics and their mutual existence in view of the infrastructures that support artistic production, the ways in which art circulates and is distributed to assorted audiences according to genres and aesthetic paradigms, and finally of how aesthetic meaning comes into being in its own right.

Realism is the main paradigm hailed by the Fascist regime as chief to its idea of State art. Indeed, realism is a way of normalizing conflict under the false pretence of a putative natural order of things the political sphere supports to elect itself to such status. By claiming that everyone is an equal, politics is the process that disputes that such partitions of the real are the outcome of nature and rather reveals their artificiality. Politics is ultimately a way of deciding, parting, what is to be acceptable as logos and what has to remain unheard as speech. Such an assertion is obviously invalidated during a dictatorship because politics happens when an entity challenges the naturalness of its position within the sensible. Only equality can guarantee politics as a means of making everyone heard, a civic right a repressive political regime naturally denies to its citizens, acting according to the logic of what Rancière describes as police. Therefore, dissensus can make the sensible not seem natural. The arts can engage in such a practice of dissensus in order to make the natural seem unnatural to varying degrees but they are always connected with politics.

In this way, Rancière stated, we are confronted with the existence of two aesthetic modes: *devenir vie de l'art* and *la forme resistante*.[8] In the first case, the aesthetic experience tends to dissolve into life; in the second, the form of resistance, the political potential of the aesthetic experience is generated autonomously from the real. Autonomy and heteronomy as separate are no longer conceivable. Art exists as art, autonomously, because art exists as a political subject, which exists in its own right, heteronomously. This is the indeterminable paradox of the regimes of the arts.

Having said that, by reformulating Adorno's position on autonomy and heteronomy in terms of regimes and interconnectivity, Rancière's theoretical apparatus aptly supports a study not only about the ways in which the aesthetic and the political spheres intersect, but about how such intersections contributed to the shaping of the totalitarian apparatus (as for example in our study of the avant-gardes). Moreover, it explains why a chronological approach to our subject matter is less fruitful than a thematic one to account for the working mechanisms of the system of the arts under the overarching policing mechanisms of the State. Accordingly, we endorse the

---

[8] Ibid., 15–25.

multilayered notion of regimes as an heuristic tool because they elude the limitations imposed by specific styles or periods. By articulating a specific relationship between words, vision and affect, each regime allows for an analysis of the varied practices which are acting simultaneously at any given time and to account for the relationships between the arts themselves, their subjects and subject matters, and the ways in which they dialogue with their audiences (including the Fascist regime).

In his recent analysis of what should be classified as 'social art' in *Aisthesis: Scenes from the Aesthetic Regime of Art* (2013), Rancierè engages with themes that were already central in the political and cultural scenarios of the 1920s and 1930s.[9] He observes that '[t]he "politics" of social art are to be found [...] in the refusal of art's own distinction, and thus also of the distinctions between the noble and non-noble arts'.[10] The Fascist regime concentrated its efforts on shaping a certain type of mass art by emphasizing the existing distinction between the popular and the elitist. This stance clashed with previous policies in this sector by earlier liberal regimes such as that of Giolittian Italy, which had invested significantly less in the development of the infrastructures supporting the arts (see Agon 2 for a discussion of the support of public exhibitions).[11] What was the regime's aim when it decided to invest in the arts? On the one hand, cultural agents and the creative industries were potentially strong political allies, instrumental in the survival of the dictatorship, which gave them visibility in return.[12] On the other, the dictatorship imposed a crucial turn on the arts by calling for a return to realism, morality and rationalization of forms in line with the forging of cultural politics which overtly aimed at constructing a political, social and cultural subject capable of thinking and acting differently from the subject envisaged by the political and economic configuration of liberalism. We see these, for example, in our discussion of the artists' participation to State-supported exhibitions or in the development of a national novel following the guiding principles of State art in Agons 2 and 1 respectively.

The aesthetic regimes, then, had to be given the same importance as the political ones in order to better comprehend the reasons behind the existence of the regime for twenty years, as art historians including Michele Dantini, Fernando Tempesti, Emily Braun and Mario de Micheli have demonstrated in their work. Drawing on Italian historian Mario Isenghi's analysis of the role of the image for propaganda purposes, Laura Malvano has paved the way with her early conceptualization of the politics of visual cultures and the discourses that sustained the political apparatus of the regime, from its inception right up to its fall. In her 1988 *Fascismo e politica dell'immagine*, Malvano introduced the concept of eclecticism in the choices of the regime, as an answer to contingent needs, rather than a rigidly designed project. She argued that it was vital to renounce the dichotomies that split artworks into polarizing categories –

---

[9] Jacques Rancière, *Aisthesis: Scenes from the Aesthetic Regime of Art* (London, Verso, 2013), 135.

[10] Ibid.

[11] Gentile, *Il culto del Littorio. La sacralizzazione della politica nell'Italia fascista* (Rome-Bari, Laterza, 2009), 161.

[12] With reference to pluralism as the main line in the regime's cultural policies, see Marla Stone, *The Patron State: Culture and Politics in Fascist Italy* (Princeton, NJ, Princeton UP, 1998), 5; Salvagnini, *Il sistema delle arti* and Giovanni Sedita, *Gli intellettuali di Mussolini. La cultura finanziata dal fascismo* (Florence, Le Lettere, 2010).

'elite and popular' cultures, or 'experimental and propagandistic' – to show how images produced historically bounded meaning when confronted with a political agenda – something we too have sought to achieve in this book.[13] In his most recent book, *Arte e politica* (2018), Dantini, in particular, has identified a gap in the existing literature, writing that 'an historical-artistic study of "political liturgy" in Italian art is only available in a fragmentary fashion, with the sole exception of the explorative and brilliant *Fascismo e politica dell'immagine* by Laura Malvano, dated 1988'.[14] If the task of covering in great detail such a vast panorama in a monograph is daunting, Malvano's work – albeit in a different format – offers a powerful methodological model to follow.

What is State art then? The term 'State art' has always been used in relation to the Italian dictatorship, but not to the Soviet Union and Nazi Germany, where 'totalitarian art' or 'degenerate art' have been the preferred terms.[15] Is this terminology useful? Or should we instead be referring to Regime art, or simply art of the fascist period; plural, repressive, experimental, totalitarian, eclectic, modern, reactionary?

Igor Golomstock's seminal account of totalitarian art is a prime example of an articulation of an analysis of the arts and politics on a transnational and comparative basis: totalitarian art, for Golomstock, was a powerful means of education for the masses, as Mussolini had declared on the tenth anniversary of the Fascist rule in his statement about the desire to unite culture and public life.[16] Wide-ranging in its coverage and despite the somehow cursory nature of some of its more specific observations, Golomstock's study helps us to ground the aesthetic within the political in order to understand better the intricacies and intersections across different embodiments of totalitarian art and, crucially, their inscription within the political agenda of four anti-liberal and totalitarian regimes. Golomstock also makes it clear that the theme of his book is not 'art under totalitarian regimes', but rather 'totalitarian art', thereby ascribing an ideological value to the whole artistic production selected for analysis.[17]

Our subject is different because we have not selected artworks which can be univocally classified: this is a study not only of totalitarian art, but a study of how the arts under the Fascist regime contributed to the totalitarian project, either autonomously or heteronomously, or both.[18] For instance, this point is particularly

---

[13] *Fascismo e politica dell'immagine* (Turin, Bollati e Boringhieri, 1988) and Emily Braun, *Mario Sironi and Italian Modernism: Arts and Politics under Fascism* (Cambridge, Cambridge UP, 2000).

[14] *Arte e politica in Italia. Tra fascismo e Repubblica* (Rome, Donzelli, 2018), 3. See also Antonello Negri, Silvia Bignami, Paolo Rusconi, Giorgio Zanchetti and Susanna Ragionieri (eds), *Anni Trenta. Arti in Italia oltre il fascismo* (Florence, Giunti Editore, 2012).

[15] Boris Groys, *The Total Art of Stalinism: Avant-Garde, Aesthetic Dictatorship and Beyond* (London, Verso, 2011).

[16] Igor Golomstock, *Totalitarian Art: In the Soviet Union, the Third Reich, Fascist Italy and The People's Republic of China* (London, Collins Harvill, 1990), 115.

[17] Ibid., xv.

[18] We have not included in our exposition a discussion of the relationship between the political power of the Church and that of the regime, or indeed of art defined as sacred, because this topic would require a different set of hypotheses and theoretical frameworks to be dealt with exhaustively. On these points, we refer for example to Monica Jansen and Luca Somigli's recent work 'The "necessary modernization" of Sacred Art: A "double vision" on Modernism and Modernity', in MDRN (eds), *Time and Temporality in Literary Modernism* (1900–1950) (Leuven/Paris/Bristol, Peeters 2016), 125–36.

evident if we take into consideration the decidedly focused study by Emily Braun of the controversial figure of Mario Sironi.[19] Reflecting on her monograph on Sironi, and on his consequent critical rehabilitation, Braun claimed that she did not want to write a 'conventional art historical monograph but an artistic and political biography that interprets Sironi's vast and diverse oeuvre in light of his ideological convictions'; that is, not only about his support of the regime but rather about his decision of using the arts to create its visual languages and mythologies. Braun is not accepting the art of Sironi as totalitarian art, not even when explicitly in favour of the regime, because she looks at the whole spectrum of Sironi's artistic production in such a way as to baffle stifling categorizations.

The configuration of Italian cultural politics during the dictatorship enabled scholars to speak of aesthetic 'pluralism', a definition which has been widely accepted. On the theme of the complexity of the organizational structure of the regime, Marla Stone's *The Patron State* has spelled out the idea of aesthetic pluralism as one of the main drivers in the relationship between the arts and politics. 'The seemingly inconsistent appearance of Fascist patronage reveals an evolving cultural politics shaped by conflicting factors', she wrote, whilst identifying futurism as a particular case in point of such 'tolerant' pluralism.[20] Such a definition could, in principle, account for (and vindicate) the relative tolerance of the regime towards a plethora of aesthetic paradigms under the umbrella of State art but not for the intersections between different artistic trends, movements and artworks, or the shape the arts assumed when conceived as a system often responding to the changes and demands of its infrastructures, as this book is seeking out to explore. Pluralism over the race for hegemony can be taken as a 'pan-category' element that encompasses everything – and its opposite – without ever reaching a conclusive amalgamation. The oppositions of, for example, futurism versus Novecentismo, the Premio Bergamo versus the Premio Cremona, *Strapaese* versus *Stracittà* are rather inconclusive categorizations to be applied to the scrutiny of the relationship between the arts and loci of power, since the latter is not oppositional in nature. One could argue that the fascist system of the arts and the fascist system *qua* system borrow eclectically one from the other without ever essentializing their practices, since every choice was functional to a specific application within a given context determined by the idea of State art.

We propose an analysis that prioritizes intersections across the three regimes we have discussed at the beginning because it can tease out in a nuanced manner the connections between the different arts, their areas of overlap and their progressive repositioning in relation to the equally changeable political apparatus. The arts cannot be simply placed either under or within the aegis of the regime, pluralistically or not, since they often functioned precisely across the notions of autonomy and heteronomy in reaction to the changes taking place at the level of the infrastructures; the arts functioned as a system of facts which partitioned the sensible and were articulated

---

[19] De Micheli, *Le circostanze dell'arte* (Genoa, Marietti, 1987) and *L'arte sotto le dittature* (Milan, Feltrinelli, 2009).

[20] Stone, *The Patron State*, 5.

according to the logics of their aesthetic regimes. By understanding the arts as a system and not as discreet fields, we hope to draw productive conclusions, and to design, with precision and from different angles, the features of the Italian artistic landscape over the twenty-year period of fascist rule.

Modern Subjectivities: Liberalism vs Fascism

Emilio Gentile has described totalitarianism as an experiment with an unknown outcome, and we have similarly followed the trajectory of 'experimentation' over a pre-configured and conclusive definition of what constitutes a totalitarian regime.[21] Gentile's view is that the regime's determination to shape a political religion around its own doctrine must be read as the primary way forward to achieve modernity, since such a vision resulted from a deep-seated crisis in the modern or bourgeois man. Such a man, having lost all faith in traditional religion, required a political religion of mass scale which could elevate the cult of nation to that of a deity.[22] The examples we offer throughout this book, and especially in the case of the new modern Italian novel (Agon 1), engage precisely with this last point: how did the arts contribute to enhancing this kind of modernity project that wanted to fuse the individual with the national, in line with myths and dogmas shaped by a political theology?

In *Fascist Modernism in Italy*, and drawing on some of the key concepts outlined above as particularly apposite for explaining the arts and politics nexus, we endorse an encompassing idea of modernity defined by Alain Touraine as '*relation, chargée de tensions, de la Raison et du Sujet, de la rationalisation et de la subjectivation, de l'esprit de la Renaissance et de celui de la Réforme, de la science et de la liberté*'.[23] Touraine's relational definition encapsulates the insoluble tensions that motivated the drive for modernity during the regime, especially within the artistic sphere since it accounts for the link between subjectivity and objectivity, individuality and collectivity, tradition and modernity itself according to the idea of a systematic order which mirrors the relationship the arts had with the regime. Moreover, such a definition also accounts for both the existence of new forms of participation of the citizen within the social sphere and a call for aesthetic rationalization as a way of representing forms of social transformation through the arts' modernity.

Luisa Mangoni's book on intellectuals at the end of the nineteenth century, Albertina Vittoria's study of 1930s cultural and intellectual debate and Mario Isenghi's definition of 'militant intellectuals and official intellectuals' are all key moments in the historiography of Fascism as a whole because they have underscored the discursive patterns shaping the regime's cultural policies and have moved the scholarly barometer from politics to culture, by foregrounding cultural modernity as a recurring topos in

---

[21] Emilio Gentile, 'Fascism as Political Religion', *Journal of Contemporary History*, 25 (1990), 229–51 and Gentile, *Il culto del Littorio*, 161.

[22] Gentile, *Il culto del Littorio*, 23–6, 108.

[23] Alain Touraine, *Critique de la modernité* (Paris, Fayard, 1992), 15.

political and aesthetic declarations.[24] Other scholars of the regime have focused on the question of modernity in general and of fascist modernity in particular: Walter Adamson and Ruth Ben-Ghiat, for instance, offer examples of skilful dissection from different viewpoints. Adamson's work on Florence has been exemplary in teasing out the manifold connections between early twentieth-century Florentine culture and the multiple cultural roots converging on and responding to Fascism and to its claims about modernity.[25] Ruth Ben-Ghiat's *Fascist Modernities*, too, puts the issue of modernity at the very forefront of its argument. If there was not one single ideological drive for the regime and for the cultural front it envisioned, the arts were nonetheless made to connect by means of a complex system of patronage within a political and ideological grand plan; one that aspired to build a national culture, a new youth culture and to craft closer bonds with the intelligentsia so as 'to create a new ruling elite that would perpetrate their models of modernity'.[26]

Modernity always echoes, and in the interwar years means, modernization. The modernization project of the regime concerned itself primarily with the public sphere and with its transformation, through well-established factors including secularization, science and technology, industrialization and urbanization, social and geographical mobility and the development of mass culture. Modernization was, firstly, an imperative that produced practical changes through reforms and interventions within the public space and legislations; and, secondly, it was embedded within a projection of trust in the regime. Such trust was subsequently to be elicited in crowds via a repertoire of images and codes, especially those manifested in the Public art frequently used to decorate functional public space, from post offices to official buildings and the 'new towns'. Aesthetically, such changes were often, but not exclusively, realized through simplified or rationalized codes and languages which defied figurative representation but which could nonetheless convey the myths and the mythology of the regime as civic religion, as for example in the case of avant-garde art (Agon 4). In our conceptualization of their role in shaping the contribution of the arts to the totalitarian project, modernity and modernization simply cannot be put asunder, or uncoupled, since they address not an individual subjectivity but a collective social body. The New Man/Woman with whom the arts were in dialogue was no longer the political subject of liberalism nor that of the total realism of the USSR,

[24] Mario Isenghi, *Intellettuali militanti e intellettuali funzionari* (Turin, Einaudi, 1979) and 'Per la storia delle istituzioni culturali fasciste', *Belfagor*, 30/3 (1975), 249–75; Albertina Vittoria, *Le riviste del duce* (Turin, Guanda, 1983) and Maria Luisa Mangoni, *L'interventismo della cultura: intellettuali e riviste del fascismo* (Rome-Bari, Laterza, 1974). And more recently Alessandra Tarquini, *Storia della cultura fascista* (Bologna, il Mulino, 2016), 42–3. Pier Giorgio Zunino's ground-breaking, *L'ideologia del fascismo* (Bologna, il Mulino, 1985) was a forerunner of a new historiographical approach to the study of the ideologies of the regime.

[25] Walter Adamson, *Avant-garde Florence: From Modernism to Fascism* (Cambridge, MA, Harvard UP, 1993); 'The Culture of Italian Fascism and the Fascist Crisis of Modernity: The Case of *Il Selvaggio*', *Journal of Contemporary History*, 30/4 (1995), 555–75 and the more recent *Embattled Avant-Gardes: Modernism's Resistance to Commodity Culture in Europe* (Berkeley, CA, University of California Press, 2009).

[26] Ruth Ben-Ghiat, *Fascist Modernities: Italy, 1922–1945* (Berkeley, CA, University of California Press, 2001), 13.

but rather a collective formation shaped through a process of political sacralization, led by a totalitarian regime that entailed rituals, shared myths and beliefs and that was supported by the arts functioning as a system.

Considering the practical operations involved in the construction of State art and its apparatuses, and deploying large volumes of archival evidence, for example, Sileno Salvagnini's *Il sistema delle arti* has illustrated how the modernization project was engineered in his comprehensive and detailed investigation of the ways in which the arts as institutions were organized as a system, and of how they functioned in mutual interdependence during the Ventennio. Salvagnini moves skilfully between diverse fields of interventions in the arts by the regime, from highly institutionalized interventions like State-sponsored exhibitions, to exhibitions in the private sphere of proprietary art galleries; and also, appreciably, to those supporting the decisions agents and artists took in their own right and that were motivated by an aesthetic enjoyment of the work of art without being contained by stifling theoretical paradigms. By allowing historical data to be foregrounded, Salvagnini's inductive picture confirms that we can read the relationship between the arts and politics as synergic moments, geared towards a political design, as well as decisions driven by artistic passions and beliefs, and the importance of an analysis which does not limit itself to a few case studies to support complex arguments.[27] In a similar vein, Monica Cioli's work on futurism does consider the broad picture – the arts as system – and does not limit her critical appreciation to futurism's efforts to prevail. By covering an impressive amount of detail Cioli paints an exhaustive picture of how futurism sought to attain a position as official State art, against other movements, most notably the Novecento movement. Cioli's argument about the longevity of futurism takes as its starting point the ability of Marinetti's movement to converge with Fascism around some common interests, such as modernity and modernization, and popular culture, in a way that no other artistic movement of the period was able to accomplish or implement.[28]

In accord with these scholars, we have privileged the idea of the aesthetic economy of the arts to clarify long-standing critical assumptions such as those about modernity and modernization we have outlined: how were exhibitions arranged, which were the public declarations voiced by agents in the field and the international visibility achieved by certain movements, and how did they develop cogent programmes to navigate the political landscape sketched by the dictatorship?

---

[27] Similarly, Massimo De Sabbata's monograph on the history of the Venice Biennale during the regime and of the exhibitions of the 1920s is a historical tour de force that offers essential information to anyone attempting to navigate the period and to anyone interested in looking at how the regime constructed its network of influence and patronage, see *Tra diplomazia e arte. Le Biennali di Antonio Maraini (1928-1942)* (Udine, Forum, 2006) and *Mostre d'arte a Milano negli anni Venti: dalle origini del Novecento alle prime mostre sindacali, 1920-1929* (Turin, Allemandi, 2012).

[28] *Il fascismo e la 'sua' arte; Anche noi macchine! Avanguardie artistiche e politica europea (1900–1930)* (Rome, Carocci, 2018) and Monica Cioli, Maurizio Ricciardi and Pierangelo Schiera (eds), *Traces of Modernity. Art and Politics from the First War to Totalitarianism* (Frankfurt/New York, Campus Verlag, 2019).

Historicizing Spectacles

The last question to debate then in what follows is: how do we situate the arts in relationship to other models of social activity and particularly, in this instance, within the social and political life of Italy during the Fascist regime? In the 1982 edited volume, *Annitrenta*, the art critic Vittorio Fagone brought together a number of established critics and art historians, seeking to map a field in which many important works by individual artists and movements could find key elements of unification that would demonstrate their salience as contributions to a collective endeavour and not simply as discrete moments of reflection.[29]

The consistent interest towards the arts as humanities in the 1920s, 1930s and 1940s has also been strongly evidenced in the many international exhibitions staged since the turn of the millennium. This revival has included shows such as *Arte italiana. Presenze 1900–1945*, curated by Pontus Hulten and Germano Celant at the Palazzo Grassi in Venice in 1989; *Milano anni trenta: L'arte e la città*, by Elena Pontiggia and Nicoletta Colombo at the Spazio Oberdan in Milan in 2004–5; and *Gli anni Trenta: Le arti in Italia oltre il fascismo*, curated by Antonello Negri, Silvia Bignami, Paolo Rusconi and Giorgio Zanchetti at the Palazzo Strozzi in Florence in 2012–3.[30] In 2009, *Futurism 1909–2009: Velocita+Arte+Azione* opened at the Royal Palace in Milan, curated by Ada Masoero and Giovanni Lista; and in 2014, Vivien Greene's *Italian Futurism, 1909–1944: Reconstructing the Universe* premiered at the Guggenheim Museum in New York.[31] These are some of the most renowned exhibitions ever staged, and there has been a further surge of interest in the last years of the second decade of the twenty-first century. 2018 saw not only Celant's aforementioned exhibition at the Fondazione Prada, whose six-hundred-plus artworks sparked lively debate, but also smaller shows including one taking Sarfatti as its subject at the Museo del Novecento in Milan and the MART in Rovereto, and another on Sironi, entitled *Mario Sironi: Dal Futurismo al Classicismo* at the Galleria Harry Bertoia in Pordenone, both igniting interest in this contested cultural and artistic heritage.[32] Again in 2018, the Fondazione Massimo e Sonia Cirulli supported an important exhibition curated by Jeffrey Schnapp and Silvia Evangelisti entitled *Universo Futurista*; and in 2019, an exhibition dedicated to aeropainter Tullio Crali, entitled *Crali e il Futurismo. Avanguardia Culturale* at

---

[29] Vittorio Fagone, 'Arte, politica e propaganda', in AA.VV., *Annitrenta: arte e cultura in Italia* (Milan, Mazzotta, 1982), 43.

[30] Germano Celant and Pontus Hulten (eds), *Arte italiana. Presenze 1900–1945* (Milan, Bompiani, 1989). Nicoletta Colombo and Elena Pontiggia (eds), *Milano anni trenta. L'arte e la città*; Antonello Negri, Silvia Bignami, Paolo Rusconi, Giorgio Zanchetti and Susanna Ragionieri (eds), *Anni Trenta*.

[31] Giovanni Lista and Ada Masoero, *Futurismo, 1909–2009. Velocità+Arte+Azione* (Milan, Skira, 2009) and Vivien Greene (ed.), *Italian Futurism 1909–1944: Reconstructing the Universe* (New York, The Solomon R. Guggenheim Museum, 2014).

[32] Germano Celant (ed.), *Post Zang Tumb Tuuum. Art Life Politics Italia 1918–1943* (Milan, Fondazione Prada, 2018); Fabio Benzi (ed.), *Dal Futurismo al Classicismo 1913–1924* (Cinisello Balsamo, Silvana Editoriale, 2018); and Daniela Ferrari (ed.), *Margherita Sarfatti. Il Novecento italiano nel mondo* (Milan, Electa, 2018).

the Galleria Comunale d'Arte Contemporanea in Monfalcone.[33] Three additional salient shows were held in 2019: one in Pisa at the Palazzo Blu dedicated to futurism, curated by Ada Masoero; and another at the Galleria Nazionale d'Arte Moderna e Contemporanea in Rome focusing on the friendship between niche poetry publisher Vanni Scheiwiller and sculptors Adolfo Wildt and Fausto Melotti.[34] On display from 4 March to 17 April 2020 at the Casa Italiana Zerilli-Marimò New York University, the exhibition *PROPAGANDA. The Art of Political Indoctrination in Italy, 1902–1950* curated by Nicola Lucchi featured works belonging to the Fondazione Cirulli and was a further moment of reflection on the unbreakable connections between arts and power around the very same notion of propaganda the show is trying to deconstruct.[35] Propaganda is something perhaps this book has tried to circumvent by privileging the idea of the system of the arts. Moreover, this last exhibition stretched the chronological boundaries to the pre- and post-fascist years in order to problematize how propaganda was not something exclusive to anti-democratic regime, thereby raising legitimate questions still to be answered.

Taken as a whole, these initiatives are noteworthy for many good reasons relating to scholarship, but it also cannot be underestimated how important such events are for introducing wider audiences to the arts and for the relentless work carried out by the creative industries, private and public ones, to preserve our shared cultural heritage worldwide. Not only do such exhibitions pay testament to the resilience of artists and movements to thrive under and during a repressive political regime, they are the testimony of an exceptional *longue durée* achieved through the establishment of an evolving relationship between those aesthetics of politics and the politics of aesthetics we are going to discuss at length in what will follow.

Agons

The book is divided into five Agons. Each Agon is subdivided into subsections with headings borrowed from futurist plays. Dissonances indicate subsections which show the seemingly contradictory meanings of the artworks under scrutiny; syntheses cover scholarly debates relevant to each part; theatre of objects sections offer an analysis of one or more artefacts; fusions deal with the historical settings of a particular artistic junction; and hypotheses illustrate theoretical stances key to the understanding of the artistic, literary and architectural movements discussed.

---

[33] Silvia Evangelisti and Jeffrey Schnapp (eds), *Universo Futurista* (San Lazzaro Savena, Fondazione Cirulli, 2019) and Marino de Grassi (ed.), *Crali e il futurismo. Avanguardia culturale* (Gorizia, Edizioni della laguna, 2019).

[34] Ada Masoero (ed.), *Futurismo* (Pisa, Fondazione Palazzo Blu, 2020), http://www.futurismopisa.it; Giuseppe Appella, Laura Novati, Carlo Bertelli and Paolo Mauri (eds), *Vanni Scheiwiller e l'arte da Wildt a Melotti* (Cinisello Balsamo, Silvana Editoriale, 2019).

[35] *Propaganda: The Art of Political Indoctrination*, http://www.casaitaliananyu.org/newsroom/propaganda-art-political-indoctrination.

In Agon 1 we look at debates on State art, on realism in the novel and at the representation of subjectivity in selected artworks. Our principal hypothesis as far as State art is concerned is that all parties in question (artists, politicians, patrons, agents, gallerists, publishers) shared the common ambition of formulating an alternative aesthetic system to that of liberal Italy geared towards artistic prose in literature, for example, along various declinations of realism coupled with a strong moral imperative. Such system simultaneously entailed a redefinition of the relationship between modernity and modernization and a shift of the fixed parameters of objectivity towards a more socially and morally aware artistic production. Both stances aimed at addressing those putative collective subjectivities predicated by the anthropological revolution promoted by the regime. To illustrate the application of those theoretical principles we will analyse novels by Alberto Moravia, Mario Soldati, Corrado Alvaro as well as some artworks by early Mario Sironi.

In Agon 2, we focus on those works that render more visible the anthropological shift that began in the mid-1930s towards the E42 and the Corrente movement. Murals, sculpture and public architecture were other expressions of this same aesthetic reconfiguration insofar as they made visible the relationship between the individual, the collective and the political message that such artworks transmitted through their experimental aesthetic syntax, and which ultimately sought to create new social mythologies consistent with the ideology of the regime. How did Public art contribute to the anthropological revolution? What was its lexicon? We explore such themes and answer these questions by reconstructing the history of public institutions supporting the arts. Specifically we pose to discuss the Palermo and La Spezia post offices, the mural paintings at the V Triennale and at the E42 and, finally, the return to realism with the Corrente movement and the Premio Bergamo and Cremona.

In Agon 3 we centre on architecture. Our analysis of the architectural landscape of 1920s and 1930s Italy follows a trajectory from individual to collective presence within the public domain, and concentrates on two main conceptual and empirical spaces: the spatial construction of the New Man/Woman's urban reality and the processes of compositional rationalization, which helped to configure the collective spectacle orchestrated by the regime aesthetically. Therefore we ask, what was the political function of architecture and how did such a function translate into aesthetic experiments? How did architecture fuse theory with empirical, lived reality to build spaces for the individual made collective? By renewing and simplifying the aesthetic rules of construction, architecture would be able to work towards a new social understanding of the living space of the individual and of the social space of the collective, as in the works of Luigi Figini and Gino Pollini, Giovanni Muzio, Giuseppe de Finetti, Giuseppe Terragni, and in the plans for new towns and neighbourhoods.

In Agon 4, we move onto the analysis of the role played by the avant-gardes within the space delineated by State art with particular reference to futurism and abstracticism. We test our hypothesis about the avant-gardes' heterodox involvement in and contribution to the State art project by analysing a series of debates which centre on their political role of vis à vis their aesthetic manifestos. Therefore, to what extent did the aesthetic autonomy of the avant-gardes gain a political signification in the race for supremacy in State art? By retelling the history of futurism and abstracticism from the point of view of their intersecting aesthetic and political agenda and that of their public life through exhibitions, we explore such intersections in the works by Fillìa, Prampolini, Thayaht, Munari and Carlo Belli. Finally, the last Agon uses the example of futurist aeropainting well into the final years of the regime to fuse together the lines of argument the book has drawn together in a seemingly coherent whole.

A Note on Sources

The primary sources for these books were mainly the artefacts listed in the corpus. The research has also taken place in archives in Italy. Namely, the Archivio del '900 (MART), held at the Museo d'Arte Moderna e Contemporanea di Rovereto e Trento, in Rovereto, the Triennale and Quadriennale historical archives in Milan and Rome, the Archivio Fondazione Piero Portaluppi, the Fondo Bardi and the Archivio Giuseppe Rivolta at the Archivio Storico Civico in Milan, the Fondo Anceschi at the Biblioteca dell'Archiginnasio in Bologna, and the Archivio Centrale dello Stato in Rome.

Agon 1: Realism and Fascist State Art

Dissonances: Geographies

'The Enlightenment is totalitarian', Adorno and Horkheimer wrote to discuss how reason enters into a state of crisis and paralysis, when used not to engage with nature but only to supress instinct as well as to repress myths, by replacing them with positivistic knowledge.[1]

During the 1920s and 1930s, the anti-liberal regimes based in Rome, Berlin and Moscow created political and ideological apparatuses for the control of individuals and citizens within the private and public spheres, seeking total control, mass consensus, social modernization and the constitution of the New Man/Woman as the foundation of a modern collective identity. Yet – crucially – they did so in different fashions when it came to the contested matter of State art.[2] As performed in Rome in particular the creation of State art was not guided by an ad hoc official legislation issued by the regime, nor did it stay unchanged throughout the Ventennio.[3] On the one hand, State art was a

---

[1] Theodor Adorno and Max Horkheimer, *Dialectic of Enlightenment: Philosophical Fragments* (Stanford, Stanford UP), 18. For two recent critiques and revaluations of Adorno and Horkheimer philosophical work in relation to the 1930s dictatorships, cf. Stefan Breuer, 'The Truth of Modern Society? Critical Theory and Fascism', *New German Critique*, 131/44, no. 2 (August 2017), 75–103 and Jeffrey Herf, 'Dialectic of Enlightenment Reconsidered', *New German Critique*, 117/39, no. 3 (Fall 2012), 81–9.

[2] For some seminal and wide-ranging interventions on art and totalitarianisms, see Golomstock, *Totalitarian Art*; Mikkel Bolt Rasmussen and Jacob Wamberg (eds), *Totalitarian Art and Modernity* (Aarhus, Aarhus UP, 2010) for a critique of Golomstock's comparative analysis, 125–26; and Groys, *The Total Art of Stalinism*. For the Italian case, see Mario Isnenghi, 'Per la storia delle istituzioni culturali fasciste', *Belfagor*, 30/3 (1975), 249–75; Fernando Tempesti, *Arte dell'Italia fascista* (Milan, Feltrinelli, 1976); Vittorio Fagone, 'Arte, politica e propaganda', in AA.VV., *Annitrenta*, 43–52; Rossana Bossaglia and Howard Rodger MacLean, 'The Iconography of the Italian Novecento in the European Context/L'iconografia del Novecento italiano nel contesto europeo', *The Journal of Decorative and Propaganda Arts*, 3 (1987), 52–65; Malvano, *Fascismo e politica dell'immagine*; Adamson, *Avant-garde Florence*; Alessandro Del Puppo, 'Da Soffici a Bottai. Una introduzione alla politica fascista delle arti in Italia', *Revista de História da Arte e Arqueologia*, 2 (1995-6), 192–204; Marino Biondi and Alessandro Borsotti (eds), *Cultura e fascismo. Letteratura e spettacolo di un Ventennio* (Florence, Ponte delle Grazie, 1996); Stone, *The Patron State*; Braun, *Mario Sironi*; Salvagnini, *Il sistema delle arti*; Ben-Ghiat, *Fascist Modernities*; Davide Lacagnina (ed.), *Immagini e forme del potere. Arte, critica e istituzioni in Italia fra le due guerre* (Palermo, Edizioni di Passaggio, 2011); Cioli, *Il fascismo e la 'sua' arte*; Alessandra Tarquini, *Storia della cultura fascista* and Dantini, *Arte e politica in Italia*.

[3] For a comprehensive overview of the legislations about the arts, see Vincenzo Cazzato (ed.), *Istituzioni politiche e culturali in Italia negli anni Trenta*, vol. 1 (Rome, Istituto poligrafico e zecca dello Stato, 2001).

theoretical formulation *in fieri* for finding a way of legitimizing the role played by the arts in shaping the totalitarian project; and, on the other, it was a practical means of defining a privileged mode for the arts themselves to exist independently from, as well as in response to, such political configuration.[4]

At least until the mid-to-late 1930s, the theoretical debate on State art took place primarily in journals and through public declarations: from those voiced by various, more or less avant-garde groups and movements to those by mainstream literary, artistic and political figures. Inquiries into State art often centred on how to develop modern artistic expressions and aesthetic paradigms that represented the modernizing fascist civilization. Such a modernity was rendered chiefly through diverse aesthetic practices converging towards realism, a paradigm deemed able to construct new forms of subjectivity-cum-objectivity within a collectivist and totalitarian understanding of the real and to challenge international debates on 'international realism'.[5]

State art was also, of course, a practical matter, and a matter of State patronage. State-funded exhibitions, such as the Triennale, the Quadriennale or the mostre sindacali, provinciali and regionali (syndacalist, provincial, regional) exhibitions, together with artistic networks revolving around privately owned art galleries in Milan, Turin and Rome (e.g. La galleria Pesaro, Il Milione, La galleria Guglielmi, La galleria Milano, La Cometa, La Galleria d'arte di Roma) played a crucial role in delineating the profile of the system of the arts, since they often followed their own logic of practice and interest – and not exclusively that voiced by intellectual arguments – and could consequently carve out spaces for artistic conversations and for international exposure. Through the multiple channels of such an articulated aesthetic system, the fascist political apparatus could in practice speak both to the masses and to the elites – and ideally to those in between, as pertinently observed by Laura Malvano when she questioned the very same idea of propaganda art as diametrically opposed to 'art'.[6]

---

[4] On these issues a considerable body of scholarly work already exists; suffice to mention: Fabio Benzi, 'Arte di Stato durante il regime fascista: una storia di fallimenti nel segno dei maccanismi del "consenso"', *pianob. Arti e culture visive*, 3/1 (2018), 162–85; Philip Cannistraro, 'Mussolini's Cultural Revolution: Fascist or Nationalist?', *Journal of Contemporary History*, 7/3–4 (1972), 134; Enrico Crispolti, *Arte e Stato. Le esposizioni Sindacali nelle Tre Venezie (1927-1944)* (Milan, Skira, 1997); De Sabbata, *Tra diplomazia e arte*; Vittorio Ferme, 'Redefining the Aesthetics of Fascism: the Battle between the Ancients and the Moderns Revisited', *Symposium: A Quarterly Journal in Modern Literatures*, 52/2 (1998), 73 in particular; and Giovanni Sedita, *Gli intellettuali di Mussolini.*

[5] In his *Teoria del romanzo*, Guido Mazzoni distinguishes three phases in the evolution of the novel from 1800 onwards: the third one, from 1900 to 1940 in particular, witnessed a constant desire of experimentation and progress which started to decline in the 1930s and to be halted in the 1950s, (Bologna, il Mulino, 2011), 53-6. On the specific issue of realism and the contemporary Italian novel, see Ruth Ben-Ghiat, 'The Realist Aesthetic in Italy, 1930–1950', *The Journal of Modern History*, 67/3 (1995), 627–65 and Pasquale Voza, 'Il problema del realismo negli anni Trenta: *Il Saggiatore, Il Cantiere*', *Lavoro critico*, 21/22 (1981), 65–105.

[6] Malvano, *Fascismo e politica dell'immagine*, 24. Other key texts addressing similar problems around the same dichotomy are Salvagnini, *Il sistema delle arti*; Cioli, *Il fascismo e la 'sua' arte*; Stone, *The Patron State* and Crispolti, *Arte e Stato. Le esposizioni Sindacali nelle Tre Venezie*; De Sabbata, *Tra diplomazia e arte*; and Colombo and Pontiggia (eds), *Milano anni Trenta*.

Our principal hypothesis is that all parties in question (artists, politicians, patrons, agents, gallerists, publishers) shared the common ambition of formulating an alternative aesthetic system to that of liberal Italy – geared as it were towards artistic prose in literature – and attuned to various declinations of modern realism coupled with a strong moral imperative. Such a system entailed a shift of the fixed parameters of objectivity towards forms of artistic production which were more culturally and morally aware of the needs of modern society. In this Agon, we will test our hypothesis by analysing the debates on State art and on modern realism. To illustrate the applications of those theoretical principles we will analyse modern novels by writers explicitly engaging with new forms of realism: Corrado Alvaro, Alberto Moravia and Mario Soldati as well as with some of Mario Sironi's artworks that challenged the conventional paradigms of figuration.

Synthesis: State of the Art

The scholarly assessment of Italian modernism has been quite vivacious in the past decade: on the one hand, reaching convincing conclusions, especially as far as a definition of the Italian brand of modernism and its chronological boundaries are concerned; and on the other, bringing the Italian case onto the same plane as 'other', more established, modernisms. While focusing on the chronology, specificities, definitions and historiography of Italian modernism, scholars have somehow avoided scrutinizing the relationship literature established with the political and public sphere, and have not carried out a sustained analysis of the interdisciplinary nature of the Italian case as opposed to a more exclusively literary take on the problem as already articulated in the Anglo-American literary and scholarly world.[7] Riccardo Castellana in particular has proposed the category of '*realismo modernista*' to explain the peculiarity of the Italian case: modernist realism is a brand of realism which engages with the real not according to a mimetic but an experimental literary paradigm. However, Castellana's probing analysis limits itself to the decade from 1915 to 1925, while we wish to expand it to cover the interwar years.[8]

Indeed, the Italian 'brand of' modernism can be more profitably situated in the context of global and comparative modernist studies where the Italian case constitutes a landmark – specifically so as far as the politics of aesthetics and the aesthetics of politics are concerned. Such Italian peculiarities derive both from how the whole State art system was arranged and how such system reiterated the significance of the

---

[7] Luca Somigli, 'Modernismo italiano e modernismo globale. Appunti per un dibattito in progress', *Narrativa*, 35/36 (2013/4), 65–75 for a study that situates the Italian case globally, while a key reference for global modernist studies is *The Oxford Handbook of Global Modernisms*, Mark Wollaeger (ed.) with Matt Eatough (Oxford, Oxford UP, 2013). On the 1930s as an age of progressive decline in narrative experimentation, see also Mazzoni, *Teoria del romanzo*, 359–60.

[8] Riccardo Castellana, 'Realismo modernista. Un'idea del romanzo italiano (1915-1925)', *Italianistica: Rivista di letteratura italiana*, 39/1 (2010), 23–45.

national dimension in relation to the peculiar relationship the arts established with the political apparatus.[9]

Pericles Lewis's work on nationalism and the modernist novels of Joseph Conrad, Gabriele D'Annunzio, Marcel Proust and James Joyce has made explicit the nexus between aesthetic aspirations and political theories during the pre-First World War years, and laid out the theoretical premises of our argument. When looking at the novel in particular and when focusing on the works of those four European high modernists, Lewis convincingly demonstrated how one of the multifaceted manifestations of the crisis of the liberal nation-State was expressed in a particular form of writing, which sought refuge from the harshness of the real not just by experimenting with formal aesthetic strategies but also by constructing a 'national consciousness'.[10]

The First World War was a watershed moment. Not only did it reverse the relationship between the inner and the outer worlds, already clearly challenged by modernist prose writing, but it also reconfigured the ways in which the novel (and the other arts) had to look at reality itself in view of the pressing needs to modernize the European social sphere and find a new 'political order'. These writers materialized their consciousness of the crisis afflicting such political, ideological and economic systems as liberalism and nationalism, by giving space in their novels to a wider factual, if not explicitly historical dimension, which ultimately provided an externalized means of decoding internal dynamics.[11] D'Annunzio's over-determination of the material aspects of the fictional worlds he constructs is a case in point.[12] Lewis's analysis illustrates the interrelationship between the aesthetic and the political during times of perceived epochal crisis, seen as a dramatic transformation of a status quo, and he thus opened up fresh interpretative avenues.

The modernist novel discussed by Lewis, along with the 1930s realists and the visual artists examined here, pursued the same argumentative

---

[9]   See the recent *Il modernismo italiano* (Rome, Carocci, 2018), edited by Massimiliano Tortora for an overview of the debate, and especially of its possible chronological boundaries (12–14). A similar debate had already taken place in the journal *Allegoria* between Tortora, Somigli, Romano Luperini and Valentino Baldi (n. 63, 2012) questioning the definition, historicity and paradigms of the Italian version of modernism. Of similar interest is another edited collection by Romano Luperini and Massimiliano Tortora entitled *Sul modernismo italiano* (Naples, Liguori, 2012). In the opening chapter, Luperini asks whether an Italian brand of modernism exists, while Raffaele Donnarumma draws a series of maps to locate Italian modernism. Worth mentioning is also Luca Somigli and Mario Moroni's assessment of the historical trajectory of modernism, dating it back to 1861, and their reading of Italian modernism as a 'complex network of relations' rather than as a self-standing phenomenon, *Italian Modernism: Italian Culture between Decadentism and Avant-garde* (Toronto, Toronto UP, 2004), 13.

[10] Pericles Lewis, *Modernism, Nationalism, and the Novel* (Cambridge, Cambridge UP, 2000), 2–4.

[11] In this respect, I subscribe to John R. Parkinson's idea of democracy that is defined by the availability of a free public space for debate, see *Democracy & Public Space. The Physical Sites of Democratic Performance* (Oxford, Oxford UP, 2012), 23–48. The modernists represented this relationship between inner and outer worlds through an account of the vagaries of the novelist-hero's consciousness of the nation-race rather than through a chronicle of the external social and political events of their era.

[12] Lewis, *Modernism, Nationalism, and the Novel*, 11.

strategy.[13] For the 1930s saw a crisis of democracy and of democratic representation in the broadest sense, which echoed that before the First World War. There was still a strong drive for social modernization and industrial development, only now advocated by totalitarian regimes; there was still a preferred aesthetic form, namely realism over decadentism, which once again marked a break with the late nineteenth century in so far as it did not put the individual produced by liberal economies at the centre of the narrative, but rather the collective body shaped, directed and orchestrated by the dictatorships. The rise of totalitarianisms imposed upon the arts a more practical end, which also translated into a need to construct society, the collective self, and build it around the idea of ethics and the common good. The call for morality in the arts and for a redefinition of the idea of subjectivity as a collective being were modern topics. The traditional, inner subjectivity of modernism could no longer be endorsed as typical of its time; this was a time of collective endeavours. The masses were soon going to be the new and decisive political formation to which the arts also had to respond.[14]

Hypothesis I: Realism at the Boundaries of Collective Subjectivities

European totalitarian and authoritarian regimes followed a similar pattern when attempting to create an aesthetic apparatus that could fuel a discursive production of the real, to use Ernesto Laclau's terminology.[15] Despite recognizing some differences in the degree of control exercised over the artistic sphere, Igor Golomstock has detailed the extent to which a comparable emphasis on the importance of a 'generically defined' realist paradigm was upheld in totalitarian regimes' modernizing plans for the public sphere as they progressively emerged across at least Italy, Germany and the Soviet Union.[16] Responding to the more liberal Ernst Bloch in the celebrated dispute on 1930s realism and the novel, even orthodox György Lukács had come to accepting the importance of the subjective, irrational, 'subversive tendencies of reality' as foundational to the rendering of objectivity'; and, we add, such 'deviances' had

---

[13] On the relationship between modernism as a literary and artistic practice and its social, cultural and political reverberations across the arts' system, Walter Adamson, 'Avant-garde Modernism and Italian Fascism: Cultural Politics in the Era of Mussolini', *Journal of Modern Italian Studies*, 6/2 (2001), 230–48; Matthew Affron and Mark Antliff (eds), *Fascist Visions: Art and Ideology in France and Italy*; and Braun, *Mario Sironi*. On the trajectory of Italian avant-gardes, see Paolo Buchignani, 'Avanguardie durante il fascismo: Umberto Barbaro, il realismo, l'immaginismo', *il Mulino*, 36/313 (1987), 724–49.

[14] On how the arts contributed to some major social experiments the regime engaged in, see Jeffrey Schnapp, '18 BL: Fascist Mass Spectacle', *Representations*, 43 (1993), 89–125 and his *Building Fascism, Communism, Liberal Democracy* (Stanford, Stanford UP, 2004) as well as Diane Ghirardo, 'Città Fascista: Surveillance and Spectacle', *Journal of Contemporary History*, 31/2 (1996), 347–72.

[15] Ernesto Laclau, *On Populist Reason* (London, Verso 2005), 3–4.

[16] A discussion on the peculiarities of the Italian idea of arte di Stato can be found in Francesca Billiani and Laura Pennacchietti, *Architecture and the Novel under the Italian Fascist Regime* (Basingstoke, Palgrave, 2019), available online: https://link.springer.com/chapter/10.1007/978-3-030-19428-4_2 (accessed 5 October 2020) and Golomstock, *Totalitarian Art*, 46–7, 49–52.

complicated the picture even further by rewriting the subjectivities of the avant-gardes within the realist paradigm.[17]

Throughout the 1920s and 1930s, vanguardism as elated subjectivities travelled across a Republic of Letters *sui generis* – oftentimes in the company of different styles of realism.[18] The roaring 1920s witnessed a proliferation of manifestos which were testimonies of ambitious transatlantic aesthetic variations of realism+avant-gardes. In 1920 Naum Gabo and Antoine Pevsner published in Moscow their *Manifesto of Realism*, conceived in aesthetic terms and in opposition to Tatlin's more practical and tactile brand of constructivism. In rebuffing futurism and cubism, Gabo and Pevsner wanted to reconstruct the aesthetic realm from its initial premises of space and time as defining constituencies. Hence, the couple sought to reintroduce the ideas: of tonality over colour, of the line as vector of the rhythms of objects rather than as descriptive or decorative factor, of the importance of depth over full volume and of kinetics defined by time over static rhythms. These were also the basic principles of any constructivist technique to follow – no colour, no line, no volume, no sculpture, no rhythm – because bare facts were to be the foundational mechanisms for the artistic experience itself.

In rapid sequence, even more exalted proclamations followed suit: the techno-constructivist groups in Russia with *The Eccentric Manifesto* (1922) published in Petrograd by the 'Depot of Eccentrics' with articles by Leonid Trauberg, Grigorii Kozintsev, Sergei Yutkevich and Georgii Kryzhitskii and hailed as a bastion of popular art; *Constructivism* (1922) by Aleksei Gan composed as a response to industrial transformation and against bourgeois art; the *Constructivism and the Proletariat* (1922) manifesto by Hungarian artist and photographer László Moholy-Nagy on the rein of the machine; the *Manifesto* issued by the Syndicate of Technical Workers, Painters and Sculptors in Mexico City in the same year against the oppression of workers and intellectuals; and the culmination of the genre with André Breton's *Manifesto of Surrealism* (1924) and Alexander Berkman's the *Now and After: The ABC of Communist Anarchism* in 1929.[19] But in Russia the avant-garde movements effectively came to an end by the mid-1920s, with their last show being held in Petrograd in 1923 and Lenin's death in 1925, to be replaced by total realism in 1927: at a time when in Italy the official cultural debate was concentrating on what constituted State art, while in Germany the Bauhaus' editions tried to keep the vanguardist spirit alive by translating and publishing Kazimir Malevich's 1915 *Manifesto of Suprematism*.

Originally written with Vladimir Mayakovsky's input and reworked five years later as *Manifesto of Suprematism*, it played an introductory role in the understanding of the shift from representational to non-representational aesthetics. By rejecting mimetic representations of reality, Malevich upheld an idea of an aesthetic declination

[17] Theodor Adorno, Walter Benjamin, Ernest Bloch, Bertolt Brecht, György Lukács, *Aesthetics and Politics* (London, Verso, 2007), 33. See also, Lukács, 'The Theory of the Novel', 1920, 227, reprinted in Vassiliki Kolocotroni, Jane Goldman and Olga Taxidou (eds), *Handbook of Modernism* (Edinburgh, Edinburgh UP, 1999).

[18] For an overview of the intersections between different avant-garde movements, see Cesare De Michelis, *L'avanguardia trasversale. Il futurismo tra Italia e Russia* (Venice, Marsilio, 2009).

[19] On the significance of the year 1922 for Italian modernism, see Remo Ceserani, 'Italy and Modernity: Particularities and Contradictions', in Moroni-Somigli (eds), *Italian Modernism*, 53–8.

which consisted in the pure expression of subjective sensations; that is, not of any form of objectivity, but rather of patterns of colours filtered through the prism of individual perception. Consequently, suprematism opened the way for theorizing non-representational sensitivities, forming shapes without any detectable aim, because they were based on the use of plastic perceptions to transpose spatial arrangements onto canvas. Still, many metamorphoses of such first waves of spurious programmes and 'dogmas' upheld by the avant-gardes came into being throughout the 1930s and complicated the picture of what modern realism was even further: for instance, the trend of idealism in Nazi Germany, which constituted a rejection of the New Objectivity; and that of second futurism in Italy. In 1931 the group Abstraction-Création was founded in Paris.[20] In 1932, the pro-Nazi municipality of Dessau shut down the Bauhaus: one chapter was open and one was swiftly closed.

In democratic France and Great Britain, literary breakthroughs marked an analogous shift towards modern realism, which was hailed as a reaction against the purported solipsism of the avant-gardes and of modernism itself.[21] Just to mention a few significant moments: at the sunset of the surrealist experience and at the dawn of the new politicized decade, in France, André Breton with *Nadja* (1928) and François Mauriac with *Leviathan* (1929), together with the likes of André Malraux, Georges Bernanos, Ferdinand Celine and André Gide, exemplified the tension between the modernists' and avant-gardes' ethos, concerned with the idea of derailing the real into new representative fashions, and the new emerging aesthetics of the real, preoccupied instead with a close portrayal of society as a whole. In England, not dissimilarly, Aldous Huxley, George Orwell, Joseph Conrad, Henry Green and E. M. Foster were faced with the challenges of narrating the modern world in such a way as not to obliterate either its consciousness or its historical meaning. Or, further afield in the USA, John Dos Passos and Francis Scott Fitzgerald were confronted with social descriptions which were offsprings of technical advancements.

In this pandemonium, the Italian case was in many ways an exception in how it played between vanguardism and realism if we consider that it was functoning under a repressive regime.[22] Italian nineteenth-century realism began to transform itself by

---

[20] Mario de Micheli, *Le avanguardie artistiche del Novecento* (Milan, Feltrinelli, 2018 [1986]), 264–90 for a detailed panoramic view of abstracticism in Russia, as well as Golomstock, *Totalitarian Art*, 30–6. For a discussion of the overlaps between surrealism, dada and futurism, see Luciano De Maria, *La nascita dell'avanguardia. Saggi sul futurismo italiano* (Venice, Marsilio, 1986), 47–63. On the international circulation of futurism, see Claudia Salaris, *Futurismi nel mondo* (Pistoia, Gli Ori, 2015), while on the local dimension of avant-garde encounters Melania Gazzotti and Anna Villari (eds), *Futurismo e Dada. Da Marinetti a Tzara. Mantova e l'Europa nel segno dell'Avanguardia* (Cinisello Balsamo, Silvana Editoriale, 2010).

[21] For a recent overview of the relationship between art, modernity and totalitarianisms across European authoritarian regimes, see Rasmussen and Wamberg (eds), *Totalitarian Art and Modernity*. For a definition of the main phenomena recurring in processes of modernization, see Alberto Martinelli, *Global Modernization: Rethinking the Process of Modernity* (London, Sage, 2005), 10–11; while for a study of the transnational reach of modernism, Wollaeger (ed.), *Global Modernisms*.

[22] Golomstock, *Totalitarian Art*, 34–6. For a series of studies detailing these shifts across Europe, see Groys, *The Total Art of Stalinism*; Mark Mazower, *Dark Continent: Europe's Twentieth Century* (London, The Penguin Press, 1998); Roberts, *The Total Work of Art in European Modernism*; James Scott, *Seeing Like a State: How Certain Schemes to Improve the Human Condition Have Failed* (New Haven, CT, Yale UP, 1999).

starting to adopt the individual, the fragment, of the avant-gardes and by trying to reinscribe it in a new form of non-univocal objectivity. Realism was a fragmented notion and obviously not a plain mirror of totality: it was synonymous with Massimo Bontempelli's magical realism coined in 1927, Carlo Carrà's mythical realism borrowed from Franz Roh and New Objectivity in 1927, Ardengo Soffici's idealist realism conceptualized in 1928, alongside the Novecento italiano's classical tradition, the Scuola romana's oneirism, the Immaginismo movement's experimental writing, not to mention booming advertising as the new glamorized real: in other words, it existed as a system of relations within the various regimes of the arts.[23] Fragmented as it was, State art had to recompose and make visible Italian modern realism into viable aesthetic paradigms. The political project of totalitarianism sought to reinvent 'the real' in order to construct a rational dimension from which to foster social modernization, and channel emotional and irrational responses.[24]

In 1930s Italy, therefore, the brand of 'new' realism under the overarching concept of State art was a combination of the modernist narrative technique of the interior monologue and of a frustrated desire to become real and reach a wider audience.[25] The personal element – which had almost been erased by nineteenth-century realism in its aim to portray totality and history and the hyper-elated subjectivism of the avant-gardes of the early twentieth century, set on embodying modernity and precarity – in 1930s Italian culture was fused into an aesthetic twinkling: between subjectivity and objectivity, between modernity and modernization.[26] In 1929 both Alberto Moravia in Italy and Alfred Döblin in Germany turned to highly fashionable New Objectivity with *Gli indifferenti* and *Berlin Alexander Platz* when called to face a similar challenge, while in Milan Margheritta Sarfatti was organizing the II Mostra del Novecento italiano to reinforce the need for '*modernità italiana*' (Italian modernity) as the paradigm for order and clear contents in the visual arts.[27] Moravia aside, even the Rome-based and underground avant-garde of Umberto Barbaro, Anton Giulio Bragaglia, Enrico Emanuelli, Marcello Gallian, Dino Terra, Vinicio Paladini, Ivo Pannaggi and the Imaginists en masse refashioned an idea of realism in terms of imagination and

[23] A probing analysis of the theoretical and political complexities of Bontempelli's 'magical realism' are discussed in Keala Jewell, 'Magic Realism and Real Politics: Massimo Bontempelli's Literary Compromise', *modernism/modernity*, 15/4 (2008): 727–34. See also Maurizio Fagiolo dell'Arco, *Classicismo pittorico. Metafisica, Valori Plastici, Realismo Magico e '900'* (Genoa, Costa e Nolan, 1991); Alessandro Del Puppo, 'Il "realismo magico" e la fortuna dei primitivi nella pittura italiana dei primi anni Venti', in Mario Sartor (ed.), *Realismo magico fantastico e iperrealismo nell'arte e nella letteratura latinoamericane* (Udine, Forum, 2005), 46–61; and Valerio Terraroli (ed.), *Realismo magico. Origini, ragioni e sviluppi di una stagione della pittura italiana negli anni Venti e Trenta* (Milan, Electa, 2018), 17, 23. For an overview of the Novecento movement, Rossana Bossaglia, *Il Novecento italiano* (Milan, Charta, 1995).

[24] For a discussion of the relationship between realism and the novel, see John Orr, *Tragic Realism & Modern Society: The Passionate Political in the Modern Novel* (London, Macmillan, 1989).

[25] Umberto Carpi, 'Gli indifferenti rimossi', *Belfagor*, 36/6 (30 November 1981), 696–709.

[26] For the theoretical debate around the idea of modernity in Italy and Germany, see Fernando Esposito, *Fascism, Aviation and Mythical Modernity* (Basingstoke, Palgrave, 2015), 27–38.

[27] *Seconda Mostra del Novecento italiano*, Catalogue, Introduction by Margherita Sarfatti (Milan, E. Gualdoni, 1929), 14.

mechanical reproduction.[28] From the margins of the peninsula, Corrado Alvaro and to a certain extent Aldo Palazzeschi did so along the lines of a return to the regional dimension of the literary novel, which realistically showed the harshness of life. If subjectivity (individualism coupled with bourgeois escapism as in modernism) and objectivity (the collective representation of the real as in realism) could no longer be separated into two fields, what then would collectivity and consciousness (of the object) consist of in this time of totalitarian regimes?

Fusions I: Towards a New State Art

Just like for every aspect of fascist culture, the debate on State art followed a precise trajectory: from the inaugural speech on 26 March 1923 at the elegant Pesaro gallery for the opening of the exhibition of the Novecento italiano movement, and the Perugia speech in 1926 at the Accademia della Belle Arti, to official 'artist' Mario Sironi's rejection of an easel for mural painting in 1933, to Bottai's programme 'l'azione per l'arte' and *Primato*.

The early manifesto, *Contro tutti i ritorni in pittura*, signed by Achille Funi, Mario Sironi, Leonardo Dudreville and Luigi Russolo and published on 11 January 1920 functioned as a forerunner of Novecento and indirectly of the debate on State art when it called for 'construction' in visual arts, after the excessive formalism of the Valori plastici movement.[29] This much-discussed *Manifesto* was a call for a return to composition, which did not, however, have to imitate the classics (or the primitives), but rather to obtain a 'synthetic plastic construction', as the futurists allegedly aspired to do since 'The deformation should not have itself as its only aim, however such an aim is or might be entirely logical. One must make sure that deformation is a rhythmical necessity for rhythmical construction [...]'.[30] In other words, the social and

---

[28] Umberto Carpi, *Bolscevico immaginista: comunismo e avanguardie artistiche nell'Italia degli anni Venti* (Naples, Liguori, 1981) and *L'estrema avanguardia del Novecento* (Rome, Editori Riuniti, 1985) remain the best overall assessment of the underground, avant-garde and experimental scene of the period. See also, Giuseppe Casetti (ed.), *Movimento Immaginista a Roma nel V anno del R. F.* (Rome, Edizioni Stampa Alternativa, 1990) and Claudia Salaris, *La Roma delle avanguardie* (Rome, Editori Riuniti, 1999). For some specific interventions, F. T. Marinetti, 'Dino Terra', *L'Impero*, (5 August 1927), 5 about an appraisal of the novelist as a young futurist, or Bonaventura Caloro 'Orientamenti di giovani scrittori', *Il Tevere*, (9 March 1928), about the ethical drive of young writers and finally Adriano Tilgher, 'Marcello Gallian e Dino Terra', *Il popolo di Roma*, (9 June 1929), 3 in relation to a critique of their fragmented narrative structure.

[29] On the history of the movement, the main reference points are Elena Pontiggia, *Il Novecento italiano* (Milan, Abscondita, 2002); *Modernità e classicità. Il Ritorno all'ordine in Europa, dal primo dopoguerra agli anni Trenta* (Milan, Bruno Mondadori, 2008); and Bossaglia, *Il Novecento italiano*. For more information about Margherita Sarfatti and her position within the artistic field of the day, see Elena Pontiggia (ed.), *Da Boccioni a Sironi. Il mondo di Margherita Sarfatti* (Milan, Skira, 1997); Fabriano Fabbri, *I due Novecento. Gli anni Venti fra arte e letteratura: Bontempelli versus Sarfatti* (Lecce, Manni, 2003); and Simona Urso's biographical study, *Margherita Sarfatti: dal mito del Dux al mito americano* (Venice, Marsilio, 2013).

[30] 'sintetica costruzione plastica', 'La deformazione non deve avere per unico scopo se stessa, per quanto sia, o sembri, essenzialmente logica. Bisogna invece che la deformazione sia una necessità ritmica per la costruzione ritmica [...]', Pontiggia (ed.), *Il Novecento italiano*, 21.

political determination of reassessing a possible identity for the Italian tradition and the aesthetic issues of rhythm and construction as means of bringing volumes and forms together in a coherent whole were cardinal to the very essence of what constituted a work of art. Such questions, bridging aesthetic and political realms, often persisted across almost every artistic field of the system of the arts of the day.[31]

Mussolini addressed the issue of State art in the famous speech at the Pesaro art gallery in Milan on 26 March 1923 at the opening of the exhibition organized by Lino Pesaro and Margherita Sarfatti to celebrate the foundation of the Novecento movement (effectively existing since November 1922) and his seven representatives: Anselmo Bucci, Leonardo Dudreville, Achille Funi, Guido Marussig, Gian Emilio Malerba, Ubaldo Oppi and Mario Sironi.[32] The Duce stated that: '[...] it is not my intention to encourage something which might look like State art. Art belongs to the individual sphere. The State has only one duty: not to sabotage art, and to provide the most human conditions for the artists to work in.'[33] If the political meaning of this statement it obvious, the aesthetic one is less so. Mussolini is equating art with individuality; for the Duce gives centre stage to the dialectics between subjectivity and objectivity and elects them as interconnected, cardinal moments in the initial stage of the debate on State art. At the onset of the reflections on the relationship between the State and the arts, one of the main anxieties the Fascist regime voiced was already that of defining its ideological position: to what extent was it convenient to the regime to impose a unique direction on the arts?[34]

By 1925 the Italian Fascist regime was concerned with how to present itself not only as the new political order but also aesthetic form, embodying in both instances modernity and social transformation.[35] On 15 January 1925 in *Critica fascista*, we notoriously read: 'The State sums up every initiative and every gesture: it assumes its own responsibilities, forces everyone into ranks.' And 'Art must be State art because

---

[31] See on the idea of latinità in architecture and the visual arts, Simona Storchi, '*Il fascismo è una casa di vetro*: Giuseppe Terragni and the Politics of Space in Fascist Italy', *Italian Studies*, 62/2 (2007), 234–35.

[32] Salvagnini notes that there had been another exhibition of the Novecento artists in November 1922 at the Bottega di Poesia gallery in Milan and it had a larger number of artworks than those exposed at the Pesaro, *Il sistema delle arti*, 178–80. He also detects a certain hostility by Pesaro towards the Novecento and Sarfatti herself. The speech will be published in *Il Popolo d'Italia* two days later. For an assessment of Novecento's origins, see Pontiggia, *Modernità e classicità*, 166–74.

[33] '*Dichiaro che è lungi da me l'idea di incoraggiare qualcosa che possa assomigliare all'arte di Stato. L'arte rientra nella sfera dell'individuo. Lo Stato ha un solo dovere: quello di non sabotarla, di dar condizioni umane agli artisti*', in Elena Pontiggia (ed.), *Il Novecento italiano*, 52.

[34] On this point, Salvagnini, *Il sistema delle arti*, 344–66.

[35] As Roger Griffin has demonstrated in his wide-ranging study of the period and of modernism, the idea that travelled across Europe, and thus was employed to describe the rise of the dictatorships, was that of 'palingenetic rebirth'. The regime and its cultural elites sought to 'modernise and break through', in view of a palingenetic rebirth – originating from the trauma of the First World War, the death of the avant-gardes and the consolidation of the regime's hegemony over popular culture in the 1930s, *Modernism and Fascism: The Sense of a Beginning under Mussolini and Hitler: The Sense of a New Beginning under Mussolini and Hitler* (Basingstoke, Palgrave, 2007), 227–48. See also the recent edited volume by Monica Cioli and Maurizio Rcciardi (eds), *Traces of Modernism* for a comprehensive examination of the role of the State and the figure of the New Man across the European landscape.

the State is the only moral and civic entity which creates coercive spaces for the individual.'[36] The role of the State, and that of the arts within it, in this instance is very clearly defined in terms of totalitarian and hierarchical control over the social sphere, something that was naturally but not propagandistically developed in Bottai's 'action for art' in the mid-to-late 1930s, when the artistic sphere was given aesthetic value and a certain degree of freedom.[37]

In the same year, in Bologna, at the Convegno per la cultura fascista (Conference on Fascist Culture) held on 29–30 March, Gentile had presided over the congress, already implicitly supporting Bottai's 'Resultanze dell'inchiesta sull'arte fascista' on the role cultural institutions needed to play to channel, sustain and protect artists and further endorsing his *Manifesto degli intellettuali fascisti* (1925).[38] At the end of 1925, on 19 December, neo-idealist philosopher Giovanni Gentile was appointed chair of the newly-established Istituto nazionale fascista di cultura (National Fascist Insitute of Culture), under the direction of the National Fascist Party (PNF).[39] Not differently than what was happening in other fields, at the start of the reforms, it was implicit that not only the institutional apparatus of the State but also the aesthetic realm of the arts had to join forces to organize forms of social life; in this initial phase, it should be noted that the arts still retained those powers of partial autonomy and control over political 'totality', which they would, in many ways, lose as the argument unfolded and the forms of State patronage became more explicit in from the mid-to-late 1930s.[40]

The debate on fascist art peaked in 1926 and reached interesting – still open, eclectic and opportunistic – conclusions. Undoubtedly, such a composite score did originate from Mussolini's second speech on 15 February 1926 at the vernissage of the I Mostra del Novecento italiano (I Exhibition of Novecento featuring 110 artists of diverse affiliations) at the Palazzo della Permanente in Milan. Mussolini famously declared that '[w]ithout art there is no civilisation. I believe art to signal the dawn of

---

[36] 'Lo Stato riassume in sé ogni iniziativa e ogni gesto: assume le sue responsabilità, costringe i singoli nei ranghi.' And 'L'arte deve quindi essere arte di Stato perché lo Stato è un'entità morale e civile che crea spazi coercitivi per l'individuo', 'Il nuovo compito', *Critica fascista*, II/2 (15 January 1925), 1.

[37] Two recent contributions on the controversial figure of Bottai are Michele Dantini, *Arte e politica in Italia*, 59–97 and Fabio Benzi, 'Arte di Stato durante il regime fascista: una storia di fallimenti nel segno dei maccanismi del "consenso"', 162–85.

[38] On 29 and 30 March 1925, the Congresso per la Cultura Fascista organized by Franco Ciarlantini was held in Bologna; cf. Tempesti, *Arte dell'Italia fascista*, 72–3. The list of participants included Sarfatti with a paper entitled 'L'arte nell'economia nazionale', Soffici with 'Il fascismo e l'avvenire nell'arte', Marinetti who proposed the establishment of a bank to support artists and finally Prampolini and Oppo.

[39] For a detailed analysis of the structure and mission of the Insitute, see Albertina Vittoria, 'Totalitarismo e intellettuali: L'Istituto nazionale fascista di cultura dal 1925 al 1937', *Studi storici*, 23/4 (1982), 897–918 and Cannistraro, 'Mussolini's Cultural Revolution: Fascist or Nationalist?', 22 for the congress' outcomes and the forging of a new alliance between the State and the cultural sphere.

[40] On this point and on Bottai's autonomous lines of action, see Giorgio Luti, *La letteratura nel ventennio fascista. Cronache leterarie tra le due guerre: 1920–1940* (Florence, La Nuova Italia, 1972), 146–7.

every civilisation'.[41] On this occasion, he remained again suitably and predictably vague on the matter of State art. More significantly, however, he announced that the most distinguished elements of the artists on display were 'the firmness and precision of the sign, the solid plasticity of objects and figures', since these mirrored the new political course taken by the country under the guidance of the regime.[42] Plasticity was once more a key word here – just like in the *Contro tutti i ritorni in pittura* manifesto and in Mussolini's speech – since it combined search for innovation with the political mission of moulding and directing the crowds.

In 1926 the Royal Academy of Italy and the Federazione nazionale dei sindacati fascisti degli intellettuali (National Federation of Fascist Syndicates of Intellectuals) were also founded, with the former encouraged by Sarfatti and the latter closing two years later. Intellectuals then gathered at the Confederazione nazionale dei sindacati fascisti dei professionisti e degli artisti (National Confederation of Fascist Syndicates of Professionals and Artists), chaired by Giacomo Di Giacomo. The arts were under the same centralizing control as the other spheres of society thorough institutionalized powers in the hands of leading personalities who upheld the regime. Nonetheless, that was not the only way to exercise control: just like everybody else, intellectuals needed to be persuaded.

The first official debate about fascist art played out in 1926–8 in Minister Giuseppe Bottai's leading journal *Critica fascista* (1925–43), but it reached no definite conclusions, other than encouraging artists to adopt a more 'constructivist' (not necessarily in the avant-garde sense of experimentation with forms), modern and less decadent attitude in their work, and inviting the State to support its artists. The 1930s battles for modern and/or totalitarian realism in the arts, when fought again in *Critica fascista* and in other more or less mainstream periodical publications, avoided all mysticism in order to champion a pragmatic idea of culture, which significantly functioned as a – more or less faithful – representation and not just as a mirror of modern society and its collective (anti-liberal) spirit.[43] The question *Critica fascista*

---

[41] '*Senza l'arte non vi è civiltà. Credo che l'arte segni l'aurora di ogni civiltà*', 'Arte e civiltà', (5 October 1926). In the afternoon of the same day, 5 October 1926, S. E. il Capo del Governo visited the Accademia di Belle Arti in Perugia, and he stated that: '*Noi dobbiamo creare un'arte nuova, un'arte fascista*'. Mussolini's speech was then published in an article by young Augusto de Marsanich, 'Rassegne di politica e cultura. Rassegna dei fatti politici', *Critica fascista*, IV/20 (15 October 1926), 394–5 as the opening of the debate on fascist art. See also Gentile, *Il culto del Littorio*, 279. In his review, Carrà described the exhibition a success, '*Il vernissage della mostra del 'Novecento italiano'*, *L'Ambrosiano*, (3 March 1926).

[42] '*la decisione e la precisione del segno, la solida plasticità delle cose e delle figure*', *Il Popolo d'Italia*, (16 February 1926), 1. Notable contributors to the debates, apart from those already cited in this article, are Antonio Pagano, Michele Pirrone, Alessandro Pavolini, Enrico Rocca, Mino Maccari, Carlo Curci, Alberto Iacopini, Julius Evola and Enrico Massis. On this point, see Benzi, 'Arte di Stato durante il regime fascista', 164–6. For more details on this event and those who took part in it, see Catherine Paul and Barbara Zaczek, 'Margherita Sarfatti & Italian Cultural Nationalism', *modernism/modernity*, 13/1 (2006), 892.

[43] On these debates, see the conclusions drawn by Albertina Vittoria, 'Le riviste di regime: "Gerarchia", "Civiltà fascista", "Critica fascista"', *Studi romani*, 28/3 (1980), 312–34 and *Le riviste del duce* (Turin, Guanda, 1983); Umberto Carpi, *L'estrema avanguardia del Novecento* and *Bolscevico immaginista*; as well as Mario Sechi, '"Critica Fascista" 1929–1932. Idealismo politico e fermenti di cultura nuova alla svolta del regime', *Lavoro critico*, 19 (1980), 271–322 and *Il mito della nuova cultura: Giovani, realismo e politica negli anni trenta* (Bari, Lacaita, 1984).

asked artists, writers and intellectuals in 1926–7 was indeed a rather simple one and one in line with Mussolini's declarations: what is the role of the arts in the fascist era? Still, a further question could be asked: to what extent had artists had to contribute to the totalitarian project, by fostering forms of totalitarian consent and by taking part in the its aesthetic economy? In the December issue of *Critica fascista*, which contained the most incisive contribution to the vexed question, Umberto Fracchia, then director of the weekly arts and culture journal *La Fiera letteraria*, emphasized how the Fascist revolution was for modernity, for the new art, a concept which he and many other contributors never quite refined and explained other than in bombastic and vague terms.[44] If taken in itself as a discursive tool, as early as 1926 and throughout the early 1930s, the fascist rhetoric constructed in *Critica fascista* was often built around the interlocking notions of construction and modernity. To this end, Bontempelli, founder in 1924 of the Novecento movement, editor of *900* and in 1930 elected to the Reale accademia d'Italia (Royal Academy of Italy), attempting once more to define fascist art, in an open letter to Minister Bottai wrote: 'because art is the only sensitive toll which had to mark and favour at the same time, express and bring to fruition the fecundating of the third epoch of civilisation: the fascist era'. Furthermore, Bontempelli believed Fascism to be an 'orientation of life: public and private: total and final regimentation', and fascist art to be the actualizing expression of this clear orientation and totalizing organizational principle, encapsulating the life of the citizen.[45]

This is one of the first and strongest points made, together with those by Ardengo Soffici and Gino Severini: the arts had to be engaged with the social and with the political sphere.[46] Mussolini himself was in contact with Soffici whom he had invited to Rome to start theorizing his own 'artistic and cultural policies'. Not surprisingly, perhaps, in his opening contribution, Soffici foresaw the importance of myth-making for State art and tellingly indicated a clear direction for the years to come, one especially clear in Sironi's own Public art and in mural painting in general. As a painter once close to the militant European avant-gardes, Soffici tackled the issue of realism, and he spoke of '*realismo sintetico*' (synthetic realism) – and not of Bontempelli's magical realism – whereby the inner world of the artist has to come into contact with the external one of fascist history through figurative language. The linearity and the constructive force of traditional Italian art had to be employed to support the national tradition and to reconcile it with the new the Fascist revolution.

In his contribution, naturally, Bontempelli advocated instead his own brand of magical realism as the chief theoretical foundation of modern art because of its anti-romantic and anti-rhetorical style, which in turn would also have an interdisciplinary

---

[44] 'Arte fascista', in section 'Opinioni sull'arte fascista', *Critica fascista*, IV/24 (15 December 1926), 453. Arts ought to be understood as '*creazione di uno che poggiava [...] su di una realtà solida*', IV/21 (1 November 1926), 393.

[45] '*perché l'arte è il sensitivo strumento che deve segnare e favorire insieme, esprimere e portare a maturazione la fecondità della terza epoca della civilizzazione: l'epoca fascista*' 'orientamento della vita: pubblico e privato: ordinamento compiuto e totale', 'Arte fascista', *Critica fascista*, IV/22 (15 November 1926), 416.

[46] On this point, see also Ardengo Soffici, 'Arte fascista', *Critica fascista*, IV/20 (15 October 1926), 384–5, and Soffici, 'Il Fascismo e l'arte', *Gerarchia*, I/9 (1922), 504–8.

application in construction; namely, in architecture and in the visual arts, as shown in the pages of the journal *Quadrante* that he edited with Pietro Maria Bardi (see Agon 3).[47] In this respect, Severini's point about 'an architectural art' in the context of State art was revealing the necessity of an artistic dimension, which could be seen as interconnected to the other arts in a system.[48] Futurist Volt, remarking on the centrality of architecture and urban planning in the regime's race for modernity and modernization, followed this streak and encouraged an interdisciplinary fusion of technique and design to avoid traditionalism and passéism.[49] The main thread uniting such diverse claims was the notion that, within the State art paradigm, realism was a pragmatic force for construction provided it preserved an aesthetic autonomous quality, even when politically and socially engaged.

Other dissonant, critical voices, such as those of Mino Maccari, Curzio Malaparte, Enrico Rocca and Alessandro Pavolini asserted that there should not be a 'fascist art' because it would imply a form of detrimental statalization of the arts' potential, resembling, according to Rocca, what was happening in Moscow.[50] By the same token, the Fascist revolution ought to avoid replicating the Soviet model, where the arts serve the State following the paradigm of total realism – something Mussolini himself neither had nor would demand. Interestingly, Margherita Sarfatti was in favour of State support for the arts but not of the unions. The artists should be free to express themselves as an elite group which could nonetheless receive patronage. Contributing to the same conversation about novelty and patronage, the iconoclast impresario and theatre director at the Teatro degli Indipendenti Anton Giulio Bragaglia added that for writers 'it will still be possible to give energy to what it has been describe as *fascist art*, in other words young people's art', and associated fascist art with modernity, construction, anti-bourgeois sentiments, social transformation and revolutionary spirits, thereby both situating the underground avant-gardes within the official debate.[51] Finally, according to Marinetti of course, fascist art was ultimately and prophetically futurist art.[52]

When programmatically summing such a plethora of voices, in his 'Resultanze dell'inchiesta sull'arte fascista', while stating that the State ought to support artists economically, Bottai also strongly advocated the separation between the aesthetic and the historical and political realms, and thus thwarted the subversive potential to the

---

[47] 'Arte fascista', *Critica fascista*, IV/22 (15 November 1926), 416–17. See also Vittorio Ferme, 'Redefining the Aesthetics of Fascism: the Battle between the Ancients and the Moderns Revisited' for a detailed discussion of the most significant contributions to the debate, 74–9.

[48] 'L'idolatria dell'Arte e decadenza del 'quadro', *Critica fascista*, V/2 (15 January 1927), 24.

[49] Aka Count Vincenzo Fani Ciotti, author of a science fiction novel entitled *La fine del mondo*, 1921, 'Nuova arte fascista', *Critica fascista*, IV/21 (1 November 1926), 398.

[50] Curzio Malaparte, 'Botta e risposta', *Critica fascista*, IV/22 (15 November 1926), 419–20; Alessandro Pavolini, 'Dall'arte fascista', *Critica fascista*, IV/21 (1 November 1926), 393–5; Emilio Rocca, 'L'arte fascista è la grande arte', ibid., 395–6; and Mino Maccari, 'Arte fascista', ibid., 396–8.

[51] '*si potrà ancora dare impulso a quella che è detta arte fascista, vale a dire arte di giovani*'. In this respect, see also Alessandro de Stefani, 'Per un'arte fascista' and Curzio Malaparte, 'Botta e risposta', *Critica fascista*, IV/23 (1 December 1926), 419; A. G. Bragaglia, 'Rassegna del pensiero latino', in section 'Rassegne di politica e di cultura', *Critica fascista*, IV/22 (15 November 1926), 436.

[52] 'L'arte fascista futurista', *Critica fascista*, V/1 (1 January 1927), 3.

arts.[53] A work of art, according to Bottai, should primarily possess an intrinsic and autonomous aesthetic value, able to transcend its historical moment, and convey an universal message that exceeded those of simple propaganda linked to the contingency of any given present situation.[54] For the arts, when it came to the aesthetic dimension, the debate was about modernity as a way of reconceptualizing the relationship of the subject with the real; instead when such a debate concerned the political sphere, it was about how to find a more direct way of addressing the realities of the people through the arts in order to construct new collective formations.[55]

Fusions II: The Peripheries, the Futurists et al.

At the fringes, aesthetic innovation was evoked as the main means of regenerating the cultural and public field against old-fashioned, centralized and incoherent artistic manifestations, going against the spirit of the fascist era, the Duce and the Fascist Party.[56] Futurist and futurist-like journals in particular were active across the peninsula in debating arts and politics from a range of different perspectives; all, however, converging on the relationship between aesthetic innovation and political revolution as interlocking moments. As early as 1923, the daily *L'Impero* (1923–33) sponsored by Mussolini and directed by Mario Carli and Emilio Settimelli questioned the relationship between the arts and the State, which were to remain independent fields of action and power. In a 1923 argument between Bruno Corra and Emilio Settimelli, the former sought an autonomous position for the arts, while the latter expected futurism and avant-garde art to be part of the fascist political programme: their roles were mutually exclusive.[57] As observed by Claudia Salaris: 'The danger perceived by futurists of *L'Impero* was, therefore, that of a certain intellectual agnosticism when it came to the regime's cultural choices' and their debates often tried to steer in the direction of State support for the arts.[58]

---

[53] Salvagnini, *Il sistema delle arti*, 348.

[54] On 3 April 1926, the law n. 563 anticipated the conclusions about syndicalism, it was rectified by a later one issued on 1 July 1926, n. 110, which divided manual and intellectual workers into two distinct categories (cf. R. D.I, 1 July 1926, n. 1130, Norme per l'attuazione della legge 2 April 1926, n. 563 sulla disciplina giuridica dei rapporti collettivi di lavoro, *Gazzetta Ufficiale*, Rome, 7 July 1926, n. 155). See for further details on other important legislations, Salvagnini, *Il sistema delle arti*, 359–60. On the legislation and status of the Direzione generale delle antichità e belle arti, see Salvagnini, *Il sistema delle arti*, 365–71.

[55] Mark Antliff discusses how the regime used the arts to shape its own mythologies according to a set of typological categories, in 'Fascism, Modernism, and Modernity', 148–69, while Emilio Gentile, in his *Il mito dello stato nuovo dall'antigiolittismo al fascismo* (Rome-Bari, Laterza, 1982), looks at these phenomena from a political and historical angle.

[56] 'Un' arte fascista', in section 'Opinioni sull'arte fascista', *Critica fascista*, IV/23 (1 December 1926), 435.

[57] Corra, 'Gli intellettuali creatori e la mentalità fascista. Risposta di Bruno Corra a Volt e Settimelli', *L'Impero*, I/237 (14 December 1923), 1; Emilio Settimelli, 'Risposta di Settimelli a Bruno Corra', ibid.; Settimelli, 'Chiusura. (A proposito degli intellettuali creatori e la mentalità fascista)', *L'Impero*, I/245 (23 December 1923), 1.

[58] Claudia Salaris, *Artecrazia. L'avanguardia futurista negli anni del fascismo* (Florence, La Nuova Italia, 1992), 69.

Even earlier than *Critica fascista*, in 1926, the Palermo-based journal *L'Arte fascista* launched an inquiry into futurism as State art, with contributions by local intellectuals Dino Vittor Tonini, Gesualdo Manzella-Frontini and the futurist Ferdinando Caioli, unequivocally entitled 'L' arte fascista sarà l'arte futurista?' and who, the following year, reiterated the message through a book with the same title published by the Edizioni de 'L'arte fascista' in Palermo.[59] Once again and on the whole, criticism from the 'provinces' was directed towards the ever growing bourgeois attitude the Rome-based fringes of the movement had been endorsing to reassert the need for futurism to make a strong claim towards its anti-bourgeoise, morally sound, national and experimental nature. As Salaris has put it, Tonini's last intervention in defence of Marinetti was of particular relevance because he agreed on the prominent role of futurism as State art when expressed as chiefly national and not as international art.[60] Contrary to the other contributors Manzella-Frontini and Caioli, who criticized the ever growing distance between Marinetti's futurism and the genuine Italian artistic traditionally morally, Tonini perceptively identified a first and a second phase in the history of the movement, – 'destructive the first one and constructive the second' – thereby not only historicizing it but also unquestionably attributing to futurism, when primarily nationally inflected, a forward-looking aesthetic leadership with regard to State art, something reinforced by Marinetti's own intervention.[61]

The same year, at the other side of the peninsula, in Turin, Fillìa published *Arte fascista* for the Edizioni Sindacati Artistici, gathering major contributions by leading figures such as the omnipresent Marinetti, old-guard Balla, Bragaglia, prominent artists Depero, Dottori, Prampolini, Volt and Soffici, Russolo, together with Fillìa himself – all arguing forcefully and more visibly for futurism to be elected to the rank of State art because of the potential for renewal of the aesthetic field the movement carried. The tone of the edited volume was varied, but there was a distinct feeling in the contributors that a hegemonic position for futurism within the system of the arts could no longer be taken for granted because of the movement's growing conservatism and progressive detachment from Marinetti. As detailed by Umberto Carpi, the left-wing fringes of futurism supported a strong bond between artistic creation and syndicalism but viewed with suspicion the relationship between the two 'Duce' – Mussolini and Marinetti – because, once again, potentially leading to a conservative, centralizing aesthetic turn which endorsed a distinctively regulatory role of the State.[62]

Besides the Rome-based intellectual circuits gravitating around *Critica fascista*, in the 1920s, more short-lived, little and peripheral magazines and occasional publications shaped the arts' contribution to the totalitarian project with their anti-liberal, anticlerical, pragmatic, inter-artistic and socialist flush of early enthusiasm and with their heartfelt

---

[59] I/1 (July 1926), 17–19.

[60] Salaris, *Artecrazia*, 81–2.

[61] Tonini, 'Prime conclusioni ad un'inchiesta', *L'Arte fascista*, 2/5 (May 1927), 179. Writing from *Il Tevere*, Edgardo Sulis finds Tonini's pro-futurism claims excessive and asks for a dissociation between futurism and Marinetti, see Salaris, *Artecrazia*, 82–3 for further details on the individual articles dealing with the issue of State art. On these points, see also, Ialongo, *Filippo Tommaso Marinetti: The Artist and his Politics* (Madison-Teaneck, Fairleigh Dickinson UP, 2015), 186.

[62] Carpi, *L'estrema avanguardia del Novecento*, 105.

mission to perpetuate intellectual freedom and experimentation over forms of political dirigisme, centralization and statalization.[63] Crucially, these journals and publications acted as counterforces to balance the Marinetti's hegemonic position towards State art by calling for an interdisciplinary understanding of the arts as a system, apt to act upon the social sphere. Founded by Marcello Gallian with Alfredo Poinelli as editor-in-chief, in the same years as the debate on *Critica fascista*, *Spirito Nuovo* (1925–6) wished for a new spirit in the arts against the conservationism of the bourgeoisie. In his two articles dedicated to State art, the impresario Bragaglia advocated the pressing issue of intellectual freedom for artists to be preserved at all costs, following a somewhat eccentric line of argument to that of Marinetti in *Critica fascista* when he officially and unsurprisingly stated that futurism was State art par excellence.[64]

Such a view was shared across other small, independent journals: *Interplanetario* and the Rome-based *I Lupi* edited in 1928 by Gian Gaspare Napolitano and Aldo Bizzarri.[65] *Interplanetario* in particular, published only for one year in 1928 under the joint directorship of Luigi Diemoz and Libero de Libero, had a different take on the politics of the arts and on their role in the framework of State art, which was paradoxically in line with both Novecento italiano and Margherita Sarfatti and Bontempelli's magical realism, and with the belief in the Fascist revolution as a permanent revolution that was never to settle for a bourgeois compromise, a view shared across the provincial fringes of futurism. The journal was acutely aware of the new political subjects emerging from the post-First World War crisis, the masses and of the need for the arts to adjust to their aesthetic and cultural demands. Therefore, the arts, and the new arts for the wide public, had to embrace a pragmatic ethos, be supported by the State and act as forces for social transformation: only in these ways the arts could contribute, as they should, to the life of the regime. These young intellectuals pictured themselves as modern artists who upheld a militant spirit, the spirit of modernity. Finally, the Rome-based, short-lived *2000. Giornale della rivoluzione artistica* (1929) edited by Marcello Gallian with Armando Ghelardini and Alfredo Gaudenzi, epitomized even further such a situation. A minor initiative, offspring of some underground circles in Rome, it nonetheless advocated experimentalism in the arts, especially theatre, with an even more radical international and interdisciplinary flair, again under the aegis of the State.[66] The praise for Marinetti went hand in hand with the criticism towards the decadence of the arts in Italy in general, thereby asking for themselves a more militant role as young artists and intellectuals. These peripheral fringes – whether geographical or not – pointed towards the topicality of the debates on State art across the peninsula and, significantly, to a view of the artists as active participants in the politics of the arts and of the arts themselves functioning as a system able to preserve their potential for

---

[63] Ibid., 154 and passim on the Giuliano futurism and its borrowings from Russian constructivism.

[64] Ibid., 98. Other earlier interventions in the debate on State art were in *Spirito Nuovo*: A. G. Bragaglia, 'La Politica delle Arti', 1/1 (October 1925), 1–2; 'Abbasso i letterati', 1/2 (November 1925), 2; Bragaglia, 'Arte di stato', 2/2 (15 February 1926), 1.

[65] Notable interventions in the debates from peripheral venues are: Umberto Barbaro, 'Una nuova estetica per un'arte nuova', *La ruota dentata*, (1927), 1; A. B. 'Stile fascista', *I Lupi*, I/3 (29 February 1928), 1; Luigi Diemoz, 'Fascismo e Novecentismo', *Interplanetario*, 2 (15 February 1928), 1.

[66] Ghelardini, 'Valutazioni', I/4 (June-August 1919), 1.

innovation as a means of fuelling the tensions between a definition of the movement either as State art or as pure art under the regime.

The years from 1927 to 1932 were on the whole the generation's defining years: the barometer was moved towards militancy and realism as transformative artistic, social and cultural practices. In 1931 the journal *L'Universale* (1931–5), edited by Berto Ricci, addressed once more the issue of State art, only to find a middle ground between the experimentalism of the avant-gardes and the traditionalism of Novecento by pushing modern realism in the arts and literature to assume a key role in the empirical definition not only of modern art but also of State art. State art should be linked to its historical context, situated socially and against academies and artistic prose they believed, hence in line with *Critica fascista* when saluting the renewal of prose fiction and the visual arts.[67] *L'Universale* issued the *Manifesto realista*, almost two years later, on 10 January 1933, written by Berto Ricci, and undersigned by a rather long list of artists and intellectuals of unshakeable Fascist faith: Ottone Rosai, Roberto Pavese, Icilio Petrone, Alberto Luchini, Mario Tinti, Edgardo Sulis, Gioacchino Contri, Diano Brocchi, Alfio del Guercio, Giorgio Bertolini and Romano Bilenchi. Despite not talking openly about the arts, this manifesto affirmed the obligation for politics, religion and culture to engage with the real. By implication, the arts were a political tool, if understood in their pragmatism, since they could act upon society to change it: intellectuals had a militant mission to accomplish according to Ricci et al. Notably, the *Manifesto realista* also obliquely declared that intellectuals and artists should not be confined in any ivory tower but should forge the social transformations unfolding within the public sphere.[68]

In 1932 the '*questione dell'arte fascista*' had already resurfaced under two guises that were informed by and looked back to the initial debate and tied in with the current one in *L'Universale* because of its focus on prose writing and realism as pivotal moments in the definition of State art. In the 1932 *Idee fondamentali e dottrina del fascismo* Benito Mussolini had himself declared that: 'Fascism politically wants to be a realist doctrine; practically, it aspires to resolve not only those problems that arise historically and as such resolve themselves. To act amongst people one needs to enter reality and conquer the forces therein in action.'[69] The idea of social progress was therefore entangled with that of control through a romanticist, irrational view of manhood (of Man upon Man and Nature), since it reinstated the real not as a fragment of an unknowable whole, but as the whole itself which, in its entirety and without borders, could be directed by the totalitarian powers of the New Man.[70] Yet again, the sense of 'construction' was linked to the fascist rhetoric of reactionary modernity. In both instances, the implication is

---

[67] Gherardo 'Opinione su Rosai', *L'Universale*, I/2 (3 February 1931).

[68] On left-wing Fascism in Tuscany (*Bargello* and Strapaese movement), see Giuseppe Iannacone, *Il fascismo sintetico* (Milan, Greco & Greco, 1999), 58–9.

[69] '*Il fascismo politicamente vuole essere una dottrina realistica, praticamente, aspira a risolvere solo i problemi che si pongono storicamente da sé e che da sé trovano e suggeriscono la loro soluzione. Per agire tra gli uomini bisogna entrare nel processo della realtà e impadronirsi delle forze in atto.*' Dottrina (point 6); see also the position on this matter voiced by Ugo Spirito, the mind behind the system of corporations, 'L'iniziativa individuale', *Critica fascista*, X/24 (15 December 1932), 474.

[70] On this point, see Dantini, *Arte e politica in Italia*, 85–6.

that the political construction of people is orchestrated with the purpose of regulating them into a pattern that can better describe the relationship between subjectivity and objectivity; and, crucially, this progressive control has to be applied to the aesthetic as well as ideological domain of the real. Realism as construction, as far as fascist political discourse was concerned, became a totality and stood for that very same hegemonic relation, which sustained totalitarianism's regressive and modernizing ideology.

On 15 February 1932, the opening article of the journal 'Esortazione al realismo' encouraged writers *in toto* to be realist, anti-bourgeois and fascist in order not only to support the national values of State art but also to be competitive at a European and transatlantic level.[71] Writers were expected to 'embrace European values', if progressive, realist and virtuous, but to reject morally degenerate literature; an example of such literature was the brand produced in the Soviet Union, which was not only ideologically but also ethically unacceptable and unsparingly referred to as a 'postribolo' (brothel).[72]

Two months later, in an article entitled 'Arte e costruzione', where he listed the core differences between the present and nineteenth-century realism and decadentism, Attilio Riccio revisited the official position emerging in the year leading to the celebrations of the Decennale, and concluded that now

It is easy to understand why the issue of realism and of its imitation does not concern the modern artist. Non only the novel is a fragment of live [...] but still a fragment of built life [since] modern spirit requires two essential factors: collaboration and construction; and those who think art is a separate realm will never be artists of our time.[73]

In 1932 Riccio introduced another important player to explicate the dynamics in action in the identity-forming process of fascist art and in shaping the profile of State art: the figure of the modern writer, who paradoxically ought to engage in a close and, appreciably, constructive dialogue with reality per se, which was fuelled by technique and morals as discussed already in 1926.[74] According to Riccio and to those belonging to the fascist left-wings, under totalitarian rule the aesthetics of the real acquired a strong ontological dimension because realism itself was synonymous with the process

---

[71] Novecento exhibitions took place in Amsterdam, Geneva, Zurich 1927, Nice 1929, Buenos Aires 1930, Stockholm 1931, Helsinki 1931 and Oslo, 1931; see Salvagnini, *Il sistema delle arti*, 53.

[72] *Critica fascista*, X/4 (15 February 1932), 61, see also Tomaso Napolitano, 'I problemi morali nella letteratura sovietica', ibid., 76. See Iannacone, *Il fascismo sintetico*, 58–71, for further insights on the debate.

[73] 'è facile comprendere perché il problema del realismo e della sua imitazione non si ponga neppure più per l'artista contemporaneo. Non solo il romanzo è un frammento di vita, [...] ma ancora è un frammento di vita costruita [since] lo spirito moderno richiede due fattori essenziali: collaborazione e costruzione; e chi crede di considerare l'arte un regno appartato non sarà mai un artista del nostro tempo', *Critica fascista*, X/8 (15 April 1932), 149. On the new writer, see also Giorgio Granata, 'Aspetti del nuovo scrittore', ibid., 152 and Dogana, 'Funzione dello scrittore' and 'Azione, realtà, idee', *Critica fascista*, X/20 (15 October 1932), 390–1. The relationship between the new Italian novel and the European novel is discussed in virtually all literary and political journals of the day, spanning *L'Italia letteraria*, *Il Saggiatore*, *Orpheus*, *Pegasus* and *Il Convegno*.

[74] Barbaro makes the same point in his essay 'Considerazioni sul romanzo', *Occidente*, I/1 (1932), 21. On the stipends to artists, see Sedita, *Gli intellettuali di Mussolini*.

of identification of the writer with the real and of their moral awareness in a fresh and modern fashion. The modern artist could, therefore, document reality in art but its artistic essence was truly 'modern' only when it remained fragmentary, transformative, elusive and not exhaustibly explicable in terms of mimesis. Riccio repeated a similar concept in *Occidente* the following year, 1933, in an article entitled 'Arte e critica', thereby reinforcing the idea of the arts' role in constructing and modernizing the public realm since *'l'arte fa nascere delle idee'* (art generates ideas) and shapes the real by engaging with international and modern prose writing.[75] Riccio's overall assessment of the role of the arts, implied a rejection of autonomy to marry an ethical dimension originating in the dialectics between subjectivity and objectivity and leading to a more modern appreciation of the foundational idea of totality as a cognitive tool, able to allow Italy to gain a more prominent aesthetic position internationally: it was a matter of construction and of plasticity as advocated aesthetically and politically since the early 1920s from Mexico City to Moscow.

Theatre of Objects I: Realisms + Avant-gardes

Two artworks exemplify the ideas of rationalization and construction that have demarcated the discussions articulated so far about how the seeds of realism were growing within avant-garde art: Pippo Rizzo's (1897–1964) *Il nomade* and Vinicio Paladini's (1902–71) *Complesso onirico n. 1* in the ways they address the representation of the New Man, central to the Fascist anthropological revolution and to an interdisciplinary notion of the arts under the regime.

In *Dialectic of Enlightenment*, Adorno and Horkheimer debated the idea of modern subjectivity and described the old Odysseus as a bourgeois man forced to repress his desires to obey a greater order.[76] By critiquing liberalism and its rationalist approach to knowledge and progress, Adorno and Horkheimer renounced any form of total understanding of the real through the eyes of the subject to embrace instead an idea of reason creating paradoxical moments almost of suspension and protest over action. Reason could only allegedly lead the bourgeois self towards modernity: the pathways of subjectivity and reason do not constitute teleological progress towards a positive conclusion since they simply educe an infinite return of the same, a waiting in vain, as embodied in any modern version of Odysseus, the disempowered bourgeois subjectivity, or in Godot. Odysseus seeks a rational abstract absolute that Adorno and Horkheimer can find only in his repression of his enjoyment of nature, and in an imposed self-control: Odysseus does not want to, or indeed cannot, listen to the Sirens, because his bourgeois logic of self-preservation and self-determination prevails over that of natural gratification. The bourgeois Odysseus that the German philosophers describe could never represent the fascist New Man since his aspirations to rational control over objectivity are inevitably doomed to fail for they inexorably

---

[75] *Occidente*, II/5 (1933), 41.
[76] Adorno and Horkheimer, *Dialectic of Enlightenment*, 40–4.

end in suspension of judgement and paradoxical assertions.[77] Rizzo and Paladini's men exemplify such a dialectical impasse between action and thought, between arts as autonomous and politics as heteronomous exercises.

Sicilian painter and sculptor Pippo Rizzo painted *Il nomade* in 1929, in a Moraviaesque setting, with a male figure aesthetically delineated and structurally shaped by clear lines. The work's style stands at the threshold between futurism and Novecento, both movements at the time racing for hegemony within State art, resonating cubism and the Bauhaus in the use of volumes.[78] The same year Rizzo was appointed Secretary of the Sindacato regionale fascista di belle arti della regione Sicilia (Regional Fasicist Syndicate of Fine Arts in Sicily). Rizzo was an artist who joined the fascist leagues and officially served the State and promoted futurism in Sicily through public exhibitions. His own artwork was greeted with success and exhibited twice: in Palermo and in Rome.[79] In 1930 Rizzo moved on from futurism and accepted Margherita Sarfatti's invitation to exhibit his works at the Novecento exhibition in Buenos Aires in 1930, thereby ending the more experimental phase of his career to embrace a return to order which was close to the example set by Carlo Carrà.

In an almost full-length portrayal, the stylized, elegantly dressed man, who is standing in front of a train with his hands on his hips and his face turned towards something we cannot see or even guess at, is the painter's friend Guido Cesareo. Rizzo's work exemplified the rationalized vision of the New Man/Woman that will emerged so prominently in the 1930s in connection with the debate on State art as well as the need for a realist and empirical approach to the subject matters of the arts. He is presented as an observer, or as a 'too assertive perhaps' modernist and modern character, waiting for something which we cannot tell will ever arrive, but who is unquestionably caught in the aesthetic of the machine, of speed. Is the train passing or has it just arrived? According to futurist '*cromocostruttivismo*', colours have a constructive power since they can be used to arrange spaces and give life to geometrical arrangements through linee-forza.[80] Strong colours – reds, blues, yellows – are assembled following volumes, and arranged not geometrically but carefully delineated nonetheless. The palette of colours gazes back at early futurism with an expressionist proclivity towards boldness, while the clearly

---

[77] Ibid., 59.

[78] Oil on canvas, 161 × 99 cm, Galleria d'Arte Moderna di Palermo. For details about Rizzo's life, writings and artwork, see http://www.archiviopipporizzo.it. (accessed 8 June 2020). This is a new resource (2019) for the study of the Sicilian artist.

[79] From 1926 onwards, Rizzo took part in the Biennali, in 1927 organized in Palermo the Mostra d'arte futurista nazionale. In 1929, he edited the single issue of *Arte futurista italiana* (Palermo, edizioni Pirullà). In 1930, he participated at the Mostra del Novecento italiano in Milan. In 1932, he was appointed director of the Accademia delle Belle arti in Palermo, a city with a particularly lively cultural milieu. He was invited to the I, II and III Quadriennale. *Il nomade* was exhibited twice in 1929: at the second exhibition it was promoted by the Sindacato degli artisti in Palermo and in Rome at the exhibition 'Due futuristi siciliani: Pippo Rizzo e Vittorio Corona', held at the Camerata degli artisti. For more details, see Sergio Troisi, *Pippo Rizzo* (Palermo, Sellerio, 1989); Davide Lacagnina, 'Politica, ideologia, militanza. Pippo Rizzo, critico d'arte e uomo delle istituzioni', in Davide Lacagnina (ed.), *Immagini e forme del potere*, 97–122; and *Anni '30. Arti in Italia oltre il fascismo* (Florence, Giunti, 2012).

[80] Marzio Pinottini, in *Diulgheroff Futurista. Collages polimaterici 1927-1977* (Milan, All'insegna del pesce d'oro, Scheiwiller, 1977), 17–18.

delineated aesthetic shapes of the human figure are instead looking to the Novecento tradition of full, imposing figures which might have attracted Sarfatti's gaze: there is stillness, there is speed, and there is a sense of mystery which recalls Giorgio De Chirico's faceless and colourful *Muse inquietanti* (1917) as well as his numerous trains on the horizon of metaphysical, enigmatic landscapes, and their waiting in vain. De Chirico's trains or boats are at the horizon, far from the centre of the scene, for they depict a journey of universal significance, which is not determined by an individual experience. Rizzo's nomad is static against a well-delineated train of realistic proportions, he is not going anywhere: his bold colours, clear lines and imposing, yet proportionate and compenetrating, volumes turn him into a pervading central image. He is a figure of modernity and not of enigma, his is the modernity of precarity and restlessness, hinting for instance at the one Ernst Ludwig Kirchner and Die Brücke movement (1905–13) had represented so well (see Boccioni's *Stati d'animo*, 1911, and also Balla's geometrical fragmentations) as well as to an assertive male figure which corresponded to the idea of traditional masculinity appealing to the regime. The criss-crossing of lines and the compenetrating of planes is also reminiscent of futurism, while the very same volumes are those Mario Sironi expanded in his *Famiglia* of the same year, and that he continued to expand and augment in the decade to follow as official State art. In 1929 this was State art: a conglomerate of influences without a clear hegemony of one aesthetic order over the other but with a distinct preference for a figurative, albeit subjective, rendering of the real, as we will see happening in *Gli indifferenti*, for example. Rizzo's nomad typifies a brand of the visual arts which married construction with realism in a figurative manner, and one which did fit with the ideas of realism-cum-avantgardes which had become prominent within the peninsula from Rome to Palermo and Turin.

At the other side of the peninsula, polyhedral and cosmopolitan Vinicio Paladini (he studied and spent time in Berlin, Vienna and New York) was born in Moscow, had a background in architecture and was familiar with the Russian avant-gardes. After starting out as a futurist and as a friend of Anton Giulio Bragaglia, Balla and futurist architect Virgilio Marchi, he progressively, if not totally, distanced himself from the movement, and after 1924 he started frequenting left-wing, politically engaged artistic groups, especially in Rome.[81] He soon adopted for himself the category of 'immaginismo', or of 'absurd painting and without an aim. This is, perhaps, the only value we can attribute to this sensory and immginist art' and renounced a rationalist explanation of the real in a way that resemanticized the very notion of realism as codified in the debate on State art.[82] Paladini contributed to several more or less mainstream journals, *Spirito Nuovo*, *La ruota dentata*, *Noi* and later *La rassegna di architettura* and *Quadrante*, always from a firm and interdisciplinary theoretical and experimental angle he borrowed from his knowledge of the Russian avant-gardes. In his first works he drew on metaphysical painting, surrealism and dada to evoke images

---

[81] Paladini was born in Moscow in 1922 to a Russian mother. He was an architect, scenographer and
      director. *Complesso onirico n. 1* (oil on canvas, 110 × 135 cm, private collection). On Paladini's
      political commitment, see Carpi, *Bolscevico immaginista*, 35–65.

[82] Giovanni Lista, *Dal Futurismo all'Immaginismo. Vinicio Paladini* (Bologna, Edizioni del Cavaliere
      Azzurro, 1988), 40.

that could elicit associations able to move the viewers beyond the limits of objective reality which is, however, rendered through distinctively geometrical patterns.[83]

Complesso onirico n. 1 (1932) is a fine sample of this wider trend: it chiefly marries surrealism with dada, expressionism and constructivism to bring an international edge to the Italian artistic culture. The oneiric atmosphere of surrealism is coupled with more explicit references to metaphysical painting: again De Chirico's coeval use of bold colours to delineate volumes and spaces is a reference point, together with the impudent nude woman in black hose and a plaster Antinous covered with a garland of white flowers, all re-enacting the impossibility of knowledge and communication in a classically composed scene. Russian constructivism also peeks through, with the volumes countered by sharply juxtaposed colours and with the generally balanced compositional scene. The act is set in a unpretentious house with modernist furniture and a lonely cactus plant, something highly topical in 1932. Matisse can also be spotted in the bedspread and rug with their striking geometry, together with a direct homage to the tradition of the female nude from Titian (*La Venere di Urbino*, 1538 and *Danae*, 1545) to Manet (*Olympia*, 1863) and Goya (*Maja desnuda*, 1797–1800). If we turn to the literary scene, Bontempelli's short novel *La scacchiera davanti allo specchio* (1922) is echoed in the mixture of geometry, recalling a chessboard, and in the oneiric and fantastic atmosphere the painting directly evokes, suspended between a highly recognizable reality and a potentially disquieting one behind an imaginary chessboard.[84] Once again, the colours chosen recall expressionist shades and tones, and the global composition of the objects is reminiscent of the teachings of the Bauhaus about architecture and composition through use of essential volumes.

Paladini's work is emblematic of a series of contradictions and intersections within the Italian visual arts: on the one hand, the arts were supposed to construct reality, and on the other reality needed to escape any form of construction. The engaged intellectual and architect Paladini moves between the imperatives of Russian avant-gardes, constructivism and his desire to present private, emotional and unconscious moments evoked by and in dreams. This work speaks of an aesthetic and a political tension, embodied at the fringes of the official culture but also within State art: a tension between the rejection of any form of bourgeois, self-referential artistic practice through rationalism and the necessity of maintaining an individual perspective through a humanistic view of the arts and a call for the arts to remain in dialogue with the international scene.

---

[83] *Anni '30. Arti in Italia oltre il fascismo*, 136. 'Estetica del sogno', *Interplanetario*, 4 (15 March 1928), 4.

[84] The echoes of mechanical art are sounding from the pages of Paladini, Pannaggi and Prampolini's *L'arte meccanica, Manifesto futurista*, published in *Noi*, series II, I/2 (May 1923), 1–2, as well as from Paladini's own 'Appello agli intellettuali', published in *Avanguardia: giornale della Federazione italiana giovanile socialista aderente al P.S.I.*, 27 (16 July 1922), reproduced in Lista, *Arte e politica. Il Futurismo di sinistra in Italia* (Milan, Mudima, 2009), 226–7. This article foregrounded the role of the proletariat which should be performed in conjunction with that of the machine, and perceived neither in opposition nor as inferior to those carried out by intellectuals, thereby expanding his original perspective. For further details on these political writings, see Angelo D'Orsi, *Il futurismo tra cultura e politica. Reazione o rivoluzione?* (Rome, Salerno editrice, 2009), 308 and Enrico Buonanno, 'Il Novecento immaginario di Massimo Bontempelli', *Studi Novecenteschi*, 30/66 (2003), 250–8.

Fusions III: Building the Modern Novel

In his preface entitled 'Discorso di Mussolini nel contesto del romanzo', the Duce presented the volume *Antologia degli scrittori fascisti*, which had been edited by former futurist and co-editor of *Roma futurista*, 'ardito' Mario Carli along with G. A. Fanelli, and which collected the best and most modern of fascist writing. In this discourse and in line with the debates on State art, Mussolini recognized the importance of the national novel for the Fascist revolution and in general for the healthy moral life of the nation.[85] With figures to hand, Mussolini had a point to make; from 1920 to 1926 in Italy an average of 6,336 to 6,341 books went into print. From 1927 to 1929, 8,154 books were published, a figure which increased to 11,431 during the 1930s, with a peak of 12,500 in 1933. From 1922 to 1945, 21 per cent of the books published were fiction and in the mid-1930s 47 to 53 per cent of the titles published by Mondadori were in translation. It is worth mentioning that, thanks to their readability and adherence to everyday or even to cosmopolitan reality, translations were the commercial success of the 1930s.[86] Previously, from 1930 to 1935, 19.19 per cent of titles were in translation, with the highest volume, 1,295, in 1933 and the lowest volume in 1939 with 705 titles. Around the same time, in Germany and in the UK, the book market had a circulation of 23,000 and 16,000 titles, respectively.[87] Foreign novels – realist and adventurous – were effectively driving the modernization and rapid industrialization of the publishing industry, and the regime was well aware of its importance in its battle to win 'nazional-popolare' hegemony over the public domain.[88]

What was then understood as the modern national novel? In the Italian literary and artistic circles revolving around literary journals of the 1920s and 1930s, cultural and aesthetic modernity was frequently, albeit generically, understood as everything that broke away from the national literary and artistic tradition and provided alternative, innovative, often foreign, models to conceptualize either aesthetic or intellectual choices.[89] The transatlantic models, repeatedly cited and reviewed across several little

---

[85] Mario Carli and G. A. Faneilli, (eds), *Antologia degli scrittori fascisti* (Florence, Bemporad, 1931). On the futurist milieu of the day, see Emilio Settimelli, *Il codice della vita energica. Ostrica d'Arno. Pensieri di arte e di vita*, in Mario Verdone (ed.), *Scritti inediti* (Cosenza, Pellegrino, 2003).

[86] Francesca Billiani, *Culture nazionali e narrazioni straniere, Italia 1903–1943* (Florence, Le Lettere, 2007), 127–41 and Christopher Rundle, *Il vizio dell'esterofilia. Editoria e traduzioni nell'Italia fascista* (Rome, Carocci, 2019), 54–62.

[87] If in 1921 26.6 per cent of the population was illiterate, in 1936 the percentage had decreased to 21.5 per cent: approximately 25 per cent in the North; 50 per cent in the South and less than 50 per cent in the centre, see Billiani, *Culture nazionali*, 152–6, for further data and for a discussion about translation policies.

[88] Billiani, *Culture nazionali*, 181–90.

[89] For example, Edgardo Sulis, 'Simbolismo italiano', *Arte fascista*, I/3 (September 1926), 1: '*Saranno tutti d'accordo nell'ammettere che il romanzo (risparmiamoci il "vero e proprio") in Italia non c'è mai stato*' (Everyone would agree that there never was a [let's spare ourselves the idea of the 'real and authentic one'] novel in Italy). He proposes the idea of an Italian historical novel that can turn facts into fantasy as happens in the great European tradition. Some eight years later, the same encouragement to build a solid national tradition by creating new audiences for the novel was forthcoming from futurist journals, see editor Lino Cappuccio, 'Arte editoriale futurista', *Nuovo futurismo*, I/1 (30 May 1934), 2; and Federica Millefiorini, *Tra avanguardia e accademia. La pubblicistica futurista nei primi anno trenta* (Pisa, Giardini editori e stampatori), 134–5.

Italian magazines of the Ventennio, were the likes of Anglo-American modernists Joseph Conrad, James Joyce, T. H. Huxley, Virginia Woolf, Henry James, D. H. Lawrence; highbrow European authors André Gide, Franz Kafka, Thomas Mann, Paul Valéry, American realist John Dos Passos, and polymath W. E. B. Du Bois, alongside Italian high modernists Italo Svevo, Luigi Pirandello, Marcel Proust and the highly fashionable New Objectivity of the Weimar Republic.[90]

Modern Italian novels also tended to fuse social with psychological realism, as we see happening, for instance, in the following works most markedly oriented towards a 1930s take on realism: Giovanni Comisso's *Giorni di guerra* (1930); Corrado Alvaro's *Gente in Aspromonte* (1931); Umberto Barbaro's *Luce fredda* (1931); Enrico Emanuelli's *Radiografia di una notte* (1932); Ignazio Silone's *Fontamara* (1933); Elio Vittorini's *Garofano rosso* (1933); Carlo Bernari's *Tre operai* (1934); Romano Bilenchi's *Il capofabbrica* (1935); and Mario Soldati's *America primo amore* (1935). Thus, when the young Alberto Moravia published his debut *Gli indifferenti* his concerns were also those of the decade to come: how to find a modern form to depict old anxieties, simultaneously avoiding 'futile' and politically unacceptable introspection.

In May 1930 in *La Cultura*, Leone Ginzburg published an article entitled 'Formalisti e Marxisti', detailing the famous polemic between *contenutisti* and *calligrafi*. The Turinese intellectual suggested a more innovative method for gaining a deeper understanding of contemporary writers, one that evaluated both form and content without reciprocal exclusion or hierarchy. Despite not favouring either of the two poles, Ginzburg's incisive intervention indicated the strong need for a redefinition of the Italian critical landscape as well as of his methodological perspective, and it was duly echoed in *Critica fascista*. On 1 May 1933, co-editor of *Critica fascista*, Gherardo Casini, after briefly dismissing the *calligrafisti*, suggested that the core problem was to determine the extent to which it was the chief task of the arts, under the regime, to bring back the 'real' to its own topic in order to realize its full aesthetic potential and, in doing so, generate artistic creations that responded to the demands of the Fascist revolution.[91] Similarly the Luciano Anceschi private papers confirm that this question has a long tail and how similar an attitude to Casini's was that upheld by young intellectuals when calling for an anti-literary mentality that they deemed sill not strong enough in Italy.[92] In his resignation letter to the editors of the Bologna-based journal *Nettuno*, Anceschi criticized the excessive literariness and the lack of political commitment of this publication. In his swift reply, young editor-in-chief Wolfango Rossi asserted that the aim of *Nettuno* was to 'represent in an indirect way the political values of the time' but that he refused to accept that direct political action was a task literature should carry out.[93]

---

90 I have sampled these authors from a selection of reviews (*Lo spettatore italiano, Orpheus, Il Saggiatore, Corrente, Fiera e Italia letteraria, La ronda, Il Convegno* and *Solaria*). On this point, see Ben-Ghiat, *Fascist Modernities*, 32–3, 44–5.

91 'Elementi politici di una letteratura', *Critica fascista*, XI/9 (1 May 1933), 161–2.

92 F. 'Anceschi', f. 'Nettuno', Anceschi to the editors of *Nettuno*, Milan, 7 May 1934, Archiginnasio, Bologna.

93 F. 'Anceschi', f. 'Nettuno', Rossi to Anceschi, Bologna, 8 May 1934, Archiginnasio, Bologna.

In the specific case of the reflection on the novel as the most appropriate genre for telling and showing modern reality, such intersections between the political and the aesthetic realms concurred around the idea of the construction of the New Man/Woman for its crucial importance to both spheres: the novel had a political meaning when documenting the lives of new men and their collective consciousness. On 1 December 1932, debating the boundaries of individual and collective consciousness, Valentino Piccioli published an article on Babbitt and American realism. Babbitt, the '*uomo* standard' from across the Atlantic, could be legitimately saved from oblivion because he embodied a document of 1930s American life. Individual consciousness, even in a corrupting society like the North American one, could become collective, as under Fascism, provided that it paid pragmatic attention to the real, better to the social real, and it avoided the pitfalls of fake expressions of democracy, hidden in ideologically vacuous concerns. Babbitt, the fragment, could be rescued if he became part of the realistically portrayed total entity of the collective envisaged by totalitarian art.[94] Similarly and equally meaningfully, on the 1 December 1932, Domenico Carella, in one of his contributions calling for renewed attention towards realism in response to the European economic crisis, argued that

> The two main problems of the new novel are realism and collectivism. Indeed, individual consciousness, differently from that of other modern societies, under Fascism can become collective only if attentive to the real and to the social elements and if it shapes itself not in response to ideological but to pragmatic and concrete issues.[95]

The kernel in this fresh view on aesthetics meeting politics was the fascist New Man/Woman – equally individual and collective, morally sound and politically devoted. Many of the debates taking place in literary journals tackled the issue of 'how to write a novel' and to what degree it had to engage with the supposed 'real'.[96] Evidence of this growing attention towards the real can, however, also be found in less expected places than the official and anti-Crocean *Critica fascista*.[97] Set up in 1932 by Armando Ghelardini – with the support of Umberto Barbaro, Vinicio Paladini and Elio Talarico,

---

[94] 'Babbitt l'uomo standard', *Critica fascista*, X/23 (1 December 1932), 456. See also Giacomo Lumbroso, 'Per un romanzo del nostro tempo', ibid., 460.

[95] '*I due problemi del nuovo romanzo sono quindi quelli di realismo e collettivismo. Infatti la coscienza dell'individuo, diversamente da quella delle altre società moderne, con il fascismo può diventare collettiva solo se è attenta al reale e al sociale e se si forma non in risposta a problemi ideologici ma pragmatici e concreti*', 'Coscienza collettiva e coscienza individuale', *Critica fascista*, X/23 (1 December 1932), 448, but also the article written with Casini, 'Nostro realismo', *Critica fascista*, XI/7 (15 April 1933), 133.

[96] For instance, *Il Saggiatore* (1930–3), *Orpheus* (1932–4), *Il Convegno* (1919–38), *Lo spettatore italiano* (1924), to cite some of the most directly linked with the debates taking place internationally.

[97] In *La ronda*, a review which was a bastion of the calligrafisti, see Billiani, 'Return to Order as Return to Realism in Two Italian Elite Literary Magazines of the 1920s and the 1930s: *La ronda* and *Orpheus*', *The Modern Language Review*, 108/3 (2013), 854–5; or in the Milanese review *Il Convegno*, one of the many Italian incarnations of the *Nouvelle Revue Française*, which championed a return to realism both as a way of protecting and of expanding the national tradition.

all former members of the editorial team of the short-lived review *La ruota dentata* (1927) and the small publishing house La bilancia (1923–5), and of Bontempelli himself – the short-lived review *Occidente* (1932–5), modernist and transatlantic in aspiration, is a case in point. Like many other small reviews of the early 1930s, from *Il Saggiatore* to *Orpheus* via *Camminare*, *Occidente* too can be aligned with the youth culture of the regime (and with its relative freedom), champion both of the idea of art as a collective enterprise and of the novel as constructing and documenting the real, without 'eloquence' and through lucid prose writing. Agent of a cultural position and vision within the Fascist regime that almost indiscriminately championed avant-garde and innovation, *Occidente* is an important agent in the field and in our argument, because it gives clear evidence of how concerns regarding the European and Italian novel went hand in hand with those regarding realism, understood in the broad sense of a political and aesthetic statement, which encapsulated the very same idea of modernity and the new forms of narrative communication.[98]

Occidente's ideal reader was a 'cultured and intelligent man', but the review's hope was also to be able to put Italian writers in touch with foreign modernist and realist writers to bridge the gap between national and international avant-garde experiences and the fresh developments in the new media communications, cinema, photography, radio and montage.[99] In the first issue of the review, we find a similar line of translations of Aldous Huxley and D. H. Lawrence, to be followed by Franz Werfel, Liam O'Flaherty, Jean Cocteau, James Joyce, Valery Larbaud, Joseph Conrad, William Faulkner, Virginia Woolf, John Dos Passos, Max Beerbohm, Waldo Frank, Hans Canossa, James Cain and Ernest Hemingway. However, we also find surfacing from the pages of *Occidente* the most progressive of Italian writing and articles by men standing at the centre of the regime as well as on its fringes: Alvaro, Bontempelli, Mario Puccini, Ennio Flaiano, Barbaro, Rocca, Paolo Orano, Corrado Pavolini, Bottai, Bragaglia, Marinetti, Salvatore Quasimodo, Vittorini, Federico Tozzi, G. B. Angioletti and Francesco Jovine.

In virtually every issue at least one article deals with the novel or with the novel in the European context. In his 'Ritratti americani', Attilio Riccio drew an incisive and forceful connection between 'Hemingway and Faulkner [who] look like each other because they are both looking for a new style', and despite being guilty of some moral slippage 'Faulkner's characters are always human beings'.[100] Individuality cannot be tantamount to self-referentiality, but must be a reflection of a socially embedded subjectivity so as to become synonymous with the same collective performance described by Enrico Rocca in his essay on 'Hermann Kesten o delle trasfigurazioni del cuore'. Rocca attributed the deep moral sense exuding from the German writer's art to his ability to

---

[98] For a discussion with copious details of the Rome-based avant-garde climate, see Carpi, *Bolscevico immaginista*.

[99] Armando Ghelardini, 'Introduzione', I/1 (1932), 1. See Alessandra Briganti, '*Occidente* e la capitale delle avanguardie', *Letteratura italiana contemporanea*, 9/25 (1988), 1–24 in relation to the position of the journal within the Rome milieu; and Briganti, 'Umberto Barbaro dall'avanguardia al neorealismo', *Letteratura italiana contemporanea*, 5/11 (1984), 187–209 for Barbaro's profile.

[100] '*Hemingway e Faulkner [che] si assomigliano perché cercano un nuovo stile*' 'I personaggi di Faulkner sono sempre esseri umani', *Occidente*, III/8 (1934), 111–17.

activate a truthful and, largely unmediated, individual performative engagement with the real. A socially and collectively – a morally and individually – entrenched novel could therefore come into existence in Italy and across European literature, since 'the children of this century are now called Glaeser, Körmendi, Liepmann, Kästner, Kesten, Süskind. Why is this? Moravia and Gambini, even?'[101] In 1933 Tommaso Landolfi, in an article on two contemporary Russian writers and satirists 'Ilf e Petrov' acknowledged precisely how inspiring Russian literature could be for Italian writers when founded on the two interlocking principles of *'costruzione e moralità'* (construction and morality), which had already been mentioned in *Critica fascista*.[102]

In a clarifying essay 'Considerazioni sul romanzo', which was also published in Telesio Interlandi's *Quadrivio* in the same year Barbaro returned to the specific debate on the Italian novel and condemned the crude techniques of the avant-gardes, protégées of the old European culture, in order to champion the rehabilitating of aesthetic constructivism:

> The need was felt to reclaim technique and a return was made to the carefully constructed and well thought-out work in its most typical from, the novel: the latter, however, like rationalist architecture and all avant-gardisms, is full of self-absorbed voracity, and now it aspires to be nothing but fantasy; nothing but technique, like in detective novels (the old anti-artistic need that Guerrazzi was already talking about long ago [...]) or nothing but sociology, morality or content, that is to say, still nothing but fantasy.[103]

Significantly, Barbaro, novelist and noted, influential film critic, judged as thoroughly pointless any overindulgence in either pure technique or straightforward realism. Both attitudes resulted in pure and dry sociological forms of identification between subject and object that simply evoked futile expressions of unproductive imagination; if something had to change in the novel as form, Barbaro added, the first

---

[101] *'I figli del secolo oggi si chiamano, Glaeser, Körmendi, Liepmann, Kästner, Kesten, Süskind, e perché no? Anche Moravia e Gambini'*, *Occidente*, II/2 (1933), 53–9. See also Rocca's article in *Critica fascista*, 'L'arte fascista è la grande arte', IV/21 (1 November 1926), 395.

[102] 'Nota su Ilf e Petrov', *Occidente*, IV/10 (1934), 59–64.

[103] *'Si è sentito il bisogno di recuperare la tecnica e si è tornati all'opera costruita e pensata, nella sua forma tipica, il romanzo: ma esso, come l'architettura razionalista, e come gli avanguardismi, è pieno di eautontimerumena voracità, oggi aspira ad essere tutta fantasia; tutta tecnica, come nei romanzi gialli (vecchio bisogno antiartistico di cui parlava già Guerrazzi [...]) o tutta sociologia e morale o contenuto, cioè ancora tutta fantasia'*, Umberto Barbaro, 'Considerazioni sul romanzo', 20. Barbaro was the author of a realist novel entitled *Luce fredda* (Lanciano, Carabba, 1931), which in many ways reflected both his interest in Soviet cinema and montage and Moravian references in the portrayal of the stifling interiors and the unforgiving characterization. For an analysis of *Luce fredda* and a comparison with *Gli indifferenti*, see Lea Durante, 'Avanguardia e realismo in *Luce fredda* di Umberto Barbaro', *Critica letteraria*, 106 (2000), 111–28; while for an overview on the reactions by fascist authorities to the publication of Moravia's novel, see Ben-Ghiat, *Fascist Modernities*, 58–9, and Maria Di Giovanna, *Teatro e narrativa di Umberto Barbaro* (Rome, Bulzoni, 1992). On Barbaro artistic profile and involvement with cinema, see Fabio Andreazza, 'Prima della specializzazione. La traiettoria di Umberto Barbaro dalla letteratura al cinema', in Raffaele De Berti and Massimo Locatelli (eds), *Figure della modernità nel cinema italiano (1900–1940)* (Pisa, ETS, 2008), 315–31.

priority any writer had to set was that of 'rifiutare forme di arte pura' (reject pure art) and 'l'arte evasione' (escapist art) (ivi). And, he continued: 'to an artist of good will these notes can offer a fresh perspective to mythologise in a modern way the lost paradise, the burst of the object which becomes the subject, of the subject which leaves himself behind'.[104] In the full-fledged age of consensus, the Italian novel had increasingly and unquestionably to look at the international scene to transform itself into the artistic form that embodied aesthetic and political modernity and commitment. Just like the claims in *Critica fascista*, *Occidente* legislated that realist aesthetic and modernizing social transformations could take place by rejecting forms of solipsistic wandering to embrace morality and a closer contact with objectivity; thus 'The new novel has to get in touch with the real since any true morality in art consists in bringing the reader back into contact with, and constraining him within, the narrow confines of the everyday. The writer has the moral duty of infusing hope in the reader'.[105] Not unlike the position emerging from *Critica fascista*, the subjective is reinstated in the objective entity of the real through moral commitment and an engaged attitude on the part of the writer towards (growing numbers of) readers, especially of fiction. The writer's task was to be that of infusing hope for social change into the reader and, in a totalitarian fashion, of making him or her affectively into an individual stance made collective. Modernist subjectivity is transposed once more into a morality-cum-individuality, while morality per se is rearranged into an expression of the social common good. In this vein, the question of the novel recaptured the same political debate over the role of the arts under the regime and its stark rejection of nineteenth-century realism in favour of a new realism, which had to be founded on solid moral ground.

Umberto Forti in 'Tecnica del mondo moderno' went a step further in this direction and, in his strenuous efforts to demarcate modern literary spaces, stated that 'A culture which is estranged from technology and science is too much like those grand old nineteenth-century houses which had two reception rooms, plenty of grand features, but not even the tiniest of bathrooms'.[106] Such literature could not address the basic demands of humanity but only frivolous accessories, lacking awareness, as it did, of the true moral engagement of the writer with the readers' demands for modernization and with the necessity of also exposing real, ordinary life (that ordinary life the regime was progressively rationalizing).

Technique and experimentalism were acceptable only and if they echoed the everyday and not if there were means of constructing alternative, individualist, aloof worlds. In 'Coefficienti nuovi nel romanzo', Elio Talarico, a 'convinced fascist',[107] reinforced a similar point when he wrote that the task of the new novel is to avoid

---

[104] '*ad un artista di buona volontà questi appunti possono offrire uno sguardo per mitizzare modernamente il paradiso perduto, lo slancio dell'oggetto che si soggettizza, del soggetto che esce di sé*', ibidem.

[105] '*Il nuovo romanzo deve entrare in contatto con il reale dal momento che la vera moralità dell'arte sta nel ricongiungere, ricostringere nelle angustie della quotidianità il lettore. Lo scrittore ha il dovere morale di infondere speranza nel lettore*', ibidem.

[106] '*una cultura estraniata dalla tecnica e dalla scienza somiglia troppo alla vecchie case Umbertine, che avevano due salotti, molte cose di pretesa, ma nemmeno una stanzetta da bagno*', Umberto Forti, *Occidente*, III/9 (1934), 7.

[107] Ben-Ghiat, *Fascist Modernities*, 57.

any 'scivolone morale' (moral slip) like Gide and sexuality, or '*sentimentalismo e intellettualismo*' (sentimentalism or intellectualism) like Huxley and all his '*mirabolante tecnica contrappuntistica*' (barnstorming technique of counterpoint), to ask his readers: 'what are we waiting, then, why don't we start building again, from right now'?[108]

Theatre of Objects II: To Carla, Michele and All the Others

Cause célèbre of the 1930s because of how it fused realism with psychologism, *Gli indifferenti* (Alpes, 1929) by young debutant Moravia marked the start of this realist era by putting its debates in practice, for he succeeded in capturing the shift from modernist self-reflectivity to the needs of narrating historical symbols of a generation and of its national consciousness on the verge of self-destruction; furthermore, he sustained his narrative efforts through an innovative technique, which anchored its subject matter to the rock of the real.[109] Read against the light of the debate on modern realism and of its intertwining ramifications with the aesthetic and political fields we have detailed, and not in its own right or in psychoanalytical terms, Moravia's novel is central to the development of the fascist culture of the real and of modernity in the 1930s. In one of the most incisive and lucid assessments of the novel, Roberto Esposito has clearly stated that a close relationship between *Gli indifferenti*'s logical and historical form with the social context of the time ('social relationships') can be drawn to achieve a sharper understanding of the novel's literary as well as political implication.[110]

If the modernist use of multiple and highly subjective narrators attempted to transcribe the stream of consciousness, the non-linear movement of time and the self-consciousness about the form of the novel, the use of hyper-realist dialogue and a unequivocal move towards a sharp social critique defined the turn towards documenting the real. The dialectical oscillations between outer and inner – as Lewis argued for the modernist pre-First World War decade and as Esposito reiterates in his analysis – in the novels of the totalitarian decade, and in *Gli indifferenti*, is rejuvenated through a process of internalization, whereby the 'inner evidence' of psychology enabled realist perspectivism, whose pre-existence modernism had been obliged to forget.[111] Michele and Carla Ardengo, the young siblings at the centre of *Gli indifferenti*, not only exemplify the moral decadence of a generation, or even a crisis beyond repair, but also an attempt at experimenting with perspectivism, especially in dialogic form and with an expressionistic use of punctuation, which reaffirmed realism as a process that weaved the individual into the collective via a set of conflicting, paralysing and affective responses.

---

[108] '*Che cosa si aspetta dunque, perché non costruire davvero, subito?*,' *Occidente*, II/3 (1933), 9. Not too dissimilar ideas as repeated in B. [Bontempelli], 'Tramonto dell'arte borghese', *Occidente*, II/5 (1933), 73; and Elio Talarico, 'Mussolini scrittore italiano', *Occidente*, II/4 (1933), 7–9.

[109] For an incisive discussion of the relationship between the 1930s novel and the fascist idea of modernity and nation-building, see Ben-Ghiat, *Fascist Modernity*, 51–69.

[110] Roberto Esposito, *Il sistema dell'indifferenza. Moravia e il fascismo* (Bari, Dedalo, 1978), 210.

[111] Ibid., 41–78.

The reality of the two young protagonists in particular exists only in their dream-like fantasies, which do not materialize in actions and largely linger at the level of projections – both Michele's attempt to kill his mother's lover Leo and Carla's illusions about a more dignified existence persist in almost hallucinatory states throughout. Yet, despite its thematic repertoire, *Gli indifferenti* is neither a purely existentialist nor a straightforward realist novel, as is often claimed. It is, instead, a complex example of the intricacies between the much theorized act of documenting the real, and affect as a driver for individual and collective self-narration and identification. The real in the novel is present through the lenses of the protagonists, perspectivism (all of them except Leo), thereby multiplying, in a very recognizable setting, its significations. However, paradoxically, the novel does reaffirm realism in presenting reality as the ultimate test for the two siblings to take. The new life the characters hope for, the realization of the 'vero' (in Michele's formulation as he ruminates about his putative trial for killing Leo) is not to be achieved or to be granted to any of the protagonists. The closing chapter of the novel sees Carla and Michele running towards their home – while the woman stops to ponder her condition: '*Le parve di essere chiusa fuori dal mondo, solo col fratello in quella scatola buia e di essere portata a grande velocità verso un luogo sconosciuto; dove? Così finivano la giornata e la sua vecchia vita: con una domanda alla quale era impossibile rispondere.*'[112] Besides the reference to an uncertain future, the image shows us the body of the protagonist trapped in a box and unable to break free from it – meteorological condition aside. Carla is mentally trapped but also realistically, physically not in control of a unified self. Over the three days in the Ardengo's upper-class house in Rome, as this final quote suggests, the reader witnesses the failure of all the characters, but especially Carla and Michele, to become a New Man/Woman, too embedded as they are in the old bourgeois neurosis of self-indulgence; or unable, once more, to come into contact with the reality of their own selves, or indeed of their own collectivity, either through rational choice and engagement or affective responses. By the end, Carla had remained confined in the same box she was at the beginning of the novel, and Michele is still adamant that the right attitude in life is that of pretending: '*Non esistevano per lui più fede, sincerità, tragicità; tutto attraverso la sua noia gli appariva pietoso, ridicolo, falso; bisognava appassionarsi, agire*' (233).

If any mental attempt at rationalizing the outer world leads not to change but to apathy and indifference, it is the portrayal of the bodies of these two protagonists, the body of this 1930s realist novel, that mostly defines their inability to become real, to create a profound symbiotic unity with their surroundings.[113] To paraphrase Roberto Esposito, their indifference manifests itself in their difference from the others around them and not simply in their inability to act upon themselves and their surroundings.[114]

---

[112] *Gli indifferenti* (Milan, Bompiani, 1949), 275.
[113] Carla's bodily imbalance is presented to the reader in the first few pages of the novel and is reiterated throughout: '"*Resti a cena con noi?*" ella domandò alfine senza alzare a testa. "*Sicuro,*" rispose Leo accendendo una sigaretta; "*forse non mi vuoi?*" Curvo, seduto sul tavolo, egli osservava la fanciulla con una attenzione aida; gambe dai polpacci storti, ventre piatto, una piccola valle di ombra fra i grossi seni, braccia e spalle fragili, e qualla testa rotonda così pesante sul collo sottile' (4).
[114] Esposito, *Il sistema dell'indifferenza*, 211.

Furthermore, their difference is not to be read as a sign of distinction, as an act of resistance, but rather as a constantly shifting dichotomy between two dialectical poles (light and shadow, inside and outside, reality and imagination).

At a political level, *Gli indifferenti* is both a chief example of decadent fascist society and of its inability to change and be submerged by the very same indifference that enabled Michele to '*cambiare ogni giorno, come altri il vestito, le proprie idee e i propri atteggiamenti*' (266) or Carla's realization that '*la vita era quel che era, era meglio accettarla, che giudicarla*' (266). In their masochistic and doomed pursuit of change, the young protagonists of *Gli indifferenti*, and of Italian fascist society as a whole, could not abandon their subjectivity to embrace 'real' objectivity, to create meaning and become the new modern individual. The system of indifference therefore would imply that Carla eventually married the wrong man and Michele continued with his logic of Olympic boredom, if not of differentiation: '*Non ho fatto nulla [...] Non ho amato Lisa [...] non ho ucciso Leo [...] non ho che pensato [...] ecco il mio errore*' (280).

That being said, the profound impasse of the protagonists of *Gli indifferenti* is encapsulated not only in their own psychological dramas but more precisely in the new logic of realism, via modernism, which fuses subjectivity into objectivity without finding a totalizing synthesis. Every character (apart from the true fascist Leo and perhaps the street-wise Lisa, or the prostitute Michele briefly encounters) lacks a trajectory towards a new idea of reality, a new conceptualization of existence for a new man, which requires action. In the tragedy-like setting and unity of time, space and action that they inhabit, the protagonists of *Gli indifferenti* document the 'real' in its self-indulgent individuality and labyrinthine autonomy, unable to transgress any border and to follow any *telos* of historical change.

Moravia's innovative realism was to mark a decade, and a trend young writers were eager to follow. In 1932 Enrico Emanuelli published *Radiografia di una notte* with Ceschina, a small publishing house based in Milan. Because of its explicitly experimental nature, spanning modernist interior monologue, New Objectivity and American realism, *Radiografia di una notte* can be interpreted as a response to the regime's call for a new Italian novel that could depict modern reality without resorting to the aesthetics of artificiality, or to the *prosa d'arte*. The novel moves through its twenty-six short chapters at a fast pace which mirrors that of modern life and use technology to reproduce the perception of objectivity: it provides an X-ray of the daily life of a group of citizens in a precise social setting. Each chapter, in rapid sequence, gives a glimpse of either the mental or external reality of the protagonists, thereby emphasizing the novel's constructive mechanisms and its anti-naturalistic take on storytelling. The narrative rhythm is determined by quick snapshots, which move without explicit continuity from one to the next and often leave the reader in a state of doubt about what precisely has been recounted. In a nutshell, modern realism entailed broken narratives, introspection and artistic juxtapositions.

A dissecting and disaffecting attitude towards the real and its temporality is that of young and versatile writer and journalist Mario Soldati in his *24 ore in un studio cinematografico*, published under the pseudonym of Franco Pallavera (Corticelli,

Milan).[115] Written between 1934 and 1935, the novel reconstructs a day spent on a film set, with a detailed analysis, akin to Emanuelli's, of the figures that populate the place. From chapter 1, 'Risveglio', dedicated to the daily routines of the diva in her existence split between glamour and solitude, we are progressively introduced to the leading characters of this world: the director, the extras, the cameramen, the technicians and the make-up artists. A fine sample of *cinéroman*, mixing technical details and documentary-style writing with intense lyrical moments, it questions the cinema industry, the most successful propaganda machine the regime had in 1935, as a fake world of illusions and turns experimental prose into a popular novel, or better into an everyday situation.

24 ore in un studio cinematografico's extradiegetic narrator keeps distant from the characters, like a handy-camera in a neorealistic film, to present an '*impressione vivace della lavorazione di uno studio*' 'a lively impression of the daily working routine of a studio'.[116] *24 ore* is a fast-paced, realist-synthetic short novel that is also highly idiosyncratic and impressionist, as the author himself claims in the introductory note.[117] However, it is also a collective, choral novel (Cesare Pavese translated Dos Passos in 1935 for the Mondadori's series Medusa), because none of the characters could exist without the author's skilful filming through the camerawork of the narrator with a distinctive meta-narrative tone. The narrator punctuates his telling by showing glimpses of the contemporary world with serendipitous comments on other films, on the art of acting, on cinema jargon, on film starts. Soldati carves out a more experimental, even more acerbic writing style, than Moravia, one which favours a completely unmediated, dialogue-based, narrative tone in order to support a closer contact with the real, which is yet unfamiliar for the reader, while maintaining the alienating and anti-compositional ethos of the avant-gardes.

Short episodes, almost like Emilio Cecchi's ephemeral cameos in *Pesci rossi* (1920), give light to figures and situations, which are not arranged around a frame: they can live individual lives or, if they so wish, collective ones united by an invisible thread. Soldati's realism recalibrates subjectivity and objectivity as mutually dependent moments. In this way, Soldati uses modern realism to surpass simple experimentation and melt into an impressionist form of realism which is also deeply embedded in interdisciplinarity and in a non-linear narrative that often derails and offers alternatives paths through an idea of technology as modernization of the arts. Soldati's characters are not in charge of the story they find themselves in, and like Moravia's characters, they cannot take control of their lives, and thus progress. Fragmented thoughts, conveyed by 'broken' (heavily punctuated) sentences litter the narrative, often making it difficult for readers to follow.[118]

---

[115] From 1931 to 1934 Soldati taught at Columbia University in New York.

[116] Mario Soldati, *24 ore in uno studio cinematografico* (Palermo, Sellerio, 2003), 9.

[117] Ibid.

[118] Ruth Ben-Ghiat, 'The Realist Aesthetic in Italy, 1930–1950', 627–65 and *Fascist Modernities*, 59–61 discuss the novel in detail. See also Francesca Billiani, 'Documenting the Real across Modernity in the 1930s: Political and Aesthetic Debates around and about the Novel in Fascist Italy', *Italian Studies*, 71/4 (2016), 477–95.

Technique is on display: how to shoot a film, or even how to apply make-up are part of the fictional snapshots of a real day. A chapter is entirely devoted to the discussion of cinematic techniques and camerawork in remarkable detail. Cinematography exists in its own right and it is different from the other arts because it is the modern art. References and comparisons with other arts are woven in the narrative: to architecture, to the visual arts (47, 59) to give an impression of reality as well as to reach outside the fading boundaries of fiction. In Soldati's words: 'We should keep in mind that one thing is cinematographer one this is literature' (65).[119] Such a demarcation between literature and cinema, and vice versa, is a declaration of distrust towards any artistic form which simply reproduces or documents reality, because reality exists only as an indefinite form of technological reproduction: reality can be documented but will always exceed its own fictional boundaries. As we will see in the case of the Mostra della rivoluzione in 1932, the artwork possesses an interactive nature which sees modernity as the outcome of new narrative and visual compositional technologies: cinema is the highest of art in this novel, as notoriously Mussolini too declared elsewhere about this art form. In combining fresh narrative techniques that reveal the artificiality of the fictional product and reportage, this novel also questions the boundaries of realist narration since what has been scrutinized is actually even too close to what a real life might be and, therefore, exceed the boundaries of the fictional world.

These novels published around the same time share a message: the degeneration of society (and of the family unit) is related to a widespread lack of any ethical mission and the pursuit of rather frivolous desires. In an implicit overlap with Luigi Pirandello and Moravia, Soldati's work indicates no escape from the circumstances the characters more or less willingly find themselves in, other than by totally accidental incidents of life.

Theatre of Objects III: The Boundaries of Realism: Constructing a Collective Subjectivity?

The 1920s had seen the start of the reconstructing of the novel form with Antonio Borgese's *Rubè* (1921), while the following decade opened with another type of realism: Corrado Alvaro's *Gente in Aspromonte* (1931). These works summarize some of the tendencies about morality and realism we have so far discussed in our analysis of the profile of State art, and the line it trod between modernity, modernization and realism.

Published in 1921 by Treves, *Rubè* was reissued in 1928 by Mondadori. It documents the moral crisis of a nation between the First World War and the rise of Fascism since the novel is not only the story of a man caught in an existential crisis, it is also a portrait of a changing historical landscape, leading to violent social

---

[119] '*Bisogna di nuovo tenere presente che altro è cinematografo e altro è letteratura*'. Guido Davico Bonino [1985] 'Nota', in *Mario Soldati* (Palermo, Sellerio, 2003), 151–5 and Massimo Grillandi, *Mario Soldati* (Florence, La Nuova Italia, 1979).

transformations. Filippo Rubè is an ambitious young man, who arrives in Rome from the provinces with a degree in law, ready to become a lawyer and then enter into the political arena. At the beginning of his new life, like many of his generation, Rubè is an enthusiastic supporter and advocate of the First World War. However, he very quickly becomes disillusioned, and after the end of the war, like many other men, he struggles to find a place in the new social fabric of the country. The novel draws a sharp connection between economic precarity and social frustration, presenting these conditions as a prelude to the dictatorship.[120] Told in four parts and twenty-four chapters, *Rubè* pioneers a potential model for a new Italian novel with a constructive dimension seen in its long-narrative, which rejected the 'frammentismo' of artistic prose for privileging the architecture of the plot; the patent failure of a generation; and the demand for social and, crucially, political change. Not only it should be read in relation to the collection of short essays entitled *Tempo di edificare* published by Borgese two years later, in 1923, but also as a frontrunner of the 1930s return to a type of realism morally inflected and socially attuned, if not imbued with local colour.

A decade later, such a narrative reframing became the *pièce de résistance* of a generation of young writers in search of a realist narrative that could give voice to their moral crisis, desire for objectivity and for experimentation. *Gente in Aspromonte*, a collection of thirteen short stories by Corrado Alvaro, published in 1931 by the Florentine publisher Le Monnier, characterizes a regional form of return to realism by foregrounding the local facet as a mirror of a national moral crisis. By tackling the *'questione meridionale'*, often from the perspective of its peasant protagonists (the *umili*), this short novel brought Alvaro critical acclaim as a national novelist and a direct comparison with Giovanni Verga. The collection's powerful exploration of the poverty, exploitation and injustice endemic in the Italian South renders it one of the finest examples of the return to realism of the 1930s. Set in the author's native Calabria, the narrative delves into the difficult realities of post-unification rural southern Italian life and shares a desire for the arts to return to the local realm of *mediterraneità* as it emerged, especially in architecture, being a more authentic living dimension.[121] *Gente in Aspromonte* responded to the call for a novel which was in touch with reality directly: a call for literature as engagement and for an active role of

---

[120] Maria Cristina Terrile, 'La narrazione dell'inettitudine in *Rubè* di Giuseppe Antonio Borgese', *Italica*, 72/1 (1995), 40–53; Gian-Paolo Biasin, 'Il rosso o il nero: testo e ideologia in *Rubè*', *Italica*, 56/2 (1979), 172–97; Timothy Campbell, '*Infinite Remoteness*: Marinetti, Bontempelli, and the Emergence of Modern Italian Visual Culture', *MLN*, 120/1 (2005), 111–36; Marco Mondini, 'The Construction of a Masculine Warrior Ideal in the Italian Narratives of the First World War, 1915–68', *Contemporary European History*, 23/3 (2014), 307–27.

[121] Corrado Alvaro, 'Moralità', *900*, 2/5 (Autumn 1927), 139–42, and 'La prosa', *900*, 3/2 (August 1928), 68–71. For a critical assessment, Walter Mauro, *Invito alla lettura di Corrado Alvaro* (Milan, Mursia, 1973); Georges Güntert, 'Né dannunziano né verista: Corrado Alvaro e i racconti di *Gente in Aspromonte*', *Esperienze Letterarie: Rivista Trimestrale di Critica e Cultura*, 29/3 (July–September 2004), 19–42 and Angelo Mele, 'Corrado Alvaro. La Calabria favolosa e lirica e la civiltà tecnologica dell'Europa borghese, l'idillio paesano e la babele urbana, fra mito poetico e saggio utopico', in *Novecento. Gli scrittori e la cultura letteraria nella società italiana*, Giovanni Grana (ed.), vol. VI (Milan, Marzorati, 1983), 5305–25.

the intellectual in changing society for the better. It was characterized by a firm moral imperative that sought to bear witness to the harshness of peasant life and to promote social change; and expected the reader to adopt an empathic relationship with the fully dramatized characters in the story.

Alvaro observed the lives of peasants in the Aspromonte region in the documentary style typical of the 1930s but with a different gaze to Moravia and Soldati's readers, narrators and characters: by refusing any ornament (indeed something architects described as a crime, for instance), in a text punctuated by essential dialogical exchanges staging the rhythm of the diegesis, Alvaro wants to bring to his readers' attention to the histories of the humbles and, at the same time, give them universal significance. Verga used free indirect speech to allow characters to speak; Alvaro instead allows direct speech to gain psychological insights.

There is no simple oneiric evocation of the past in Alvaro's writing. Rather, the hope for a social and historical change is the *trait d'union* across the thirteen individual short stories which in this respect continue the tradition of the nineteenth-century novel. Contrary to previous '*letteratura meridionalistica*' (literature from the South), Alvaro's text had an almost militant ambition in its profound historicity of the South: his writing was an effort to record and raise awareness of the social condition of those obscured and not seen by history itself, of those who chose to remain in their lands and not emigrate to the North to try and improve their living conditions. Despite its roots in a mythical dimension, such an ideological aspiration embraced the idea of modernity as progress that could change and modernize the social sphere and welcome those left behind, by uncompromising traditionalism. The success of *Gente in Aspromonte*, four years after Alvaro's *debut* novel *L'uomo nel labirinto*, strongly indicated how literary writing needed to be reviewed as far as its subject matters and execution were concerned by hailing a turn to collectivity and historicity as opposed to the solipsism of the *prosa d'arte* and of the early avant-gardes.

Realism was no longer an expression of chronological linearity: it had been fragmented and multiplied by a strong subjective element at its core – and was therefore in need of finding a way of reassembling its parts as the debate on the choral novel singled out. In 1934, a young publisher, Valentino Bompiani, launched the editorial campaign 'Invito Editoriale' to promote the project of a putative Italian novel that could be choral, realist and social: a counterblast to *Critica fascista*'s official position on arts, politics and the national novel.[122] In the press campaign that followed this initiative, the collective novel was presented as an expression of the Italians' bright, open character, as opposed to the reserved and introverted personalities of northern Europeans. If European literature of the crisis presented Man as tormented by Freudianism, swinging freely between Proust's psychologism and Dos Passos's collective documentary, the national collective novel had to borrow eclectically from them in order to revisit and rethink the very notion of nineteenth-century *verismo*, which now had to be the mirror of the spirit of healthy humanity, driven by a collective and constructive attitude towards the real and towards society. In the young publisher Bompiani's position we

---

[122] Bompiani Valentino, 'Invito editoriale al romanzo', *Gazzetta del popolo*, (14 March 1934), 3.

can hear echoes of the regime's rhetoric of competition with other European countries. Such rhetoric was ready to recognize the importance of the pattern set by foreign literature for the renewal of the novel, the genre that was uniting the nation in common reading habits.

Many writers and intellectuals of different political orientations participated in the debate, many who had also written for modernist *Occidente* and then contributed to the debate on State art in *Critica fascista*. For example, Bontempelli criticized the collective novel as failing to interpret Italian modernity, whereas Luigi Chiarini portrayed it as the coming into being of Fascism's true social consciousness. In general terms, however, the vast majority of those who took part in the contest supported the collective novel. Despite its allusions to foreign writers of sometimes 'dubious' leanings – Proust, Joyce, Döblin – in its Italian and fascist embodiment the collective novel could represent the honest, objective, modern and social essence of the regime. However, in the usually long and lively discussions taking place, some dissenting voices protested at the failure of fascist art in its aspiration to find a trajectory for a solid and innovative novel, as well as the inability of Italian writers, as compared to foreign ones, to engage with real life.[123] In 1934, initiating this dispute on the future of the Italian and fascist novel, Bompiani confirmed the need to move towards a national novel which could respond to a widespread sense of frustration with any sort of introspection, whether right-wing or left. If, due to external pressures and progressive marginalization on the international arena, the rhetoric of the regime was becoming increasingly imperialist, that of the literary field had to follow suit; but not without rewriting the modernist perspective into the collective of modernity.

By a strange temporal coincidence, realism, tackled in Italy as State art at the peak of the regime's national popularity, achieved full recognition at the Soviet Writers' congress held in Moscow in 1934 as total realism, the same year as Bompiani's campaign in support of the Italian collective novel. By reading the participants' contributions to the discussion, it becomes clear that in Europe and beyond, the 1930s brand of realism was by no means univocal or easy to define. Nevertheless, it was equally crystal clear that it represented exactly what modern prose and poetry aspired to achieve when they fashioned themselves as heavily politicized. The Austrian, international communist leader Karl Radek, when asked to discuss James Joyce as a socialist writer in the section dedicated to World Literature, asserted: 'Realism does not mean the embellishment or arbitrary selection of revolutionary phenomena; it means reflecting reality as it is, in all its complexity.'[124] In Italy, it rather meant State art when it constructed modern subjectivities and collectivities through experimental linguistic and formal codes

---

[123] See, 'Medusa', *Corriere Adriatico*, (7 April 1934), 'Passaggi a livello. Ancora del romanzo collettivo', *Tribuna*, (19 April 1934). Amongst the contributors to the debate, Evola and Moravia, championed a realist novel with an heroic ethos able to narrate the epics of modern society. Others who participated in the discussion which spread across other journals (*Quadrivio, Oggi, Domus*) were Bontempelli, Piero Gadda Conti, Giovanni Titta Rosa and Giovanni Comisso.

[124] Gorky, Zhdanov, Radek, Bukharin et al. (eds), *Soviet Writers' Congress 1934: The Debate on Socialist Realism and Modernism in the Soviet Union* (London, Lawrence and Wishart, 1977), 156–7.

which enabled writers and readers to engage ethically with a modernized society. It also meant experimenting with the real as dissociation of facts from fiction.

Theatre of Objects IV: Embodied Modern Subjects

In what was conceived as a constructive effort within the system of the arts, from the 1923 speech at the Pesaro gallery until *Primato*'s call for the azione dell'arte, endless reconfigurations of and experimentations with the idea of subjectivity meeting objectivity within a realist paradigm could also be found in many important visual artists, as a further indication of its centrality within the choral search for State art.[125]

As early as in 1921, in an Italy transformed by the First World War and filled with disillusionment, Mario Sironi joined Novecento and Sarfatti and put an end to his futurist days. He painted a series of *Paesaggi* set in the suburbs, while he himself settled in Via Pisacane in the outskirts of Milan.[126] Critics Fabio Benzi and Elena Pontiggia recognized in Sironi's *Paesaggi* a oneiric aura, which reiterates Massimo Bontempelli's lesson on magical realism and the spurious aesthetic and to a certain extent political atmosphere of the early 1920s.[127] The theme of suburbs will be a constant preoccupation for him, attuned as he was to an idea of modern classicism which allowed for the exploration of social realities.

As the titles evoke, these post-futurist *Paesaggi* often depict solitary landscapes where the somewhat familiar scenes invite an emphatic response from the onlooker. Sironi's suburban areas are painted in darker, more intimate and more inquisitive tones than those used by Boccioni's in *La città che sale* (1910) or by Gino Severini in *Ballerina in giallo* (1912).[128] By articulating an antithesis between rural and city life, these artworks ascribe meaning to modernization through oneiric, dynamic and distinctively dialectical oppositions, preluding to his more politicized atmospheres of the 1930s. Like for many other artists and novelists of the interwar generation, the aesthetic transformation is only gradually becoming political after the First World War and with the establishment of a more pervasive political discourse. Yet, as early as the immediate post-First World War years, Sironi is interested in the 'now', in the everyday, because the new artistic – and crucially political – subjects and subject matters are the masses: those disoriented and mysteriously wrapped in solitude crowds, or else those alienated beings, one can clearly see in the many versions of the *Periferie* and those which will become the New Man/Woman of the totalitarian regimes of the 1930s.[129]

---

[125] We discuss these scholarly contributions throughout the book but as main references, see Pontiggia, *Modernità e classicità*; Colombo and Pontiggia (eds), *Milano anni trenta*; Bossaglia, *Il Novecento italiano*; and Benzi (ed.), *Mario Sironi, 1885–1961* (Milan, Mondadori Electa, 1993).

[126] Fabio Benzi, *Dal Futurismo al Classicismo*, 137–8 for details about the exhibitions of these artworks and on Sarfatti's role in shaping Sironi's career.

[127] Ibid., 22 and Elena Pontiggia (ed.), *Sironi: Il mito dell'architettura* (Milan, Mazzotta, 1990), 7.

[128] On Sironi's departure from futurism, see Benzi, *Dal Futurismo al Classicismo*, 158, and 169 on the use of perspective in the landscapes.

[129] Ibid., 146, 149 and Braun, *Mario Sironi*, 77.

In the 1920s *Paesaggi* – *Paesaggio urbano con camion* (Brera) and *Paesaggio urbano con camion* – the barren industrial landscape is left virtually unbroken, devoid of human presences: there are no metaphysical undercurrents, other than a static landscape, and reality stands almost monolithically in the geometrically encircled picture to capture the viewer with all its solitude and anguish.[130] In the Brera *Paesaggio*, for example, such linearity is only disrupted by a pedestrian, who is about to cross the street in what might seem an aimless wondering or a suppressed attempt at reclaiming social significance for people in the suburbs of Milan. A black lorry is immobile, just like the human, faceless figure standing in precarious equilibrium. The early futurist cities, full of lights and people – Boccioni's *Rissa in galleria* (1910) – have vanished to be traded with unforgiving and immobile sketched moments of popular life in despair. Other *Paesaggi* paint human figures, who in turn are labelled according to their profession, such as *Paesaggio urbano con ferroviere* (*c.* 1924), to mark the awareness of the precarious living conditions of these citizens.[131] Because of its fugitive perspective, this urban landscape resembles the dynamism of futurism with augmented a-rhythmic volumetry, a somehow distorted sense of proportion, and a return to anthropomorphic figures, such as in the drawing *Figure e paesaggio urbano* (1920) which will resurface in his fully realized Public art murals coupled with an aura of classical and geometrical composition.[132] Just like the monumental men and women of the 1930s, these human figures are reduced to tactile volumes without action (a Montalian '*immoto andare*') to speak to the drama of the protagonists, and to their powerlessness to change their social condition.

Compared to the previous works, a slightly later *Paesaggio urbano* (1922) fulfils the prerequisites of modernity: the life of the modern man had won over solipsism by assuming a collective and communitarian dimension, which could annihilate individualism.[133] The small houses of the previous landscapes have been replaced by city dwellings, the modern *palazzi*, arranged over several floors, conceived to accommodate many more people and many more families, and able to change the social composition of the public sphere: indeed, lack of housing for the workers, strikes and raising unemployment were widespread problems in many Italian cities after the end of the First World War. Public transport could have helped revitalize such neglected and peripheral areas and allowed for movement of people: here trams, for example, were to be viewed not as a modernist means of self-exploration but rather as a privileged means of modernization and development of a new society, which could cement the urban solidarity over further disintegration. The network of electric tramlines in Milan had been expanding since the war years to support the industrial growth of the city and its progressive expansion due to the arrival of people from provincial towns and villages. The dark, melancholic colours and the volumetric

---

[130] Beginning 1920, oil on canvas, 44 × 60 cm, Pinacoteca di Brera, Jesi collection, Milan, in Benzi, *Dal Futurismo al Classicismo*, 137 and beginning 1920, oil on canvas, 50 × 80 cm, private collection, in Benzi, *Mario Sironi*, 148–9.

[131] Oil on paper applied on a table, 54.4 × 51.7 cm, private collection.

[132] Ink and tempera on paper, 274 × 218 cm, private collection.

[133] Oil on canvas, 56 × 76 cm, Sarfatti collection, Rome.

compositions of the buildings mimicked both the human condition and a social problem, that of the deprived urban areas increasingly in need of new housing plans. This political matter was to be tackled systematically in the mid-to-late 1920s and 1930s plans for urban development in Milan and in other Italian cities, aiming to reach out to those citizens living in provincial towns, in new territories of the Italian empire, and in the new towns.[134]

Emily Braun has observed the extent to which Sironi's urban landscapes capture the political tensions of the period and the climate of insurrection of the Red Biennial, thereby linking Sironi's art simultaneously to the rendering of a human condition and to a political plan, while Elena Pontiggia has described them as '*disiecta membra*' and suggested a connection with Borgese's *Tempo di edificare* (1923), as a manifesto for the reconstruction of the compositional aesthetic order in the arts, as we have discussed in the case of the novel around the same temporal juncture.[135] Emily Braun has interpreted these works against a political milieu, while accepting the dangers of drawing too close a connection between text and context, e.g. the social turmoil of the Red Biennial: Sironi did politicize his paintings but he also completed an artistic transition which can be recognized in the unfinished tones and in the ambiguity of these works where an anxious modern human condition stands firmly forefront of the composition.

By the early 1920s Sironi had completed his transition from futurism to Novecento. In *Nudo con lo specchio* (1923), for example – exhibited at the 1924 Biennale in Venice together with the *Allieva*, *Venere* and *Architetto*, in the room 'Sei pittori del Novecento' (Room 22) – in Margherita Sarfatti's words, Sironi 'above anything else always aspires to the synthesis of forms'.[136] And, moreover, he followed the principles outlined in *Contro tutti i ritorni in pittura* for solid 'construction' embedded in reality and in three vertical rectangles and their diagonals with a plastic echoing.[137]

Within a short period of time, Sironi brought his art to a new high, close to State art. He executed two artworks on the theme of family, pondering even more didactically than before on morals, construction, rationalization and the social good, dilemmas which were very much welcomed in official settings because their contents were in line with the aesthetic debate taking place within fascist circles. *La famiglia* (1930) is set against a deserted and barren, cycloptic landscape, characters gaze over from a close perspective, with three of them in the foreground: father, mother and son.[138] In 1931 Sironi was given a room for himself at the I Quadriennale as a mark of respect for a national artist of fascist faith. In the *Famiglia del pastore*, exhibited the following year at the 1932 Venice Biennale, the same figures we see in the *Famiglia* can be identified

---

[134] See Braun, *Mario Sironi*, 46 for the artist's own illustrations on these matters. Sironi, *Il tram*, 1920, oil on canvas-backed paper, 72 × 92 cm, Civica Galleria d'Arte Moderna 'Empedocle Restivo', Palermo. Gian Claudia Ferrari, *Sironi. Opere 1919-1959* (Milan, Charta, 2002) and on Sironi's early works, see Pontiggia, *Sironi: Il mito dell'architettura*, 10–15 and Braun, *Mario Sironi*, 54–6.

[135] Braun, *Mario Sironi*, 62–3 and Pontiggia, *Sironi: Il mito dell'architettura*, 9.

[136] '*sopra ogni cosa tende sempre*, [sic] *alla sintesi della forma*', 'Presentazione', *Catalogo della XIV Esposizione Internazionale d'Arte della Citta di Venezia*, 1924, 77.

[137] Benzi, *Mario Sironi*, 166.

[138] Oil on canvas, 104 × 83 cm, Galleria Nazionale d'Arte Moderna, Rome, exhibited at the I Quadriennale in 1931.

with an addendum of the Holy family (Joseph, Mary with a blue veil and the Christ Child).[139] After the Venetian show, this painting was purchased by one of the most prominent architects of the regime, Marcello Piacentini, to be displayed in his villa in Rome in another homage paid by the State to one of their more loyal artists and as a seal of approval for future collaborations, namely the decoration of the windows of the Palazzo delle corporazioni in Rome. The regime was concurrently and progressively moving towards the promotion of the family as the pillar of society, culminating in the pro-natalist campaign, and of work as a way to dignify one's existence; perhaps not surprisingly, Margherita Sarfatti showed significant enthusiasm for the *Famiglia*.[140] Yet, in the *Famiglia* these are simply profane nudes, with no religious connotation; these are monumental, squarely depicted, softly diffused figures which could belong to the everyday rather than the heavenly.

The *Famiglia* is a hymn to fertility and to the role women are obliged to perform in private and in public. This artwork foregrounds fecundity as the most natural mode of cementing, constructing and building society, because is it at the centre of the normalizing political discourse. The epic tones of the composition, with augmented volumes and imposing frontal figures dressed in white, magnify the scene. The family is a monumental unit which has to be publicly displayed. The subjective element, even of motherhood, has become a public matter in Sironi's work. By mixing a solitary, yet monumental, presence of an almost lost subjectivity in what appears to be a deserted, while recognizable landscape of classical proportions, Sironi condenses his own as well as the early 1920s artistic transitions between futurism and Novecento, with echoes of expressionism and new realism, the latter defined by morality, construction, rationalization and concern for the modernization of society. Sironi realizes the idea of 'monumental classicism' in the context of Sarfatti's Novecento, inclined towards Picassian neoclassicism albeit with political and expressionist contents, and in opposition to the Rome-based version of the return to order of 'Valori plastici'.[141] His theorization of the line avoids the pitfalls of *verismo* and gives the figures an earthly presence, enhanced by the burned terracotta colours and his rosso. As Braun has concluded about Sironi's pragmatic project about fascist art, he 'incorporated his virile and archaizing figures – bodies mythic and politic – into his public art projects of the 1930s'.[142] In his Novecento and classical period, Sironi developed his empathic and committed attitude towards the social narrative of his time, expressed in a new moral code for the artist: his take on classicism and monumentality was geared towards the human experience, which he still understood in isolation in the early 1920s while

---

[139] Sironi realized several variations of this painting between 1927 and 1934. *La famiglia del pastore* became part of the collections of the Galleria d'Arte Moderna, while *La famiglia* of those of the Galleria Nazionale d'Arte Moderna, both in Roma. *La famiglia*, 1932, is held at Villa Necchi in Milan as part of the Fondo ambiente italiano.

[140] Benzi, *Mario Sironi*, 212. As evidenced in a document in the Rivolta archive entitled f. '44-Discorso del Podestà alla "Famiglia meneghina" (6 June 1932)', AGR, the family was the key social player and therefore the State had to preserve its physical and mental health by developing adequate infrastructures.

[141] Benzi, *Dal Futurismo al Classicismo*, 192.

[142] Braun, *Mario Sironi*, 131.

progressively moving towards themes close to the official debates on State art as one can clearly see in his more distinctively 'political' works preceding his transition to mural painting. And from 1933 onwards Sironi's new credo in Public art did consolidate the power interactions between the State and the arts.

Between the early 1920s and the early 1930s the spirit of the time was modernity, a concept which deliberately eluded definitions in order to encompass a broad range of aesthetic and political orientations and formalizations. Because of its reconceptualization in terms of a fusion of subjectivity and objectivity without synthesis, realism could function as the aesthetic paradigm of modernity and of social modernization, and thus be the act of documenting, representing figuratively, shaping and enchanting the totality created by European totalitarianism. 1930s realism also had to be the act of inscribing subjectivity into objectivity and a response to new political orders and social configurations. To this end, subjectivity had to be redefined either in terms of collectivity or in terms of the profile of the New Man/Woman created by the regime's anthropological revolution. As the debate in the journals discussed outlines, as Alvaro, Moravia, Soldati prove with their novel, and as the artists portray in their liminal figures, the aesthetics and politics of the 1930s real had to transgress the boundaries between subjectivity and objectivity, while concurrently collating them into collectivities and into their precarious futures. Only through an act of remoulding the 'real' could a new aesthetics of subjectivity made collective document, shape and dismantle the real to politicize the arts and to free them from politics per se: this happened from Rome to Moscow and Berlin, and across modernity and modernizing social projects.

Agon 2: The Fascist New Man/Woman and the Bourgeois Ulysses

Synthesis: What is Public Art?

In one of the most astute and persuasive assessments of artistic perception as a vehicle for a deeper comprehension of the cultural moment in which the artworks live, and to which they give life, Michael Baxandall has described the conventions we use to interpret images, writing that:

> The first convention is more immediately related to what we see, where the second is more abstract and conceptualised – and to us now rather unfamiliar – but they both involve a skill and a willingness to interpret marks on paper as representations simplifying an aspect of reality within accepted rules.[1]

In the case of Public art, what the 'period eye' – in its focus on the socio, cultural and economic conditions of its time – can see is how artworks are depicted or constructed in the most accessible and clearest of forms and shapes. Such a figurative disposition ought to make explicit and codify the sometimes liminal, sometimes explicit and obvious ideological and propagandistic messages encapsulated in artworks operating in their own right. Furthermore, for Public art, the relationship between the image and the abstract meaning, the codes, is key to its definition. Public art is a dynamic field of evolving aesthetic and cultural practices, transforming in response to a changing understanding of the notion of the public space and of citizens' participation in the public sphere(s). Therefore, Public art problematizes not only the relationship between art and life but also between art, life, history and politics; and in so doing, provides a broader conceptualization of the ways in which the arts act within the public spheres, with the aim of speaking to collective bodies. Such a nexus becomes even more prominent when manifested under a totalitarian regime that aims at constructing a collective public space according to a clear set of rules categorized, in this case, in

---

[1] Michael Baxandall, *Painting and Experience in the Fifteenth-Century Italy* (Oxford, Oxford UP, 1988), 32.

the *Dottrina del fascismo* (1932) or in the State art paradigm, and that is structured according to institutions hierarchically organized with the main purpose of moulding a State patronage apparatus.

Political and propaganda art and Public art are potentially slippery concepts in terms of their respective aesthetic forms, languages and spaces. Political and propaganda art under a totalitarian regime imply art which resounds figuratively or not, realistically or not, a definite State-owned ideology in order to invoke consensus. Furthermore, such art should be able to make specific ideologies available to targeted groups of people through different linguistic and formal codes. Public art takes the same varying forms: from representational to anti-representational; from figurative to non-figurative, from the monumental to small everyday objects of consumption, but does not respond to a pre-codified ideological meaning.

How does Public art convey a political or ideological message without becoming necessarily political or propaganda art? How did Public art contribute to the anthropological revolution? What was its lexicon? To what extent did Public art represent the regime? And, to what extent did it create instead an autonomous space for citizens? We explore such themes and answer these questions by reconstructing the history of public institutions supporting the arts and by looking at artworks which aspire to become the total work of art (e.g. the Mostra della rivoluzione) by combining architecture with the visual arts. Specifically we pose to discuss Mussolini's heads, the Palermo and La Spezia post offices, the mural paintings at the V and VI Triennale and at the E42. At the fringes of this cultural landscape, other transformations were underway: a final return to realism, prompted by a disillusioned generation whose aim was to destabilize the regime in pursuit of political change, such as in the return to realism with the Corrente movement and the Premio Bergamo and Cremona.

Dissonances: Heads of Mussolini

In his speech at the opening event of the 1938 Biennale, Giuseppe Bottai maintained that art is always socially useful when it is good art.[2] He proposed there to be a strong connection between aesthetic and political meaning and relevance: a connection that could not easily be undone. Such an association becomes particularly enlightening when we look at Public art.

In the 1920s, the cult of the Duce was an official theme sponsored by Press Office of the regime: consequently, artistic representations of the head or bust of Mussolini proliferated during the Ventennio, because the Duce embodied not only the Fascist revolution but also the New Man/Woman that stood firmly at its core. The project of Public art was precisely that of transforming the individual monument into a collective experience through a process of aesthetic rationalization, popularization

---

[2] Stone, *The Patron State*, 187.

and simplification of images and shapes, and the recalibration of the classical tradition into a national one.[3]

In 1923, Margherita Sarfatti commissioned the sculptor Adolfo Wildt to make the first *Maschera di Mussolini*, to celebrate the inauguration of the Casa del fascio in Milan and to mark the first anniversary of the March on Rome: a space and an event destined to initiate the process of political sacralization through enhanced visibility of the totalitarian project. Between 1924 and 1928, Wildt produced several further iconic portraits of Mussolini in bronze and marble.[4]

Mussolini was rendered like a Roman sculpture, in white and green marble, eye sockets carved full out, and around his head, the white woollen band (*infula sacerdotale*) traditionally worn by Roman emperors like Augustus. Wildt's early abstract versions of the head of Mussolini became the symbol of the regime: an almost de-individualized message, designed to favour communal enjoyment of the artwork, which functioned as transhistorical allegory of political power. Wildt's mask of Mussolini was also modernist, Pirandellian in its nakedness: there was an affective drive in Wildt's portrait, an impetus which could guarantee an emotional response towards the leader. While the *Maschera di Mussolini* retained an aesthetic value, it was one of the first attempts to deploy the arts and their potential as a political tool to promote consensus in the public sphere, without being reduced to a mere instrument for propaganda. As Public art, it illustrated how the arts could be used in support of the totalitarian project, converting the latter's ideological dogma into images that could speak to the collective body of its citizens and its nation, suspended as both were between modernity and modernization on the one hand, and tradition and stagnation on the other.

By the mid-1930s, the machine of consensus was in full swing and images of Mussolini proliferated. Masks of Mussolini appeared everywhere and were often displayed in public buildings to sacralize the regime and its *Condottiero*, most notably – but not exclusively – during the period of the Mostra della rivoluzione and afterwards with the Casa del fascio in Como and the Universal Exhibition in 1942. Emilio Gentile has also assessed the extent to which the regime was an experiment which initiated not merely a political, or even cultural, revolution per se, but an anthropological one.[5] The Fascist revolution had not simply changed the political landscape and rescued Italy from the liberal State; it had also to produce a new civilization, whereby the

---

[3]   The topic has recently been amply debated, but we refer to W. J. T. Mitchell, *What Do Pictures Want? The Lives and Loves of Images* (Chicago, The University of Chicago Press, 2005) for a theoretical assessment of the question.

[4]   After this first, successful commission, Wildt sculpted various versions of the same subject, using different materials and framings (60 × 49 × 22 cm, Carrara marble on slab of green marble). Eight of them are busts and four are masks, as the *Maschera di Mussolini* here analysed, where the framing tends to highlight the abstract and almost visionary expression of the Duce. The one considered here is the sample acquired in 1928 by recently opened Galleria d'Arte Moderna in Milan and still pertaining to the museum: a fragment composed by a green marble slab, behind a Carrara marble mask portraying Mussolini. Furthermore, one can find Wildt's *Maschera* exhibited in some of the main artistic events of that time – from the 1924 Biennale in Venice to the 1925 Exposition Internationale des Arts Décoratifs et Industriels Modernes in Paris.

[5]   Emilio Gentile, *The Struggle for Modernity: Nationalism, Futurism and Fascism* (Westport, CN, and London, Praeger, 2003), 80–3.

Figure 1 Adolfo Wildt, *Maschera di Mussolini*. Credits: Wikicommons: https://commons. wikimedia.org/wiki/File:Adolfo_wildt,_maschera_di_mussolini,_1923-25.jpg.

minds of the Italians, whose primary attribution as individual citizens was now that of being fascists, had been transformed. The New Man/Woman's choice to be fascist was not only based on rational economic or political reasons alone, since their belief in that new – or better – world order the dictatorship represented was commensurate to that promised by any given religion, and thus governed by faith and affect. The outcome of this anthropological revolution could not have been but to be the New Man, who was quintessentially 'serious, intrepid, tenacious' within a larger political and social project.[6] Or, the anthropological revolution, therefore, transformed the idea

---

[6] Simonetta Falasca-Zamponi, *Fascist Spectacle,* 51.

of subjectivity, from a form of self-sufficient individual existence, into an individual existence, which could only come into being as connected collectivity.[7]

Since its inception, futurism had explored the abstraction and anti-representational codes of the *universo meccanico* but, by the mid-1930s, such a theoretical stance had to come to terms with the everyday, and the everyday was political and closely linked with the search of figurative modes of expression to visualize Mussolini. A comparison with another rendering of a bust of Mussolini may further clarify the aesthetic and political dynamics of public representations of power as the New Man shaped by the Fascist revolution. Anglo-Florentine artist Thayaht's (aka Ernesto Michahelles) *Dux con pietra miliare*, exhibited at the XVII Biennale in 1930, was his first official futurist artwork on a Fascism-related theme.[8] Made in 1929, the year that the artist officially aligned himself with the regime, the sculpture took the form of a metallic knight's head on a *pietra miliare*, or stone pedestal, bearing the inscription *Dux*.[9] The *Dux*, conceived of in 1928 and first realized in an alloy called 'creat', was perfected the following year and cast in *ghisa acciaiosa*, cast-iron steel, and set on a *pietra miliare* or milestone base, for presentation at the national competition at the Palazzo Vecchio in Florence in 1929.

The sculpture is an example of Thayaht's use of the straight line to arrive at a rationalized anthropomorphic rendering of the New Man – in this case, even to the point of sacralization of the Duce as 'priest' of a new political 'religion'. Within an overtly geometrical, functional understanding of the artwork, the human remains a central element. There is a fundamentally anthropomorphic take in this sculpture, whereby the lines converge in a well-defined image of Mussolini: one that can, precisely because of its aesthetic patterns, assume a universal significance. The *piani-volumi* are arranged according to continuous rhythms and plastic interpenetrations that are formed over shapes reproduced from abstract compositions. Historical significance, as Scappini has pointed out, is certainly part of the meaning of the *Dux*, but it is not the only meaning: the sculpture fuses aesthetics and politics in one material, representational accord.

---

7   Tarquini, *Storia della cultura fascista*, 134–7.
8   Antiqued plaster on metal base, 289 × 142 × 142 cm, CLM Seeber collection, Rome. 'Man is a linear and geometrical form in its essence, it a crystalline form. Hermetical mask of a man who does not know his destiny yet', Alessandra Scappini (ed.), *Thayaht. Vita, scritti, carteggi* (Milan, Mart-Skira, 2005), 25 and note 41. Thayaht national breakthrough coincided with the invitation to exhibit at the Galleria Pesaro in Milano in October 1929, at the Mostra dei trentatré artisti futuristi. Subsequently, together with Antonio Marasco, he co-organized the Mostra futurista Pittura–scultura–aeropittura held at the Florence's Galleria in 1931, for further details see Scappini, ibid., 24.
9   On the metamorphosis of the Dux, see Mauro Pratesi (ed.), *Futurismo e bon ton. I fratelli Thayaht e Ram* (Milan, Leo S. Olschki editore, 2005), 49. See, for instance, *Thayaht, Paesaggio aereo e pali della luce*, 1931, and *Il grande nocchiere aeropittura del grande timoniere*, 1939. The success of this iconography, celebrated by Mussolini himself, also persists in Thayaht's following career as a painter. In 1929 the artist painted *Madonna di Montenero*: a painting on paper that, even if dedicated to a different subject – a sacred one – clearly echoes *Dux con pietra miliare*, both chromatically and formally. Rosso's sculpture payed homage to the *Manifesto dell'arte meccanica futurista* as well as contemporary artworks such as Archipenko's sculptures and Léger's paintings. Léger's works were exhibited for the first time with those by Jules Pascin at the Il Milione gallery, 10–20 December 1932. Another fitting example is Prampolini, *Sintesi plastica* (1926 exhibited at the Biennale), a 'ritratto spirituale', through composition and decomposition of colours and volumes.

Figure 2 Thayaht, *Dux con pietra miliare.* Credits: *Emporium* 430 (1930): 232.

The static and reassuring image of the Duce, *il Condottiero*, was to induce confidence and trust in citizens; but such an authoritative, indeed severe, image also needed to remain mysterious and sacred, since Fascism functioned in the style of a civic religion, seeking consensus not by reason but by faith. In 1934, the Turin-based futurist sculptor Mino Rosso produced an iconic portrait of Mussolini in his Léger-machine-like *Architettura di una testa (Mussolini)*.[10] As with Enrico Prampolini's mechanical depiction of the Duce, for example, Rosso abandoned a realist mode for his portrait in favour of an abstract fragmentation into mechanical components: an oversized wrench around a screw on an irregular perforated background. Rosso's sculpture in wood and aluminium was therefore both State art – with futurism progressively affirming itself as one of the hegemonic artistic movements of the era – and Public art: both movements engaged in finding a new way to visualize the regime. Different to Wildt's bust, Rosso's Mussolini is identifiable, but not in an obvious way. It is a stylized, non-figurative, industrialized rendering of Mussolini as the New Man; crucially, there is no emphasis on grandiosity or virility. Mussolini is a precariously assembled, but functioning, modern machine (as he is, too, in Marinetti and Prampolini's portraits): not yet the emblem of static authoritarianism but balanced, rather, in an almost perilous equilibrium, playful but rationalized. Rosso's *Mussolini* was a heretical – albeit officially acceptable – portrait that sat, just like Wildt's, at a crossroads of multiple contrasts; an interweaving of errant lines in a compositional framework with both full and empty spaces, and without a univocal message.[11] Public art enabled artists to model assorted formulations of their understanding of the regime, experiment with forms, codes and with languages, and fuse together different artistic fields; and thus elicit a variety of responses.

Hypothesis I: The Total Work of Art

The total work of art is as a synthetic work which aspires to integrate all its parts into a coherent whole. As such this concept dates back to the nineteenth-century Wagnerian *Gesamtkunstwerk*, which suggested the reunification of all arts.[12] Through its many manifestations and embodiments, the total work of art also found fertile ground in the social and aesthetic discourse upheld by the dictatorship since, as David Roberts puts it, '[t]hese projects expressed a common will to recover the lost public function of

---

[10] Léger's works were exhibited for the first time with those by Jules Pascin at the Milione gallery, 10–20 December 1932.

[11] For further details about a relatively less studied figure who was part of the Turinese circles, see Sandro Alberti, *Mino Rosso. Scultore e pittore 1904–1963* (Turin, Editris, 1993) and Beatrice Buscaroli, Roberto Floreani Fabbri and Anna Possamai Vita (eds), *Scultura futurista 1909–1944. Omaggio a Mino Rosso* (Cinisello Balsamo, Silvana Editoriale, 2009).

[12] For a detailed discussion of Wagner's use of the world and its political reverberations, see Sanna Pederson, 'From Gesamtkunstwerk to Drama Music', in David Imhoof, Margaret Eleanor Menninger and Anthony J. Steinhoff (eds), *The Total Work of Art: Foundations, Articulations, Inspirations* (New York/Oxford, Berghahn, 2016), 43–6. For examples within the Italian context, see Ezio Godoli, *Guide all'architettura moderna: Il Futurismo* (Rome-Bari, Laterza, 1983), 45 and Vivien Greene, 'The Opera d'Arte Totale', in Vivien Greene (ed.), *Italian Futurism 1909–1944*, 211–13.

art, a will that pointed beyond the aesthetic revolutions of the avant-gardes to political revolutions as the promise of a complete reunion of art and life'. In this regard, Roberts has shown how the modernist dimension of art should be considered not merely an attempt to tame the irrational and romantic tendencies of society through processes of technological and productive rationalization.[13] The 1930s total work of art needed not only to account for the change in the relationship between subjectivity and objectivity but also to embody publicly the sacralization of the New Man/Woman through the arts. In other words, creating a total work of art was the aim of every dictatorship, for it brought together often in the shape of Public, and not simply political or propaganda, art all artistic fields, all corners of the social sphere(s) in a concerted attempt to be functional to the very same existence of the arts and of their regimes.[14] Two artworks can illustrate how the total work of art could be at the same time Public art and political art. Yet, Public and political art do not necessarily have to become one because, when functioning as a system of the arts, they elude stifling categorizations such as autonomous vs heteronomous, pluralistic vs monadic and are thus able to fulfil diverse functions at once.

After 1932, the key player in the system of the arts was the total work of art as Public art, or art which visibly expressed a totalizing ideology. The synthesis of artistic currents under the superior order to the State became strikingly obvious during the Mostra della rivoluzione, which had to be hypermodern and audacious in conception and visual realization.[15] In 1932 the young Adalberto Libera and the more experienced Mario de Renzi, 'war veterans from the second exhibition of rationalist architecture', planned the external façade of the Palazzo delle Esposizioni (built in 1882 by Pio Piacentini) for the Decennale. With its volumetric precision, a 30 × 30 metre gigantic cube divided by four 'fasci' held together by an entry shelter imposed an aesthetic rhythm to the wholeness of the design against a red background covered with the Roman symbols of the Littorio. It projected a forceful, yet futuristic, vision of the totalitarian goal of the regime; it was shocking and pervasive.

In the most important room of the Mostra, the Sala O of the year 1922, Giuseppe Terragni created his futurist-fuelled montage of the collective spirit of the regime, using avant-gardist tropes such as writings, slender grids and supporting constructions in structural steel.[16] Adalberto Libera and Antonio Valente created the *sacrarium* of the martyrs of the Revolution, while futurist artists such as Fortunato Depero, Enrico Prampolini and futurist architect Emilio Marchi had been invited to contribute their

---

[13] David Roberts, *The Total Work of Art in European Modernism* 2–5.

[14] Ibid., 2, 5.

[15] On the Mostra several important works have appeared, see Libero Andreotti, 'Architecture as Media Event: Mario Sironi and the Exhibition of the Fascist Revolution', *Built Environment*, 31/1 (2005), 9–20; Cioli, *Il fascismo e la 'sua' arte*, 185–93; Giorgio Ciucci, 'L'autorappresentazione del fascismo. La mostra del decennale della marcia su Roma', *Rassegna*, 4/10 (1982), 48–55; Diane Ghirardo, 'Architects, Exhibitions, and the Politics of Culture in Fascist Italy', *Journal of Architectural Education*, 45/2 (1992), 67–75; Jeffrey Schnapp, *Anno X: la Mostra della rivoluzione fascista del 1932* (Pisa, Istituti editoriali e poligrafici internazionali, 2003); Stone, *The Patron State*, 128–76.

[16] Dino Alfieri and Luigi Freddi, *Partito Nazionale Fascista. Mostra della Rivoluzione Fascista* (Milan, Industrie Grafiche Italiane, 1982), 188.

works throughout the entire exhibition and Sironi completed the Sala R (Salone d'onore), emphasizing the lettering, that modernist-rationalist style reappearing for the V Triennale.[17] Diane Ghirardo has rightly pointed out that every space was 'full' as to trap the viewer in a mesmerizing universe of proliferation of forms hierarchically orchestrated; and Flavio Fergonzi that the Mostra was a way of creating a '*totalità visiva*' by repositioning sculpture and monuments from a stance of classical isolation to one of modern pastiche.[18] On this highly charged political occasion, the arts functioned as a total work of art because they were acting as a system, and in doing so, they set a precedent.

In Rome in May 1932, futurist Mino (Stanislao) Somenzi debuted his *Futurismo* (1932-3) in a futile attempt to return to an original *sansepolcrismo*, that is, to the true revolutionary and anti-bourgeois roots of futurism. The journal was more convenient to Marinetti's apparitions for architecture as State art, still in the name of Sant'Elia, but with influential contributions by artist Prampolini, Fillìa and architects Gino Levi-Montalcini and Alberto Sartoris. The newly born journal devoted considerable attention to the slim presence of futurists at the Mostra della rivoluzione, for the show came to symbolize the total work of art.[19] Detached from Marinetti's growing conservativism, Somenzi claimed the supremacy of futurist art by looking at the USSR as a place where the State directly sustained the arts through a well-constructed system of patronage; and in this way he indirectly endorsed Bottai's wish for the artists to be supported by the State.[20] Somenzi's far-sighted political ambitions were to turn avant-garde art into a mass phenomenon in order to speak to those audiences Marinetti had neglected to address as key political subjects. In their respective analyses of the modes of social and cultural existence of the dictatorship Mabel Berezin, Simonetta Falasca-Zamponi, Emilio Gentile and Jeffrey Schnapp pointed out why and how masses ought to be seen as the new political presence of the 1930s totalitarian age. Such new political and politicized subjects should primarily be understood as spectacularized, and not simply aestheticized as gazed-over ones; rather the massed ought to have been reframed as

---

[17] Photomontage was particularly popular in 1930s Italy – Diulgheroff, Depero, Fillìa, Paladini. For example, visible art critic Roberto Papini, in 'Arte della Rivoluzione', *Emporium*, LXXVII/460 (April 1933), 197 maintains that there is clear link between architecture and sculpture as expressions of an ideal synthesis. Other contributions which highlight synergies between the arts are: Prampolini, 'Artisti futuristi e futuristizzati alla Mostra della Rivoluzione fascista', *Dinamo futurista*, I/1 (February 1933), 6-7, Margherita Sarfatti, 'Architettura. Arte e simbolo alla Mostra della Rivoluzione', *Architettura*, fasc. 1 (January 1933), 1-17; Fillìa, 'L'opera futurista di Prampolini alla Mostra della Rivoluzione', *Futurismo*, I/10 (November 1932), 1-7.

[18] Ghirardo, 'Architects, Exhibitions, and the Politics of Culture in Fascist Italy', 69; 1-17; and Flavio Fergonzi, 'Dalla monumentalità alla scultura arte monumentale', in Flavio Fergonzi and Maria Teresa Roberto (eds), *La scultura monumentale negli anni del fascismo. Arturo Martini e il Monumento al Duca d'Aosta* (Turin, Umberto Allemandi, 1982), 185.

[19] F. T. Marinetti, 'Evviva il genio futurista di Benito Mussolini', *Futurismo*, I/8 (28 October 1932), 1.

[20] 'Il Futurismo batte il cubismo in Russia. (Intervista con S. E. Marinetti)', *Futurismo*, I/3 (15-30 July 1932), 2. The agency A.L.A. divulged the news that cubism has been banned in Russia, leaving futurism as the only legitimate avant-garde. Ojetti started a polemic on the cosmopolitan sympathies of futurism, to which Somenzi replied by claiming the political function of futurism over a merely artistic one: 'Fascisti, siate futuristi in arte! La funzione politica dell'Arte', *Futurismo*, I/3 (15-30 July 1932), 1.

artistic beings in themselves because of their active contribution to the coming into being of the political experiment the Fascist regime was.[21]

It was very easy for Marinetti to salute the Mostra della rivoluzione as the triumph of futurist art (it was not, truly), and to use the occasion to reconnect the movement to its original spirit of bravery and strength as well as to Prampolini's new plastic dynamism and to mechanical art – since both were total works of art.[22] Quite; the whole assemblage was a mixture of pre-monumentalism, Russian constructivism, futurist photomontage, rationalist architecture, static film, embodied the latter in the use of the straight line – 'the beauty of functional lines and the honesty of the machine' – and the former in the heavy and square volumes delineating the whole complex.[23] According to the ideologies of the totalitarian regimes of the 1930s, the total work of art materialised their aspiration to be fulfilled not only by the fusion of different artistic disciplines but rather by its ability to impact on people's perceptions of political power. The sacralized total work of art of the Mostra della rivoluzione set the scene for Public art: it enjoyed great civilian participation, with 3.7 million visitors over two years; it witnessed the beginning of the more practical involvement of the avant-gardes, the futurists, within State art in an elective effort to reach the crowds at the peak of the regime's consensus; and marked the official inauguration of the arts as tools for consensus and propaganda through the creation of collective myths to sacralize the regime. In essence, the total work of art was straightforward Public art once used to visualize and sacralize the regime via a complex aesthetic assemblage of discordant elements.

By comparing the Mostra della rivoluzione with the earlier, first Pavilion of futurist Architecture for the I Mostra di architettura futurista designed by futurist Enrico Prampolini, we can measure the increased politicization of the arts in their more overt totalitarian claims. In October 1928, just a few months after the MIAR exhibition in Rome, the I Mostra di architettura futurista opened in Turin, with Prampolini, Pannaggi, Depero and the newly converted to futurism Sartoris amongst the contributors together with the Turinese group en masse (Fillìa, Ugo Pozzo, Diulgheroff, Beppe Ferdinando and Mino Rosso). Prampolini designed the Pavilion of Futurist Architecture for the I Mostra di architettura futurista, held at the Valentino park and directed by architect Giuseppe Pagano – who was somewhat hostile towards the futurists.[24] On the same occasion, architect Sartoris joined the futurist movement and brought with him the magisterial lesson of De Stijl's neoplasticism, with its recourse to colour as a means of making visible the dimension of time and space; and also that more illustrious of his correspondent Theo van Doesburg, with the dynamism of their architectural solutions towering over a simply functionalist and mechanical ones, as one can see in Sartoris's 'Studio per un centro universitario a Torino, 1925–27' with its anti-cubic assemblages as per De Stijl 1923 *Manifesto V*, points II and V on full display.[25] Of

[21] Berezin, *Making the Fascist Self*, 28.

[22] *Futurismo*, I/9 (1932), 1–2.

[23] Rancière, *Aisthesis*, 147.

[24] In some private notes, Thayaht viewed the Lingotto in Turin as a skyscraper: a '*magnifica espressione davvero di un problema tecnico genialmente risolto*', in Scappini, *Thayaht*, [Le case in serie, 1931], 427.

[25] Prampolini's architectural projects are catalogued in Federica Pirani, 'Prampolini e gli allestimenti', in Enrico Crispolti (ed.), *Prampolini: dal futurismo all'informale* (Rome, Edizioni Carte Segrete, 1992), 272–7.

particular significance as far as this brand of interdisciplinarity is concerned, is the relationship between Sartoris and Van Doesburg: both were interested in neoplasticism and elementarism when conceptualised as practices which made pure basic elements converge towards coherent wholeness.

The Pavilion functioned as a total work of art and as collective art, since Prampolini's guiding principles were choral and polymateric: an abstract–geometrical vision of volumes and shape, colours (he was well-acquainted with German expressionism), asymmetrical volumetric juxtapositions and intersections to give continuity to abstract plans, discontinuous lines and marked angular solutions. The Pavilion was planned according to geometries following volumes assembled orthogonally, behind a façade with a superimposed staircase *a gradoni*, and monumental signage. Outside, dancers performed impromptu ballet inspired by Prampolini's choreographies, and Zdenka Podhajská's *danze sportive*, with music by Silvio Mix, *Tennis*, Frantisek Mitâil Hradil, *Foot-Ball*, Balilla Pratella, *Vortice* and Franco Casavola, *Danza dell'elica*. In a Marinetti-scenario of a *teatro totale futurista* and Godoli's formulation:

> The successful episode of the futurist Pavilion at the Turinese expo, with the employment of Depero's 'typographical architecture' and the Deco inflected neoplasticist researches proposed by Mallet-Stevens positions itself half way between architectural experimentation, an ephemeral mounting, a spectacularising of space through the interaction of diverse elements-manifestos, light, colours, letterings, recreational equipment.[26]

Godoli's analysis adds to the equation the spectacular element, one consistent with the programme of the total work of art while pointing out some shortcoming of Prampolini's choreography. Paradoxically, such a *teatro totale* recalls Erwin Piscator's political theatre promoted by Bragaglia in Italy and framed as a new form of artistic and political enjoyment.[27] Godoli praises the influence of Mallet-Stevens's neoplasticism and of his 1922 theorization of the modern city on futurist architecture, especially that of Prampolini and Diulgheroff. But, he continues, in no part of the installation there was any three-dimensional perspective, all remained regrettably unidimensional, failing to become a true polymateric machine.

If architecture were to be elected to the highest ranks of State art as the total work of art instead, the relationship between form and design must be not only functional but rational, lyrical and spiritual – as one could see, for instance, in the bar of the Odescalchi theatre by Marchi, in the 'edifici scultura' by Marchi and Prampolini, in the bar Bal Tic Tac by Balla, in Depero's 'architetture pubblicitarie' or in Diulgheroff interior designs.

---

[26] Crispolti (ed.), *Prampolini: dal futurismo all'informale*, 274. Other important pavilions were those by Fortunato Depero: Progetto di padiglione della Venezia Tridentina alla Fiera Campionaria di Milano (1924), Il padiglione del libro, III Mostra internazionale di arte decorativa, Monza (1927), 'Progetto di padiglione pubblicitario' (*c.* 1927), 'Progetto di padiglione tricolore' (*c.* 1927), 'Progetto di padiglione fascista' (*c.* 1927), 'Padiglione Campari (sketch)' (1933).

[27] Anton Bragaglia, 'Propaganda politica nel teatro tedesco. I', *L'Impero*, (3 September 1932).

Another example of just such an agenda was the adjacent Cappella Bar-Futurista with its dissolution of continuous large volumes and an interlocking montage – *ad incastro* – of basic volumes which echoed educationalist Friedrich Froebel's game. On the second floor of the Pavilion, there was an Esposizione di architettura moderna, which showcased projects for 'houses, villas, working-class houses, factories, plants, and more as well as photographic documentation about the most important achievements worldwide in the architectural field', in a spirit that anticipated the theory and practice of the rationalists in Monza and then Milan; but which also looked towards an idea of aesthetics which of necessity could encompass the whole spectrum of human activities, from clothing to decorations, tapestry to photography.[28] In totalitarian terms, the total work of art within an interdisciplinary understanding of the artistic creation (be it in political, aesthetic or rather in interchangeable terms) is to be comprehended as a process of aesthetic rationalization of syntax and structure, blending different artistic fields in a unity of meaning, which could speak to the single citizen and to the masses alike, in more or less unambiguously politicized tones.

Fusions I: Spaces of, and for, Public Art

The existing infrastructures supporting the arts in 1920s Italy were in a rather derelict state, and unable to sustain any further development. Therefore, change was needed and the syndicates of fine arts seemed an apt institution to achieve it. The regime wanted to create a system of patronage for the arts: through legislation and reform naturally but, more importantly, through networks of artists and intellectuals, State-sponsored exhibitions, competition for public buildings, mass-gathering events and the Corporate State.

Bottai had started designing his corporative project slowly and progressively to direct artists towards the State through newly planned infrastructures and a series of State-sponsored exhibitions (sindacali and regionali, chiefly), which culminated in the 1926 inauguration of the Ministero delle corporazioni, in the 1927 Carta del lavoro (Charter of Labour), and in the 1934 law on corporations. Bottai was in turn Undersecretary to the Ministry of Corporations, when constituted, Minister of the Corporations from 1929 to 1932, and initially responsible for the Charter of Labour, which was finally signed by Alfredo Rocco in 1927. The first *Critica fascista* debate indicated a more direct intervention of the State as patron and sponsor of the artists of the 'Stato-fascismo', and both the 1926 and the later one on syndicalism tackled similar problems: the extent to which the State had to intervene in artistic matters, as well as to what degree artists could act independently from any infrastructure or State apparatus. In his 1928 article 'Arte e sindacalismo', Mario Tinti reiterated the ethical and technical mission of the corporations in line with the speech 'Discorso dell'Ascensione' and the

---

[28] '*case, ville, abitazioni popolari, fabbriche, opifici, oltre a una documentazione fotografica sulle più importanti realizzazioni mondiali in campo architettonico*', Fillìa, *Il padiglione futurista. Volantino* (1928), in Crispolti (ed.), *Prampolini: dal futurismo all'informale*, 278.

'*andata al popolo*', a confluence of ambitions, which anticipated the arts working as a system for the common good. Precisely, Tinti maintained that the arts played a role if functioning as a system, had a moral value and emphasized the importance of artistic technique as a means of constructing meaning and form.[29]

Within the project of corporativism, from its inception in November 1928, the Confederazione nazionale dei sindacati fascisti dei professionisti e degli artisti acted as a propulsive centre. Subdivided in twenty-one syndicates in total across the arts, it administered the whole system. The national Sindacato fascista delle belle arti (Fascist Syndicate of the Fine Arts) was one of these twenty-one syndicates. In itself it grouped the arts into eighteen more syndicates administered at provincial level and it was the body which authorized and scrutinized all plans for exhibitions. The national syndicate was run by its own Secretary and Directorate, with representatives on all the local and national commissions for the fine arts, including on the National Council of Corporations and in Parliament. These national and regional structures were connected by individuals with membership at both levels; that is, the national syndicate was constituted by members of the provincial syndicates.[30] The syndicates supported three types of exhibitions, aligned with the regime's *piramide espositiva*: provincial, inter-provincial and national. As noted by Salvagnini, from the early 1920s, the local mostre sindacali rather than any of the national organizations formed the core of the institutional system of the arts, for, as observed by Malvano, the sindacali exhibitions were charged with growth and politicized: 'multiply the volume of the artistic power'.[31]

All member artists could exhibit at least one work at the provinciali, held in the major cities, and the best ones would be then shown at the more numerous interprovinciali. Over the Ventennio, more than two hundred large inter-provincial exhibitions were staged. These gathered the works of artists across a specific region; these works were then sent to be exhibited at the sindacali. In this way, the regime could scrutinize the artistic production in a somewhat capillary manner, but 'such an intervention did not act directly on the artistic production, rather on the "working and living conditions of the artists"', as Bottai had anticipated since the debate in *Critica fascista* in 1926-7.[32] The mostre interregionali were, however, unable to launch artists onto the national and international scene, and the provinciali 'mostly of little notice and often the result of the arbitrary decisions of some local notables'.[33] From 1928 to 1932, the mostre sindacali progressively lost their influence. In 1933 they began to decline both in popularity and in artists' participation. And from the early 1930s there was significant expansion of the national networks, with larger exhibitions of national art and the I Quadriennale in Rome, which was founded by the governorate of Rome in 1927 around the time of

---

[29] Mario Tinti, 'Arte e Sindacalismo', *Critica fascista*, VI/17 (1 September 1928), 328–30.

[30] Key texts on these points, are Cioli, *Il fascismo e la 'sua' arte*; Stone, *The Patron State*; and Salvagnini, *Il sistema della arti*. For the legislation on the arts, especially in the late 1930s, see Cazzato, *Istituzioni politiche e culturali*.

[31] Malvano, *Fascismo e politica dell'immagine*, 37.

[32] Salvagnini, *Il sistema delle arti*, 21 footnote 23, citing R. Melli, 'Gli Statuti del Sindacato artisti', *Il Tevere*, (24 October 1933).

[33] Ibid., 21–2.

the debate for State art in *Critica fascista* and opened his doors on 3 January 1931.[34] The national circuit was organized in less selective Sindacali (I, 1933 in Florence; II, 1937 in Naples; III, 1941, Milan); Biennali in Venice (1895-); Triennali in Milan (1933-); and finally Quadriennali in Rome under the aegis of the Governatorato (1931-). Together with State-sponsored exhibitions, several galleries began staging individual or collective exhibitions, primarily in Rome, Turin and Milan.[35] With the rise of the Quadriennali, Biennali and Triennali, the mostre sindacali began to lose their power and impact.[36]

Artistic syndicalism – the State organization in charge of orchestrating such a system – was Bottai's creation active since 1929 and the second chapter of the debate on *Critica fascista*. The mostre sindacali essentially mapped out the field of Italian art as it would later be exhibited at national level in Rome and Venice.[37] The two men in charge of the sindacalismo artistico were painter and art critic Cipriano Efisio Oppo, who dedicated himself to fighting all extra-syndicate organization and was appointed General Secretary in 1929; to be replaced in 1932 by sculptor and critic Antonio Maraini, previously Secretary of the Sindacato regionale toscano, who aligned himself more directly with the demands of the State, thereby securing Mussolini's support and diluting any risk of youth dissent.[38]

On 20 July 1932, Maraini was nominated Commissario Straordinario of the Sindacato fascista delle belle arti. To avoid endemic corruption at local level, Maraini instituted the national Quadriennali sindacali from 1933 to grant talented artists, who had exhibited at regional level, national exposure. On the same day Maraini was appointed, Bottai resigned from his role as Minister of Corporations after Ugo Spirito, the mastermind of corporativism, was accused of Bolshevism at the May congress in Ferrara.[39] Subsequently, Mussolini appointed himself Minister of Corporations, but the original ethos of that particular political project was lost in favour, instead, of a process of centralization of the artistic apparatus, and of direct financial dependence of the artists on State support.[40] After a brief period (1932–5) as President of the Istituto nazionale per la previdenza sociale, Bottai was chosen as Governor of Rome in 1935, and of Addis Ababa in 1936, before becoming Minister of Education from 1936 until 1943. Oppo directed the Quadriennale (1931–43), and Maraini the Biennale

[34] Ibid., 13–16, 14, 21–4. And Daniela De Angelis, 'Il Sindacato Belle Arti. Una ricerca sui documenti dell'Archivio delle Stato dell'E.U.R. a Roma' (Nettuno, Gruppo 88, 1999). 'Exhibitions such as the syndacalist aimed at easing such tensions and, like in the case of the Quadriennale, at creating an artistic and geopolitical equilibrium', Vittorio Fagone, 'Arte, politica e propaganda', *Annitrenta*, 48.

[35] For details about sales and numbers of works exhibited, see Stone, *The Patron State*, 28 and Alessandro Sandorfi, 'Aquisti pubblici e privati alla II Quadriennale', in Carlo F. Carli and Elena Pontiggia (eds), *La grande Quadriennale 1935. La grande arte italiana* (Milan, Electa, 2006), 248–61.

[36] Salvagnini, *Il sistema delle arti*, 161.

[37] Crispoli, *Arte e stato*, 22.

[38] See ibid., 27 on Maraini's belief in syndicalism as propulsive for good art and his efforts to apply the regulations fairly when secretary of the syndicate in Tuscany. He was in charge of the first Quadriennale sindacale held in Florence in 1933 and then in Naples in 1937.

[39] Alessio Gagliardi, *Il corporativismo fascista* (Rome-Bari, Laterza, 2010), 21–5; and Gianpasquale Santomassimo, *La terza via fascista: il mito del corporativismo* (Rome, Carocci, 2006), 60–70.

[40] De Sabbata, *Tra diplomazia e arte*, 54 for details about legislations.

(1928–42), for the whole Ventennio; and if Maraini was conservative and at times despotic, Oppo proved to be a more forward-looking artistic and political figure.[41]

The I Biennale had opened in Venice in 1895, so by the 1920s the exhibitions had an established programme as well as an international profile. Vittorio Pica, General Secretary of the Biennali from 1900 to 1926, had no particular affiliations with the regime: he was a man of letters and ran the Biennale as a platform for the elites, introducing to Italy the high art of, for example, Degas, Cézanne, Archipenko, as well as the Novecento movement and, in 1926, the futurists in their first appearance, in a separate pavilion. In outlook, of the three major national exhibitions, the Biennali were overall the more upper-class, conservative and international, and they privileged the international scene over the national.

In early 1927, Maraini, Sarfatti and Oppo were selected by the government to sit on the exhibition's governing body to drive change and organize the arts world according to a more hierarchical structure with Rome at the top. From 1927, Maraini started a process of '*andata al popolo*' to fulfil the regime's aspirations. The arts were charged with affiliating themselves with this ideal process, and engaging more directly with the real to accord more fully with the tastes and aspirations of the public.[42] However, from the Biennale of 1928, the regime began to take an interest in the Venetian show, with the aim of integrating it entirely within its programme of 'regimentation' and centralization of the arts in support of the totalitarian project. Under the direction of Maraini and of industrialist and politician Giuseppe Volpi, I Count of Misurata, the Venice Biennale was turned into a national endeavour, no longer linked with regional support of Venice since, 'like a commercial enterprise, Fascism's Biennale had to cater to the market'.[43] A royal decree of 30 January 1930 put the Biennale under State control. Financial sponsorship came directly from the government, in a fixed sum, and from other institutions, thereby transforming it into an *ente autonomo* with nationalized funding, and its administration placed under the control of Mussolini.[44] From the 1920 show to the one in 1926 the Biennale sold artworks for about 2.6 million lire, while from 1928 to 1938 it registered a steady decline with an average of about 1.5 million lire of sales. The least successful shows were the 'State-run' ones in 1934 and 1936 with sales below a million lire.

Maraini was granted greater authority and power, including a say on the selection of artists and works for the show. Another important difference was that on 27 October 1930, at the Consiglio direttivo, Volpi proposed a return to the old system of invitations, giving more power to the director – in this case, Maraini – and started introducing themed competitions about the successes of the regime.[45] The invited artists had to have already participated in a Biennale and were to present works which

[41] Ibid., 45–58.
[42] Ibid., 73–6 for data and citations.
[43] Stone, *The Patron State*, 33.
[44] Ibid., 39.
[45] Venezia, A. S. A. C., Verbali adunanze, vol. 1 (from 27 February 1930 to 7 December 1931), 12–13, cited in Salvagnini, *Il sistema delle arti*, 39, footnote 81.

had never previously been exhibited in Italy. The State supported the Biennale through a sustained pattern of acquisitions of Italian art, especially futurism in the 1930s.

The Biennale was in direct competition with the Quadriennale, and artists were forced to choose one or the other in this ideal *piramide espositiva*. Artists such as Giorgio De Chirico, Corrado Cagli, Virgilio Guidi, Mario Sironi, Gino Severini and Arturo Diazzi declined the Biennale invitation in 1934 in order to take part in the II Quadriennale, the pre-eminent hall of fame.[46] In 1931, the first Quadriennale in Rome testified to the triumph of national art, gathering in Rome different expressions of State art. The work of some five hundred artists, with the futurists on show collectively in Sala XIII (Benedetta Cappa, Thayaht, Fillìa, Prampolini, Fortunato Depero, Mino Rosso, Giacomo Balla, Gerardo Dottori, Bruno Munari), were on display. Other important artists presented were Funi, Renato Guttuso, the *Italiens de Paris*, Mario Tozzi, Severini, Filippo De Pisis, Campigli, with solo exhibitions for Arturo Tosi, Carlo Carrà, Felice Casorati and Sironi amongst others. While 'others proposed the content: specifically, technicians, art critics and politicians', those invited to participate were chosen because of the artistic value of their work and not their name or affiliation to a particular artistic movement.[47] One of its former members, Oppo himself, defended the movement, but Novecento's decline was imminent.[48] Despite director Oppo being more interested in the artists' potential and in the artworks than in the regime's rhetorical statements or expectations, it is nonetheless true that no previous government had invested so much in the support of the arts.[49] Notably 'artworks for a value of over a million and a half lire of the day were sold. There were two hundred thousand visitors, and profit was of two and a half million lire, against circa two million lire of expenditure; with a final return of half a million lire.'[50] The first prizes went to Tosi for painting and to Arturo Martini for sculpture.

From 1932 onwards, the Biennale began to decline and was perceived more as a showcase for international art.[51] There were several reasons for this weakening but its elitism and political neutrality may have ultimately left it isolated within the national field. The year of the mass celebrations of the Decennale's witnessed the start of a

---

[46] Ibid., 39, footnote 79 for a list of the government's legislation on the arts, see also 113 and passim.

[47] Ibid., 25–6. The law to establish the Quadriennale as an *ente autonomo* was issued by the Governatorato di Roma on 24 December 1928 and 2 July 1929. On the role played by prizes in the success of the I Quadriennale, see ibid., 87–93. 'On average, it emerged that in Italy no less than one million lire were distributed yearly in prizes. This at least was on paper. In reality, with the sole exception of Rome, the situation was not at all rosy. Milan, for instance, did distribute prizes for almost 150 thousand lire but in fractions', ibid., 98. For an assessment of the arts' market, see Nicoletta Colombo, 'Il sistema dell'arte a Milano 1930–40. Pubblico e privato', in Colombo and Pontiggia (eds), *Milano anni trenta*, 39–65.

[48] Francesca Morelli (ed.), *Cipriano Efisio Oppo. Un legislatore per l'arte* (Rome, Edizioni De Luca, 2000), 341.

[49] Salvagnini, *Il sistema delle arti*, 26–7.

[50] On the State intervention to support financially the Quadriennale, with the establishment of the enti autonomi of the Biennale and Quadriennale, see ibid., 26–7. For details about sales and attendance, see Efisio Oppo, 'Discorso per la chiusura ufficiale della Prima Quadriennale d'Arte Nazionale. Dattiloscritto con aggiunte a mano, protocollato dall'Ente Quadriennale in data 11 gennaio 1932, n. 984. Archivio Oppo', in Morelli (ed.), *Cipriano Efisio Oppo*, 155–9.

[51] Salvagnini, *Il sistema delle arti*, 111.

forceful campaign against the Novecento at the XVIII Venice Biennale, because the movement was starting to be perceived as betraying the national spirit and for being dangerously close to Mussolini, and thus potentially too powerful and harmful for the other groups. The 1932 XVIII Biennale was put under heavy fire from the fascist newspaper *Il Regime Fascista* by the hand of Guido Sommi Picenardi, who accused the jury and Maraini himself of favouring certain artists and groups, such as Novecento, through the system of direct invitation. If such an attack was somehow expected, Lino Pesaro's article in *Il Regime Fascista* against Margherita Sarfatti, whom he had initially supported so vigorously, was not at all foreseeable: Novecento contended the Milanese gallery owner was too elitist to reflect the new course of Italy from 1932 onwards. Even the participation of futurists artists was reduced in number and the themed competitions lacked innovative flair. As Monica Cioli noted, another minor event mirrored the tendencies expressed in this artistic and political milieu. The Convegno fascista dell'arte took place at the XVIII Biennale with official reports delivered by a range of artists and intellectuals: by the secretaries of the National Syndicate of Fine Arts Antonio Maraini, of architects Alberto Calza-Bini, of musicians Giuseppe Mulè, of authors and writers Marinetti and by prominent figures such as Oppo and Pirandello.[52] It was again an eclectic meeting of minds and artistic tendencies aimed at showing how the arts functioned more efficiently as a system rather than as separate fields: something futurism understood better and applied much more pragmatically to the situation than all the other artists and artistic movements.[53]

Stone has written that 'by 1934, State patronage constituted a defining aspect of officially sponsored exhibitions', with a clear increase in State acquisitions of artworks and Mussolini's first purchase 'worth 43,000 lire' at the Biennale, a trend inaugurated in 1932 which will continue until the 1940s.[54] The II Quadriennale was even more successful than its predecessor with some 350,000 visitors and some five hundred works sold for a record profit of one million lire. The success enjoyed by the II Quadriennale also had something to do with the prizes awarded: one hundred lire each for painting and sculpture; two second prizes of fifty lire each; and four third prizes of twenty-five lire; a way of securing support, as Bottai had long proposed, for the artists who were part of the State art system and thereby key to its development. The first prize for sculpture went to Marino Marini for his *Bagnante*; and the one for painting to Severini.

On 1 July 1937 the Quadriennale followed suit in becoming an *ente autonomo* under the auspices of the Ministero delle corporazioni. Simultaneously, Bottai was appointed Minister of Education, from his former position as Governor of Rome. If Hitler was launching his campaign against degenerate art in Germany, in Italy, Farinacci's *Il Regime Fascista*, Arturo Francesco Della Porta's *Il Perseo*, *Quadrivio*, *Il Tevere* and Telesio Interlandi's *La difesa della razza* were its echoes, but they did not have the same political power that equivalent voices had in Germany. In 1938, to counteract the mounting ostracism of Jewish artists, Marinetti organized a conference at the Teatro

---

[52] Cioli, *Il fascismo e la 'sua' arte*, 191 for the other participants.
[53] On Farinacci and Pesaro's attack against Novecento at the Venice Biennale, Salvagnini, *Il sistema delle arti*, 44.
[54] Stone, *The Patron State*, 77.

delle Arti di Roma on the theme of 'L'italianità dell'arte moderna', which he used to defend modern art, and Jewish art as itself a part of modern art. No differently from the first two Quadriennali, the III Quadriennale in 1939 was crowded; but it did not put onstage the whole spectrum of Italian art, since many Jewish artists were excluded – Cagli, Roberto Melli, Resita Cucchiari, Ulvi Liegi. Others left Rome: Antonietta Raphaël, Carlo Levi and Cagli himself. The III Quadriennale was not a representative exhibition of Italian art; it was its diminished version.[55]

In parallel with the works exhibited, the visual presentations, the *allestimenti* (mounted displays) of the Palazzo delle Esposizioni were illustrative of an aesthetic transition from eclecticism to univocal statalization. The mounted displays followed aesthetically the regime's political trajectory: from the proto-rationalist designs of Pietro Aschieri and Enrico Del Debbio's in 1931 that mixed liberty-style, classicism and modernity (in the winter garden, for example) to Aschieri's staging of the II Quadriennale artworks which followed the rationalist paradigm en vogue with the

Figure 3 Rotonda, III Quadriennale. Credits: Fondo Archivio storico Quadriennale di Roma – Serie Materiali visivi diversi – Busta/unità Dono Puppo.

---

[55] In his speech 'L' Arte e il Regime' at the opening of the I Quadriennale, *La Tribuna*, (4 January 1931), 3, Oppo spelled out how the regime intended to '*inquadrare*' and '*ordinare*' artists and exhibitions within the State system and under an '*aspetto nazionale più facilmente riconoscibile*'.

Rotonda framed by geometrically arranged compositions of lines in a much more geometrical organization of space. The staging design in 1939 for the III Quadriennale, by Mario Paniconi and Giulio Pediconi, was instead an indication of rationalism's progressive decline. It delivered a monumental, decadent setting, with imposing melancholy statues of the King and Queen at the entrance, in the Rotonda, and in an alcove at the rear looking back through the corridor.

In 1939, Italy was moving towards a regimented idea of the arts which needed to represent in clear and self-evident terms the seat of power in the country. The III Quadriennale's King and Queen were mournful figures in the gloomy atmosphere of the eve of the Second World War.

As Bottai hinted at during the 1926–7 debate in *Critica fascista*, the relationship between the arts and politics is not exclusively about State art, rather about art produced within the structures forged and created by the regime since 'every artwork might have a value which is directly proportionated to its artistic quality'.[56] Bottai presented his argument about the arts in two later important speeches: in Venice, at the opening of the Biennale on 1 June 1938, 'Lineamenti di una politica dell'arte'; and in Rome, at the congress of the Soprintendenti alle antichità e belle arti, in his 'Direttive per la tutela dell'arte tecnica e moderna', on 4 July 1938. In these two interventions, articulated ten years apart from each other, Bottai wanted to separate the real of the arts from that of politics. His was an attempt to divide art from propaganda in such a way as to maintain the autonomous value of artistic creations, appositely guided by the State-organized system of patronage. In his theorization of the relationship between aesthetics and politics, Bottai upheld the aesthetic value of technique in realizing a work of art over an imperative for the artist to represent a particular subject in line with political narratives. With a protracted and pressing economic crisis looming, Bottai was in favour of increasing exports of artworks, under the control of the State. Scrutiny in itself was never anticipated as a mechanism to be exercised over the specificities of artistic creation, only over the patterns of its circulation. Artists were to be free to participate in the private circuit to sell their work and not be dependent only on State intervention which, however, did buy significant amounts of arts and promoted national and internationals sales. The arts and the State should collaborate, while maintaining a degree of autonomy from one another. Such matters were discussed in *Le Arti*, a journal published from 1 October 1938, whose aim was to abolish the distinction between *arti antiche e moderne* (the classical and the contemporary arts), since the arts as a whole, as a system, should contribute to the *andata al popolo* and to citizens' education (Bottai had by then become Minister of Education).[57]

---

[56] 'ogni opera d'arte valga in ragione diretta alla sua qualità artistica', *Politica fascista delle arti*, 85, cited in Vito Zagarrio, *Primato. Arte, cultura, cinema del fascismo attraverso una rivista esemplare* (Rome, Edizioni di storia e letteratura, 2007), 140. See Dantini, *Arte e politica in Italia* for an analysis of the mystical aspects of Bottai's political theorizations, 80–6.

[57] For the legislations which paved the way for the change in direction, see Salvagnini, *Il sistema delle arti*, 370 and passim and Marino Lazzari, 'Arte e modernità', *L'azione per l'arte* (Florence, Le Monnier, 1940), 163–7.

Le Arti, from 1940 directed by Marino Lazzari, was supported by such distinguished figures as Bontempelli, Carrà, Maraini, Roberto Longhi, Oppo, Soffici and a very young critic Giulio Carlo Argan. Through his contributions to this official journal, Bottai expressed his own views on the arts: *Le Arti* was in favour of independence for intellectuals and artists provided they all worked together *in concordia* for the well-being of the fascist State, as would be reiterated in *Primato*. At the beginning of 1940, the Ufficio per l'arte contemporanea was established at the Direzione generale delle antichità e belle arti. This office not only would sponsor the Premio Bergamo; but also mark the division highlighted between the classical and the modern fields. In 1938, the arts were synonymous with action and education for the collectivity; they were to remain aesthetically faithful to their mission, but had to be socially useful in order to modernize the public spheres and sacralize the regime (albeit not Mussolini at this stage).[58]

Hypothesis II: Monumentalism: Visualizing Subjectivity and Objectivity

The closer the arts grew to the regime, the more they embraced its ideological positions; namely, the rejection of 'bourgeois autonomous' art and the aspiration to continue in permanent revolution, emblematically revealed in the case of mural paintings. After the 1929 crisis, muralism was a worldwide phenomenon that under different guises stretched as far as Mexico and Russia; for instance, in Italy Gino Severini was as early as the 1920s familiar with Diego Rivera works. In 1932, Ivo Pannaggi in *La casa bella* penned an interesting article about 'pittura murale' in Germany, drawing a parallel between architecture and 'quadri murali' and pointing to the strand of muralism emerging from the Bauhaus experimentations in Dessau. He traced back to Willy Baumeister 'Mauerbilder' and to Archipenko 'scultopittura' the link between architecture and muralism since they functioned along the pathway threaded by Léger and Ozenfant credo about the 'antidecorative absolute', which elevated geometry and colours to rule over any figurative rendering of contents and subject matters. Regrettably, if Severini was to be invited to decorate the Palazzo di Giustizia and take part in the V Triennale in Milan, Pannaggi's sophisticated avant-garde outlook was not to be practiced widely and remained confined within limited circles.[59]

Mural paintings, with their striking aesthetics – lines tracing augmented bodies in artfully arranged volumes, often dressed in classical attire and suspended in an a-temporal dimension – were only one of the many cases in point. Sironi articulated similar points in several articles: in his article 'Pittura murale', published on 1 January 1932 in *Il Popolo d'Italia* (later republished in *L'Arca* and *Domus* in 1932) and a year later

---

[58] Lazzari, 'Nuova organizzazione e attività della direzione generale delle arti' and 'La direzione delle arti e l'ufficio per l'arte contemporanea', *L'azione per l'arte*, 143–56, 157–62.

[59] See, for example, Pannaggi's outlook on European muralism, 'La pittura murale in Germania', *La casa bella*, II (May 1932), 32–6.

in another article, entitled 'Architettura ed arte', in *Il Popolo d'Italia* on 8 January 1933, when he made explicit the connection between rationalist architecture and the other arts, since any theoretical separation between the arts was no longer conceivable.[60] By his understanding, mural painting, sculpture and architecture were designed to enter into dialogue with one another, and to reject a merely decorative function in favour of a social and political one. Sironi argued that his coeval artists had to follow the civic example set by classical artists, glorious and foundational as they were to mould an Italian tradition that could function across architecture, the visual arts and sculpture in its pursuit of total wholeness.[61] On this occasion, Sironi drew a parallel between painting and architecture because both relied heavily on construction and structure, which he again addressed in several of his writings: for him, the artworks assembled in a 'grande decorazione', along with architectural projects, were forms of collective constructions.[62] Regrettably, however, what consisted the magisterial lesson of the classics was not much more clearly defined other than in opposition to the Umbertine style. In this contribution to the debate in particular he drew a trajectory, whereby the field of painting had rejected nineteenth-century realism in favour of the wall itself, where a new type of 'real' could be found, 'an accord of masses, surfaces, lines, colour that wave a new reality in their invisible, and yet very firm, thread'.[63] Mural painting was monumental art: it was an artistic mode that represented the totalizing politics of the regime. It was total art, and in a sense totalitarian art, because it absorbed all the arts and involved the whole reality of Man.

Just a few months later, young Corrado Cagli circulated his own manifesto, *Muri ai pittori*, in May 1933 in the first number of *Quadrante*, demanding a fusion of the arts and 'a closer and steadier connection between the modernization of State infrastructures and modern artistic production'.[64] Sironi followed suit in December of the same year with his *Manifesto della pittura murale*, released in the first issue of *Colonna*, a journal founded and directed by cosmopolitan, surrealist Alberto Savinio, and signed by Campigli, Carrà and Funi. Sironi's *Manifesto* – published in Milan, not in Rome – was his final response to the fierce criticism he had received during the V Triennale, throughout the year 1933.[65] It synthesized the debate up to the end of 1933 and delineated some guiding principles:

1) Fascism is a lifestyle. [...] Fascist art is the plastic expression of the fascist spirit.
2) In the fascist State art has a social function: an educational function.

---

[60] *Domus*, V/53 (May 1932), 248–9. Sironi, *Scritti*, 111–15.

[61] Sironi, *Scritti*, 137–8.

[62] Elisabetta Longari, *Sironi e la V Triennale di Milano* (Nuoro, Ilisso edizioni, 2007), 138, footnotes 213 and 214 for a critique of the Triennale by J. Campistron, 'La Peinture murale à la Triennale', *L'Architecture d'aujourd'hui*, 8 (October–November 1933), Paris, 33–4.

[63] De Micheli, *L'arte sotto le dittature*, 59. Pontiggia dates it back to 1925. See Pontiggia, *Sironi: il mito dell'architettura*, for earlier statements on mural painting, 18–21.

[64] 'un rapporto più stretto e organico fra strutture statali e produzione artistica', *Quadrante*, I/1, 19–20. Cagli returned to the issue of pittura murale on two more occasions, 'Corsivo', 13, I/2 (1933) and in the October issue.

[65] Malvano, *Fascismo e politica dell'immagine*, 176.

3) Any individualist notion of art for art's sake is over.

4) Mural painting is the social painting par excellence

5) From mural painting will originate the new 'fascist style', the new civilisation will be able to identify itself with.[66]

Emily Braun has pointed out in her monograph on the Sardinian artist that Sironi returned to the wall, as his close friend architect Giovanni Muzio did, and both embodied in their works two cardinal principles of the fascist system of the arts, of State art and of the arts under this totalitarian regime: construction, visualization and sacralization.[67] Sacralization, and the creation of a State religion and of its myths when oriented socially, required a change in language, a rethink of its forms and a renunciation of the idea of autonomy for the arts. He believed mural painting captured how modern artists explained and made sense of the social sphere to contribute to its transformation. Thus the artist's task was to perform a militant role, in stark contrast to bourgeois and autonomous art, which had taken easel painting as its chief expressive language.[68] Easel painting, the quintessential mode of bourgeois painting, ought to be converted into public mural painting that adopted a visually striking iconography to communicate with the masses. Bourgeois intimism should be metamorphosed into collective aesthetics. Mural painting was collective in its aesthetic core but, interestingly, it was modern and contradictory: it was often disproportionate, yet disposed in bands, and it did not cleave to classical notions of geometrical harmony. When Public art fulfilled a solely didactical function instead, there could not have been shadows nor breaks in the narrative order, only continuous perspective.[69]

Fusions II: Visualizing Visions, 1933 V Triennale

The Triennale exhibitions were inaugurated in 1918, initially as biennial events and, from the IV in 1930, as triennial. With the law of 21 December 1930, the Triennale was also made an *ente autonomo*. By the early 1930s, the Triennale had gained a fairly prominent position within the system of the arts because of its practical disposition towards the arts in general and towards State art in particular. The Milanese Expo was not about pure art, nor art for art's sake; rather, because of its focus on the applied arts and scientific developments, it showcased and supported the regime's inclination for technological innovation as a foundation for a new civilization and society.

---

[66] '*Il Fascismo è stile di vita [...]. Arte fascista è l'espressione plastica dello spirito fascista. Nello Stato fascista l'arte viene ad avere una funzione sociale: una funzione educatrice. La concezione individualista dell'arte per l'arte è superata. La pittura murale è pittura sociale per eccellenza. Dalla pittura murale sorgerà lo 'stile fascista', nel quale la nuova civiltà si potrà identificare*', summarized and analysed in Fagone, *L'arte all'ordine del giorno*, 19, 26–32.

[67] Braun, *Mario Sironi*, 160.

[68] Andrea Sironi (ed.), *La grande decorazione* (Milan, Mondadori Electa, 2004), 14.

[69] Longari, *Sironi e la V Triennale di Milano*, 82.

In 1933, the Triennale moved from the Villa Reale in Monza to Milan, where it was housed in the newly built and imposing Palazzo dell' Arte, designed by Muzio with contributions by Sironi, who was also a member of the Directorate, along with secretary of the consortium Carlo A. Felice and Giò Ponti and chaired by the Commissario Straordinario del Consorzio Milano-Monza-Umanitaria Giulio Barella. The need to regulate all artistic institutions under the powers of the State motivated the decision of moving all exhibition in a new building. Following this move, the Triennale was renamed the Esposizione internazionale delle arti decorative e industriali moderne e dell'architettura moderna (International Exhibition of Modern Decorative and Industrial Arts and Modern Architecture), echoing in full the nomenclature of the Paris Expo. The Triennale followed the German Werkbund's and the 1925 Paris Expo models of exhibition, both of which witnessed the Italian delegation being outshined by other participants. The German and the French exhibitions were organized around types of mass-produced objects, which had nonetheless gained momentum outside their own national contexts of production or design.

The Mostra della rivoluzione in 1932 and the Milanese V Triennale in 1933 (attended by a total of 641,126 visitors over 175 days, including some 24,000 foreign visitors and 300,000 'with a reduced-price train ticket arriving from every station of the Kingdom', and with ticket sales totalling five million lire) were in this respect period-defining mass events because they both used Public art in its classical and modern syntax to publicize and visualize the ideology of the regime across assorted groups of visitors. A significant financial investment was sustained for publicity for a total sum of 1,056,743,20 lire, of which 306,743 lire were destined for advertising the exhibition abroad, which generated welcome returns since tickets sold exceeded the expectations and represented the major source of income for the State from the event.[70] The Triennale was also successful in modernizing the economic infrastructures of Milan, especially shops, as Giulio Barella clarified on 28 February 1934 to Alberto Jannitti Piromallo at the Ministero delle corporazioni.[71]

After the Mostra della rivoluzione, the totalitarian project required a more distinct and universal language as far as art in general and as far as Public art in particular were concerned, and the murals of the Triennale in 1933 typified such a trajectory towards frank monumentalism, funded by the government.[72] All these artworks were temporary installations to be destroyed in 1934, in advance of the VI Triennale of

---

[70] For a comparison with the Mostra della rivoluzione, see Salvagnini, *Il sistema delle arti*, 71. 'provvisti di biglietto ferroviario a riduzione per provenineza dalla stazioni del Regno' (1.2. Conto consuntivo della V Triennale, Milan, 23 February 1934, Triennale).

[71] Letter from Barella to Alberto Jannitti Piromallo (5. Corrispondenza relativa ad Alberto Jannitti Piromallo, Erasmo Caravale, Adolfo Stazi e Antonio Cascio, Triennale). See also for reactions to the Palazzo dell'arte, Vittorio Fagone, 'La V Triennale di Milano', in Giovanna Ginex, Tulliola Sparagni and Vittorio Fagone, *Muri ai pittori. Pittura murale e decorazione in Italia 1930–1950* (Milan, Mazzotta, 1999), 113.

[72] Letter of the Direttorio to Mussolini, Milan, 15 May 1931 (3. Corrispondenza indirizzata al capo del governo, Benito Mussolini, Triennale). This document outlines the strategy and vision of the Triennale and asks for governmental endorsement.

1936, to cede space to the Mostra dell'aeronautica and therefore could be treated as provisional statements about the arts which would not have a long-lasting impact.

Sironi had been serving in the Triennale Directorate since 1927 together with Sarfatti and Ponti. At the IV Triennale in 1930, Sironi had started experimenting with mural painting together with a group of eight artists. Giulio Rosso, Raffaele De Grada and Gigiotti Zanini had decorated the walls of the Galleria delle decorazioni; Funi and Giuseppe Pizzigoni had worked on the upper vestibule but, then, the dominant aesthetic was still neoclassical with some metaphysical undertones and an undeniable decorative grace. Thanks to the influence of Sarfatti and Ponti, the founding editor of *Domus*, Sironi's participation became more prominent during the V Triennale, with the first complete display of mural painting in the form of frescoes, bas-reliefs and mosaic.[73] He was responsible for the design of the six arches in Vicenza stone and the monumental entrances to the main building, for some of the settings, for some preparatory sketches and for the programme and invitations.[74] In 1933, *pittura d'affresco* (mural painting) as hypothesized by Sironi and Cagli entered the official sites of State patronage for the first time, sparking the ensuing battle between monumentalism as political and collective and decorativism as individualist and bourgeois.[75] By 1933, the tone of the event had drastically changed. Sironi called together artists in different fields and invited them to work towards the creation of the largest exhibition of mural painting ever staged in Italy. This included a number of sculptors (Arturo Martini, Lucio Fontana, Marino Marini, Libero Andreotti, Timo Bortolotti, Leone Lodi, Ivo Soli, Gigi Supino, Carlo Pizzi, Carlo Sessa, Antonio Majocchi) and some thirty artists, together with Lenor Fini, providing a mosaic based on a design by Funi. The artists were granted complete artistic freedom, but the one main theme was the suitably vague and equally suitably political: '*il lavoro*'.[76]

The V Triennale elicited a great deal of critical response and customarily, because of the many economic and political interests in action, not all of it positive. Roberto Farinacci, of *Il Regime Fascista*, launched an attack against the Novecento movement, at its peak of fame with Mussolini as well as with the international artistic circles, and against Sironi for being too heavily influenced by European art and insufficiently concerned with the national tradition. He reinforced these accusations through the noted reactionary Sommi Picenardi.[77] Mussolini himself

---

[73] Fergonzi, 'Dalla monumentalità', 189, on the importance of the bas-relief as another way of realizing mural painting.

[74] For a description of the Triennale in Braun, *Mario Sironi*, 172–6.

[75] As concluded by Salvagnini, 'the State would have got the most rebellious young artist, those who could feature at the syndacalist exhibitions, and perhaps even in more important ones: provided they were not too well paid', *Il sistema delle arti*, 45.

[76] Amongst the thirty artists we can count Contardo Barbieri, Pompeo Borra, Cesare Breveglieri, Cagli, Campigli, Amerigo Canegrati, Carrà, De Amicis, De Chirico, De Grada, Depero, Funi, Elena Fondra, Alfio Graziani, Dante and Giuseppe Montanari, Enzo Morelli, Gabriele Mucchi, Enrico Paulucci, Prampolini, Esodo Pratelli, Mino Rosso, Alberto Salietti, Savinio, Severini, Primo Sinopico, Emilio Sobrero, Sosso, Silvano Taiuti, Gianfilippo Usellini. See Colombo and Pontiggia, *Milano anni trenta*, 282 on the staging of the exhibition.

[77] Marinetti, prominent gallery owner Leo Pesaro used the occasion to criticize and destabilize Margherita Sarfatti.

reportedly found Sironi's 'piedoni' and 'manoni' aesthetically unpleasant in their modern use of perspective.[78]

In October 1932, Lamberto Vitali had criticized mural painting for having moved away from monumentalism to embrace lyricism in an inadequate exemplification of the modern age. Yet Vitali was not entirely negative: he saw potential in Sironi, and in a 1933 article on the Triennale itself he praised the murals in the Sala delle cerimonie for their stylistic refinement 'un chiaroscuro potente', whilst retaining some scepticism about the results presented by the artists exhibited in the corridors (contrary to Pagano's judgement, on this occasion) and about the sheer numbers of artists selected.[79] In Quadrante, Bardi was unable to praise the works at the Triennale – Cagli excluded because he was a friend of the journal and a relative of Massimo Bontempelli – in view of their Novecento-esque classical motives which he deemed too international and painfully close to becoming the official State art if Margherita Sarfatti was able to win the race. Writing in Casabella, Giuseppe Pagano was ambivalent: he did not see the relationship between architecture, for him a social device, and painting as being fully realized since the visual arts had lost their popular appeal, too entrenched in mythologies alien to the everyday.[80] Even for the typically far-sighted and cosmopolitan art critic Sigfried Giedion, or indeed Sironi's supporter Margherita Sarfatti, mural painting was a retrograde step rather than a modern or enticing way of capturing reality.[81] Roberto Papini, in Emporium, criticized muralism's lack of cogency, declaring it a random assembly of artworks with no didactic purpose, a brand of Public art which does not communicate meaningfully with its audience.[82] The only uncharacteristically supportive voice was that of Ugo Ojetti, the notoriously traditionalist, conservative and nationalist critic who, in his column in the Corriere della Sera of 20 May 1933 emphasized, on this occasion, the aesthetic merit of these works because of their 'largo respiro, la solenne semplicità del comporre' (large respite and simple solemnity of composition).[83] These reactions from leading cultural critics were testimony to the lack of aesthetic trajectory and coherence as far as State art was concerned and of its still pluralistic and even more pronounced inter-artistic ethos, at least for the next three years.

Halting these protracted skirmishes, Sironi himself wrote an exasperated reply, succinctly entitled 'Basta', on 31 May 1933. In response to the heavy criticism of Picenardi and Farinacci, he defended Novecento, listing the movement's contribution towards the creation of national art (while not diminishing, naturally, the learnings to be derived from the international scene), concluding that the only fascist artists were the novecentists because faithful to the arts' mission of supporting the regime, by creating an artistic economy comprising exhibitions, public declarations, international

---

[78]   On the unfolding of the polemic, see De Micheli, Le circostanze dell'arte, 169.
[79]   Vitali, 'La pittura murale alla Triennale', Domus, VI/66 (June 1933), 288.
[80]   'La villa', Casabella, VI/7 (July 1933), 2–3.
[81]   Sigfried Giedion, 'Osservazioni sulla Triennale', Quadrante, 3 (July 1933), 24–6.
[82]   'La quinta Triennale a Milano. Ispezione alle arti', Emporium, LXXVIII/468 (December 1933), 331–84.
[83]   Corriere della Sera (20 May 1933), 3.

visibility and a cogent aesthetic programme.[84] The outcome of this fierce debate, waged across May and June of that year, was the *Manifesto della pittura murale*, published towards the end of 1933, alongside the call for a unitary style for the arts to be conceived of as a system where the aesthetics of politics and the politics of aesthetics existed in mutual relation to one another.[85]

The V Triennale operated as a total work of art in the traditional sense since multiple art forms and fields were involved as well as in the totalitarian sense since it was a political act that aimed to change the social sphere and to educate its audiences in a particular ideology.[86] In his contribution on the Triennale in *Domus*, Giò Ponti made exactly such a point: 'modern architecture, and everyone from Piacentini to Figini, from Muzio to Pagano agree on this, seeks to give back to the painter and to the sculptor the power and authority figurative arts have in architecture, if they are realised exclusively by means of artworks representing true painting and sculpture': or, otherwise, orchestrated as parts of a system shaped by the notion of State art.[87]

In the Salone delle Cerimonie, Campigli engaged with the theme of women at work with *Le madri, le contadine, le lavoratrici*; De Chirico focused on *il lavoro* in the context of *La cultura italiana*; and Severini's mosaic looked at *Le arti*.[88] Sironi's own selected works for the Salone delle Cerimonie celebrated the morality of *il lavoro*, suspended between tradition and modernization, alongside the idea that the arts must perform a moral function in line with the broader discourse on State art.[89] These 1933 murals marked Sironi's official debut as a mural painter, and his own murals experimented especially with scales, chiaroscuro and composition.[90] *Il lavoro, o Le opere e i giorni* echoed a didactic poem by the Greek poet Hesiod and sounded like an admonishment to the viewer about the social power of art. Albeit not Sironi's first façade work, being predated by his window for the Ministero delle corporazioni for which he had prepared the *cartoni* two years previously, it was certainly his first declared mural painting. Its 111 square metres were filled with a monumental synthesis of fascist civilization,

---

[84] Sironi, *Scritti*, 142–8. Farinacci replied to Sironi with an article 'Ma che basta!', *Il Regime Fascista*, I/6 (1933), and Sironi wrote again on 3 June 1933 with an article 'Tanto peggio', *Il Popolo d'Italia*, with more conciliatory tones. The debate continued till October, see *Scritti*, 149–50, 144.

[85] About the critique to the bourgeois in Sironi's illustrations for the *Popolo d'Italia* as early as 1920–4, see De Micheli, *Le circostanze dell'arte*, 173, footnote 28. On the Corporazioni delle Arti Decorative under the auspices of architecture, see Salvagnini, *Il sistema delle arti*, 30, and specifically Mario Tinti, 'Architettura e arti decorative', Roma, vol. 2 (1922–3), 318.

[86] On the Padiglione della stampa and the destruction of all mural, see Longari, *Sironi e la V Triennale*, 115–24.

[87] 'L'architettura moderna, e qui da Piacentini a Figini, da Muzio a Pagano son tutti d'accordo, vuol restituire al pittore ed allo scultore l'imperio e l'autorità delle arti figurative nell'architettura, realizzate esclusivamente attraverso opere d'arte di vera pittura e scultura', 'Architettura-Pittura-Scultura', *Domus*, VI/66 (June 1933), 285.

[88] For a list of participants to the Triennale, see Longari, *Sironi e la V Triennale*, 137, footnote 196 – including the non-controversial sculptures. On Sironi's direction, ibid., 83. On Severini's contribution to the debate on mural painting see Braun, *Mario Sironi*, 160.

[89] For technical details about the type of paint used, see Longari, *Sironi e la V Triennale*, 90–2.

[90] Sironi realized over thirty mural decorations throughout his career. To note, *Il fascismo risolleva i simboli di Roma*, 1932, Mostra della rivoluzione; *Dux*, 1932, Mostra della rivoluzione; *Il lavoro nei campi (L'Agricoltura)* and *Il lavoro in città (L'Architettura)*, 1933, oil on canvas, 3.5 × 3.5 m each, Palazzo delle Poste, Bergamo.

bringing to fruition themes explored in his previous works (including some of his symbolic characters, such as women with baskets of fruits, virile men and female nudes representing the arts).[91]

Set against a de-historicized urban and industrial landscape, *Il lavoro* was crammed with figures arranged on several levels and all occupied in some form of productive activity.[92] Some of these figures are recurrent in Sironi's artworks: virile men engaged in physical work, pensive, standing still alongside nude women. The spatial arrangement of Sironi's mural is of particular interest, as it combines rationalization of aesthetics with classical references to Michelangelo's *Giudizio universale* and to Masaccio's *Cacciata dal paradiso terrestre* in the Cappella Brancacci, with a 'compositional intelligence', or an 'irreversible plastic determination', and to Piero della Francesca and Paolo Uccello in a mural painting which is about new civilizations and utopias.[93] As Fagone has justly observed: 'Sironi's utopia was to establish a live measure of "style" which could totally permeate a new "figurative civilisation".[94] *Il lavoro* positioned at its centre the New Man or New Woman as well as an idea of work as labour and *fatica* (effort), set against the backdrop of an industrial – not agricultural – landscape of anguished and anxious modernity punctuated by reference to classical architecture and culture (the centaur and the canephors, for instance). Moreover, the static and imposing classical dimension and scale of the figures and of the compositional elements were an indication of the grandiosity of the conception of mankind enhanced and facilitated by the dictatorship and brought to the people by Public art as per propaganda art; still there is more to be uncovered in this debut.

The object and the aim of mural art of Public art were the contemporary: it had to represent the now but not univocally.[95] In this phase of his career, Sironi mode of realism was modern in its rejection of mimetic figuration, in its anguish, in its growing fear of the future and favour for a nostalgic look at the past, and in its layering of multiple spatial dimensions, with internal symmetries as well as variations, whilst simultaneously adopting a highly representational but distorting perspective that did not favour verisimilitude. Sironi's typical melancholic tones especially in the female figure and urban landscapes embraced his twenty-one individuals, who often stood in pairs, one next to the other without any apparent connection, isolated and unable to communicate, cunningly recalling Giorgio De Chirico's silent mannequins and

---

[91] In 1928 he completed the *Uomo con vanga*, in 1929 I *Costruttori* and in 1932 *La carta del lavoro* for the windows of the staircase of the Ministero delle corporazioni (a mosaic sponsored by Bottai himself). In all these works, men were engaged in daily activities to improve their own personal condition and modernize society collectively.

[92] In 1931, Diego Rivera realized a similar fresco at the San Francisco Art Institute: *The Making of a Fresco Showing the Building of a City*. It showed a buzzing city *in fieri*, build around the collective values of a society working together for the common good.

[93] On Sironi's decoration at Bergamo post office, see Longari, *Sironi e la V Triennale*, 99, 95, 104 for his 'compositional intelligence' and Vittorio Fagone, *L'arte all'ordine del giorno*, 19.

[94] Ibid.

[95] As Fagone has fittingly observed, with mural painting there is an indirect return to the contemporary, which becomes the real subject matter of the artistic creation, but this said contemporary is highly political, ibid., 30.

muses immersed in waste lands. The gigantic scale of his murals, the cycloptic nature of the landscapes conversely resonated the constructivism of the Russian avant-gardes, the volumes of an architectural composition and their mechanical view of reality over a figurative and linear narrative Sironi had already used in the photomontages of the Mostra della rivoluzione; in his public works, Sironi recomposed unity with the fragmentary nature of life while echoing the profound fragility of the human condition.[96] Libero Andreotti has perceptively analysed the Mostra della rivoluzione through the prism of the aesthetics of shock, and especially of Wagner's, featured in Sironi's contribution and in his hazardous juxtaposition of forms and colours, to reframe the relationship between the avant-gardes and consumption of culture by means of simulacra. According to the architectural scholar, 'Sironi's work might thus be seen to exemplify a modern structure of perception that elevates the experience of shock to a general principle.'[97]

Sironi resemanticized such an aesthetic of shock according to a monumental aesthetic paradigm and one which looked to the Quattrocento and Cinquecento to put forward a more subdued view of humanity and one which had renounced the heroic and bombastic tones of the Mostra della rivoluzione. His use of scale and his almost expressionistic rendering of the human body, however, with the classical figure of the canephor bearing the fruits of the earth right at the centre, fractured the compositional order and contrasted powerfully with a didactic, conciliatory manner of delivering a political message to the masses: if Sironi was indeed devoted to composition as a unifying moment of his artistic creation, for him understood as Public art, he was equally weary of linear, simplified narratives and still entreating the idea of total work of art as assemblage he had practiced for the Mostra della rivoluzione. The centaur is another instance where hybridization, chthonic time and darkness of a pagan civilization emerge from this mural which glorifies the Christian civilization of a regime whose survival depends on the Concordat with the Roman Church. Sironi's Public works were a combination of avant-garde aesthetics fused into muralism, voided of any of the cosmological and abstract facets used by, for example, Prampolini, in his highly stylized figures, or Depero, in his playful chromatism, both of whom had been invited to take part in the Milanese show. Sironi championed a form of Public art which made and unmade its ideological and educational message. Soon afterwards, he resigned from the Directorate because of the prominence Pagano with Piacentini's backing had given to architecture. Sironi and Pagano ended up disagreeing not so much on the public role of the arts, but instead on their hierarchy within the system: despite being in favour of the simultaneous use of architecture and painting to create an artwork, for Pagano the abstract nature of architecture rendered it superior to mural painting.[98]

---

[96] For instance, Tatlin's Monument to the III International (1922), see De Micheli, *Le avanguardie artistiche del Novecento*, 284 and for Germany's take on monumentality, Benzi, 'Sironi e l'architettura', in Pontiggia, *Sironi: Il mito dell'architettura*, 81.

[97] Libero Andreotti, 'Architecture as Media Event', 20 and 'The Techno-aesthetics of Shock: Mario Sironi and Italian Fascism', *Grey Room* (2010), 38–61.

[98] 2. Consiglio d'Amministrazione, f. 'Verbale della seduta del Consiglio d'Amministrazione del 13 dicembre 1933', Milan, Triennale.

The author of the other Manifesto was the other star of the Triennale. Corrado Cagli's *Preludi della guerra* covered 30 square metres, and carried on with the same theme of nationalism, on this occasion in its belligerent aspect, and vitally continued to deconstruct a political message through the use of politicized artistic codes.[99] Cagli's tonalism exuded that sense of ambiguity in perception and judgement that is intrinsic to human nature. Set in an unidentifiable past and realized on a two-dimensional perspective, the painting depicts men waiting to go to war: a sleeping man, three horsemen and people of varying ages ready to depart. They are about to leave their homes to fight for their country, enacting a fairly obvious and propagandistic patriotic act. Cagli's primitivist style was also indicative of temporal transgressions: references to classical Greece (the profile of the horses recalls Greek ostensible 'vascular' painting) were coupled with the more typical references to Giotto and Masaccio in a static, yet tense, pose.[100] Once again, *Preludi della guerra* added an oneiric dimension to muralism because it stretched the boundaries of realism in response to the limits of the discerning view of the audiences. What Cagli and Sironi had in common is their choice of the mural as medium for their shared desire for construction and commitment to figuration, the former in particular was also closely connected with the architectural project. They nonetheless interpreted the human condition differently: for Sironi it was about collective labour, pain and anguish; for Cagli, meditation, sacrifice and a mystical shared destiny.

The further key point we have identified in the discussion on State art was its need to create new myths, supporting the sacralization of politics engineered by Mussolini's regime. As far as the visual arts were concerned this happened according to various aesthetic guises. For instance, through the use of broken lines and empowered colours, as we can see in the Scuola romana and in the works of one of its most distinguished members, Cagli again, from easel paintings to murals. The Scuola romana came into existence when, in 1927, artist Marino Mazzacurati met painters Scipione, Mario Mafai and Antonietta Raphaël and they set up camp in Via Cavour; art critic Roberto Longhi called it 'La scuola di via Cavour'. Together they founded the Scuola romana and for the whole of 1931 the journal *Fronte*, a strong adversary of Novecento that was in dialogue with European art movements such as cubism. Via Cavour soon turned into the meeting point of many leading artists and writers, Giuseppe Ungaretti, Carlo Carrà, Riccardo Barilli, Libero de Libero, Vincenzo Cardarelli, Alvaro, Moravia and Saint-John Perse, for the first time presented to the Italian public.[101] One of the traits that distinguished the Scuola romana was their understanding of classicism, which was used in anti-classical terms to express the relationship between a dismembered Ungaretti-like subject who needed to approach and face an unknowable and hostile reality.

[99] Or *Preparativi alla guerra*, as Fabio Benzi documents it, *Corrado Cagli e il suo magistero. Mezzo secolo di arte italiana dalla Scuola Romana all'astrattismo* (Milan, Skira, 2010), 22.

[100] On Cagli's muralism and rationalist architecture, see Crispolti, 'Il Cagli "romano": traccia per una ricostruzione', in Enrico Crispolti (ed.), *Cagli e la 'Scuola di Roma' 1927–1938* (Milan, Electa, 1985) 26–7.

[101] On the Italians in Paris, Colombo-Pontiggia, *Milano. Anni trenta*, 22–3.

In the 1930s, State art became a matter closely linked to the Quadriennali, Triennali, regionali and sindacali exhibitions, but also to private galleries acting as agents in the construction of a network of artistic expressions that could fit the regime's grand social and ideological design, albeit loosely conceived. When working in Rome, Bardi endorsed the Scuola romana by inaugurating his new Galleria Romana in Via Veneto with a show dedicated to Andrea Spadini, an artist marginalized by Roberto Melli during the supremacy of the Valori plastici group. In November 1930, Bardi had decided to start exhibiting works by Mafai and Scipione, to be followed by those of Carlo Levi, Francesco Menzio and Enrico Paulucci. In 1932 Bardi again had staged the first solo exhibition by Cagli, which was followed by a collective one, the 'Cagli, Capogrossi and Cavalli' show at his Galleria del Milione in Milan. Melli instead supported the Scuola romana as a new frontier in Italian art, and he did so by publishing his opinions in leading journals such as *L'Italia letteraria* and *Quadrivio*. In 1933 Cagli signed the manifesto of mural painting for the V Triennale in Milan, while in 1934 his relationship with the arts as a system of interlocking spheres (literature, the visual arts and architecture) was less pronounced. In October of the same year Emanuele Cavalli, Giuseppe Capogrossi and Melli signed the *Manifesto del primordialismo plastico* (1933), which marked the birth of the Scuola romana, as endorsed by Persico and by Polish, Paris-based, art critic Waldemar George after the group exhibited at the gallery Bojean in 1933, in opposition to official mural painting. The primordialismo plastico marked by prominent tonalism, was about spirituality and tones of colour which together can prompt emotions in expressionist waves while maintaining a figurative approach which discards abstracticism.

From 1935 to 1938, this nouvelle vague gathered in Rome at the Cometa gallery directed by Libero de Libero, who decided to host a show of Cagli's drawings, after meeting the young artist through his uncle Bontempelli. Cagli was naturally close to Bontempelli and then to *Quadrante*, edited by Bardi and Bontempelli himself; he shared their ideas about the need for the arts to create myths, and implicitly in this way to facilitate the regime's discourse on State art by means of figuration.[102] For Cagli it was the idea of primordial, different to that of primitive, which could inspire artistic lyricism and practice: that is the condition of beginning, of innocence, which allows the creation of knowledge through myths, or of an 'auroral mythopoetic condition: that is the awareness of a possible and needed new life in art'.[103] Cagli's idea of realism was a commingling of figuration, magical realism, read as a fresh way of perceiving objectivity, and the reinsertion of the Italian tradition as advocated by Novecento within a figurative tradition moved by a multiplicity of different logical patterns as active in the creation of myths and mythologies.

Cagli's *Neofiti* was completed in 1934 and exhibited on several occasions, amongst which the II Quadriennale in 1935 in the room dedicated to the artist (the sixth room

---

[102] On the *Neofiti*, *Annitrenta*, 110.

[103] Giuseppe Appella and Fabrizio D'Amico (eds), *Roma 1934* (Modena, Panini Edizioni, 1986), 15 and Enrico Crispolti, 'Il Cagli "romano": traccia per una ricostruzione', in Enrico Crispolti (ed.), *Cagli e la 'Scuola di Roma' 1927–1938*, 15 on the notion of primordio and the creation of new myths.

to be shared with Carrà and in the Rotonda).[104] The *Neofiti* fits perfectly with the school's attention towards expressionism, figuration and its anti-naturalistic take on reality. On that occasion, however, the young Cagli was also invited to exhibit four 4-metre-tall mural panels depicting the reclamation of the Pontine Marshes as one of the chief social campaigning the regime promoted in the mid-1930s to show its focus on the development and bonification of rural areas.[105] At the II Quadriennale, the Scuola romana was also championed by Scipione (Gino Bonichi who died in 1933), with a retrospective of his work, and a solo show of Mario Mafai with twenty-nine oil paintings. Other notable presences were Fausto Pirandello, Emanuele Cavalli and Giuseppe Capogrossi – and taken all together the II Quadriennale witnessed the triumph of tonalism over Novecento and to a certain extent futurism.

In *Neofiti*, Cagli experiments with the ancient technique of encaustic tempera used in Pompei on a large square wooden table (61 × 61 cm). The wood could guarantee a stable support while the wax gave plasticity and solemnity to the brushstrokes with similar effects as in mural painting. Explicit sources of inspiration for Cagli's epic version of this famous theme were the *Bathers* by Cézanne (1906) and the *Seated Bather* by Picasso (1930), together with the other artworks by the *fauves* group. The Italian artist drew upon the *fauves* predilection for monochromatic palettes, a penchant which could also be linked to Picasso's pink or blue periods. The Italian Quattrocento also provided direct inter-artistic inspiration. Cagli visually refers to Masaccio (*Battesimo dei neofiti*, 1425–6) and Masolino (*Battestimo di Cristo, c.* 1435), and even more significantly to Piero della Francesca (*Battesimo di Cristo*, 1445), with the unequivocal reference to the character on the right-hand side, for their analytical realism, entrenched in mystery-fuelled scenarios drawn with geometrical precision. The three elongated figures of men figuring in the painting are about to enter the water, their bodies move with natural fluidity against the backdrop of an undefined landscape, for it is a magical, a-temporal moment: an almost familiar moment in every persons' life. Such rendering expresses how the arts can sacralize the everyday by sharing individual myths and yet universalize through a sense of mystery. We do not see the faces of the men, they are standing, getting undressed with their back to the viewer, a choice which contributes to the aura of mystery exuding from the painting. The men to be baptized are entering something they do not know, a new religion which will guide them by faith and not only by rational explanation. There is nothing disturbing about the three naked men together. The composition of the artwork, with its ochre tones and subtly and continuously changing tonalities, encourages a slow rhythm of observation in the viewer, ordinary and solemn at the same time. The image is easy to read and to interpret figuratively, the atmosphere is tranquil: these are New Men ready to accept their new lives together as a collectivity. The *Neofiti* is a rite of passage from one order to another but such a transition is made to be a moment to share with a universal meaning, unrestricted by ambiguity but filled with mysticism and religious faith.[106]

---

[104] Carlo F. Carli and Elena Pontiggia (eds), *La grande Quadriennale 1935*, 217.

[105] Ibid., 28–9.

[106] For further readings, see Franco Russoli and Raffaele De Grada (eds), *Cagli* (Milan, SEDA, 1964) and Fabio Benzi (ed.), *Corrado Cagli e il suo magistero*.

This brand of Public art was indisputably not a straightforward expression of the fascist State; rather it was a manifestation of its codifications through a specific linguistic and iconographic repertoire. All the murals discussed briefly so far have fused architecture and the visual arts, three-dimensional and two-dimensional perspectives, and unusual techniques such as encaustic painting (hot wax painting) used in ancient Greece and in Pompei, to bond with the classical, mainstream, official and internationally recognized Italian tradition, turning the results almost into a catalogue of images visualizing and monumentalizing a de-historicized and universal contemporary world.[107]

Fusions III: Visualizing Visions, 1936 VI Triennale and X Biennale

On planning the following Triennale, on 4 January 1934 Oreste Bignardelli wrote to the President of the Triennale to encourage a steady support for all future shows because such events could create new jobs, attract foreign visitors and investors.[108] Towards the end of the year, on 7 December 1934 Pietro Mazzucato (head of the Ufficio Stampa e Propaganda in Milan) also penned a long report on what the exhibition should be about and how it should be organized. First of all, the VI Triennale was intended not exclusively as an artistic event, rather as a 'tourist event' to praise and publicize the regime nationally and internationally, or even better as a form of propaganda. To this end, the publicity was directed to two audiences divided by their social class and economic power, 'the first one of high standard, noble, hyper-modern, the second of touristic, almost popular type'.[109] To boost publicity, the Triennale and the Biennale ought to collaborate and work in synergy: Venice with its international appeal and Milan with its productive one were asked to complement each other. The newly-built railway stations were selected as points from where to publicize the events and a considerable amount of resources were to be allocated to wall advertisements, in a much anticipated 'return to the walls'. The Istituto Luce was to contribute to the propaganda machine with its newsreels. In 1936, with falling consensus, art exhibitions and Public art more in general were means of reaching wider and multiple audiences, and thus impactful on Italian citizens and on the faith in the regime. Notwithstanding such comprehensive plans for maximizing visibility and returns, the VI Triennale was much less well attended than the V and generated more expenses and considerably less profit.[110]

---

[107] Encaustic Art Institute, https://www.eainm.com/what-is-encaustic/ (accessed 25 June 2020).

[108] 6. Comunicazioni alla stampa e a personalità dello Stato, relative alla VI Triennale, Triennale.

[109] *'la prima di genere elevato, nobile, modernissimo; la seconda di genere turistico a tipo quasi popolare'*, 2, in f. 'Appunti sulla campagna propagandistica per la VI Triennale', 7 December 1934, Milan (16. Carlo Alberto Felice, Triennale).

[110] f. 'Verbale della seduta del Consiglio d'Amministrazione del 19 dicembre 1933', 3–4, Milan (2. Consiglio di Amministrazione, Triennale) and letter from Riccardo Motta to Mussolini, 15 September 1936, Milan (6. Comunicazioni alla stampa e a personalità dello Stato, relative alla VI Triennale, Triennale). The total profit during the VI Triennale was 1.5 million lire against the 5 million lire during the V.

On 14 August 1935, for the VI Triennale in Milan, Sironi invited futurist and popular Depero to realize 'an organic programme of mural paintings and room decorations', or one that they could describe as a totalizing work of Public art with social utility.[111] Depero had made his name through advertisement and had the right profile to fulfil the VI Triennale ambitions. Moreover, as a result of Pagano's role in the Directorate, the VI Triennale was more inclined to showcase the social mission of the arts, architecture and the visual arts joining forces even more than before to produce a socially useful art which needed to be disseminated widely through the right channels. Besides mural painting, then, the VI had rooms dedicated to practical matters: urbanism (Mostra internazionale di urbanistica), home furnishing (Mostra dell'abitazione) organized by Pagano and Prampolini's pavilion of stagecraft (Mostra internazionale di scenotecnica teatrale), in an ideal assemblage of the total work of art as we have defined it so far and of mass-produced objects for improving citizens' living standards.[112]

By comparison with earlier incarnations of the Milanese exhibition, the previous star of the show, muralism, was sidelined in favour or more accessible artefacts: only Sironi, Casorati, Carrà and Cagli were invited to design murals for the Palazzo dell' Arte.[113] For this instantiation of the Triennale, as expected, Sironi completed one of his most important murals: *Il lavoro fascista*, for the grand stairway. Planned as a work of 12 × 8 m, time constraints meant that Sironi finished only the central section, with its monumental female form representing Italy, together with a fascio littorio and the more diminutive figure of a builder in the lower part of the composition. Pagano described the mural as pervaded by an 'heroic sense of composition', and declared it to hold a striking power over the observer.[114] For the first time, Sironi deployed a new technique, mosaic, that he had written about in his *Racemi d'oro*.[115]

On this occasion, the Salone d'onore of the VI Triennale was given over to Marcello Nizzoli, Giancarlo Palanti, Edoardo Persico and Fontana's *Sala della Vittoria* (Victory Hall).[116] Predictably, it was a celebration of the great leadership of Italy which combined rationalist architecture and monumentalism for a modern twist: with photo-mechanically reproduced portrait busts of Caesar, Scipio, Augustus, Trajan and Constantine, as Ponti stated: 'the authority of this artwork [...] is a manifestation of metaphysical art', and one could add of avant-garde art, whereby the power of the regime is elevated to a higher standing by means of a visionary power similar to that

---

[111] '*un organico programma di decorazioni murali e di ambiente*' (F. 'Depero', Dep. 3.2.21.79, f. 'Corrispondenza sciolta 1935', MART).

[112] At the Exposition Internationale des Arts et Techniques dans la Vie Moderne in Parigi in 1937, if Picasso presented his *Guernica*, Sironi his *L'Italia corporativa* displayed in the pavilion designed and coordinated by Piacentini and Pagano. *L'Italia corporativa*, 1936–1937, mosaic on panels, 350 × 565 cm, Milan, Palazzo dell'Informazione, VI Triennale. See, https://www.wikiwand.com/en/Exposition_Internationale_des_Arts_et_Techniques_dans_la_Vie_Moderne</URI> (accessed 24 June 2020).

[113] Colombo and Pontiggia (eds), *Milano anni trenta*, 283–6 for the internal settings, especially the Padiglione della stampa and architettura.

[114] Braun, *Mario Sironi*, 179.

[115] (March 1935), *La Rivista illustrata del Popolo d'Italia*, Sironi, *Scritti*, 191–4.

[116] Raffaello Giolli, 'VI Triennale di Milano. La "Sala della Vittoria" (M. Nizzoli, G. Palanti, E. Persico)', *Casabella*, IX/102–103 (June–July 1936), 14 on Fontana's innovative language, able to infuse lightness into monumental sculpture.

Figure 4 Lucio Fontana, Marcello Nizzoli, Giancarlo Palanti, Edoardo Persico, Sala della Vittoria, VI Triennale, photo: Crimella. Credits: Triennale Milano – Archivio Fotografico.

we had seen operating at the Mostra della rivoluzione.[117] The walls of the room were made of partitions which let the light through; the reflection of light on the dark, colour-contrasting marble floors illuminated the room with geometrically aligned,

---

[117] 'l'autorità di quest'opera [...] è manifestazione d'arte metafisica', 6. Comunicazioni alla stampa e a personalità dello Stato, relative alla VI Triennale' f. 'Giro del Palazzo delle arti', foglio 6, Milan, Triennale. Ponti, 'La sala della Vittoria' *Domus*, VI/103 (July 1936), 7. For the press presentation of the Salone della Vittoria, see folder 6. Comunicazioni alla stampa e personalità dello Stato, f. 'Palazzo dell'Arte. Padiglione dei tessili e giardino', foglio 6, Triennale.

rationalist-like luminous beams arranged in a black and white, type-like repetition. The focal point was the white statue of Victory, positioned at the end of the room. This *Victory* was an amalgam of obvious classical references, animated by a modern impetus – a very different *Victory* to Thayaht's highly stylized one for the I Quadriennale, which Marinetti had hailed as a masterpiece of futurist art as State art. The classical whiteness of the *Sala della Vittoria* was a juxtaposition without synthesis which visualized many of the arguments advanced in this Agon thus far: by 1936, rationalism had come to terms and clashed with classicism, and in turn they had to meet the demands of the masses in an almost disorganized and derivative fashion. This was not a victory, rather the regime was about to lose more and more consensus following the victory in Ethiopia in 1936 up until the 1938 racial laws. This particular Victory Hall, however, still described elements in equilibrium, a balance soon to degenerate in racial hatred – as when, for example, Foreign Minister Galeazzo Ciano would order the destruction of the murals by Cagli, who had been so supportive of the regime up to that point, but who was Jewish.[118]

From 1936 onwards, as for all the other exhibitions, the role played by the State changed: for example, Maraini refreshed the format of the competitions with a greater emphasis on a more popular approach driven by fascist bureaucrats 'breaking down traditional patronage patterns and in challenging the power of the established celebrities of the art world. Good workers, party hacks, and malleable young artists replaced the stars of the art world as primary recipients of State patronage.'[119] From 1932 to 1934, during Maraini's direction, the profile of the Biennale altered drastically: it endured a process of nationalization, marginalization of leading intellectual figures from the committee, preference for more conservative art and an end to group invitations and a general reorientation of the artistic barometer towards Rome. In a last-ditch attempt to regain recognition as a national event and to reach beyond the elites, and with Ojetti's blessing, the 1936 Venice Biennale exhibited some Public art and the most appreciated artist was Menin because of his war painting. That year, Maraini issued two competitions: one for 'seven frescoes'; the other for 'eight statues to decorate a central hall chosen for this purpose'. The theme was 'Fascist life' and, as Stone has observed: 'Most importantly regulations stipulated that participating muralists and sculptors present preliminary sketches, giving the jury pre-emptive power over a possible disappointing outcome': thereby instituting a progressive form of regulation or censorship through a more didactic and less polysemic artistic language.[120]

A final State manoeuvre in the Biennale's Directorate took place on 21 July 1938, when the presence of figures appointed by the State in the Consiglio di amministrazione was requested.[121] In 1938 the trend was even more self-evident. That year, the system of invitations changed because the Biennale proposed six opportunities (competitions

---

[118] Tempesti, *Arte dell'Italia fascista*, 214–19 and Braun, *Mario Sironi*, 185 with further references, note 107.
[119] Stone, *The Patron State*, 196.
[120] Ibid.
[121] De Sabbata, *Tra diplomazia e arte*, 24–6.

for frescoes, bas-reliefs, portraits, landscapes, engravings and commemorative medals) open to any artist belonging to the Sindacato fascista delle belle arti, with the theme, once again, being 'Fascist life'.[122] Having given up the idea of inviting artists via the mostre sindacali to evade the routine personal preferences and exchanges of favour, and opting instead for a direct competition, the Biennale ended up listing twenty-four murals, sixteen of which came from young artists who had won the competitions, and six bas-reliefs on the theme 'Eventi e aspetti della vita italiana nell'era fascista'. Despite the surprisingly high number of submissions, the final invitations were sent to fewer artists than before and preference was accorded to those who either had some noted reputation or who had built their profile through national competitions. In his conservative choices, Maraini minimized any potential dissent and favoured the status quo created by the patron State: thus, in order to stress the importance of Public art, the main rooms in the grand central hall were dedicated to the most politicized winning frescoes and bas-reliefs (similar to the grand stairway of the VI Triennale, for instance), and preference was given to young artists.

In the same year, from 25 to 31 October, the Accademia d'Italia organized the VI Convegno Volta took place in Rome on the subject of the relationship between architecture and mural decoration with delegates of high calibre such as Henri Matisse, André Lothe, Willem Dudok and Marinetti. Contrary to the more regimented and propagandistic trend set by the last Triennale, Le Corbusier's intervention at the Convegno posited a separation from the visual arts, contending that architecture could function on its own terms; arguably, with his words the Swiss architect created an unprecedented hiatus between the two fields which had been closely associated under the umbrella of State art. Of the many other interventions at that Convegno, we might also single out Maraini's, taking as it did an opposite position to Le Corbusier and encouraging more consistent collaboration between architecture and the visual arts along the lines the regime had been following in, for example, the Ministero delle corporazioni, the Città universitaria, the Casa madre dei mutilati and many other buildings where 'the ability of bringing back the figurative arts to their monumental tasks affirms and reveals itself as achievable' and Marinetti's defence of his own 'plastica murale'.[123]

Theatre of Objects I: Mail and Rails

In their race for hegemony in the arts, futurists tried to reiterate their position within the debate, on mural art and Public art, on aesthetic grounds that were officially different from Sironi and Cagli's, but that in reality shared much in common. Throughout the debate, the leitmotif was an ideal juxtaposition between the national and the

---

[122] Ibid., 201–3.

[123] 'la capacità di riportare le arti figurative a compiti monumentali si afferma e si dimostra attuabile', 'Ritorno delle arti figurative ai compiti monumentali', *Convegno Volta* (27 October 1936), in Alessandro Masi, *Un'arte per lo stato. Dalla nascita della Metafisica alla Legge del 2%* (Naples, Marotta & Marotta, 1991), 204.

international traditions, with futurism as the ideal advocate for Italian supremacy because of its long-term disposition towards innovation across all the artistic fields and its cosmopolitan outlook.[124]

On 6 February 1932, supported by Pippo Oriani, Fillìa started publishing *La Città nuova. Sintesi del futurismo mondiale e di tutte le avanguardie*. In the issue of 1932 Fillìa edited by himself, dedicated entirely to architecture, Prampolini republished his manifesto, *Architettura futurista*. According to Godoli, despite simply rehearsing Virgilio Marchi's points, Prampolini's manifesto still put forward a distinctive paradigm for futurist architecture, in the context of the debate and battles for State art since 'the lyrical view of the architectonical idea finds in plastic dynamism its equivalent stylistic counterpart. Futurist architecture is therefore the style of the movement realised in space.'[125] If Prampolini and Fillìa asserted the importance of futurist architecture because of its lyrical and spiritual mode, use of new materials, collaboration with the visual and plastic arts and interest in urban studies: in his contributions Alberto Sartoris tried to mediate between the two camps, the rationalists and the futurists, once more in the name of a united front. In the same year, 1932, Sartoris published his *Gli elementi dell'architettura funzionale* with a preface by Le Corbusier and selection of the best architectural milestones across the globe, including the proceedings of the CIAM's first meetings held at the castle in La Sarraz in 1928.[126]

On 10 September 1933, Prampolini reinforced the position-taking exercise by the futurists by publishing the articles 'Dalla pittura murale alle composizioni polimateriche', and a year later, 'Al di là della pittura, verso i polimaterici', where he elaborated on the very concept of *polimaterico*.[127] Such was Prampolini and the futurists' own take on Public art, embodied in the *plastica murale*, which he envisaged as the result of mixing as many as twenty different types of materials; thus, in Giovanni Lista's words, 'artists [...] give back the central role of composition to the creative organisation'.[128] According to Prampolini, the plastica murale was a way of renewing the Italian tradition as well as its infrastructures. In order to ascertain the italianità of mural painting, Prampolini attributed the aesthetic preference for visual fragmentation of the subject matter to France: an artistic disposition and sensibility 'European' futurists à la Marinetti et al. had vigorously contributed to defeat through their own 'brand' of mural painting:

---

[124] Marinetti, 'La "Tensistruttura" grande invenzione futurista Fiorini', *Futurismo*, II/20 (22 January 1933), 6.

[125] '[l]a visione lirica dell'idea architettonica trova nel dinamismo plastico l'equivalente stilistico [...]. [L]'architettura futurista è quindi lo stile del movimento materiato nello spazio', 'Manifesto dell'architettua futurista dinamica, stato d'animo, drammatica', *Roma futurista*, III/72 (29 February 1920). And Prampolini 'L'architettura futurista', *La Città futurista*, (February 1928).

[126] Peppino Ghiringhelli in a letter to Belli describes Sartoris's work as being of much better quality than that of Fillìa (F. 'Peppino Ghiringhelli', R. 42/c. 172, 25 April 1932, Milan, MART).

[127] In *La Terra dei vivi*, (10 September 1933) 6, 2–4, and then republished in *Stile futurista*, I/2 (August 1934), 8–10. And a few months later he signed with Ambrosi, Andreoni, Benedetta, Depero, Dottori, Fillìa, Marinetti, Munari, Oriani, Mino Rosso and Tato, 'La plastica murale futurista. Un manifesto polemico', *Stile futurista*, I/5 (December 1934), 3 to continue to ascertain the importance of plastica murale as Public art.

[128] Lista, *Enrico Prampolini futurista europeo* (Rome, Carocci, 2013), 236.

Mural plasticity has overtaken perspective, because it is in its essence anti-muralist, together with all chiaroscuro optical illusions and foreshortenings, attached to reality. Geometry possesses our creation, like syntax does possess literature. [...] the formal element intervenes with its evocative power, that of the self-standing chiaroscuro; namely, as such it is understood not in its deceiving volumetric perspective, but as a constructive plastic value which can both break and contrast what might be too geometrical and render human the abstraction of architectural surfaces. [...] The analogies and reflections of continuous action, between objectivity and subjectivity, contribute to the creation of a vibrant compositional alternation. Polymateric composition are meant to replace future mural paintings (The Mostra della rivoluzione was a tangible example of their endless potential applications).[129]

Mural painting was a characteristically Italian art form which 'Italian' artists had perfected because of the centrality architecture had long assumed in their artistic and civic traditions. Moreover, Prampolini's polymateric art employed every type of material; being as such a form tending, then, towards the total work of art.[130] Hence, if new futurist architecture could only flourish in response to innovative decorative languages and techniques; the notion of *polimateria* provided a probing solution, because it was both theorised and constructed as a means of fusing the aesthetic and the social realms.

Around the same time, as customary for every new declension of the futurist paradigm of aesthetic-cum-politics, Fillìa set up *Stile futurista* (1934–5), designed to problematise the relationship between architecture and the visual arts, particularly in relation to the newly emerging question of the *plastica murale*. In Fillìa's article 'Plastica murale', architecture is formally inscribed through the grand narratives of cosmic lyricism and *arte polimaterica* into the new fascist construction, *edilizia*. The futurist version of *plastica murale* consisted of the incorporation of colour into the plaster, and the decoration was achieved by applying layers of different colours over the preparatory cartoons. No such technique had ever before found a practical application. The new art to come was polymateric and, naturally, Public and, naturally, political.

In 1934, Prampolini and Giuseppe Rosso organized the I Mostra di plastica murale, held in Genoa under the patronage of Mussolini and of Marinetti; its catalogue was published by *Stile futurista*, sanctifying such an alliance in the context of a much bigger

---

[129] *La prospettiva si può considerare come superata dalla plastica murale d'oggi, perché di se stessa antimurale, e con essa tutti gli illusionismi ottici del chiaro-scuro e degli scroci, aderenti alla realtà. La geometria presiede le nostre creazioni, come la sintassi la letteratura. [...] elemento formale interviene con la potenza evocatrice, del chiaro-scuro-autonomo, cioè, intenso non nella sua ingannevole prospettiva del volume, ma come valore plastico costruttivo, per rompere e contrastare ciò che potrebbe persiste di troppo geometrico, e umanizzare l'astrazione delle superfici architettoniche. [...] Queste analogie e riflessi di azioni continue, fra oggettivismo e soggettivismo, contribuiscono a creare un'alternanza composita e vibrante [...]. Le composizioni polimateriche sono destinate a sostituire tutte le pitture murali future (La Mostra della Rivoluzione è stato un esempio tangibile della loro infinite possibilità)*, 'Dalla pittura murale alla composizioni polimateriche', Natura, (February 1936), 28–30.*

[130] Prima mostra nazionale di plastica murale per l'edilizia fascista, Genoa, Palazzo Ducale (November–December 1934), 10.

shift in aesthetics and politics and thematizing architecture and the visual arts as a totalizing political moment with social impact and to demote Sironi's murals. Rosso, Osvaldo Peruzzi, Pietro Gaudenzi, Prampolini and Depero created public artworks, which centred around social themes: 'the corporative state', 'case del fascio, della piccola italiana, and del balilla', 'Mussolini', 'the Fascist revolution', 'war as hygiene', 'civiltà del littorio' and even 'the conquest of space', 'colonie estive', 'gyms' and – momentously – 'motorways, stations and airports', all projects modern architecture had to turn to as a means of social development.

In this assorted variety of social projects for the well-being of Fascist citizens, stations and post offices stood out because of the alliance between Marinetti and architect Mazzoni and because they had been a central preoccupation for the regime since its early days in power. In an article published in *Augustea* in May 1934 and in view of such networks becoming more prominent after the 1933 mural turn, Prampolini advocated sustained involvement of the Syndicate in public competitions in order to guarantee transparency, fairness and meritocracy which, he implied, were no longer the main criteria regulating competitions. While he naively suggested the dismissal of art exhibitions, more productive was his recommendation for an active involvement of the Syndicate in selecting committees to guarantee better quality for art commissions in general.[131]

Manifestos were quick to be penned to seal off the debate and politicize even more futurist architecture. In the same year, Mazzoni and Somenzi's *Manifesto futurista dell'architettura* and Mazzoni, Marinetti and Somenzi's *Manifesto futurista dell'architettura aerea* appeared – and indeed neither could nor did say anything particularly new, other than highlighting the futurist city as the home of the collectivities hailed as one of the breakthroughs of futurist architecture as well as of the regime's anthropological revolution because of its use of new materials and innovative architectural strategies.[132]

From 1928 to 1932, the State spent 25 million lire on public works (streets, railways, new towns, public buildings, monuments, archaeological excavations), peaking at five million lire in 1931–2. This was more than had ever been invested before in developing public infrastructures.[133] From 30 April 1924 Galeazzo Ciano, Minister of Communications, started a programme of modernization of the postal and railway network services, which would continue to expand for twenty years with new buildings, in similar fashions to those the Germans had adopted to modernize their motorway system and the Soviet their underground.[134] Santa Maria Novella station in Florence was the culmination of Ciano's plans as well as the first public commission

[131] Enrico Prampolini, 'L'arte-vita. Per una riforma sindacale', *Augustea*, 9 (15 May 1934).

[132] See also, Angiolo Mazzoni, 'Ampliare la città', *Sant'Elia*, II/5, 1.

[133] Salvagnini, *Il sistema delle arti*, 361. For a breakdown of individual contributions to the enti autonomi, ibid., 362–3.

[134] Edith Neudecker, *Gli edifici postali in Italia durante il fascismo (1922-1944)* (Latina, Casa dell'architettura edizioni, 2007), 49–65 and Edoardo Altara, *Compendio storico-tecnico delle ferrovie italiane*, vol. I (Cortona, Galosci, 2012), 123–31, and 314–21.

secured by the rationalists, in 1934, with the usual polemic that ensued.[135] Santa Maria Novella encapsulated the three main principles that positioned architecture firmly within the system of the arts in question: it was a collective space for the ideal New Fascist and the Italian citizen; it was the result of a more comprehensive attempt at modernizing the public sphere; and it was grounded in the idea of the ethical mission of architecture – stylistically anti-decorative and anti-romantic. Yet, it was not monumental but experimental in conception; and thus it was not the only possible or even most long-lasting implementation of State art since it did not employ decoration to convey any ideological message to the crowds of passers-by.[136] Florence station marked the decline of modern and rational architecture that gave way to Piacentini's monumentalism and to Marinetti's Public visions.

Mussolini's other official architect was Angiolo Mazzoni at the Ministero delle corporazioni.[137] On 14 May 1934 Mazzoni joined the futurist ranks as announced in *Futurismo*, which from that moment onwards he will co-edit. The architect was instrumental in Marinetti's attempt at gaining hegemony for futurism over the Novecento movement, and in modernizing the professed 'Italian social sphere' by building stations and post offices across the country, from Agrigento to Bolzano, with the support of futurist mural art. Somenzi and Marinetti endorsed Mazzoni's project through *Sant'Elia* and liaised with the Duce for their formal approval. Such 'friendship' between Marinetti and the architect of the Ministry of Communications lasted until 1935. In his correspondence with Bruno Zevi, Mazzoni made a clear point: despite his squabbles with Marinetti, he approved of futurism as an aesthetic movement but disapproved of it when implicated with the political sphere, as was happening more

---

[135] Andrea Giuntini, 'Management e progetto nelle ferrovie italiane tra le due guerre', in Mauro Cozzi, Ezio Godoli and Paola Pettenella (eds), *Angiolo Mazzoni (1894-1979): architetto ingegnere del Ministero delle Comunicazioni* (Milan, Skira, 2003), 99–110 for the plans of development of the railway system. Florence train station marked the peak of the rationalist front's success. Angiolo Mazzoni was originally entrusted with the project. However, after a heated debate due to Mazzoni's project being considered ambiguous and not modern enough, a public competition was announced in 1932, which was won by the Gruppo Toscano's project. The polemics started with two letters from sculptor Romano Romanelli (who was not known for his modernist leanings), published in the newspaper *La Nazione* in 1932. In these, Romanelli questioned the validity of Mazzoni's project, arguing that the railway station of a city like Florence, rich in history and artworks, should not be monumental but on the contrary, functional and self-effacing, like a lift in a beautiful palace. The argument continued to rage and the debate over the station's construction received unprecedented public coverage, becoming the object of popular interest on a local and later a national level. On 12 March 1933 an exhibition was opened at the Palazzo Vecchio, in Florence, displaying the 102 projects submitted for the competition. In just one day, forty thousand people visited the exhibition. The leading supporters of the rationalist front participated in the debate, almost unanimously praising the Gruppo Toscano's project for its modernity and for applying the precepts of rationalist architecture. It was Mussolini himself, however, who gave the Gruppo Toscano's project his seal of approval, after seeing the models of the station.

[136] Claudia Conforti, Roberto Dulio and Marzia Marandola, "'La stazione di Firenze è bellissima'", in Claudia Conforti, Roberto Dulio, Marzia Marandola, Nadia Musumeci and Paola Ricco (eds), *La stazione di Firenze di Giovanni Michelucci e del Gruppo Toscano, 1932-1935* (Milan, Electa Architettura, 2016), 11–41 for a resumé of the whole project and its repercussions.

[137] Although his project for the station was rejected, Mazzoni designed the heating plant and main control cabin, recognized as a masterpiece of futurist architecture.

evidently in the mid-1930s.[138] Many of the post offices Mazzoni realized in collaboration with Roberto Narduzzi were monumental and abundantly decorated; two of the most illustrative examples of such artistic synergistic efforts were the Palazzo delle Poste in La Spezia and in Palermo, together with those of Trento and Bergamo.[139]

The Palazzo delle Poste in La Spezia was built in just three years between 1930 and 1933 (decreed by the Ministero delle comunicazioni, law n. 10100 bis, 8 August 1930), in the central part of the city – Piazza Verdi – that had once been occupied by the humble residential neighbourhood nicknamed the Torretto. Like the Palermo post office, it was meant to solve the problem of rapid urban development of the area which was included in the new urban plan for La Spezia, signed by the Gruppo urbanisti romani (Luigi Piccinato, Gino Cancellotti, Alfredo Scappelli, Eugenio Fuselli, Giuseppe Nicolosi), completed in 1923 and approved on 29 May 1938. The new plan for urban development gave more spaces to public buildings and offices and created connections between the modern and the nineteenth-century side of the city.

The post office fit its purpose. Mazzoni's building evoked the medieval period when the *comuni* (municipalities) ruled Italy, being a modern reinterpretation of the historical *broletto*, a political seat usually located in the main square of the city, as well as the hypermodernity of Gaudi's oneiric plasticity.[140] It was solid in appearance in its main body flanked by a lateral clock tower (a recurrent feature of Mazzoni's designs as, for example, in Sabaudia) but it was also patently modern, especially in comparison with the other building because of its play of full and empty volumes and its internal decorations.

Local discourse played a significant part in the whole project, boosted by the rapid economic growth of La Spezia. In terms of traditions and materials, the building supported the principle of autarchy, especially cherished by the Fascist regime after the Society of Nations' sanctions against the crimes committed by the Italian army in Ethiopia. The cladding used for the exteriors was made of stone from nearby Tuscany (stone of Monsummano) that with its pale yellow tones seemed to pay homage to the colourful vernacular architecture of Liguria. According to Richard Etlin, 'the architectural symbolism [in the post office design] evokes both traditions of the founding of Rome and of its imperial glory', both immediately visible on the façade of the building, indexed by a massive colonnade and a series of round arches that framed the entrances.[141] The interior was dominated by plain gigantic spaces, and the architect elected to create a contrast between bricks and local marble – for example, a black marble from La Spezia (*marmo nero di Portoro*), *cotto* and *travertino* – that was reminiscent of a profane 'church' open for its 'public' of clients. Mazzoni also used

---

[138] F. 'Mazzoni', letter to Zevi, Rome, 5 December 1966, MART.

[139] Mazzoni wrote to Zevi that his most innovative works were the post office of Agrigento, the Siena train station and the project for Florence (F. 'Mazzoni', 1688.902, 'Lettera Riservata e Personale all'arch. Bruno Zevi', Rome, MART).

[140] F. 'Mazzoni', 1688.902, 'Lettera Riservata e Personale all'arch. Bruno Zevi', Rome, MART.

[141] Richard Etlin, *Modernism in Italian Architecture, 1890–1940* (Cambridge, MA, MIT Press, 1991), 89. The Palazzo delle Poste was slightly modified during the Second World War (a lateral water tank was substituted by a passage leading towards an air raid shelter). Both the building and the mosaic were recently restored (2009) and the post office is still in use.

modern materials, such as aluminium, *ceramiche greificate* (greyified ceramic) and *intonaco Terranova* (Terranova plaster).

Once the building was close to completion, Mazzoni commissioned Fillìa and Prampolini to design the interior of the clock tower, two walls each: using brightly coloured ceramics from Liguria, they created a huge mosaic, possibly sketched by Mazzoni himself, on the theme of communications, a work entitled *Le comunicazioni terrestri e marittime*.

This continuous composition depicts five main episodes in a reprise of the chronicle of mural painting. Fillìa designed the routes of terrestrial and maritime communications, Prampolini the telegraphic, telephonic and aerial. Their design was a counterstrike to rationalist architecture's disparagement of the decoration of buildings and it aimed at expanding the perceptive boundaries of viewers to empower and irrationally attract them. This totalizing and augmented elegy to the communication system could be read as a futuristic reinterpretation of Trajan's Column in Rome: a geometric narrative of movement and velocity and a symbolic ascension to the sky, with simultaneous aerial views – an example of the theory of simultaneity of sensations and spaces Marinetti had developed for the theatre.[142] The vibrant colours of the composition, rendered within a stylized context filled by lines and geometry, resulted in images dominated by a series of representative elements, occasionally tending to the geometric abstraction that Fillìa and Prampolini had elaborated elsewhere at that time (in, for example, the *Spiritualità aerea* series and Fillìa's *Plastica* and *Paesaggio aereo*). *Le comunicazioni* spoke both to State art as art that needs to bring people together under the praxis of the totalitarian State, and to the aesthetic desire for innovation and a non-figurative language.[143]

As discussed at length in his public contributions, Fillìa's *Le comunicazioni terrestri e marittime* continued the futurist exploration of patterns of compositional syncretism, while Prampolini's *Le comunicazioni telegrafiche, telefoniche e aeree* tested the limits of how divergent aesthetic perceptions, when fused together, could activate an aerial perspective on muralism and mosaic, which 'aims at erasing details without compromising the clarity and recognizability of figurations and that uses close-ups the to give communicative strength to the images' (a perspective achieved also through the use of vertical windows).[144] This combination of architecture with decorative mosaic, already popular for centuries, was repeated in at least one other comparable example: the

---

[142] In 1931 at the Manzoni theatre in Milan, Marinetti premiered *Simultanina. Divertimento futurista in 16 sintesi.*

[143] Gabriella Chioma, 'La sfida di Marinetti a tutti i poeti d'Italia e "L'Aeropoema parolibero del golfo della Spezia": Precedenti e cronaca analitica', in AA.VV., *Futurismi, Aeropittura. Aeropoesia, Architettura nel golfo della Spezia* (La Spezia, Cassa di risparmio della Spezia, 2007), 174–5.

[144] Fillìa, '*punta ad azzerare i dettagli senza compromettere la riconoscibilità nelle figurazioni e usa i primi piani per dare forza comunicativa alle immagini*', 'Il rapporto pittura architettura', *Il Lavoro Fascista*, (8 February 1933), republished in *La Terra dei vivi*, 1 (25 June 1933). Marzia Ratti, 'Cromatismo architettonico e plastiche murali. Fillìa e Prampolini artisti per Angiolo Mazzoni', in *Futurismi*, 107; and Crispolti, *Fillìa. Fra immaginario meccanico e primordio cosmico* (Milan, Mazzotta, 1988), 58–9.

Palazzo delle Poste in Alessandria, a building with a mosaic façade decorated by the futurist artist Severini (1939–41).[145]

The problem of the 'line' as the path to a new anti-figurative and anti-representational language was indeed much more central to the debate on monumentalism that it might have first appeared and brought back architecture onto the stage as Public art. In a 1931 article published in *Casabella*, entitled 'Del "monumentale" nell'architettura moderna', Pagano cited a piece written by Piacentini for *Dedalo*, 'Dove è irragionevole l'architettura razionale', in which the architect traced a connection between the horizontal line and the vertical line.[146] According to Piacentini, rationalist architecture used horizontal lines for building houses, but monumental architecture was about ascension, and therefore needed a vertical measure of space. Pagano was sceptical about the validity of this argument: Stuttgart rail station, Düsseldorf's Planetarium, the skyscrapers by Antonio Sant'Elia were all, to his mind, examples of vertical monumentalism. At stake in this indirect dialogue between Pagano and Piacentini was the very definition of monumentality. If we were to accept a standard definition of monumentality, argued Pagano, such scale could only be achieved when the relationship between mass and volume was of grandiose proportions, when the human scale was taken as a unit for measuring the building itself, and when the rhythm of construction was simple and plain. But there was more to this, he continued, in relation to how we look at modern architecture, which was neither about pragmatism nor the mysticism of classical monumentality; it was about morality and building spaces to improve the living conditions of the citizen, and therefore, he concluded:

> The rhythm can be viewed as a logical consequence of series work, the grandiose *dimension* can be viewed as an economic consequence, the new scale of highly contrasting associations between large amalgams and small silhouette could be a consequence of utilitarian thinking, but one should not forget [...] that is art and *style*.[147]

Monumentality was not to be denied, wrote Pagano, provided it was put at the service of the collective to improve living conditions, and not at the service of any ideological and political apparatus, such as a totalitarian State. Pagano and Piacentini were both committed supporters of the regime back in 1931, but their points of

---

[145] In his 1950s personal correspondence from Bogotá with architecture historian Bruno Zevi, Mazzoni always maintained that as an architect he prioritized art over politics (F. 'Mazzoni', 1688.902, 'Lettera Riservata e Personale all'arch. Bruno Zevi', Rome, MART). Etlin, 'Italian Rationalism', *Progressive Architecture*, (July 1983), 86–94 and Mauro Cozzi, Ezio Godoli, and Paola Pettenella (eds), *Angiolo Mazzoni*, on Mazzoni's complete words. For other examples of post offices built in Italy during the Ventennio, see Neudecker, *Edifici postali*, 204–5.

[146] XI/3 (January 1931), 527–40.

[147] '*Il ritmo potrà essere una conseguenza logica del lavoro in serie, la dimensione grandiosa potrà anche essere un conseguenza economica, la nuova scala di rapporti fortemente contrastanti tra grandi masse e piccole sagome potrà essere anche conseguenza di un ragionamento utilitario, ma non bisogna dimenticare [...] che è arte e stile*', Pagano, 'Del "monumentale" nell'architettura moderna', *La casa bella*, IV/40 (April 1931), 14.

view were diametrically opposed: one called for a rationalized, mechanical view of architecture as a way of shaping a better living space and social sphere; the other evoked an imprecisely defined 'Italian spirit', foundational to the act of building.

Commissioned by the Ministero delle comunicazioni, Mazzoni designed the Palazzo delle poste in Palermo between 1928 and 1934. It was inaugurated on 28 October 1934, on the occasion of the twelfth anniversary of the March on Rome. A monumental reinterpretation of an ancient temple, it was built on a huge parcel of land (in excess of 5,000 square metres), with a façade marked by ten 30-metre-high columns and flanked by a massive sculpture, representing a fascio littorio (by the artist Domenico Ponzi and destroyed after the First World War), over a C-shaped *pianta* developed around three courtyards. Yet the scheme was still reminiscent of the traditional post office, as well as of the German embassy in Saint Petersburg by Peter Behrens in 1911–13. In this Palazzo, Mazzoni brought together polymateric architecture, Greek linearity, Roman monumentality and Renaissance harmony, whilst avoiding any concession to the local styles of the day (italo-greco, arabo siculo, arabo normanno and neobarocco).

Another huge parallelepiped structure was inserted almost forcibly in the area, it was made from reinforced concrete clad in a layer of local grey marble, *tortora maculato*, quarried from nearby Mount Billiemi. The building was triumphal in its majesty and had the support of the middle and upper classes close to the regime. It was visually and publicly imposing on the district, which had been in sore need of redevelopment after the aristocracy had moved out of the city centre; and thus once again fitted squarely with the regime's plans for regeneration of the urban fabric of Italian cities. It was accessible to all as required: a point of service delivery, it communicated a political message to everyone it served, but it was also entirely detached from its urban context because of its size. If the exterior of the building hinted at a return to orders of proportion and scale, the interiors were full of interesting chromatographies thanks to the varieties of materials used. The great hall for the public was embellished by a *volta a crociera* (cross-vault) and monumental *finestre termali* (thermal windows) which echoed, as Mazzoni himself admitted, those in Stuttgart station by Paul Bonatz and Friedrich Eugen Scholer (1911–28) and by Karl Moser and Robert Curjel in Basel (1913).[148] The interior spaces – both public and private – were enriched by precious marbles (varieties included *nero del Belgio, maculato di cipollino d'Elba, rosso fiorito, libeccio* and *marmo rosso di Trapani*) used, for example, in the elliptical stairway (typical of Mazzoni as for example the one in the post office in Pula) of red and black marble, as well as in modern details designed by the architect himself.[149] In the Sala del consiglio (the boardroom) were works by futurist artists such as Tato and Benedetta Cappa with their *Plastica futurista, Sintesi*

[148] Neudecker, *Edifici postali*, 69.

[149] Lima drew a parallel between Mazzoni's use of marbles and that of Mies for the Barcellona Pavilion, 'Il palazzo delle Poste di Palermo', in Mauro Cozzoli, Ezio Godoli and Paola Pettenella (eds), *Angiolo Mazzoni*, 252.

delle comunicazioni aeree, ferroviarie e marittime applied to the wall in homage to mechanical civilization.[150]

The climax of this ideological and totalitarian discourse was almost hidden in a detail on the upper part of the façade: Napoleone Martinuzzi's bas-reliefs denoting two winged figures, one on either side of the *Poste e Telegrafi* inscription. They can be read as simple messengers, embodying a national and nationalistic 'communication system' established in 1862, immediately after the unification of Italy in 1861; while, at the same time, recalling the iconography of the 'winged Victory', one of the most recurrent characters of this period (see Martini's *Vittoria* within the Palazzo delle Poste in Naples). Mazzoni's design used a polymaterial approach for the structure. The internal spaces were, in turn, strongly symbolic and hierarchically appointed: both the public and private rooms were respectably elegant, with a prevailing linearity and extensive marble decoration; yet they could reach an authentic refinement only within the 'elite' environments. Mazzoni himself designed all the interiors; his influences included both the Dutch De Stijl movement and Piet Mondrian for colour combinations: melting and demarcating shadows of blue, red, yellow, black and golden chestnut, beige and white, marked the rhythm and scale of the spaces.

The heart of the building was the boardroom, beaming with the vivid colours of futurist artworks (paintings by Benedetta Cappa, Tato and Piero Bevilacqua; curtains designed by Bruna Somenzi; a sculpture by Corrado Vigni) and of the precious furniture. At the centre of the room, towering over the space, an oblong table was reminiscent of a marble aeroplane (and therefore the futurist aeropainting); further, 'architectural bands and frames highlight the geometrical relationships and the dimensions of the walls and for this reason are essential to the compositional process', as Lima has written.[151] Tato's grand painting codified themes of fascist youth and work; Benedetta Cappa's five mural frescoes were dedicated to *Le vie delle comunicazioni marittime, terrestri, aeree, telegrafiche and telefoniche*; and Bevilaqua's painting, to television. Cappa resorted to a non-figurative language to express the power of communication, the frescoes were in her typically evocative style – blending movement with a perceptive depth given by the palette of blues; the result were mystical journeys that united viewers along visual and emotional dimensions, not simply 'propagandistic' moments of efficiency and modernization. Cappa's work visualized the regime's power not in terms of affirmation and forceful movement, or else in the style of Boccioni's *linee-forza*; rather in terms of mystical unity and an almost religious faith, one that exuded hegemony rather than imposing it, and distinctively in line with 1930s expressions of futurist Public art devised to sacralize the regime.

Theatre of Objects II: E42

The last major collaborative architectural project the regime embarked on was the self-styled E42, the *Esposizione del 1941–1942*, that celebrated twenty years of fascist rule

---

[150] Damaged by a fire in 1988, the Palazzo delle Poste was subsequently restored and still serves its original public function. Since 2017 it has also become a destination for visitors interested in its historical, architectural and artistic values.

[151] Lima, 'Il palazzo delle Poste di Palermo', 253.

in Italy and was designed to be reassigned as a set of public buildings in order to help recover the costs of such investment in the long term.[152] All the leading architects of the day were invited to submit designs for another total work of art which hoped to revive the spirit of the early days. After the Città universitaria, Piacentini was again in charge with the support of other notable architects and urbanists Luigi Piccinato, Ettore Rossi and Luigi Vietti, in his capacity of Soprintendente ai servizi per l'architettura, whilst Pagano was increasingly sceptical about classical monumentalism as practiced up to then. The E42 was to be the triumph of classicism with Marcello Piacentini against Giuseppe Pagano and Giuseppe Terragni's clear ostracism to the project.[153] Other established and emerging architects were involved in the E42, including Pietro Lingeri, Terragni and Cesare Cattaneo (second stage, Palazzo dei congressi, 1938–9); Mario Ridolfi and Wolfgang Frankl (Palazzo della civiltà italiana, 1937); Adalberto Libera (Palazzo dei ricevimenti e dei congressi, 1937–43); Giovanni Guerrini, Ernesto La Padula and Mario Romano (Palazzo della civiltà italiana, 1938–54, finished after the Second World War); Giovanni Muzio, Mario Paniconi and Giulio Pediconi (model for the imperial door of the palazzi dell'INA e dell'INPS, 1939–40, completed after the Second World War); and the BBPR's eccentric, highly modern and rationalist post office.[154]

In addition to the many buildings, Oppo, who had served on the committee too, selected Prampolini and Depero to realize two public murals. Prampolini completed *Le Corporazioni* in 1941, a large mural situated on the external wall of the Museo nazionale delle arti e tradizioni popolari, that depicted the *civiltà dei produttori*: a classless society representing a *terza via* between liberalism and Communism. The mosaic was materially realized by the Cooperativa mosaicisti di Roma, following Prampolini's detailed instructions about sizes (between 10 × 10 and 20 × 30 metres) and materials of the tiles which were made of marble, stones, glass paste and enamels.

In a clear Prampolini style which continued from the murals in the La Spezia post office, the work was a clear homage to one of the most important economic and cultural projects of the regime, namely, the twenty-two *corporazioni* united in the Consiglio nazionale delle corporazioni, presided over variously by Mussolini or the Minister of Corporations, and finalized on 20 March 1930.[155] Corporativism had been a highly controversial, much-debated topic in many circles since the mid-1920s and had found an ideal realization for the arts in the projects for the corporativist city. In its idea of 'the corporation', the commercial field was little different from the political field: just like the arts, business had to work with politics to create a new order and a new civilization, as per Bottai's formulation, whereby 'corporativism assumed [...] the function of governmental instrument to regulate social disputes as well as the dialectics between social foci and State interests'.[156] The Camera dei fasci e delle

[152] Salvagnini, *Il sistema delle arti*, 30 and passim on the relationship between architecture and mural painting.
[153] Paolo Nicoloso, *Mussolini architetto: propaganda e paesaggio urbano nell'Italia fascista* (Turin, Einaudi, 2008), 198–214.
[154] Giorgio Ciucci, *Gli architetti e il fascismo: architettura e città 1922–1944* (Turin, Einaudi, 2002), 33
[155] D.L. 2 July 1926; D.L. 21 April 1927, n. 718; and 14 July 1927, n. 1347, were the official decrees which formalized the corporations.
[156] Gagliardi, *Il corporativismo fascista*, 13–25, 15.

corporazioni in 1939 had replaced the Camera dei deputati: a project which Bottai saw as a way forward after the inevitable fall of Mussolini. By 1940, however, the *mito corporativo* had significantly declined; deemed as a part of the State machine, but not its main part. The corporations in this particular artwork included representatives of commerce, credit, agriculture and industry: pillars of the new economic order that Fascism had created and which were either depicted as automata and machines or were reduced to vanishing geometrical symbols.[157] Indeed, Ugo Spirito's first wave of corporativism had emphasized the contradiction between agriculture and industry as crucial to the Italian case to favour a more organicist view of corporativism over the rationalized and structured one preferred by the regime in the second half of the 1920s and onwards.[158] Prampolini's mosaic was an important visual manifesto, a Benjaminesque *Angelus Novus*: a late example of how fascist-sponsored art could still be monumental propaganda and symbolic innovation at the same time, especially when reaching backwards at the origin of corporativism and looking to the end which was perceived to be near, and thus Mussolini's preference for classicism and pure monumentalism was becoming ineffective.

Depero's *Le professioni e le arti* saw the light a year later and was installed opposite to Prampolini's mosaic on the external wall of the Museo della scienza, now the Museo nazionale preistorico etnografico 'Luigi Pigorini'. The mosaic depicted the professions and the arts under the regime. Typical of Depero's style, the composition was punctuated by emblems and figures recalling a pastoral tradition and representing justice, music (the lower part) and theatre (the upper part), next to a fascio littorio. Each part of the rigidly arranged quadripartite composition was framed within an abstract architectural cornice: the pentagram for music or the fascio littorio. Depero did not adopt any original perspective, and borrowed from the classical mosaic tradition, including Ravenna's fifth and sixth century Sant' Apollinare nuovo and San Vitale, to shape motionless figures and a static choreography of icon-like personifications against a neutral background. Both Oppo and the architect in charge of the project corresponded with Depero to ask him to tone down the rigid symmetries of his composition to blend it better with the fluidity of lines in Prampolini's. But with little luck because the final result remained quite didactic. The symbols on the background evoke the guilds while the two main symbols in the front are rather unambiguous: Fascism is rendered by an imperial eagle, and justice by a woman with a sword and scale in a very straightforward rendering of fascist ideology. The relationship between the religious tradition of the mosaics and the sphere of politics is here somewhat obvious: fixed, easy to interpret and unequivocal. The iconographic language of this mosaic delivered a well-defined message though highly compartmentalized and visually soft signs, which aspire to elicit from the viewer a response of trust in the future, of reassurance in the civic religion the regime embodies and which have most certainly abandoned the aesthetic of shock and of totalizing experience the Mostra della rivoluzione had pioneered. In a nutshell, this Public artwork is a telling example

---

[157] In 1992 the mosaic was restored thanks to a contribution of the Banca di Roma.
[158] Santomassimo, *La terza via fascista*, 119.

of how politics were sacralized by the arts (be it music, poetry and theatre included), which in turn on the one hand borrowed from the classical tradition and, on the other, from pre-eminent futurism in its more popular and codified embodiments.

Hypothesis II: The Reality of the New Man/Woman

In January 1940, Bottai established the Ufficio per l'arte contemporanea, following the rivalry between the Ministero per l'educazione artistica and the Ministero per la cultura popolare, with the aim of rejecting classicism and the *stile littorio* by corroding the barrier between modern and classical art.[159] By the early 1940s, the arts had to coincide with contemporary arts and not with classicism.[160] As noted by Vito Zagarrio, Bottai should not be viewed as an 'enlightened administrator and "dissident" intellectual', invested in reconciliation of arts and politics; we should recognize that the 'positivity of Bottai's revisionism consisted in its openings towards "alternative" spaces rather than in any direct intervention to question the regime'.[161] Such alternative spaces were, for Bottai, youth culture and a return to realism, as he imagined with the Premio Bergamo, in its opposition to Roberto Farinacci's Premio Cremona.[162]

Persico had anticipated this direction in his conference entitled 'Mistica dell'Europa', held in Milan on 5 June 1934. In his intervention, Persico evaluated the importance of youth culture within the system of the arts. In essence, he concluded that youth culture played a cardinal role in the system of the arts because it introduced an element of novelty, an important aspect of the modernization of the aesthetic field, and thus acted as a driving force in keeping freshly alive the theoretical conceptualization of the New Man/Woman. In Mario Sechi's words:

> The political and institutional framework firmly embedded in the Fascist revolution, which was deemed able to express the realist (hence anti-ideological) disposition foundational to all forms of modern social State, was of no interest to these young intellectuals (as it will be for those gathering around the *Orto* in Bologna and *Orpheus* in Milan).[163]

Youth culture, then, was particularly active through journals such as *Orpheus* in Milan and *Il Saggiatore* in Rome, which had a strong philosophical strand, and the *Littoriali della cultura*, which promoted competition amongst the most promising young Italians. At the opening of the III Congresso Nazionale Istituti Fascisti di

---

[159] Lazzari, 'I due regni dell'arte', in *L'azione per l'arte*, 3–31. On the Ufficio dell'arte contemporanea modes of support for private galleries, see Pia Vivarelli, 'La politica delle arti figurative negli anni del Premio Bergamo', in AA.VV., *Gli anni del premio Bergamo. Arte in Italia intorno agli anni Trenta* (Milan, Electa, 1993), 33.

[160] On Bottai and modern architecture, see Nicoloso, *Mussolini architetto*, 214.

[161] Zagarrio, *Primato*, 162

[162] Law of the 2% (1941), see Masi, *Un arte per lo Stato*, 261–4 for the debate. In essence, 2 per cent of the total amount of funding awarded to public works had to be used to decorate such buildings.

[163] Sechi, *Il mito della nuova cultura*, 67.

Cultura on 24 April 1933, the podestà of Milan Visconti di Modrone stated that a solid culture amongst the young fringes of the regime was going to be the direction of travel from that moment onwards with the aim at foregrounding not only the economic and political revolutions but also the cultural one.[164] Primarily through such channels, youth culture encouraged both a new idea of realism and a vision of art as a social phenomenon, thereby marking the transition to post Second World War. More specifically, originating from the fringes of the regime's youth culture and following the philosophical thinking of Antonio Banfi, a Professor of philosophy at the Università Statale in Milan, the young intelligentsia rejected the individualism of Benedetto Croce's idealist aesthetics in favour of a socially aware aesthetics and an understanding of the arts as interdisciplinary endeavour.[165] A raising young intellectual star, Luciano Anceschi, clearly expressed the need for his generation to historicize, to make real and to question, what was taken as absolute. He wrote:

> The littoriali of culture are part of the new culture when free from rhetorical ornament. For the new youth culture, Fascism is not a static thing, rather something real, in constant evolution towards a new culture which will affirm itself more and more as revolutionary, in the only possible time, in the social time.[166]

Favouring corporativism as a new moral compass governing a moribund capitalist system, Anceschi and many of his contemporaries (futurists included) saw Fascism as a revolution which could address that social problem that had been created by the individualism of previous liberal governments and the arts as moving in the direction of 'collectivity, historical realism, new objectivity and functionality'.[167] In this wake, in 1934, Anceschi published a novel entitled *Romanzo elettrico o romanzo collettivista* in the *Ambrosiano* and described it as a representation of a new attitude towards reality and life according to a fresh set of morals.[168]

The cultural *rappel à l'ordre* of the dictatorship transformed itself into a return to the logical acceptance of art as an autonomous form of collective expression, albeit one closely embedded in the social reality of its production and circulation.[169] By drawing such an unbreakable connection between text and context, youth culture moved away from Croce's aesthetic reflection and decadentism's lack of moral standing and historical awareness and closer instead to European experiments such as the German new objectivity, transatlantic modernism or rational and functionalist architecture we had seen dominating the 1920s literary and artistic circles.

---

[164] F. 'Rivolta', f. '50–III Congresso Nazionale Istituti Fascisti di Cultura (24 April 1933)', Milan, AGR.

[165] Alessandro Del Puppo, *Egemonia e consenso: Ideologie visive nell'arte italiana del Novecento* (Macerat, Quodlibet, 2019), 65.

[166] F. 'Anceschi', f. 'Nettuno', 1934, Archiginnasio, Bologna.

[167] Ibid.

[168] Ibid.

[169] For a critique of *Il Saggiatore* as too conservative in outlook, see Antonio Gramsci, *Pensare la democrazia* (Einaudi, Turin, 1997), 30–1.

Alongside the rejection of Croce's philosophy and aesthetics, youth culture was also responsible for a change in direction from rationalism.[170] In a 1936 enquiry in *Domus* entitled 'Dove va l'arte italiana?', there were signs of a cultural impetus towards an almost heroic and romantic historicism. Lamberto Vitali posed five questions in the article: one about the relationship with classical art, one about the Novecento movement, one about the major aesthetic trends of the day, one about pure art and the validity of frescoes, and the last about how to react to a 'return to order'.[171] Young artists Fausto Pirandello, Renato Birolli, Luigi Veronesi, Italo Cremona, Gianfilippo Usellini and Aligi Sassu all replied. Of course their responses varied in tone, but if Novecentism was a thing of the past, if classical art was not problematic, if pure art was to be dismissed as drastically as mural painting, plain returns to order were also radically dismissed on the grounds of individual moral imperatives over political ones. Of most interest, perhaps, were the responses regarding current artistic trends: romanticism for Birolli and romanticism and impressionism for Sassu in the modern anguished sense of the word which placed the individual in dialogue with a hostile real, abstracticism for Veronesi, surrealism for Cremona and no specific answers for the others. For all concerned, however, it was the relationship of the self with objectivity that determined their preferences and inclinations as, for instance, one can see in the expressionist use of colours that defined a more tormented relationship between Man and nature as for example in Sassu's *Fucilazione nelle asturie* (1936). The painting represented the killing of Garcia Lorca by the Spanish Falangist movement.[172] It was a forerunner of a left-wing (red) expressionism which described the explicit political critique moved to the regime by a generation of intellectuals that had just started to question the regime after the Spanish civil war (1936–9), as discussed in Corrente openly.

One of the key journals supporting such an 'realist' aesthetic paradigm was precisely *Vita giovanile*, later renamed *Corrente di vita giovanile*, founded by Ernesto Treccani in 1938, and suppressed by the regime in 1940.[173] Corrente looked back to the expressionist trend in Italian culture (for example the Scuola romana) and the debate on realism that had taken place towards the end of the 1920s (for example with the new novel). The first public exhibition of the Corrente group occurred three years later, in March 1939, at Milan's Permanente; the second, at the end of the same year at the newly founded Galleria Grande, also in Milan. At the Permanente, alongside the Novecento group – Carrà, Tosi, De Grada, Marussig, Bernasconi – were invited Birolli, Valenti, Badodi, Cassinari, Migneco and Cherchi. Guttuso participated in the second

---

[170] Gabriele Scaramuzza, 'Antonio Banfi tra "arte vivente" e "crisi dell'arte"', in Sileno Salvagnini (ed.), *Banfi e l'arte contemporanea* (Naples, Liguori, 2012), 66–8 on how the Milanese philosopher theorized autonomy and heteronomy and passed his aesthetic reflection to his students (Luciano Anceschi amongst them) at the Università Statale in Milan, thereby shaping a future generation of Italian thinkers and scholars.

[171] *Domus*, VI/108 (December 1936), 54–5.

[172] Sassu, 'Il colore è poesia', *Prospettive*, VI/25–26 (15 January–15 March 1942), in Elena Pontiggia (ed.), *Il movimento di* Corrente (Milan, Abscondita, 2012), 31–2.

[173] The most recent, exhaustive contribution positioning the movement in the contest of the system of the arts is Katia Colombo, *Il 'foglio in rossetto e bistro'. 'Corrente' tra fascismo e antifascismo* (Udine, Mimesis, 2020).

exhibition, together with a larger group of artists including Mafai and Pirandello. This exhibition also saw the debut of new artists such as Broggini, Santomaso and Piero Prampolini: it was a preparation for the 'fucilazione' of the regime.

The *Corrente* group was one of the first coherent attempts at surpassing fascist State art nationally. We can observe how this began to be explored and theorized through, for example, Birolli's amorphism as a rejection of rationalism and geometry, or Sassu's chromatism and Guttuso's plasticity. These artists understood the relationship between subjectivity and objectivity in a more militant, even sociological way, and a related sense of anguish and restlessness is conveyed through the use of colour.[174] *Corrente* was driven by a moral over a stylistic imperative: the arts had to have a social impact, similar to what Bottai had proposed in his own understanding of the arts as social intervention. Birolli's choices, as he also stated in his replies to the *Domus* survey, privileged a dialogue with European modern contemporary culture over the Italian classical tradition or the classics in general; he was not alone in adopting such a position. If the Corrente's aesthetic paradigm was shaped around ideas of construction and realism accomplished with an expressionist use of colour, then the foundational models had to be Weimer, or Vincent Van Gogh, or James Ensor and not Marinetti and futurism (barely discussed in one or two contributions), because they were far too compromised with the regime. Abstract artists were sources of inspirations for their free artistic language and structural use of chromatisms. And for them Bottai was deemed as a strategic possibility to overcome Mussolinism and change the nature of Fascism itself.[175]

The natural progression of *Corrente* was the Premio Bergamo (1939–43) which, established by the Fascist Provincial Union of Professionals and Artists of Bergamo, Bottai sponsored and promoted in an attempt, on the one hand, to modernize the arts, and on the other, to defeat the powerful Ras of Cremona, Roberto Farinacci. The most notorious case in the competition was the blasphemous *Crocifissione* by Guttuso, which was awarded second prize in 1942 but winners included noted artists such as Filippo De Pisis, Pio Semeghini and Mario Mafai. How Guttuso used expressionism to manifest a universal sense of anguish is well known: but his choice should be evaluated against youth culture's call for and response to the need for radical political change, which was reverberating across European art after the end of the Spanish civil war. If much has been said about the Premio Bergamo (1939–42) and Guttuso, there has been less interest in the Premio Cremona (1939–41), the brainchild of Farinacci, who was always close to Nazi Germany as far as politics on the arts were concerned and was modelled upon the nineteenth-century anonymous themed competitions. The Premio Cremona exemplified totalitarianism insofar as it encouraged representations of populism, realism, fascist life and anti-intellectualism as key themes of its competitions. The vast majority of artists participating in the competition were local and amateur ones with the exception of Anselmo Bucci, Felice

---

[174] On racists attacks against metaphysical artists from *Il Tevere* and *Quadrivio*, see Vivarelli, 'La politica delle arti figurative negli anni del Premio Bergamo', 29.

[175] Ernesto Treccani, 'Bottai o delle competenze', *Corrente di vita giovanile*, III/8 (30 April 1940).

Carena, Ardengo Soffici and Arturo Tosi summoned to act as judges. Gaudenzi's *Il grano*, a mural triptych produced in 1940, won first prize in the second of that year's Premio Cremona competitions.[176] The large mural resorted to a very basic iconography: of the three parts, the central one featured a man drying his sweat, and the two lateral ones depicted women returning home from the fields. As a sterile response to autarchy, Mussolini had revamped the failing *battaglia del grano* he had launched in 1925 as a consequence of a failed harvester, and *Il grano* was a public representation of such battle.

There was nothing particularly innovative about this mural, apart from an implicit indication of the imminent fall of the regime. The language of Public art had by this point been reduced to its basic propagandistic aims. Gaudenzi took first prize simply because he followed the guidelines. *Il grano* was a pedestrian rendering of nineteenth-century realism, with a nod to Giotto and the Macchiaioli deployed solely for propagandistic use. It was no longer Sironi's take on lavoro as dignity, but a simplistic view of it as obedience. Everyone had to endure sacrifice to make Italy great, as soldier and as religious believer, as indicated in the choice of a church style triptych.[177] By 1940, the sacralization of politics through Public art had lost its polysemic meaning and its ability to use multiple codes to enter into dialogue with different audiences. It was no longer a total work of art, rather a totalitarian rendering of a univocal understanding of reality.

---

[176] Wall paint on plaster applied to masonite, 249 × 434 cm, Museo civico 'Ala Ponzone', Cremona.

[177] Giuseppe Azzoni (ed.), *Fascismo a Cremona e nella sua provincia: 1922–1945* (Cremona A.N.P.I., 2013), and Michele Bernardi, Alessia Cadetti et al. (eds), '*Il grano* di Pietro Gaudenzi. Stato di conservazione e problematiche di intervento', *IV Congresso Nazionale IGIIC – Lo Stato dell'Arte* (L'Aquila, Accademia Di Belle Arti di L'Aquila, 2016) and Rodolfo Bona, *Il Premio Cremona (1939–1941) Opere e protagonisti* (Piacenza, Edizioni Scritture, 2016).

Agon 3: Architecture and the Arts in the Public Domain

Synthesis: *Arte di Stato* and the Art of Building

Architecture was the highest of arts because it had the power of transforming individuals into collectivities through an aesthetic experiment in language and in space, 'resolving their structure into a number of component parts', wrote Walter Gropius.[1] Such a fusion of subjective and objective within the public sphere is a notion well encapsulated by Le Corbusier too, when he acknowledged that '[a] mass is enveloped in its surface, a surface which is divided up according to the directing and generating lines of the mass; and this gives the mass its individuality'.[2]

In a similar vein to that of the novel and the visual arts, the architectural project could be condensed into: rational construction expressed in a new language. The common basis of the three disciplines consistently was their constructive effort, founded on the rationalization of forms (a 'return to the simplicity and essentiality of expressive means'), an adherence to the real, the use of anti-subjective, anti-romantic aesthetic codes, new materials and new linguistic and chromatic compositions. New architecture was chiefly synonymous with a new compositional syntax, as architect Giuseppe Terragni wrote to architect Gino Pollini:

Architecture: mass ± colour

or

Rhythm of colours = Rhythm of volumes

or

Rationalism or Functionalism?

---

[1] Walter Gropius, *The New Architecture and the Bauhaus* (London, Faber & Faber, 1968), 20 and 39.
[2] Le Corbusier, *Towards a New Architecture* (Hawthorne, CA, BN publishing, 2013), 35.

[...]
What do you think?[3]

Three concepts are central to our argument: construction, rhythm and rationality, a combination of which constituted a new aesthetic language for architecture and one that would visualize the political unity of Italy. Mussolini the architect's grand projects were of different sizes and of a multifaceted nature but they all revolved around the ideas of renovating the urban landscape by remodelling the past and of visualizing the supremacy of the Italian nation according to a modern architectural language; of sacralizing the political sphere by building its public presence; and of creating new shared and individual spaces in response to the need of the fascist citizens.[4] Owing primarily to its public presence and its potential to build 'a national identity', architecture was considered the art that was most likely to embody the political and aesthetic ethos of the State, and thus bring forth the total work of art and construct new spaces for the individual and for the collectivities expressed by the anthropological revolution. In his *Mussolini architetto*, Paolo Nicoloso advanced the hypothesis that architecture became an indispensable tool for the totalitarian turn of the regime; since '[i]n the first half of the Twentieth-century no State has invested politically in public architecture as much as Fascist Italy'.[5]

Our analysis of the architectural landscape of 1920s and 1930s Italy focuses on two main conceptual and empirical spaces: the spatial construction of the New Man/Woman's urban reality and the processes of compositional rationalization, which helped to configure the collective spectacle orchestrated by the regime aesthetically. First, we analyse the main architectural debates (rationalist, Gruppo 7, futurists chiefly) which have speculated on how an aesthetic transformation could impact on the political discourse, and secondly we discuss different typologies of houses and urban plans, which have implemented the newly theorized relationship between aesthetics and politics. By renewing and simplifying the aesthetic rules of construction, architecture would be able to work towards visualizing a new social understanding of the living space of the individual and of the social space of the collective. Therefore, what was the political function of architecture both as a private and public practice and how did such a function translate into aesthetic experiments which combine State art and the art of building? How did architecture fuse its theory with empirical, lived reality to build spaces for the individual made collective?

---

[3] Architettura: massa +colore
    oppure
    Ritmo dei colori = Ritmo dei volumi
    oppure
    Razionalismo o Funzionalismo?
    [...] Cosa ne dici?
    F. 'Figini-Pollini', Letter from Terragni to Pollini, no date, Fig.-Pol. 5.1.03, MART.
[4] Nicoloso, *Mussolini architetto*, XIII, XIV.
[5] For a detailed account of Mussolini's relationship with architecture as a site to build a national identity, see Emilio Gentile, *Fascismo di pietra* (Rome-Bari, Laterza, 2007) and Nicoloso, *Mussolini architetto*.

Fusions I: Architectural Functions, 1923–36

Mussolini's interest in architecture started at the beginning of his rule over Italy. Between 1922 and 1923, Margherita Sarfatti initiated the Duce into the cult of *romanità* and introduced architect Armando Brasini to him, a man who was an instrumental figure in building various commemorative monuments and triumphal arches, such as the Monument to Vittorio Emanuele and the crypt to the Unknown Solider of the Great War that stands adjacent to the 'said' monument.[6] On 21 April 1924, Mussolini received the 'Roman citizenship' and started a campaign of regeneration of the city to make it a modern and colossal metropolis, the notorious 'third Rome'; the projects and revisions of Rome's urban planning dragged on until 1931 but the real work only began in the early 1940s with the E42 project.[7] Monumentalism and collectivism were predictably part of Mussolini's plans for architecture since the very beginning of his rule. According to Nicoloso, Italy's dictator's relationship and involvement with architecture was often expressed through personal visits and collective rituals, including a tour of the north of Italy from October to November 1932 on the occasion of the celebrations for the Decennale, and thus used as a means of shaping consensus and creating assorted social mythologies.[8] Architecture was a instrument, just like the other arts, to build a civic religion and a social mythology, both apt to support the ideology of modernity and the plans for modernizing the public sphere the regime started drawing as early as 1924 and to advance ultimately State art under the banner of a socially useful art.[9]

The reality of the prestige Italy enjoyed internationally was palpably less glamorous. In 1925, Sarfatti, in charge of the Italian delegation, selected a friend, the 'traditionalist' Brasini, as the official architect at the 1925 Expo in Paris, with the Italian Pavilion standing in front of Konstantin Melnikov's Russian constructivist one. At this event, which was important for the regime in order to show its cultural strength after the 1924 crisis internationally, it became even more obvious than it already was for the visual arts that Italian architecture was officially lagging behind those of other European nations; and it therefore needed to be considerably updated both in terms of technique and of plans for urban development, but above all it needed a new language to express its visions.[10]

---

[6] Carlo Cresti, *Architetti e architetture dell' 'Era Fascista'* (Florence, Angelo Pontecorboli editore, 2015), 7–22; Kirk, *The Architecture of Modern Italy/Visions of Utopia, 1900–Present*, vol. 2 (New York, Princeton Architectural Press, 2005), 67–141; Aristotle Kallis, *The Third Rome, 1922–43: The Making of the Fascist Capital* (Basingstoke, Palgrave, 2014), 19–41; Nicoloso, *Mussolini architetto*, 33–8 on the relationship between Sarfatti, Mussolini and Brasini.

[7] Nicoloso, *Mussolini architetto*, 38–9. One of the first and most monumental of these projects is Giancarlo Palanti, Progetto per la Mole Littoria a Roma, first project, 1924. To note the skyscraper-like shape of the building which, because of its costs, will never be realized, Nicoloso, *Mussolini architetto*, 41–2. As reported by Cresti, *Architetti e architetture*, the Mole was first designed by Brasini when in Buenos Aires, 91.

[8] On this point, see Nicoloso, *Mussolini architetto*, 5, 45–7.

[9] Ciucci, *Gli architetti e il fascismo*; Silvia Danesi and Luciano Patetta (eds), *Il razionalismo e l'architettura in Italia durante il fascismo* (Milan, Electa, 1988 [1976]); Cesare de Seta, *La cultura architettonica in Italia tra le due guerre* (Naples, Electa Napoli, 1998); Denis Doordan, *Building Modern Italy: Italian Architecture, 1914–1936* (Princeton, Princeton Architectural Press, 1988); Etlin, *Modernism in Italian Architecture*; Diane Ghirardo, *Italy: Modern Architectures in History* (London, Reaktion Books, 2013); and Nicoloso, *Mussolini architetto* are comprehensive studies of Italian modern architecture.

[10] Kirk, *The Architecture of Modern Italy*, 63.

In Italy from 1926 until 1936, battles raged between rationalist, Novecento, futurist and functionalist architects, all of them against each other in their search for a modern and rational *logos*. These skirmishes peaked with the establishment of the Gruppo 7, Giuseppe Terragni's opening of his apartment block Novocomum in 1927, the foundation of the MIAR (Movimento italiano di architettura razionalista) with the group's arrival at the 1927 Monza Triennale, and two MIAR exhibitions – a search for new lexicon and syntax which would culminate with the competition for the Stazione di Firenze and that for the Palazzo del Littorio, and would start to decline with the hegemony of the Rome-based Marcello Piacentini and of the *stile littorio* as evocative of official architecture, especially after the promulgation of the empire on 6 May 1936.[11] These conflicts ultimately aimed at launching architecture as State art under the banner of a socially useful art.

The Gruppo 7 (Ubaldo Castagnoli, replaced by Adalberto Libera in 1927, Luigi Figini, Sebastiano Larco, Gino Pollini, Carlo Enrico Rava and Giuseppe Terragni) were seven friends and graduates of the prestigious Polytechnic in Milan who used to meet at the house of Carlo Enrico Rava. Dissatisfied with the traditionalist education they had received there under the supervision of eminent Camillo Boito, they were all firmly anti-culturalists and rather more interested in the new languages and in the technical aspects of architecture.[12] They made their vision of architecture heard in a series of articles, a four-part manifesto, published in the little-known journal *Rassegna italiana* (directed by Tomaso Sillani) around the same time of the debate in *Critica fascista* on State art between 1926 and 1927. For the Gruppo 7: 'The new architecture, the true architecture, must result from a rigid adherence to logic', reaching the conclusion that '[w]e must succeed in this: to ennoble with indefinable and abstract perfection of pure rhythm the simple construction, which alone would not constitute beauty'.[13] Likewise, Adolf Loos's pronouncement about ornament as crime was a starting point for many young Italian architects of the day; new architecture had to suppress ornament to legitimize the frank revelation of modern materials, such as reinforced concrete, and the simple, strong geometric forms typical of much of contemporary industrial architecture, just like the Parthenon did with its 'the rhythms of Greek purity', for in this respect the '[t]he Parthenon has a mechanical value'.[14] With its pure linear,

---

[11] On these points and for a detailed account of the early days of Italian rationalist architecture, see Mariaida Talamona, 'Primi passi verso l'Europa, 197–1933', in Vittorio Gregotti and Giovanni Marzari (eds), *Luigi Figini, Gino Pollini: opera completa: [1927–1991]* (Milan, Electa, 1997), 55–81; Ciucci, *Gli architetti e il fascismo*, 132–6, 139–46.

[12] Rava hosted many of the meetings in his house in Milan and played a leading role in shaping the Gruppo direction. On the old-fashioned teaching of architecture as well as on the intransigent protection of the privileges of the architect's caste, see Ezio Bonfanti and Marco Porta, *Il gruppo BBPR nella cultura architettonica italiana 1932–1970* (Milan, Hoepli, 2009), 7. For a detailed account of the relationship between new architecture and the establishment, see Paolo Nicoloso, *Gli architetti di Mussolini* (Milan, Franco Angeli, 1999), 120–9.

[13] 'La nuova architettura, la vera architettura, deve risultare da una stretta aderenza alla logica, alla razionalità. Un rigido costrutivismo deve dettare le regole' Gruppo 7, 'Architettura I', *Rassegna italiana* (December 1926), in Michele Cennamo, *Materiali per l'analisi dell'architettura moderna* (Naples, Fausto Fiorentino editore, 1973), 40.

[14] 'ritmo di purezza greca' 'Partenone ha un valore meccanico', ibid., 43.

balanced compositional conceptions and averting of any excess, the beauty of Greece had to win over that of Rome.[15]

Stranded between Le Corbusier and Gropius, they wanted to embrace a vaguely defined but deeply felt new spirit, echoing that of *Towards a New Architecture* (1923), develop a new compositional language and chose anonymity and group-work over individuality and stand-alone creative genius as marks of their social commitment. For the Gruppo 7, the new spirit that Italy could infuse into modern architecture was that of abstraction embodied in groupiesque typologies, which were the fundamental bricks for construction, the assembling of which could give coherence to the structure of the building.[16] The new language of architecture ought to be interdisciplinary and should not have been developed without considering correspondences between national traditions and between artistic fields, and the Gruppo 7's solution to this conundrum: 'Therefore it does *exists*, particularly in architecture, a new spirit? And how about Italy? Undoubtedly we can notice some correspondences [...]: for instance there is a certain affinity between Bontempelli's abstractions and some of De Chirico's, Carrà's and Sironi's painting.'[17] The Gruppo 7 references points were Le Corbusier and Gropius as well as Cocteau – united by the idea of aesthetic clarity and purity – and their view of architecture was political when it moved across the system of the arts and did not stand still as a self-contained practice.[18]

In this vein, it is worth considering Umberto Barbaro's intervention from *La ruota dentata* in the debate specifically about the universal value of architecture and its historicity. Crucially, Barbaro highlighted some parallels with both literature and the visual arts as far as the development of a new architectural language was concerned, thereby adding a further dimension to the Gruppo 7 manifesto. In his article 'Razionalismo nell'architettura', Barbaro denied that in Italy there was ever an avant-garde in architecture, and he argued that only the Imaginists had attempted to theorize avant-garde art in view of their hybridizing conceptualization of the relationship between reality and imagination.[19] According to Barbaro, the idea of architectural beauty as something chiefly 'functional and harmonic' the rationalists put forward as radically new was instead simply a reiteration of Hegel's aesthetic categorizations of the embodiment of the Spirit in History with this time an empirical and not universal application. Rationalism as such was nothing particularly innovative unless viewed against the backdrop of an interdisciplinary take on its applications in society.[20]

---

[15] Ibid., 40–1.

[16] Ibid., 40.

[17] '*Dunque esiste, particolarmente in architettura, uno spirito nuovo? E in Italia? Senza dubbio anche da noi si possono notare corrispondenze [...]: ad esempio esiste una affinità fra certe astrazioni di Bontempelli e certa pittura di De Chirico, Carrà', Sironi*', ibid., 38. Such an idea is repeated in the third article: '*Cocteau, Picasso, Stravinsky, Le Corbusier, in ogni forma d'arte ci danno una risonanza armonica di semplicità, concisione, chiara e serrata*', ibid., (February 1927), 52.

[18] Gruppo 7, 'Architettura I', *Rassegna italiana*, (December 1926), in Cennamo, *Materiali per l'analisi dell'architettura moderna*, 37.

[19] Barbaro, 'Una nuova estetica per un'arte nuova', *La ruota dentata*, I (1927), 2–3.

[20] Paladini, 'Estetica dell'Immaginismo', solo exhibition at the Casa d'arte Bragaglia held in February 1923.

Trained in Turin at the prestigious Scuola Superiore di Architettura, artist Paladini also contributed to the debate in a series of articles from the *Interplanetario*, essentially trying to historicize new architecture along a trajectory, which moved across historical times from the beginning of the nineteenth century with the Eiffel tower to the new spirit of Le Corbusier. He praised the Gruppo 7 and the Turinese architects but he warned them about seeking too close an imitation of foreign models.[21] Architecture was undoubtedly an historically situated artistic expression, which could not but answer any social call through innovative and not simply functional aesthetic solutions. On the whole, Paladini's position was moving between nationalism and internationalism but it was effectively grounded in the idea of architecture as a universal expression of morality and of sociability, which perfectly endorsed the cardinal hypotheses sustaining the project of State art but not its ideology.[22]

Theoretical debates aside, as well as a result of those, the first most significant event organized by the Gruppo 7 was the I Esposizione di architettura razionale, held in Rome in 1928 at the Palazzo delle Esposizioni, with the opening speech delivered by Emilio Bordero, the very supportive Undersecretary for Public Education, friend of Massimo Bontempelli and P. M. Bardi and with a direct line to Mussolini. Under the direction of Adalberto Libera and Gaetano Minnucci, the new architecture was finally defined by the 'the Roman heritage of constructive power. It was profoundly rational, practical, industrial.'[23] Implicitly addressing their social concerns and claiming a political role for themselves, the Gruppo 7 proposed the theme of the 'casa italiana in serie' as a unifying thread for the exhibition: however innovative such a choice might have been, that was, and would largely remain, a type of house exclusively for the middle classes as it was never going to be made available to the working classes. The exhibition hosted projects by forty-one architects from across the whole of Italy but only five were realized in the end (amongst them the Edificio per la cura razionale dei bagni di sole built by Duilio Torres and the Lido in Venice). Notwithstanding its 'social and political' limitations, the exhibition gave national visibility to the group; so much so that in the same year the rationalist architects were able to found the MIAR (Movimento italiano per l'architettura razionale), which pulled together architects from all over the country and obtained the support of the left-wing fringes of the PNF. The contitution of the MIAR allowed these up-and-coming architects to act as a united front, politically aligned with the regime, while calling for a resemantization of the architectural language, especially that used to design houses as rationalized spaces for the individual.[24]

[21] Paladini, 'Architettura razionale', *Interplanetario*, 5 (1 April 1928), 2 and 'Architettura razionale', *Interplanetario*, 7–8 (1 June 1928), 6.

[22] For a detailed analysis of the contents of these articles and the exact influences on Paladini, see Christina Brungardt, *On the Fringe of Italian Fascism: An Examination of the Relationship between Vinicio Paladini and the Soviet Avant-Garde*, PhD thesis (CUNY, New York University, 2015).

[23] '*retaggio romano della potenza costruttiva. E profondamente razionale, utilitaria, industriale*', *Prima esposizione italiana di architettura razionale* (Rome, De Alberti editore, 1928). See David Rifkind, *The Battle for Modernism: Quadrante and the Politicization of Architectural Discourse in Fascist Italy* (Vicenza, Centro internazionale di studi di architettura Andrea Palladio; Venice, Marsilio, 2012) for the support by Bordero, 30.

[24] Kirk, *The Architecture of Modern Italy*, 81.

In other words, the MIAR brought together the imperative of construction with that of rationalization, a synthesis which pledged to the same claim towards modernity that informed the brand of Sate art theorized in *Critica fascista*.[25]

The establishment's reactions to the event were not entirely negative: much of the press covered the exhibition, with contributions by Umberto Barbaro, Marinetti, Paladini, Oppo, Arturo Lancellotti and Roberto Papini. Piacentini was sceptical but not hostile. He naturally spoke against the MIAR's European outlook, specifically against their universal types, since these were conceived of as abstracted from their own physical environment, something that was essential to his own view of architecture and of his idea of State art as a pragmatic force for construction.[26] Still, he ultimately did not intend to cause any damage or antagonize these young architects – on this occasion.[27] On the contrary, Marinetti and Fillìa were instead ready to respond more vigorously and start their own campaign for futurist architecture as State art.

Theatre of Objects I: The Novocomum

Amongst the many (perhaps too many according to some people) projects presented at the second exhibition of rationalist architecture, we can certainly count the Novocomum and list it as a period-defining building: aesthetically innovative, modern, in dialogue with the international scene and its chief aim was that of modernizing society by designing new spaces for the individual and the collective.

Although firstly commissioned in 1927 to his elder brother Attilio, this lake-facing apartment block, nicknamed the Transatlantico and sponsored by the Società Novocomum in Como, was the first building of this type Giuseppe Terragni completed in 1929. Because it had to be placed next to an existing neo-Baroque-style building, Terragni initially presented a more 'conservative design' to the city council to be modified during the realization of the apartment block. The reception was not all positive because of how radically the final result deviated from the original plan. On this occasion, Pagano programmatically wrote in *Casabella* that the Novocomum was a modern masterpiece and that a new aesthetic was born.[28] The Novocomum has a five-storey reinforced-concrete-frame construction with a flat roof, which is not dissimilar to the Mattè-Turco futuristic idea for the Fiat Lingotto in Turin with a test track on the

---

[25] Libera-Minnucci, 'Introduzione all'esposizione' (Catalogue, Rome, 1928), in Cennamo, *Materiali per l'analisi dell'architettura moderna*, 105. See Oppo's positive assessment (apart from the excessive number of projects), 'La prima mostra di architettura razionale', *La Tribuna*, (29 March 1928).

[26] Piacentini, 'Difesa dell'architettura italiana', *Il giornale d'Italia*, (2 May 1931), 3.

[27] Riccardo Mariani, *Razionalismo e architettura moderna. Storia di una polemica* (Milan, Edizioni Comunità, 1989), on those rationalist groups who were closer to Piacentini, 153–7. For a detailed account of the relationship between new architecture and the establishment, see Nicoloso, *Gli architetti di Mussolini*, 120–9.

[28] Kirk, *The Architecture of Modern Italy*, 78. The debate on the Novocomum was predictably vivacious, see G. P., 'I benefice dell'architettura moderna. (A proposito di una nuova costruzione a Como)', *La casa bella*, III/27 (March 1930), 11–14; Ponti, 'Una modernissima costruzione in Como', *Domus*, 11 (April 1930), 28–31; and *Architettura*, fasc. V (January–February 1931). The Novocomum was discussed in Bardi's *Rapporto*, and in the II Mostra d'architettura razionale catalogue.

Figure 5 Giuseppe Terragni, Novocomum, Como. Credits: https://www.flickr.com/photos/trevorpatt/6318806190/.

roof: the latter was a fine implementation of industrial architecture that, when it was first presented as a plaster prototype in the Sala IV (Turin) of the 1928 and 1931 Esposizione italiana di architettura razionale, stood out for how it combined symmetry with speed, coupled as they were with the moral purpose of achieving better working conditions.[29]

---

[29] Kirk, *The Architecture of Modern Italy*, 76. In his review of the Exhibition, architect Alberto Neppi defined the Fiat building as '*un notevole insegnamento di nuda sincerità pratica e, in un certo senso, sociale*', 'La prima esposizione italiana dei "Razionalisti", *Il Raduno*, (7 April 1928). The building was cited by Le Corbusier already in 1924 as 'one of the most impressive sights in industry' (Le Corbusier, *Towards a New Architecture*, 1924, 287) and considered 'an incomparable building made out of plain forms […] able to express the principle of order' by the Italian critic Edoardo Persico, de Seta, *La cultura architettonica*, 124.

The Novocomum was an architectural milestone because of the Bauhaus-like symmetry of the lake-facing façade and of its alternating chromatic patterns (originally blue, ochre), its cantilevered volumes, plain walls and open corners.[30] It was a realized example of the Gruppo 7's programme for the renewal of the languages and forms of architecture: it demonstrated how the Italian tradition entered into dialogue with the Bauhaus and Le Corbusier, while creating a space (and this became even clearer in the Casa del fascio) where the individual citizen, still prominently and privately represented, perceived the real through glass walls. Within this context, dominated by spatial and light-and-shadows contrasts, colours and materials played a significant part too in shaping the overall composition of the Novocomum. In order to highlight the linear identity of the building, Terragni decided to use different nuances: hazel and yellow for the façades, orange for the recesses of the structure and the windows, and blue for the balcony railings, while the structural parts were left in concrete. More or less the same idea is applied to the materials – reinforced concrete for the frame, glass for the staircase-cylinders and for the windows, metal for the window fixtures – which, together, contributed to the embodiment of a new way of living.

The interiors reprised a conventional 'intensive housing' outline: hinged along a central axis (a long corridor that goes through the entire length of the building), they all differ from each other, having thus different light, space and view conditions.[31]

In a note to Figini and Pollini, Terragni described the Novocomum as follows:

Technical notes on the house owned by the Novocomum society (Como, Viale G. Sinigallia)

[…]

PANORAMA:

For the first one: use of a concrete structure (recommended also by the condition of the terrain subject to water infiltrations from the lake) and development of the plan of the bodies protruding towards the courtyard.

For the second: development of balconies facing the lake and the public gardens, large windows, verandas on the edges.

[…]

Lightening – atrium and staircases diffused and reflected lights.

This project replaces the first one which was never authorised by the building commission of Como.

The flats are divided externally on the balconies with irons frameworks with think and double glazed hammered windows.[32]

---

[30] On Terragni's borrowing from the design of the Zuyev Club (1926–8) by Golossov in Moscow see de Seta, *La cultura architettonica*, 133 and Thomas Schumacher, *Surface & Symbol: Giuseppe Terragni and the Architecture of Italian Rationalism* (New York, Princeton Architectural Press, 1991), 87.

[31] Gruppo 7, 'Gli stranieri', *Rassegna*, in Cennamo, *Materiali per l'analisi dell'architettura moderna*, 51.

[32] *PANORAMA: Per il primo: adozione della struttura in cemento armato (consigliata anche dalle condizioni del terreno soggetto alle infiltrazioni delle acque del lago) e sviluppo della pianta in due corpi avanzati verso corte. Per il secondo: sviluppo di balconate verso il lago e verso i giardini pubblici, finestre ampie, verande sugli angoli. […] Illuminazione – atrio e scale (relay) luce diffusa e riflesso. Questo progetto sostituisce il piano arretrato del progetto primitivo, piano che non fu autorizzato dalla Commissione edilizia di Como. Gli appartamenti sono divisi esternamente sulle balconate con telai*

In his book on the Como-born architect, Thomas Schumacher analysed three versions of the Novocomum project (two in 1928 and the final one in 1929) to illustrate how the changes in his designs moved towards a new language for architecture. He argued that, in the planning of the apartment block, Terragni shifted from a markedly Lecorbusian-inflected initial design, sliding across a more classical and traditional one. The final compromise between the two, consisting in a mix of complete volumes, but without the experimental flair of a 'prominent central glass-cylinder hovering above the entrance floor and connected to an elaborately developed roof-terrace' that he had once included.[33] In the last version of the Novocomum, new materials and the newly designed structures in functionalist apartments meet the anticipations of a bourgeois condominium. The Novocomum was ultimately stripped of any of the more experimental solutions adopted in the planning of a rationalist villa; yet it preserved its constructivist and geometrical syntactical order for the building to function as a real house.[34] For instance, the sharp edge of the top floor creates a distinct contrast with the cylindrical shape of the ribbon windows of the second and third floors and an oxymoronic symmetry with the full and round edge of the first floor. In merging these elements together, Terragni replicated a constructivist theme, which was also being reshaped by Piero Portaluppi in the curvilinear space he inserted of the angular main block of his Casa Radici di Stefano (1929–31, Via Ulisse Aldrovandi, 3, Milan). It is not insignificant therefore that, amid the heated controversies about the Novocomum, Pagano took Terragni's side because he could see the potential for concrete innovation of such a design and consequently the political uses of modern architecture: and, moreover, the potential for modern architecture to become State art when engaging with probing dialogues at international level and when deliberately trialling forms, languages, colours and materials.[35] The Novocomum propelled other changes in the visual arts: Como became the leading centre not only for modern architecture but also for rationalist arts with local artists Mario Radice and Manlio Rho to be involved in the decorations of the Casa del fascio shortly after.

---

in ferro e doppio vetro martellato a grosso spessore. Le tre scale sono riunite e collegate in basso da due passaggi coperti in ferro e vetro (smontabili nella stagione estiva) (F. 'Lettere di Figini e Pollini', Fig.-Pol. 5.1.03, MART). In Persico's words, the '*transatlantico*' is in line with the designs of modern European architectures, while la Casa del fascio in Como is a step backwards, in 'Gli architetti italiani', Giulia Veronesi (ed.), *Edoardo Persico. Tutte le opere (1923–1935)* (Milan, Edizioni di Comunità, 1964), 149.

[33] Schumacher, *Surface & Symbol*, 75.

[34] On the sources of inspiration for Terragni, from Russian constructivism to Sartoris, see Schumacher, *Surface & Symbol*, 87.

[35] Pagano defended the Novocomum and described it as a fine example of a *machine à habiter*, 'I benefici dell'architettura moderna. A proposito di una nuova costruzione a Como', *La casa bella*, III/27 (March 1930), article cited in Giuseppe Pagano, *Architettura e città durante il fascismo*, de Seta (ed.), 133–5.

Fusions II: Towards a New State Art:
From Milan to Rome via Turin

Upon the success of his controversial exhibition 'Carrà e Soffici' staged at the Galleria Bardi in Milan in 1930, Bardi moved to Rome to take up his strategic position as director of the Galleria d'arte di Roma with the support of Mussolini and of the then director of the Sindacato nazionale fascista delle belle arti, Giuseppe Bottai, thereby manoeuvring his campaigns in favour of architecture as State art from both 'capital cities' and in opposition to Sironi's lead. Bardi lamented that architecture was marginalized from the I Quadriennale held in the capital city. From the Milanese *L'Ambrosiano*, in 1930, Bardi for the first time addressed directly Mussolini by sending him a petition about the need to renew architecture: his was the first sustained attempt at theorizing the political meaning and weight of architecture on the basis of the aesthetic potential the Gruppo 7 and the modern architects of the MIAR had started vocalizing since their public first pronouncements. He openly declared that the State had so far appeared too neutral towards architecture, which, because of its importance in the public domain, should instead be elected as State art.[36] From Como, Terragni responded to Bardi; and rejected the centralizing role the Milanese had attributed to the State as patron of the arts and of architecture as the most important of them, to vindicate independence of execution. The architect should remain the project leader and local committees should be free to decide on the most appropriate of solutions for any given architectural matter in accordance to their own necessities and objectives.[37]

Turinese futurist Fillìa too replied to Bardi. Between 1928 and the dissolution of the MIAR, the relationship between the Milanese and Turinese groups was cordial: both fringes were seeking to theorize their own brand of new architecture, to establish a mutually beneficial dialogue and to be recognized internationally. Just like the debate in Milan, in Turin it had begun as early as 1928 and if then it was predominantly about urbanism, it would soon turn towards State art, in line with Pagano's view of architecture as a socially attuned project. Before Bardi's intervention in the field, in 1929 Fillìa had written the editorial article 'Futurismo e fascismo', and argued for futurist architects' leadership in State art in the name of Sant'Elia's earlier *Manifesto* in 1914, as he had already done in the pamphlet *Arte fascista* he edited in 1927.[38] However, his programmatic article, published in the little-known Turinese journal *La Città futurista* he edited with Alberto Sartoris for about a year, could not have as wide a reach as required.[39] In contrast to an idea of a centralizing role of the State, Fillìa favoured local governmental bodies in making decisions about suitable urban plans

---

[36] Bardi, 'Architettura. Arte di stato', *L'Ambrosiano*, (14 November 1930).
[37] Rifkind, *The Battle for Modernism*, 39, footnote 63. The articles originally published in the *Ambrosiano* will be expanded into the pamphlet *Rapporto sull'architettura (per Mussolini)*, which was published on the occasion of the Second Exhibition of Rationalist Architecture in March 1931.
[38] *La Città futurista*, I/1 (1 April 1929), 1.
[39] He organized the exhibition with the participation of the futurists (first exhibition of futurist architecture in Turin, 1928) and he was the author of 'plastiche murali' and murals in La Spezia, 1935.

and architectural design; moreover, he attributed to the press the moral function of educating the people to a new understanding of the art of building: for the futurist State art required decentralization and regional autonomy.[40] In order to pursue his idea of futurist State architecture, Fillìa disputed that the Bauhaus 'fabbricazione in serie', or the repetition of the same typology implemented by rationalists, for instance, could be detrimental to the idea of beauty, which had rather to be attained in the name of a more mystical and lyrical take on the art of building based on plasticity, colours and, evidently, on Sant'Elia metropolitan visions. If much of this argument is obvious, more pertinent is the Turinese group opinion on the relationship between local architects and the State.

Gino Levi-Montalcini published an article explicitly entitled 'Architettura arte di Stato' in *Futurismo*. After the usual assessment of the new trends within the European landscape, Levi-Montalcini evaluated the aesthetic quality of futurist architecture. He asked for more public competitions for urban plans to be staged in order to select the most talented of architects to help modernize the country, thereby endorsing the State as a commissioner and the architectural practice itself as the leading art within State art.[41] Fillìa and Levi-Montalcini insisted on two crucial points: interdisciplinarity and the characteristically lyrical component of futurist architecture over the technical one, which was rather blatant in its rationalist incarnation. They, however, did not present futurist architecture in opposition to rationalist architecture. Their core argument was: futurist architecture could prevail over rationalism in the race for State art, since its aesthetic mechanics were more appropriate for representing modern society such as in the designs of Sartoris, Diulgheroff, Levi-Montalcini, Pagano, Cuzzi, and Aloisio without neglecting to include work by members of the MIAR (Pollini, Figini, Terragni, amongst others). The tension was clearly between architecture as a centralized national project in the hands of the State in Rome and architecture as a regional project in the hands of the architects themselves: the former favoured the politics, the latter the aesthetics but both were aware that the two could not be disentangled from each other.

Despite these cries for independence coming from Como and Turin, the II Esposizione di architettura razionale supported by the MIAR opened on 30 March 1931, took place at Bardi's gallery in Via Veneto in Rome, with Mussolini in attendance, and proved itself to be a means of solving the hiatus between State and architects.[42] On this occasion, Bardi did not speak with the National Syndicate of Fascist Architects

---

[40] Fillìa, 'Architettura di Stato', *L'Ambrosiano*, (12 February 1931).

[41] Levi-Montalcini, 'Architettura Arte di Stato', *Futurismo*, I/14 (11 December 1932), 6. Another minor, yet significant futurist journal, because it dealt with similar matters is *La Terra dei vivi* (1933), edited by Fillìa himself and published in La Spezia. To note the contributions by several key intellectuals and architects, united in a claim quite generic in tone towards architecture as State art, see Millefiorini, *Tra avanguardia e accademia*, 150–1. In the same issue, Prampolini republished an article 'Architettura futurista' to support the synergy between lyricism and plasticity in architecture as one of the defining features of futurist architecture. In the following article 'Architettura moderna', Sartoris argued for an international dimension of modern Italian architecture in line with that of the futurist movement itself ('Architettura moderna', (18 December 1932), 6).

[42] Rifkind, *The Battle for Modernism*, 35–8. Giuseppe Terragni, 'Architettura di Stato', *L'Ambrosiano*, (11 December 1931).

but he directly addressed Mussolini with his *Rapporto sull'architettura (per Mussolini)*, published in the exhibition catalogue; in this pamphlet he demanded once again that rationalist architecture was the only legitimate modern architecture to become State art.[43] Bardi's 1931 *Rapporto* was the first and most wide-ranging attempt at politicizing architecture by references to a newly codified aesthetic paradigm which acknowledged the importance of classical architecture for creating rational forms and calling for a major change of direction. While declaring the rationalists as the modern architect par excellence and encouraging Mussolini to intervene proactively and practically with commissions in defence and support of the new architecture, Bardi intentionally acknowledged the central role played by the futurists in reaching such a goal but not an aesthetic similarity between futurism and Fascism, which could justify any prominence of their architecture, since his was an attempt at uniting all fronts as one (Paladini, Sartoris and Diulgheroff were also invited together with the Aloisio, Cuzzi, Gyra, Chessa, Levi-Montalcini, Sottsass, Pagano and Vedres). Moreover, through to the first few months of 1931, Bardi began a campaign to revive the role of Sant'Elia as a forerunner of rationalist architecture, irritating Marinetti who wanted to ascribe this pioneering figure to the ranks of futurist architects.[44] The polemical debate was not late to begin.

As Rifkind noted, even in his aspirational *Rapporto*, Bardi himself, at the centre of several networks of power, was careful enough not to upset Marinetti because of his long-term 'connection' with Mussolini and, unlike the Gruppo 7's manifested hostility towards the chaos and professed individualism of futurism, he was willing to recognize the role played by futurism in regard to the anti-bourgeois revolution initiated by the regime.[45] Furthermore, in his interventions Bardi invited the State to support practically his architects, a key point since it corresponded to Bottai's view on the way the State needed to act as patron of its own artists. In return, Bottai published Bardi's *Rapporto* in *Critica fascista*, thereby officially endorsing – though unfruitfully – his petition to the Duce. In the *Rapporto* and later in tune with Bontempelli in *Quadrante*, Bardi wished for a new united aesthetic front, and in his attack against the establishment he coherently acted in an analogously concerted manner to that chosen by Terragni for the Sala O of the Mostra della rivoluzione: he pursued a tacit aesthetic and political compromise with futurism on the one hand and with the establishment of the 'traditionalists' on the other.[46] Architecture could become State art because of its moral dimension – in Bardi's model, if all architects accepted the centralizing role

---

[43] Bardi is on good terms with Bottai who seems to appreciate his anti-Farinacci's attitude, see Francesco Tentori, *P. M. Bardi: con le cronache artistiche de 'L'Ambrosiano' 1930–33* (Milan, Mazzotta, 1990), 46.

[44] Bardi's friends included Pagano, Aschieri, Figini and Pollini, BBPR, Muratori, Ridolfi, Angnolodomenico Pica, and especially Sartoris. Bardi had a working relationship with Oppo, but not with Sironi, since he endorsed the many points of Oppo's speech on the arts pronounced at the Camera in 1929.

[45] Rifkind, *The Battle for Modernism*, 41.

[46] According to de Seta, Terragni does borrow from futurism to arrive at Lissitzky and Malevich, and thus avoid purism in his architectural choices, *La cultura architettonica*, 139.

of the State as patron, and if in return the State gave rationalist architects more official commissions: a trend that will be fallowed in many projects to come directed toward the modernization of the public sphere, such as Rome university in 1935 or the E42.

Bardi's attempt at politicizing and uniting architecture in the name of a putative total work of art in the hand of the State crashed immediately at the II Esposizione italiana di architettura razionale. Bardi's *Tavolo degli orrori*, a dada-constructivist photomontage of the horrors of Italian architecture and of Brasini's shameful 1925 Pavilion at the Paris exhibition, emblematically positioned as in the 'saletta polemica', not only ridiculed the old guard of Brasini's but also the untouchable Piacentini; and thus stirred a colossal controversy. As Rifkind pointed out, Bardi's *Tavolo degli orrori* was influenced by dadaists, such as the pioneering photomontage of the Berlin-based artists Hannah Höch and Raoul Hausmann, by Dutch Paul Citroen and his 1923 photomontage *Metropolis* and, as expected, by architect, photographer and constructivist Russian artist Ed Lissitzky's *Proun* series (1919–23).

Naturally, Bardi's confrontational cultural politics and equally aggressive argument (supported by Terragni, Sartoris, Libera and Belli) were neither universally liked nor shared outside rationalist circles.[47] The result was twofold: a straight collusion with the sindacato nazionale fascista architetti (National Syndicate of Fascist Architects) and Mussolini's silence. Piacentini was too powerful to be ridiculed in public and he had the architectural and, to a certain extent, political establishment on his side. His reaction was predictably bellicose.[48] Still, the MIAR had enough influence to pursue its aims and to try and structure the new architects into a national organization, however short-lived that was.

The press campaign that covered these two exhibitions revels some strategic discourses which will define the future of modern architecture during the Ventennio: in essence, from right, left and centre, virtually all contributions focused on modernity vs classicism, originality vs imitation and, more crucially, nationalism vs internationalism. The practical outcomes of this provocation and of the second exhibition were threefold: the dismantling of the MIAR, Minnucci's resignation from his academic post at La Sapienza and Piacentini's new programme for 'a very modern architecture, in line with the social, civic aspirations of today's Italy', as outlined in the opening page of the newborn *Architettura*, the official journal of the sindacato nazionale fascista architetti, with active collaborations with convinced rationalists such as Libera, Michelucci, Pagano and Fagoni.[49]

---

[47] For the detail and reach of the polemica, Rifkind, *The Battle for Modernism*, 45–6.

[48] '*E mettiamo subito in chiaro – che è l'argomento più importante – il fattore politico*', Marcello Piacentini, 'Difesa dell'architettura italiana', *Il giornale d'Italia*, (2 May 1931), 3. Vinicio Paladini, 'Questioni sul razionalismo', *Il Tevere*, (7 April 1931) argues for the practical (the energy of the new material) and theoretical (new concept of space for the modern Man) nature of new architecture, in the aftermath of the II Mostra di architettura razionale.

[49] '*una architettura modernissima, concorde con le aspirazoni sociali, civili dell'Italia di oggi*', *Architettura*, fasc. 1 (1 January 1932), 1–2.

Theatre of Objects II: *Case Brutte, Case Economiche, Case Tipo*

'The architecture of the house is not only an artistic problem, it is a problem of civilization', stated Giò Ponti in his first editorial for *Domus* in January 1932.[50] For a country like Italy, which was experiencing a serious problem with urban development, the house was of fundamental importance for gaining consensus and from 1929 the economic crisis that hit Italy as well as the rest of the world made it even more central.

In 1931 Rome had 916,858 citizens, from a grand total of 209,222 in 1871, and of 511,076 in 1911, registering a heavier population concentration in the suburban areas.[51] From 1926 onwards, groups such as Gruppo urbanisti romani (GUR) (Luigi Piccinato, Eugenio Faludi, Eugenio Fuselli, Emilio Lavagnino, Luigi Lenzi, Gaetano Minnucci and Cesare Valle) began to debate the issue of how to renew Italian cities with their first plan for the regeneration of Padua and later on in 1931 with that for Rome. The GUR vision entailed the need to deal with their historical past, and the equally pressing need to build social housing.[52]

The beginning of the aesthetic renovation in the concept of the house, culminating in the mid-1930s *case tipo*, could be traced back to Muzio's Ca' brutta in Milan.[53] Throughout his long and productive career, Muzio's architectural mission was always that of bringing together different traditions under the overarching Italian one which will be embodied in architecture as State art. Such a career's path will allow Muzio to become one of the leading architects of Milan before and after the regime.[54] Precisely, Muzio's debut, the Ca' brutta, was the epitome of modernity and tradition: where modernity surfaced in the linear, geometrical construction of the building and its series of windows, and where gravitas was accomplished in the attachment to both the Italian and the classical tradition.[55] This thousand-unit development at the corner of the Via della Moscova was effectively a modern apartment block for the Milanese bourgeoisie. It consisted of seven floors divided into three horizontal zones, each made of different

[50] '*L'architettura della casa non è solo un problema d'arte, è un problema di civiltà*', 'Quale sarà la nostra casa, domani?', *Domus*, 49 (January 1932), 1.

[51] Ciucci, *Gli architetti e il fascismo*, 78, footnote 2. Le Corbusier visited Rome in 1933. Bardi organized the visit but Mussolini did not eventually meet him because of the opposition coming from most intransigent fringes of the regime, Nicoloso, *Mussolini architetto*, 84–5, and on Le Corbusier's failed attempt at presenting a project for the planning of Addis Abeba to Mussolini, 94.

[52] Cennamo, *Materiali per l'analisi dell'architettura moderna*, 32–3. In the late 1920s, the problem of urban development was often discussed in journals such as *Architettura e arti decorative, Il giornale d'Italia, La Tribuna*. See even Arturo Bianchi, 'Nuovo piano regolatore', *Emporium*, LXXVIII/466 (October 1933), 223–35.

[53] The debate on the *casa popolare* and *casa minima* takes up considerable space in many leading journals (*Architettura e arti decorative, La rassegna di architettura, Casabella-Costruzioni, Edilizia moderna, Quadrante*) often in dialogue with European developments (Holland, Germany, Hungary, USSR).

[54] Giulia Veronesi on the significance of the Ca' brutta for the Milanese intellectual milieu. She details how the prominent art critic Giolli defended the Ca' brutta against the attacks from the establishment for its innovative design, *Difficoltà politiche dell'architettura in Italia, 1920–1940* (Milan, Christian Marinotti edizioni, 2008), 26–9.

[55] Fulvio Irace, *Giovanni Muzio 1893–1982: opere* (Milan, Electa, 1984), 15.

materials (travertine marble for the basement, natural cement for the middle floors, and marble and quicklime for the cornice); and it was the first house in the city to include an underground car park and a central heating system.

Muzio's use of a reinforced-concrete frame, of pillars, of cantilevered bays and of an alternation of squared and arched windows gave the building an imposing aura over Via Moscova. The Ca' brutta's grand volume was composed of seventeen different façades (each with a symmetrical axe) divided according to the maximum heights allowed by the building regulations of the time. In order to break the monotony of his Novecento geometry and the squareness of his plans, Muzio varied the patterns of the windows so that every occupant could easily recognize their own flat and, to this end, he inserted 'a decorative system of classical motifs applied to the exterior in inventive patterns' of autonomous architectures. The result was a severe structure which was at the same time an example of order as well as a disguised example of traditional forms of composition and linear patterns. There are subtle variations in the repetition of similar patterns across all the apartments, and within the same apartment, even when they belong to separate blocks: just like the new poetics of realism, the space had clearly been transformed from the house of the single person to the house of the collective, where individuality could be retained. Such a shift had occurred thanks to a new aesthetic organization: modernity as fragmentation and tradition as a continuity of patterns and geometry, as per the *Contro tutti i ritorni in pittura* manifesto.

The Ca' brutta was divided into two main blocks which were joined together by an archway with a 'severe Palladian motif of an arcuate centre bay framing the view of the narrow street and flanked by smaller treadbeated bays [that] recalls Vasari's use of a similar device for the Uffizi in Florence'.[56] In this respect Richard Etlin has noted the mannerism in the Ca' brutta alongside its metaphysical, encyclopaedic and kaleidoscopic nature.[57] The metaphysical qualities of the Ca' brutta, suspended eclectically, or encyclopaedically, between the Valori plastici and their return to order and the magical realism of Novecento, needed to be harmonized since, as Vittorio Gregoretti noted, 'while on the one hand the need to find an architectonic format for the new typologies (such as the condominium) proceeded thought as series of expansions of a compositional syntax made of classical elements, on the other it was the same pattern of urban connections to question the traditional volumetry of the building'.[58] But what sort of 'expansion' was that?[59] On the one hand, Muzio called for a return to order as a return to poised compositions in line both with metaphysical paintings by De Chirico and, in literature, with arrangements championed by Vincenzo Cardarelli and *La ronda*. On the other hand, he attempted to dismantle the compositional syntax of the building by expanding it through irregular geometric repetitions, only made uniform by the still neoclassical-Palladian chromatism of greys, blue-greys and pale pinks. Muzio's 'experiment' therefore exceeded the parameters of a simple return to

---

[56] Doordan, *Building Modern Italy*, 32.

[57] Etlin, *Modernism in Italian Architecture*, 176–7, 184–7.

[58] Vittorio Gregotti, 'Milano e la cultura architettonica tra le due guerre', in Danesi and Patetta (eds), *Il razionalismo e l'architettura*, 17.

[59] Ibid.

order in a neoclassical fashion, by fusing order with syntactical asymmetry. Once the scaffolding was removed, the Ca' brutta received at best a lukewarm reception; but its clear and linear geometry became a symbol of an era to come.

Together with Muzio's work, Giuseppe De Finetti's Milanese Casa della meridiana (1924–5, Via Marchiondi 3) is another image of modernity seen as a 'variation' within traditional forms, achieved by using different geometrical arrangements, in this case of cornices for every level of the edifice, a new language, that of the Viennese school of Loos, and an interdisciplinary understanding of the working mechanisms of the arts as a system.[60] Painter and architect Gigiotti Zanini added the sun dial. De Finetti had studied with Loos in Vienna (his only Italian student) and in 1934 he published in *Casabella* his translation of 'Ornament is crime', '*Ornamento e delitto*'.[61] Loos's teachings could be detected in the precision of the discrete cornices, which define each of the ascending parallelepipedal blocks.[62] The Casa della meridiana recalled Loos's 1912 Scheu House in Vienna and, just like the Ca' brutta, played with modern architecture: for instance, by replacing the traditional staircase with an elevator, a decision also forced by the small size of the lot.[63] De Finetti too opted for mural architecture, or for continuity between the friezes and the patterns which run through the façade of the house, while leaving the luxury for the interiors. The geometry of the façade with jutting cornices and the simple lines of the severely cut and orderly arranged windows were precursors of the Gruppo 7's claim to functionality and to their equally solid desire for purity of forms, as per Le Corbusier's programme. Compared to the Ca' brutta, the Casa della meridiana achieved aesthetic harmony because of its startling juxtaposition of empty and full volumes: it was an exercise in volume composition where the only criminally ornamental concession could be found in the pillars in the first floor balcony. By virtue of its geometrical equilibrium of volumes enhanced by the rhythmically ascending sequence of its parallelepipedal blocks and straight perpendicular lines.[64]

However, above all these pertinent observations, the Casa della meridiana's and the Ca' brutta's modernity was a test in urban planning (its construction continued the real estate expansion of the axis between the city centre and the old Central Station), in the understanding of collectivity and muralism, and in the process of reworking the very notion of tradition from a process of careful realignment rather than of explosive outburst and dismantling of syntax.[65] Such a further transition from classicism to

---

[60] Doordan, *Building Modern Italy*, 35–6.

[61] 'Ornamento e delitto (1908)', *Casabella*, VII/73 (January 1934), 2–5.

[62] On Loos's influence on Novecento, see Doordan's analysis of the Pizzigoni House, 1925–7 in Bergamo, *Building Modern Italy*, 38.

[63] See on this point, Cesare de Seta, *Architetti italiani del novecento* (Milan, Electa, 2006), 82. In this respect it is also worth mentioning Piacentini's only Milanese building, Palazzo Missori (1933–8), Giuliana Gramigna and Sergio Mazza, *Milano* (Milan, Hoepli, 2005), 179.

[64] Kirk, *The Architecture of Modern Italy*, 69.

[65] Persico was highly critical of Muzio because he believed that his classicism denied the social role of architecture, 'Razionalismo di Muzio', *Casabella*, VII/80 (August 1934), 36–7, and '*A tanto reagisce la casa di Palanti: con uno schema castigatissimo, e con una esemplare sobrietà dei mezzi di costruzione*', 'Una casa a Milano (arch. Palanti)', *Casabella*, VIII/96 (December 1935), 6. See for technical details, Alessandro Isastia and Orsina Simona Pierini (eds), *Case milanesi 1923-1973. Cinquant'anni di architettura residenziale a Milano* (Milan, Hoepli, 2017), 478.

composition could also lead to a realist interpretation of the 'real', as for example in the 1937 upper-class Casa Bonaiti and Malugani by Muzio, which rejected any neoclassical element in favour of a streamlined geometrical pattern and the use of new material like red klinker, and in frequent collaborations with Sironi in the planning of the Palazzo dell' Arte or of the Arengario.[66] Finally and tellingly, the Casa della meridiana and the Ca' brutta were a 'subdivided property', and one of the first models for a proper condominium in Milan where the growth in population was rapid.

Since the early 1920s the matter of *case popolari* was on the table more prominently than in Rome.[67] The Lombard capital was hosting the 'Club degli urbanisti milanesi' and, in 1903, MP Luigi Luzzatti had created the Istituto per le case popolari (ICP, later the Istituto autonomo case popolari IACP) and built 4,500 houses from 1919 to 1922, while in 1924 the regime founded the Istituto per le case economiche, followed in 1926 by its Rome-based equivalent run by Gustavo Giovannoni, Innocenzo Sabbatini and Massimo Piacentini, with plans such as the development of the Garbatella district.[68] In 1930 the first Istituto nazionale di urbanistica (National Institute for Urban Studies) was established, while in Milan in 1929 architect Cesare Chiodi started teaching a university course entitled 'Impianti urbani', soon to be renamed 'Tecnica urbanisitica' and then 'Urbanistica' in the 1930s under the tutelage of Muzio and Griffini. Such intitatives developed in Rome under the heading of 'Edilizia cittadina', a university course taught by Piacentini himself.

One early example of research into new homes as a means of solving social problems were the affordable houses. Architect and painter Gigiotti Zanini applied some of the technical solutions seen in the Casa della meridiana and the Ca' brutta in the construction of a Casa economica (affordable house) ad Affori in the Milanese district of Dergano in 1926. This mid-1920s Casa economica, one of the first houses designed by Zanini, was an early example of fusion between middle-class and popular architecture, admittedly with mixed results. The classical Palladian motifs and colours sweep across a rationalized façade, punctuated by sequences of differently shaped (square, tympanum, porthole and oval) windows appointed on every floor. An aesthetic solution which one could also note later in both Ponti's *case tipiche*, especially in the Casa Onoraria, and that was already present in the distribution of tympanums in the upper three floors of Muzio's Ca' brutta.[69] Because of the incoherent assemblage of architectural motifs, Cesare de Seta has described this house as 'grotesque' and has unfavourably compared it with futurist and constructivist Casa Zamponi, built in 1925–6 in Macerata by Ivo Pannaggi for a local industrialist.[70] Such mixing of styles without a clear innovative direction disappears in Zamponi's futurist-constructivist project.

---

[66] A later reinterpretation of the Ca' brutta is the Casa Borletti (1926–7) by architects Giò Ponti and Emilio Lancia.

[67] On urban development in Rome from the early 1920s through the initiatives of the ICP, see Ciucci, *Gli architetti e il fascismo*, 86–92.

[68] N. D. R, 'Casette modello. Costruite dall'Istituto per le case popolari di Roma alla borgata-gairdino "Garbatella"', *Architettura e arti decorative*, IX, fasc. V (January 1930), 254–75.

[69] Antonio Nezi, 'Nostri Architetti d'Oggi', *Emporium*, LXXVII/462 (June 1933), 349–52.

[70] Cesare de Seta, *Architetti italiani del Novecento*, 72.

Volumes, chromatisms and new materials are part of Zamponi's infrastructure and represent its pioneering interpretation of Italian architecture. Assessing the aesthetic value of these houses is beside the point: more significant is how affordable houses can illustrate the relationship between society and its inhabitants. Zanini's house has a political meaning, Pannaggi's house does not. The former is a visualization of how the upper-class ethos and language of the Novecento style could be applied to an affordable house. Only taken together, however, these two houses show the contradictions within Italian architecture of the mid-1920s: thorn between the political message for the people and the avant-garde for the upper and middle classes.

From 1925 to 1930, in Milan the urban policy was to push the lower working classes outside the city into the alleged satellite neighbourhoods (twenty-two in total had been built), which had to be well connected to the city centre, increasingly occupied by the upper and middle classes.[71] In the Lombard capital, not only were the working classes were progressively thrust out to the peripheries, but the ICP started to build new households for those middle classes hit by salary cuts. Hygiene and functionality were the unquestionably main characteristics for a modern house for the popular and middle classes alike. Overall though, the housing situation continued to be quite static, with Mussolini trying to keep citizens either in the countryside or in the big cities both to stop and police internal immigration and to exercise progressively centralized control over movements of people.[72]

Better housing and improved working environments for all social classes was the mission of social architecture as early as 1927.[73] The problem of new types of housing had appeared in the first instalment of the Gruppo 7's *Rassegna* in 1926 since 'meaning of the house should be [...] simple construction which can mirror through its exterior the spirit of necessity from which it originated'.[74] German architecture was taken as an landmark of this, exemplified in Gropius's factories as shown in Dessau in 1914, where from 'those two bodies made of steel and glass [...], of an hypermodern aesthetic, derive the beautiful and rational solution of Arthur Körn sketch for the competition of the "Districts of the Department Stores"'.[75] Just like the three pairs of semi-detached houses Gropius built in Dessau, the houses develop a building programme based on the typological repetition of minimal units, through the use of similar material

---

[71] For a list of *case popolari* built in Milan in the first half of the 1920s, Gramigna and Mazza, *Milano*, 83, 92.

[72] Maurizio Grandi and Attilio Pracchi, *Guida all'architettura moderna* (Milan, Libraccio, 2008), 126–31.

[73] The second instalment of the *Rassegna italiana* brought to the fore comparisons with other national traditions: Austria, Germany, France, Russia, the Netherlands and Switzerland. See Ciucci, 'Lo stile di Libera', in Giorgio Mascherpa (ed.), *Adalberto Libera. Opera completa* (Milan, Electa, 1989), 62–5, about his contribution to the journal *Stile* and on how some of Libera's architectural schemes 'edifici modello' were adopted during the post-war reconstruction.

[74] 'il senso della casa, che dev'essere, [...], costruzione semplice e rispecchiante attraverso la sua veste esterna lo spirito di necessità da cui è nata', Gruppo 7, 'Architettura III', *Rassegna*, in Cennamo, *Materiali per l'analisi dell'architettura moderna*, 57–8.

[75] 'quei due corpi di ferro e vetro, [...] di estetica tecnica ultramoderna, deriva la bella e razionalissima soluzione del bozzetto di Arthur Körn nel concorso per "Quartieri di Grandi Negozi"', Gruppo 7, 'Gli stranieri', ibid., 45.

and minimal geometrical variations.[76] However, the house for the Gruppo 7 was not supposed to function as a machine because 'the house will have its new aesthetic dimension, just like the airplane has got one, but the house will not have the same one as the airplane': the house has to privilege the living necessity of the individual, a statement which marked a distance from architecture understood as social mission.[77]

Modern architecture sought to combine a clear conception of the social obligation of the architect with an equally lucid understanding of the aesthetic dimension, to be working as a socially transformative force which needed to put the idea of collectivity and not of individualism first. In 1927, the Gruppo 7 with Libera, Sartoris, Figini and Pollini were invited to take part in the epoch-defining Stuttgart Weissenhof Exhibition organized by Mies van der Rohe; internationally, they obtained poor results, if one considers, for instance, the rather limited ambition of Libera's Alberghetto di mezza montagna (1927), especially evident when compared with German and modern architecture's aesthetic and social objectives for achieving urban regeneration and improvement of living standards upheld by Le Corbusier, Gropius, Hans Poelzig, Ludwig Hilberseimer, J. J. Oud and Max Taut.

After their return from Stuttgart, the Gruppo 7 created some prototypes for affordable houses for the 1928 I Esposizione, with about ten different house plans. At this early stage of their careers, the Gruppo 7 still presented prototypical projects to be shown collectively and anonymously.[78] Trying again to resolve such a paradox, on this occasion, Libera designed the 'Tipo di casetta economica italiana in serie per soggiorno estivo da lire 40.000' to illustrate a typology 'tipi fondamentali' of houses for everyone at a reasonable price.[79] The *case tipo* were made of fundamental units, which could be combined over and over: social architecture was not the result of a flight of genius but the upshot of a collective game of combinations, according to an infinite number of spacial variations, which could produce social change.[80] In practice therefore, the *case*, which were built by assembling the minimal units needed for obtaining good living standards, could be a fruitful application of rationalist theories and practices but they had to defy established and hostile views about their lack of aesthetic qualities over their perceived mere 'usefulness'.[81] Despite their public declarations, the Gruppo 7's programme and

---

[76] Gruppo 7, ibid., 51. Other examples of the use of glass are the House of Cactus at the Palmgarten in Frankfurt by Ernst May and Martin Elsaesser, the Press Pavilion in Cologne by Hans Schumacher, Villa Falkestein in Hamburg by K. Schneider and The Glass Exhibition in Stuttgart by Mies van der Rohe.

[77] '[l]a casa avrà una sua nuova estetica, come l'aeroplano ha una sua estetica, ma la casa non avrà quella dell'areoplano' 'Architettura', 'Gli stranieri', ibid., 41

[78] Doordan spoke of 'renunciation of individualism', *Building Modern Italy*, 50. To note that in 1927 a decree about the division of roles and tasks between architects and engineers and their direct relationship with the syndicate was passed (R.D.L. 27 October 1927, n. 2145, 'Norme di coordinamento della legge e del regolamento sulle professioni di ingegnere e architetto con la legge sui rapporti collettivi di lavoro, per ciò che riflette la tenuta dell'albo e la disciplina degli iscritti', Architettura e arti decorative, (1927–8), 193–6, cited in Salvagnini, *Il sistema delle arti*, 358, note 95.

[79] See for instance the plan for the Case economiche a Tor di Quinto and Casette economiche a Tripoli by Libera and the article N.D.R. 'Esito di Concorsi: il concorso per Case tipo da costruirsi a Tripoli', Architettura e arti decorative, IX, fasc. VII (April 1930), 373–9.

[80] See for instance the Case di Ostia and the Mostra per le colonie estive e assistenza all'infanzia or the working-class houses in Bolzano in 1936.

[81] Riccardo Mariani, *Razionalismo e architettura moderna*, 155, 183.

its applications remained focused on the individual sphere: theoretical and abstract in nature and essentially bourgeoisie in conception, since they lacked strong grounding in the everyday practice of construction. Despite their new spirit and ambition, Persico criticized some of the most internationalist statements of the Gruppo 7, and he labelled them as having 'amateurish positions'.[82] If providentially Carlo Carrà himself (later also a supporter of monumentalism) had not intervened in favour of the Gruppo 7 with his article 'Necessità di un'architettura nuova' to endorse the start of the battle for a new architecture that he perceived as a necessary condition of the renewal of the applied arts, these young Milanese architects' attempts – bourgeois or amateurish as they might have been – at modernizing the art of building would have gone unnoticed.[83]

Theatre of Objects III: Rationalist Villas

Since the 1927 Triennale, the interest in applied arts at the 1930 Triennale had increased. By the early 1930s, the main centre for rationalist architecture was Milan; Pagano had moved there and Bardi was still active and connected to the influential art galleries (the Pesaro and Il Milione gallery) of the Lombard capital. In Milan, *Quadrante* (1933–6) edited by Bardi and Bontempelli and *Casabella* (1928–present) edited by architects Pagano (chief editor), and Giancarlo Palanti and art critic and journalist Edoardo Persico set the scene for the domestic and public role of home creation.[84]

The theme of the IV exhibition was 'a modern vacation home for a single family that rules out either the low-budget cottage or the luxury villa, but leaves open, at least within reason, the scale and the setting' and it will be continued in the following one in 1933.[85] In 1930, forty-eight projects in total were submitted to the competition and the jury was composed of Alberto Calza-Bini (president of the Sindacato fascista), Pietro Betta, Enrico Griffini and Marcello Piacentini. On this occasion, in the park of the Royal Villa Luigi Figini and Gino Pollini built a prototype of what they called the Casa elettrica, which was expected to become the star of the exhibition because

---

[82] Edoardo Persico, 'Gli architetti italiani', *L'Italia letteraria*, (6 August 1933), in Giulia Veronesi (ed.), *Tutte le opere (1923–1935)* (Milan, Edizioni di Comunità, 1964), 145–50. Piacentini, too, intervened in the debate and elaborated further on some technical considerations on the new architecture, which he deemed not suitable to the Italian landscape, see 'Prima internazionale architettonica', *Architettura e arti decorative*, VII/12 (August 1928), 546–8, in Pisani, *Architettura moderna*, 127–33. 'Dilettanti' was used by many of the Gruppo 7 detractors as evidenced in the press campaign.

[83] Carrà, 'S'è aperta la Mostra di Monza', *L'Ambrosiano*, (31 May 1927). In reviewing the III Biennale in Monza, Carrà appreciated new architecture but considered the Gruppo 7 excessively purist and intransigent in their aesthetic preferences. For an earlier supportive intervention by Carrà, see 'Architettura nuova', *L'Ambrosiano*, (23 October 1924).

[84] In 1928 Guido Marangoni is the first editor of *La casa bella*, renamed *Casabella* by new editor Pagano in 1933. In 1935–6 Persico co-directed the journal. In 1938 it becomes *Casabella-Costruzioni*, and in 1943 *Costruzioni-Casabella*. It had a considerable distribution while *Quadrante*'s maximum print run was five thousand copies, Rifkind, *The Battle for Modernism*, 14.

[85] The exhibition catalogue was entitled *Esposizione internazionale delle arti decorative e industriali moderne, 36 progetti di ville di architetti italiani* (Milan-Rome, Bestetti and Tuminelli, 1930).

Figure 6 Giò Ponti and Emilio Lancia, Casa per le vacanze, 'Domus Nova', IV Triennale. Credits: Triennale Milano – Archivio Fotografico.

of its fashionable display of modern technology to improve the living standards of a modernized society. In 1930, Mussolini himself paid a visit to the park of the IV Triennale and to the Palladian Casa per le vacanze by Ponti and Lancia and to the Casa elettrica by Figini and Pollini. Before leaving, he complimented directors Ponti and Sironi on their results.[86]

Figini and Pollini designed the structure of the Casa elettrica, while architect Piero Bottoni the kitchen.[87] Adalberto Libera and Guido Frette were responsible for the furnishing for the whole house: it was a collective effort. Sponsored by the Edison Company, this Taylor-inspired project had on display forty different models of the latest technology in home appliances, stressing that: 'architectonically is the most modern expression of the house; because of its precise organisation of services […] the classical disposition of lines, for the denunciation of any unnecessary decoration.'[88] In this informative brochure, the company elucidated in great detail the practical use of each domestic appliance in every room. Of particular note were the illustrations of the

[86] Nicoloso, *Mussolini architetto*, 19.
[87] For a discussion on the 'rationalist kitchen', see Arch A. B. 'Le cucine razionali', *La casa bella*, I/9 (April 1928).
[88] 'Architecturally this is the most modern expression of a house; because of its precise disposition of services, […], the classical lines, the renunciation of any ornament', Illustrative brochure, 'An Electric House', Edison to his users, August 1930.

Figure 7 Luigi Figini and Gino Pollini, Casa elettrica, Vetrata della serra vista dal soggiorno e dalla sala da pranzo, project by Guido Frette and Adalberto Libera, IV Triennale, photo: Girolamo. Credits: Triennale Milano – Archivio Fotografico.

kitchen appliances for maximizing time and minimizing effort: technology needed to be deployed to shape a new family configuration where the woman of the house could gain greater control over her environment. Bottoni's kitchen was directly inspired by Margarete Schütte-Lihotzky's 'Frankfurt Kitchen' (1926) and by Erna Mayer and J. J. Oud's demonstration kitchen of the Deutscher Werkbund.[89] In spite of describing itself as a house for everyone, there is a room for a maid, a little detail which would have excluded a large chunk of the population who could not have been able to afford a domestic worker.

Not only the latest technology, the Casa elettrica also contained a walled greenhouse with an extraordinary display of succulent plants, and water could be taken from the lake and purified for drinking purposes. The greenhouse was an intrinsic part of the villa and echoed the offices of the Frankfurt's Palm Garden, realized in 1929 by Ernst May and Martin Elsaesser.[90] As pointed out in the technical review published

---

[89] On the various architectural influences see Rifkind, *The Battle for Modernism*, 91. See also, Piero Bottoni, 'Cromatismi architettonici', *Architettura e arti decorative*, VI/1–2 (September–October 1927), which is virtually identical to the original article 'Cromatismes architectoniques' Bottoni presented at the exhibition Die Farbige held in Zurich in August–September 1917 and published as 'Cromatisme Architectural', *Das Werk*, XV/7 (July 1928), 219–22.

[90] Ornella Selvafolta, 'Introduzione', in Luigi Figini, *L'elemento verde e l'abitazione* (Milan, Libraccio editore, 2012), xviii.

in *La casa bella*, this was the first case of extensive use of windows as walls, concrete pillars with circular section and insulation with eternity.[91] Lighting, too, was used as constructive element in a range of applications: direct light, reflected light, diffused light to shape the separate volumes of the house, across its open-plan space. The Casa elettrica was the textbook of what new architecture wanted to achieve: it was a functional space for the modern man and woman where they could transform their daily lives in accord with the demands of modernity, as seen in Mies's Tugendhat house in Brno and Le Corbusier's house at Weissenhof in 1927. The Casa elettrica received national and international praise, with its inclusion, as the only Italian contribution, in the Hitchcock and Johnson catalogue of the International Style exhibition which ran at the MoMa in New York in 1932. Function and volumetric rhythm in assonance with technological innovation shaped the Casa elettrica, which could in this way mould the human presence in a modern dialogue between modernized space and existential quest.[92]

To measure the innovative value of the Casa elettrica, it is worth considering Figini and Pollini's contribution to the following V Triennale which hosted in the park the 'Mostra dell' abitazione moderna'. At the grand V Triennale in 1933, Figini and Pollini, with Guido Frette in charge of the utility rooms, played the leading role again with the Villa studio per un artista (diploma d'onore by the international jury), which was described in the official press review as follows: 'it is a relatively small building, with only one floor. The Villa studio per un artista is characterised by a simple and linear architecture on the outside, while it is a masterpiece on the inside because of the arrangements of the rooms which retain significant intimacy'.[93] Despite the critical acclaim of this house, it would be safe to add that apart from their own brand of Italian rationalist design – which did not add very much to the Casa elettrica one – Figini and Pollini followed slavishly the Le Corbusier credo of Villa Savoye (Poissy, 1928–30), Villa Stein de-Monzie (Garches, 1926–7) and the Pavillon de l'Esprit Nouveau (Paris, 1925) with their ribbon windows and open-plans: but, in 1933, Le Corbusier's programme was no longer something particularly new.[94] Contrary to the Casa elettrica's gardens which used modern materials and where part of the infrastructure of the building,

---

[91] III (November 1930), 83–4.

[92] See also Pollini, 'Il vetro nell'architettura moderna', *Natura*, (April 1930), 51–5 and Bottoni, 'Illuminazione dell'architettura', *Illuminotecnica*, I/3 (March 1929), 6–9.

[93] '*è una costruzione relativamente piccola, ad un solo piano, di un'architettura semplice e lineare all'esterno, è però un capolavoro per la disposizione interna degli ambienti pieni di raccolta intimità,*' *Casabella*, VI/6 (June 1933), 5–9, special issue on the V Triennale.

[94] Other important landmarks of the new architecture which, while catering for the upper-middle classes at the same time reflected the new aesthetic spirit of rationalization, were the houses by Griffini, Figini and Pollini in via dell'Annunciata. The first proper rationalist experiment in Milan, the Casa a ville sovrapposte by Figini and Pollini (Milan, 1932–4) were a series of large apartments with long, narrow balconies facing the gardens of Borgonuovo. The composition of the front of the houses used a coherent symmetry, with access balconies '*balconi a uscita*' on the right-hand side and ribbon windows in the duplex apartment on the top floor. In all though, for the period, only the Casa a ville sovrapposte and the little Villa Figini built for himself at the Villaggio dei giornalisti applied in full Le Corbusier's five points about the new architecture, such as external staircases, ribbon windows, roof-top gardens, open-plans and pilotis, to maximize the minimum space required for the standard of living of the modern man.

the two gardens in the Villa studio per un artista were walled inside in harmony with the purpose of the house to facilitate artistic creativity and in a more explicit, and far less striking, homage to *romanità* and the Pompeian gardens, both exemplified in the cortile a impluvio and the cortile del pruno rosso (the red prison tree) one can see in the Casa di Loreio Triburtino in Pompei and Casa del tramezzo di legno in Herculaneum. The house developed an H-shaped plan, with a living room, the artist's gallery, the kitchen and the dining area. The colours are pale (shades of greens), the floors are white marble, the crystals are pink. The artist's atelier has different colours: black linoleum and light blue and green walls. Despite its official recognition, this was a middle-class house which had lost its aesthetic and political topicality and meaning, especially at a time when visual artists where rejecting easel painting because they perceived it as too bourgeoise: the Villa studio per un artista could only be of interest to a very limited number of users, if any at all, and could not impact on the understanding of modern living and could not transform the social sphere by producing real spaces for the collectivity.

Having said that, more interesting to detect, in our discussion of the arts functioning as a system under the overarching concept of State art, are the artistic intersections, which emerged from the artworks arranged in the interiors. One of most striking aspects of this Villa studio was the integration of different art forms by painter Angelo Del Bon, sculptors Fausto Melotti's *Senza titolo* and Lucio Fontana's *La Bagnante* and

Figure 8 Luigi Figini and Gino Pollini, Villa studio per un artista, V Triennale (mostra dell'abitazione), photo: Crimella. Credits: Triennale Milano – Archivio Fotografico.

abstracticist painter Gino Ghiringhelli's *Composizione*. In the years between the two Triennali, Figini had become interested in photography as a way of capturing the shadows of human presence within reality: the outcome was a more lyrical and less functional architecture. Fontana's light and plastic sculpture of a reclining woman stood on the side of the swimming pool, pensive and tranquil in contrasting bright colours; Melotti's equestrian sculpture with its black and white chromatism was positioned in the courtyard opposite the artist's atelier, in a very domesticated version of an equestrian statue, while Del Bon's return to the fresco of the red prison tree in the garden was a more rationalized and classically composed rendering of Cagli's *Neofiti*.[95] The fresco was at the same time an homage to the classical tradition and a strong gesture towards the new political trends in the visual arts. These artworks not only complemented the house's arrangement by providing a focal point of observation, which shaped the surroundings as sources of light, but also by allowing these young artists a modern take on the living space which entered into dialogue with the classical tradition without simply replicating it.[96]

Another element to add to the politics-cum-aesthetics of the Villa studio was a distinct return to a Mediterranean understanding of architecture, which implied an attention for the local elements of construction as indicated by the official lines of the government and therefore very much supported by the Direttorio of the V Triennale: the landscape primarily with its colours and materials, as one can see culminating in the Villa Malaparte in Capri or at the Foro Mussolini (now Foro Italico in Rome) and in accordance to *Quadrante*'s *Programma per l'architettura*.[97] As rightly observed by Rifkind, the Villa studio was an able compromise: between mediterraneità and modernity (if not modernization on this occasion) 'in the use of courtyard terraces and gardens to organize the flowing interior spaces of the plan libre' and in the 'use of geometric proportions similarly invoked classical and contemporary precedents simultaneously'.[98]

Aesthetically and politically and both, the V Triennale was a major undertaking and it featured prominently the rationalist villas alongside mural painting, as almost *verbatim* reported in a document dated 13 December 1932, which assessed the contribution to be made by architecture and its architects to the Triennale and to the overall aesthetic economy of the years of consensus. The podestà Visconti di Modrone in his political speech at the reception at Palazzo Marino for the participants to the

[95] Guido Lodovico Luzzato, 'Scultura ornamentale per l'architettura nuova', *Casabella*, VI/8–9 (August–September 1933), 30–4.

[96] On the critical reaction to the event and on Pica's enthusiastic assessment, see Eleonora Trivellin, *1933, la villa razionalista: BBPR, Terragni, Figini e Pollini* (Florence, Alinea, 1996), 104–5.

[97] Alberto Sartoris, 'Architettura standard', *La casa bella*, II/28 (November 1929), 9–14. Sartoris praised the Bauhaus and Le Corbusier because of the formal unity of their designs, adaptable to the needs of several different individuals; see also Giancarlo Palanti, 'Gruppo di elementi di case popolari. Arch. E. A. Griffini e Piero Bottoni', *Edilizia moderna*, 10–11 (August–December 1933), 28–31 for another positive assessment of new architecture. Other later implementations of such an architectural credo are the BBPR 'Una casa qualunque' (1934) for the corporative living or the Stabilimento Cima by Baldessari, 1930–2, as well as Ponti and Figini and Pollini 'Case unifamiliari a schiera per i dipendenti della Olivetti a Ivrea', in 1940.

[98] Rifkind, *The Battle for Modernism*, 95–6.

Congresso degli Architetti on 16 September 1933 made a similar point about the role of architecture: to promote aesthetic innovation and modern techniques while supporting the economic and structural development of the country.[99] The podestà explicitly stated that tradition does not mean returning to the past; rather that new building material, techniques and mechanical tools can offer profitable opportunities to young architects that were unknown to their predecessors.[100]

The regime's clear objectives in sponsoring the Triennali were: to develop the job market, to support local business and activities at national level. Such developments had to be put in practice by the town and provincial administrations, often involved or visited during the planning of the events. The results were 24,074 foreign visitors from thirty-seven different countries worldwide, and the composition was: 4,000 artisans, 12,000 militaries and 26,000 students from primary school to university. The list of notable personalities attending the event included royals, ministers, industrialists and bankers from Italy and abroad, thereby making the Triennale a key player in the aesthetic economy sparkled by the arts.

Another comparison could help in clarifying matters further and illustrate the multiple uses of houses: from aesthetic statements voiced through new languages which can or not acquire a political meaning, to aesthetic formulations that only tangentially touch on politics, to arrive to uses of architecture which show the progression and modulation of the relationship between aesthetics and politics as intersecting moments. The Gruppo comasco, a collaboration of architects led by Giuseppe Terragni and Pietro Lingeri, participated in the V Triennale and presented their own version of the Casa per le vacanze di un artista sul lago (Adolfo Dell'Acqua, Gianni Mantero, Oscar Ortelli, Carlo Ponci, Mario Cereghini, Pietro Lingeri and Gabriele Giussani, awarded the Gran Premio with congratulations of the international jury together with the Padiglione della Stampa).

The project stemmed from Lingeri's commission by the Accademia di Brera to realize a group of artists' houses on the Isola Comacina, donated by the Belgian royal family to the Academy, on Lake Como. The Casa per le vacanze di un artista sul lago stretched over two floors over 7 metres to host the artist's family. The artist had a room of their own in the building, which was connected to the rest of the house via a courtyard and a balcony.[101] In this villa project, lighting played an important role as inspirational to the artist, and the design was intended to foster artistic creation through highly innovative technological means, such as a mobile bridge that could help the artist to paint from a higher standing point. In the pavilion's villas, Terragni explored various combination of glazing – clear glass and glass block, gliding, double hung and casement sash – all of which were used in later projects. As Rifkind wrote, '[t]he juxtaposition of clear-glazed sash and expensive glass masonry in the studio wing, for example, reappeared in the Casa del fascio and Casa Rustici, as did flat floors

[99] F. 'Rivolta', f. '58–Ricevimento a Palazzo Marino dei partecipanti al congresso degli architetti (16 September 1933)', AGR.

[100] F. 'Rivolta', f. '58–Ricevimento a Palazzo Marino dei partecipanti al congresso degli architetti (16 September 1933)', AGR.

[101] Trivellin, *1933, la villa razionalista*, 81.

Figure 9 Giuseppe Terragni, Adolfo Dell'Acqua, Gianni Mantero, Oscar Oltelli, Carlo Ponci, Mario Cereghini, Piero Lingeri, Gabriele Giussani, Casa per le vacanze di un artista sul lago, V Triennale (mostra dell'abitazione), photo: Crimella. Credits: Triennale Milano – Archivio Fotografico.

punctured by expanses of glass block and double-hung windows of unprecedented breath'.[102] The design exuded a sense of transparency (glass block walls and ribbon windows) for the benefit of every artist, and an idea of transparency as conducive to communication which will be developed further in Casa del fascio and in the Casa Rasini apartment block. Artists were involved in the decoration of the interiors, with another fresco by Marcello Nizzoli entitled *La vita sportiva sul lago*, which lacked the empathic feeling of the Villa studio because it simply repeated some nautical motifs already present in the frame of the house, and a diptych fresco by Mario Radice. The two architects applied straight rationalist principles to their projects: in the choice of ribbon windows, window doors used to amplify volumes (in the Lavezzari house), or in the fragmentation of the core blocks of the house to recompose them in relation to the plot of land available and the building context.[103]

The plan of the Casa Rustici in particular was highly innovative and summative of the outcomes of works of rationalist architects. The project was significantly conditioned

[102] Rifkind, *The Battle for Modernism*, 99.
[103] The collaboration between the Como-based Terragni and Pietro Lingeri produced some more notable rationalist results in Milan for the middle classes: Casa Rustici, 1933–5 (corso Sempione, 36), Casa Ghiringhelli, 1933–5 (piazzale Lagosta, 2), Casa Lavezzari, 1934–7 (piazza Morbegno, 3), and Casa Comolli Rustici, 1934–8 (via Guglielmo Pepe, 3). For details, see Gramigna and Mazza, *Milano*, 158–9.

by the small size of the trapezoidal lot. The façade of the building coherently joined together two distinct architectural units in one. Yet, the somehow fragmentary nature of the house split into two blocks was homogenized through the use of slabs of white Lasa marble and orange-rose stucco and by a carefully calibrated disposition of full and empty areas throughout. The whole structure played with geometrical steel arrangements in the balconies (*'balconate a ponte'*) and in the façade, as well as with the linear repetition of the square windows according to highly regular patterns (*Il collegamento tra i due volume era consentito dal una sequenza di passarelle aeree con parapettini in metallo*). The Casa Rustici could well be described as one of the best results of the 1930s rationalist architectural experimentations – somewhere between Pagano's Istituto di fisica at the Sapienza University and Terragni's Casa del fascio – because it maintained a novel tone, a fragmentary nature, but showed nonetheless the tensions between its rationalist and visible infrastructure and the rhythm of the full and clearly shaped (by new materials like stucco) volumes, which make up those very same buildings.[104] These houses are testimony of how rationalist principles for architecture and its language filtered through to the everyday after being somehow neutralized of the political significance they had acquired at the beginning of their escalation to the ranks of State art with the Gruppo 7 and the MIAR.

A few years later, however, the language of the private space is metamorphosed into political language. Transparency, prominent structural frame and inter-artistic collaboration were the signs of distinction of Terragni's Casa del fascio (1932–6) where he deployed novel techniques and artistic compositions to create a singular space for the citizen in a concerted effort across the arts, as Manfredo Tafuri has amply demonstrated in his 1978 essay on how Terragni build the modern style by staging an architectural language, made of syntactical composition with accumulation coupled with sliding and change of scale (*autonomizzazione*) of elements.[105] The glass block is the most important of all materials because it allows for transparency and luminosity as imperatives with regard to the main public function the building had to fulfil. Yet,

---

[104] 'Una casa d'abitazione in Milano degli Arch. Lingeri e Terragni', *Domus*, 102 (June 1936), 1–11.

[105] The Casa del fascio has been the subject of intense academic scrutiny. Some key texts are: Giorgio Ciucci, *Gli architetti e il fascismo* and as editor, *Giuseppe Terragni. Opera completa* (Milan, Electa, 1996); Enrico Mantero, *Giuseppe Terragni e la città del razionalismo italiano* (Bari, Dedalo, 1993); Ada Francesca Marcianò, *Giuseppe Terragni. Opera completa 1925-1943* (Rome, Officina edizioni, 2008); more targeted studies are Diane Ghirardo, 'Politics of a Masterpiece: The Vicenda of the Decoration of the Façade of the Casa del Fascio, Como, 1936–39', *The Art Bulletin*, 62/3 (1980), 466–78; Jeffrey Schnapp, 'The People's Glass House', *South Central Review*, 25/3 (2008), 45–56; Simona Storchi, '*Il fascismo è una casa di vetro*: Giuseppe Terragni and the Politics of Space in Fascist Italy', 231–45. On the accusation of plagiarism, see Mantero, *Giuseppe Terragni e la città del razionalismo italiano*, 169 and Terragni's correspondence held at the MART (F. 'Giuseppe Terragni', R. 50/C. 290, MART). On the theoretical aspect and place of Terragni within the history of architecture (spanning Le Corbusier's purism, Gropius's spirally shapes factories, Mies's neoplasticism, constructivism and the machine), see Peter Eisenmann, 'Giuseppe Terragni e l'idea di testo critico', in Giorgio Ciucci (ed.), *Giuseppe Terragni*, 139–48 and Bruno Zevi, 'Terragni cospiratore modenista', in Ciucci (ed.), *Giuseppe Terragni*, 9–17. Cf., Sileno Salvagnini, *Il teorico, l'artista, l'artigiano del Novecento. Bontempelli, Terragni, Sironi* (Verona, Bertani editore, 1986) for an analysis of the relationship between Bontempelli and Terragni, 71–81. On the technical aspects of the Casa del fascio, Federica Dal Falco, *Stili del razionalismo: anatomia di quattordici opere di architettura* (Rome, Gangemi, 2002), 14–32.

there is not only glass in the Casa del fascio, there are also many varieties of marbles in different colours (nero di Col di Lana, giallo adriatico or calcare botticino), reinforced concrete and plastic, iron, aluminium, glass blocks and a highly structured system of natural ventilation and, because of all these elements, the house can be inscribed in the list of building which most successfully practiced the language of architecture to varying degrees of politicization.

Consistently with the idea of a politicized total work of art on this official occasion and for an actual building to be completed and used by citizens, Terragni invited once again abstract artist Marcello Nizzoli and Mario Radice to decorate the Casa del fascio: the first was in charge of the interior with his photomontages (like he did in the Sala O of the Mostra della rivoluzione) and the second was responsible for the main façade with a monolithic marble slab engraved with the words *Credere, Obbedire, Combattere*. It is worth adding that, in 1936, abstracticism was at its aesthetic peak in Italy while still struggling to gain political weight. David Rifkind's discussion of the works by Radice and Nizzoli to decorate the building properly suggests how these installations cut across artistic realms from photography to typography whilst toying with traditional applications of bas-relief, mosaic and fresco.[106] Nizzoli ideally wanted to decorate the front with metallic plaques painted with momentous fascist events (a project that was never realized). Mussolini's head was integrated into the composition by Radice in his typical abstract style.[107] Federica Dal Falco's technical analysis of the house has brought to light how 'the façades four have the same dimensions, but are diversified in the distribution of full and empty volumes and in the composition of some elements: the portico, the loggia, the window, the parapet, the pillar, the architrave. The unity of the different architectural motives is given by the stylistic continuity in the building structure' and the plan was that of a 'court scheme'.[108] Technique was unquestionably, it would seem, synonymous with a new political and aesthetic language as anticipated by the Gruppo 7 in their 1926–7 manifesto articles.

Theatre of Objects IV: *Case Minime, Case Popolari*

After six years of debates about new languages and new designs, houses for multiple uses but respondent to the needs of modern citizens were plausibly to be the central piece of the V Triennale exhibition since 'architecture is the applied art that best represents modern and fascist civilization', as a report directed to Mussolini also declared.[109] Many

[106] David Rifkind, 'Furnishing the Fascist interior: Giuseppe Terragni, Mario Radice and the Casa del Fascio', *History*, 10/2 (2006), 181.

[107] On the decoration of the Casa del fascio, see Cristina Casero, 'La Casa del Fascio di Como e la sue "decorazioni". Uno strumento di comunicazione del potere', *Ricerche di S/Confine*, I/1 (2010), 118–134; Rifkind, 'Furnishing the Fascist interior', 157–70, and Luciano Caramel (ed.), *Mario Radice. Catalogo generale* (Milan, Electa, 2002), 16–18.

[108] Dal Falco, *Stili del razionalismo*, 22.

[109] 1.1. Consiglio di Amministrazione', f. 'Triennale di Milano. Allegato A', Milan, 13 December 1933, and folder 3. Corrispondenza indirizzata al Capo del Governo, Benito Mussolini, Giulio Barella to Mussolini, Milan, 15 May 1931, Triennale and for the propagandistic and economic return of the Triennale, see folder 3, Corrispondenza indirizzata al Capo del Governo, Benito Mussolini, Giulio Barella to Mussolini, Milan, 1 September 1931.

Figure 10 Giuseppe Pagano, Franco Albini, Renato Camus, Giancarlo Palanti, Giuseppe Mazzoleni, Giulio Minoletto, Casa a struttura d'acciaio, V Triennale (mostra dell' abitazione), photo: Crimella. Credits: Triennale Milano – Archivio Fotografico.

of the prototypes were of interest because of the themes they addressed, spanning classes and professions to account this time for much more varied groups of users and assume a political and social value: La casa media by Vallot, Rossi and Rusconi, La casa minima by Cairoli, Varisco and Borsani, La casa di campagna per uomo di studio by Moretti, Damiani, Pediconi, Tafuroli and Zanda, La casa per gli artisti decorativi by Ziveri, Canevari, Di Cocco, Mafai, and Fazzini. Despite their principal 'purposes' and despite their middle-class destination of 'use', the houses exhibited at the V Triennale aimed to cover the whole spectrum of the life of a citizen or indeed of a human being.[110] The ville were certainly a stab at organizing the lives of citizens across their whole spectrum of everyday activities. Their function was therefore 'aesthetic' but could not be separated from a political aim.[111]

[110] '*semplici costruzioni come queste case per vacanze, le quali, prima cosa, sono quel che sono, (ma sono intanto assai carine): si costruiscono, seconda cosa, in poco tempo: costano, terza cosa, poco: servono, infine, i nostri desiderii tanto sani di vita indipendente e semplice in contatto con la natura*', Giò Ponti, 'Case per Vacanza', *Domus*, 66 (June 1933), 292.

[111] La casa appenninica (Bego, Legnani, and engineer Rampon); Casa sul golfo (Lanino, Cases, Chiaramonte and Larnica); Casa dell'aviatore (Scocciomarro, Zanini, and Midena); Stamberga per dodici sciatori (Vietti); Casa dopolavoristica (Prof. Luigi Lovarini); Casa coloniale (Piccinato) are examples of the typologies of houses presented.

In his highly critical article on Italian architects' contribution to the 1933 V Triennale, Persico stated that he could not see any practical application for them, other than a cerebral and theoretical *divertissement*, which implicitly marked the end of the movement understood as a new social, political and aesthetic force.[112] He praised Pagano (and Albini, Camus, Mazzoleni, Minoletti and Palanti) and their Casa a struttura d'acciaio (not the rationalist villas) built under the auspices of the Associazione nazionale fascista industriali metallurgici italiani.[113] Pagano et al. were truly interested in the practical problems of architecture and they were faithful to their moral ambition of creating a better living space in a way that would transform the existence of many Italian citizens across class boundaries.

This house was effectively an experiment in the use of modern materials to build the whole supporting structure.[114] Gropius-like use of geometrically assembled volumes and of ribbon windows together with the elevation of the horizontal tower frame created the most rationalized and economically possible scheme, as well as a 'lesson in modesty', as per one of the requirements of State art.[115] Pagano applied the criterion of rigour to this project while also sponsoring the use of materials such as aluminium, a material which increased in consumption in Italy by eight thousand tonnes to forty thousand tonnes in ten years. Pagano's assessment of the rationalist villa is an ideal summary: he argued that the success of the villa at the Triennale was a clear sign that the bourgeois was accepting the modern world represented by the regime and that the State had therefore to elect architecture to the rank of State art.[116] Furthermore, Pagano's architectural project fitted squarely with the regime's policies about the use of new resources in general as these were becoming more stringent, even before the invasion of Ethiopia because of the high tariffs on imports and the imposition of the fixed value 90 to the lira against the pound sterling. The lira 90 and the tariffs on exports favoured steal, armaments and shipbuilding industries. Housing expansion was soon turned into an autarchic imperative and

---

[112] Pagano is highly critical of the houses at the V Triennale because they lack coherence and show a 'fragmentary inspiration' and in general a taste and style heavily borrowed from European examples: Le Corbusier in the Villa Savoye, and Mies van der Rohe at the Barcellona Pavillion Exhibition or in the Tugendhat house in Brno, 'Gli architetti italiani', *L'Italia letteraria*, (6 August 1933), 148–50. Pagano was critical of Loos, see 'In memoria di Loos', *Casabella*, IX/106 (October 1936), 171. According to de Seta, this article was written together with Pagano, *La cultura architettonica*, 185–6.

[113] The review in *Domus* highlighted the modern conception of the house which gives greater space to living room and kitchen over the bedrooms. This house is the ideal reflection of the needs of the modern man, who enjoys an active lifestyle. To note the use of new building materials, and of colours for marking different floor spaces. 'La "Casa a struttura d'acciaio"', *Domus*, 68 (August 1933), 474–7.

[114] He will only start taking distance from the regime in 1936 with his resignation from committee of the VI Triennale.

[115] Giuseppe Pagano, 'Ignazio Gardella. Una lezione di modestia', *Casabella*, X/111 (March 1937), 2–6. This is a narrative Pagano used to describe how the altar to the fallen by Ignazio Gardella was an example of the moral value of architecture, ibid., 4. Articles about the advantages of '*costruzioni in acciaio e finestre in ferro*' populate the pages of *Casabella* after the V Triennale.

[116] Giuseppe Pagano, 'La Villa', *Casabella*, IV/7 (1933), 2–3.

into the corporativist city.[117] At that moment in time though, if Pagano was still close to Mussolini, a member of the elite Scuola di mistica fascista, he was no longer very much respected by the rationalist cadres of Il Milione and Bontempelli-Bardi.

The same social-cum-political-cum-aesthetic motivation could not be perceived, according to Persico, in the Gruppo di elementi di case popolari Griffini and Bottoni created for the V Triennale, because that work merely adhered to distinctly derivative formulations and not to the deeply felt moral and ideological conviction that characterized the work of Pagano.[118]

Figure 11 Enrico Griffini and Piero Bottoni, Gruppo di elementi di case popolari, V Triennale (mostra dell'abitazione), photo: Crimella. Credits Triennale Milano – Archivio Fotografico.

---

[117] Ugo Ojetti, 'La quinta Triennale di Milano', *Corriere della Sera*, (26 May 1933) and Giuseppe Pensabene, 'L'architettura alla Triennale di Milano', *Il Tevere*, (8 July 1933), who did not have the respect of Bontempelli and Bardi.

[118] 'Gli architetti italiani', *L'Italia letteraria*, (6 August 1933), 147–8. Another example can be found in Gramigna and Mazza, *Milano*, 155, while for other houses by Muzio and Giancarlo Palanti, ibid., 156–7. See also Anon., 'La "casa minima" alla Triennale', *Domus*, 68 (August 1933), 418–19. The house was designed by Alessandro Cairoli, G. Battista Varisco, and furnished by the furniture maker Borsani in Varedo.

Griffini and Bottoni's project 'conceived domestic inhabitation in accord with the existenzminimum concerns of II 1929 CIAM congress (Congrès Internationaux d'Architecture Moderne) in Frankfurt and the empirical housing studies of Alexander Klein', rather than with the specific needs of the Italian occupants in minds.[119] A formula seen before than at the Weissenhofsiedlung in 1927 in Stuttgart, and later on at the 1933 IV CIAM congress in Athens, or in Le Corbusier's maison Citrohan and the Immeubles Villas and Fiorini's visions Le case di abitazione in serie tipo 'A' e 'B'.[120] Moreover, the *case minime* were the minimal unit for building what Le Corbusier illustrated at the IV CIAM congress in 1933 in Athens under the heading of 'the functional city'. The *Quadrante* group (Pollini, Figini, Terragni and Bardi) were the only Italians in attendance and, during this trip, they proposed a Mediterranean view of architecture with the rationalist house at its centre, as issue 5 of *Quadrante*, entirely dedicated to the event, reports.[121]

The whole idea that informed the *casa minima* was the use of minimal space for functional and healthy living to raise awareness of the problem of urban development and of more accommodation needed in the city centre.

The minimal houses were completely furnished in a manner which recalled the interior arrangements of Bruno Taut and Ernst May, and in a manner which accounted for the smallest details of modern living. The concept of *case minime* and that of the standardization of units as a form of collective living, however, dates back to Muthesius and the Deutscher Werkbund, whose mission Rancière recapitulated as:

> An ethical function of art is being affirmed here in the strictest sense: its mission is to produce objects best suited to practical needs, but also ones that are most likely to place the symbols of a common way of inhabiting a world within each home, thus educating individuals in common culture.[122]

As an art critic this time, Persico judged the houses deficient in original aesthetic value since the six apartments were a mere repetition, with minimum expense, of the same patterns.[123] Despite the lukewarm reception received by leading figures, the Gruppo di elementi di case popolari gained a certain recognition amongst the

[119] Rifkind, *The Battle for Modernism*, 102 and Massimiliano Savorra, *Enrico Agostino Griffini: la casa, il monumento, la città* (Naples, Electa, 2000), 79–80. Sartoris was invited to the 1928 CIAM congress in La Sarraz (Switzerland).

[120] Rifkind, *The Battle for Modernism*, 102.

[121] P. M. Bardi, 'Viaggio di architetti in Grecia', *Quadrante*, 5 (September 1933), 1. See also some variations of the *case tipiche* Guido Fiorini, 'Progetto di casa di abitazione in serie', *Quadrante*, 1 (January 1934), 17 and 'Progetto di casa di abitazione in serie per scapoli', ibid., 18 and later Bottoni, 'La standardizzazione dell'abitazione collettiva', ibid., 9 (September 1935), 20–3. Reports on working-class houses were arriving from Poland, Barbara Bukalaski 'Abitazioni operaie in Polonia', *Quadrante*, 8 (December 1933), 28–35.

[122] Rancière, *Aisthesis*, 148. See Hermann Muthesius, 'Propositions', in Charlotte Bentono (ed.), *Documents: A Collection of Source Material on the Modern Movement* (Milton Keynes, Open University Press, 1979).

[123] On top of the Triennale's contribution, the project was also funded by the ICP, by the Consorzio antitubercolare and by other firms, Rifkind, *The Battle for Modernism*, 103; Savorra, *Enrico Agostino Griffini*, 186 and Enrico A. Griffini, 'La casa popolare', *Quadrante*, 3 (July 1933), 19–25.

specialists because of their 'usefulness', and their potential for practical use. These houses were aesthetically and politically somewhere between the necessity for purity and rationalization and the demand for a morally sound effort on the part of the architect to realize something useful for the citizen. Besides their theorization and prototypes though, none of these young architects had a real idea of what the shortage of housing was really like in Italy, and their visions stayed as such.[124] The two architects publicized the *case popolari* quite widely. In November 1933, Bottoni in particular realized a short docufilm, *Una giornata nella case popolare*, where he details, just like Soldati in his novel, life in a modern house over the twenty-four hours of a typical day. As Rifkind has noted the main themes addressed in this film were hygiene, light, green spaces, affordable furniture serially produced, Taylorized kitchens and sanitary services.[125] The idea was that of universalizing the message of *case popolari* as *case tipiche* which can accommodate the demands and necessities of every citizen by normalizing them into repetitive frames.

The debates on the *case minime* and *case popolari* and some enactments of their incarnations allows us to zoom in on the intricacies of the practical use of modern architecture before the monumental turn.[126]

The issue of the *case minime* versus *case popolari* was felt in various circles. Bottoni was in correspondence with Giuseppe Gorla at the Istituto delle case popolari di Milano who was very interested in the potential application of such a design which will feature with the support of Giulio Barella, in the exhibition of urban studies at the following VI Triennale. When Bardi left *L'Ambrosiano* to set up *Quadrante*, Crocean art critic Raffaello Giolli succeeded him. Despite his Crocean education, Giolli was attentive to the social aspect of the arts and in 1934 he published an article by novelist Elio Vittorini entitled 'Architettura funzionale – Case popolari e case minime'.[127] The young and politically engaged (but not yet anti-fascist) writer and intellectual Vittorini was adamant about the moral role modern architects had to provide a house for everyone.[128]

Other voices were equally assertive on this matter. Persico, in 'Case popolari a Bologna', praised architects Albini, Camus and Palanti because they brought together the desire to embellish people's lives with the need to give them some moral 'standing' or 'guidance' as the essence of modern style and modern architecture, and of totalitarian

---

[124] Rifkind, *The Battle for Modernism*, 102–6.

[125] Ibid., 106.

[126] See 'an ideal small house' designed by Ponti in 1939, in Lisa Licitra Ponti, *Giò Ponti: The Complete Works 1923–1978* (London, Thames & Hudson, 1990), 105. Other notable examples of *case popolari* by noted architect in the late 1930s, Giuseppe de Finetti and Enrico Agostino Griffini and Griffini himself with Giovanni Manfredi are described in Gramigna and Mazza, *Milano*, 120–1.

[127] Elio Vittorini, 'Lo stile *novecento*', *L'Ambrosiano*, (2 May 1934), in Luciano Patetta (ed.), *L'architettura in Italia 1919–1943*, 104–7.

[128] See Mariuccia Salvati, *L'inutile salotto. L'abitazione piccolo-borghese nell'Italia fascista* (Turin, Bollati e Boringhieri, 1992) for the debate in specialized journals, 106–16 and Annalisa Avon, '"La casa all'italiana": modernità, ragione e tradizione nell'organizzazione dello spazio domestico dal 1927 al 1930', in Giulio Ernesti (ed.), *La costruzione dell'utopia. Architetti e urbanisti nell'Italia fascista* (Rome, Edizioni Lavoro, 1991), 52–4, about the rationalization of domestic labour and innovative kitchen layouts to facilitate it.

Figure 12 Alessandro Cairoli, G. B. Varisco, Osvaldo Borsani, Casa minima, Zona giorno, V Triennale (mostra dell'abitazione), photo: Crimella. Credits: Triennale Milano – Archivio Fotografico.

politics.[129] In the project of *case popolari* the question of arts' morality, as per State art, could be fully realized and put into practice in the regeneration of peripheral areas whose political support was greatly needed, he firmly argued. In the same year, Ponti changed the tone of the debate by introducing the problem of demographic growth and of the symbolic value of construction. It was not simply a problem to be addressed as 'size' but as architectural design which had to be functional, yet at a reasonable price, to meet the needs of larger (and not exclusively working-class) families. Houses, Ponti added, were a political matter because they informed the regime's strategic attempt to 'perfect the family as a form of unity'.[130] The resulting collective city had to be not simply a chaotic mass but a coherent whole made of similar *case tipo*. According to the Milanese architect, something like that was already happening in Sweden with

---

[129] See also Giancarlo Palanti, 'Nota sulle case popolari', *Casabella*, VII/78 (June 1934), 6–11, 275–6.

[130] Giò Ponti, 'Case per le famiglie numerose', *Corriere della sera*, (19 April 1934), republished as 'Interpretazioni dell'abitazione moderna: case economiche ed appartamenti grandi', in *Domus*, 75 (May 1934), 8–9. In May 1934, ibid., 1–3, *Domus* launched the inquiry, 'Responsabilità dell'edilizia', to praise the regime's contribution to the development of Italian cities and the completion of many new urban plans. Overall the responses from the readers called for the development of new towns, the preservation of the historical heritage, and for cities not divided by class.

new working-class neighbourhoods such as Hjorthagen, Kristineberg, Eriksdal, Lidköping or even the island Kvarnholmen as a masterpiece of industrial architecture. Ponti's intervention is significant because the house is presented as a social concern; nurseries and other similar structures were a further instantiation of buildings which could weave and cement together the social fabric, as in Terragni's rationalist nursery Sant'Elia (1935–7) in Como, for example.

Two years later, in 1935, Giuseppe Samonà published a book dedicated to the *casa popolare* (Epsa, Naples) where he clarified further the difference between the *casa minima* and the *casa popolare*: the first one adjusts its plan to the needs of the minimum operative space, the second adjusts its needs in relation to economic matters.[131] The *case popolari* and *tipiche* were certainly the most innovative applications of rationalist and modern architecture, since these houses could have effectively transformed architecture into a tool for initiating social change through the modernization of the urban fabric but did implement the view of the art of building as a new language. The aesthetics of the politics of architecture remained mostly unexploited within the context of already existing city landscapes, but they found another embodiment in the corporativist cities while envisioning these initial experimental visions.

Theatre of Objects V: New and Old Towns: Urban Planning

One of rationalist architecture's most pivotal contributions to State art was the debate on urbanism. This debate was long-standing, reaching back as far as early expressions of futurist architecture with Sant'Elia (reviewed on several occasions by Fillìa and then Marinetti) and forward to Alberto Sartoris's international style applied to the Studi urbanistici for un quartiere Stadium and Orbassano in Turin (1925–6) – echoing Cornelis van Eesteren's plan for Rokin in Amsterdam, or his Studio per un centro universitario in Turin (1925–7).[132] Sartoris later attended the first and founding meeting of the I CIAM in 1928 at La Sarraz and, together with the Gruppo 7 & Enrico Rava, the second meeting in 1929.

Urban developments were clearly at the forefront of all this since the mid-1920s. In 1926–7 Marco Semenza and Portaluppi won the competition for Milan's new urban plan with *Milano com'era/come sarà*, now a metropolis growing in census from 818,000 in 1921 to 961,000 in 1931 to reach 1,116,000 in 1936. According to the political agenda of the day, urban development should have freed space in the centre of town to allow for the expansion of tertiary activities, and hence the plan concentrated on the development of public transport with ten metro lines and a green belt on the outskirts of the city.[133]

---

[131] See also Anon., 'La "casa minima" alla Triennale', *Domus*, 68 (August 1933), 418–19. The house was designed by Alessandro Cairoli, G. Battista Varisco, and furnished by the furniture maker Borsani in Varedo.

[132] Godoli, *Guide all'architettura moderna*, 62.

[133] Jeffey Schnapp, 'Piero Portaluppi's Errant Line', in *Modernitalia*, Francesca Santovetti (ed.) (Bern-Oxford, Peter Lang, 2012), 60–2, 66–7.

Jeffrey Schnapp identified Portaluppi's project for a city plan for the monte Amarillo district in the imaginary city of Allabanuel as the 'inspirational source' for Semenza and Portaluppi's own idea.[134] The utopic and visionary proposal for a Latin American city comprised of identically repeated and assembled cubic blocks (each building is made of nine identical blocks [8 + 1] symmetrically repeated). However, as Schnapp observed, in the new plan for Milan Portaluppi changed direction: no more functional, symmetrical linearity but a city where imagination could also play a constructive part.[135] In this way, the Milanese architect proposed a thought-provoking interpretation of urban visions because his design granted an alternative take on the straight lines of the rationalists: he reversed the micro-dimension of architecture one finds in linearity and symmetry to accommodate the baroque and imaginative sense of wholeness, which one can see in his villas or in his Planetario, not to mention the other imaginary Hellytown.

Portaluppi's Hellytown in Argentina (1926, pencil and ink on paper) is a dystopian image of the ideal city drawn in 1914 by Sant'Elia. The repetition of the cubic units follows a vertical organization that forms a grid of empty and full geometrical arrangements. The effect is disturbing and alienating, since the volumes are not arranged in a linear ascending mode, which could give way to a light, hopeful view; instead it presents a metropolis where rationality does not follow a linear path (again the errant line over the straight one). The ending is precarity, as Portaluppi himself said: 'with few concrete crutches the house could hold all its horizontal structures: every acrobatic feat is statistically allowed'.[136] Schnapp further notes that at the time of Hellytown, Portaluppi was preoccupied with the notion of '*sistemi di abitazioni*', a word he uses in *Milano com'è ora/come sarà* to justify how the act of building had to move beyond that of the single house to create a planning system: but his system was not arranged according simply to linearity and symmetry but by 'collapsing the opposition between ornamental and static-constructive systems'.[137] The sources for this proposal were also Dutch social architecture and the work of the architect Otto Wagner, whom Portaluppi had visited in 1913. As early as 1923 in *Architettura e arti decorative*, Gaetano Minnucci had written a detailed account of modern Dutch architecture and its Italian reception. Oud, he emphasized, was socially committed and intended to fuse together aesthetic and formal elements to realize architectural projects able to improve the structures of the public sphere.[138] De Stijl had collaborated with Valori plastici – and Piacentini held highly Dudok's work. Furthermore, in the 1930s young architects increasingly started to look to Scandinavian examples (of Sven Markelius or E. Friberger for instance) as inspiration for socially aware, functional architecture that was in touch with the citizen.[139]

---

[134] 1920, ink on paper, Fondazione Portaluppi, Milan.

[135] Schnapp, 'Piero Portaluppi's Errant Line', 60–1.

[136] '*con poche stampelle di cemento armato la casa regge tutte le sue strutture orizzontali: ogni acrobazia è statisticamente permessa*', Portaluppi, *Architettura moderna*, 22, in Schnapp, 'Piero Portaluppi's Errant Line', 64.

[137] Schnapp, 'Piero Portaluppi's Errant Line', 68, 69.

[138] Minnucci, 'Architettura moderna olandese', *Architettura e arti decorative*, II fasc. XI (July 1923).

[139] Published in Stuttgart, *Moderne Bauformen* was the German periodical mostly read in Italy at the time, with Terragni amongst its many assiduous readers.

For the Quadrante group urbanism was almost synonymous with State art as far as modernization of old cities, development of transport networks, improvement in public services and new urban plans were concerned.[140] Starting out with the financial support of Terragni and of abstract painters Mario Radice and Gino Ghiringhelli, again in Rifkind's words, the journal's mission was explicitly 'social' and it 'championed modern architecture as an explicitly fascist mode of construction' and supported new urbanism in particular.[141] Belli, Cattaneo, Pietro Lingeri, Manlio Rho, Mario Radice, Terragni (aka gruppo comasco), Luciano Baldessari, Figini, Pollini (aka gruppo bar Craja), Sartoris, Ciocca, Olivetti, Del Bon, De Amicis, Persico, Ezio D'Errico, Fausto Melotti, with the likes of artist Willi Baumeister and José Caballero and art critic Juan Ramon Masolinier – to name but a few – all revolved around *Quadrante*.

In his detailed study of *Quadrante*, Rifkind has summarized the journal's position within the discourse on the arts because '[m]ore than any contemporary European publication, *Quadrante* dealt with the vexing question of how modern architecture could meet the regime's ideological need for formal representation'.[142] *Quadrante* was pivotal in the debate on the system of the arts because it provided the guiding principles to draw connections between the novel and architecture in relation to the issues of realism, morality and new narrative and stylistic techniques.[143] Therefore, *Quadrante* comfortably occupied a central position within the architectural discourse, or better within the understanding of the artistic project as an interdisciplinary endeavour, and its ability to make multiple aesthetic discourses converge towards the political field granted the journal an influential voice.[144]

One of the most militant and forward-looking steps the *Quadrante* group took towards a new architecture was their decision to give prominence to the relationship between architecture and urban and town planning – 'corporativist urbanism' – with the support of leading industrialists such as Adriano Olivetti and architects Piero Bottoni, the BBPR group, Gaetano Ciocca and Terragni himself.[145] This was probably

---

[140] Rifkind, *The Battle for Modernism*, 134. F. 'Rivolta', f. 'Progetto di Mostra nazionale di urbanistica Milano 1934', AGR. *Quadrante* published the urban plans for Pavia, Como, Sabaudia, Algiers (November 1933). The n. 7 of the Quaderni di *Quadrante* is dedicated to new urbanism and n. 5 to Le Corbusier functional city. To note, Guido Fiorini 'Piano regolatore di Algieri', *Quadrante*, 7 (November 1933), 30 and Enrico Peressutti, 'Urbanistica corporativa. Piani regolatori', *Quadrante*, 10 (December 1934), 1–2. The new urban plan for Novara appeared reviewed by Pagano in *Casabella*, VII/74 (February 1934) followed by Persico's 'Introduzione a Le Corbusier' about the political significance of the Swiss architect urbanism, *Casabella*, VIII/85 (January 1935). In *Architettura* were published articles on the urban plans of Monza, Busto Arsizio, Gallarate, Mantova, Como, Pistoia, Terni, Castel Fusano and Imperia.

[141] Rifkind, *The Battle for Modernism*, 10–11

[142] Ibid., 12.

[143] Massimo Bontempelli, 'Principii', *Quadrante*, 1 (May 1933), 1 and Francesco Monotti, 'Antiletteratura', ibid., 4–5. For a reconstruction of the debate based on archival evidence, see Franco Biscossa, '"Quadrante": il dibattito e la polemica', in Giulio Ernesti (ed.), *La costruzione dell'utopia. Architetti e urbanisti nell'Italia fascista* (Rome, Edizioni Lavoro, 1991), 67–89.

[144] Billiani and Pennacchietti, *Architecture and the Novel*, 105–11.

[145] On the expansion and renovation of the Olivetti factory in Ivrea (1934–40), Rifkind, *The Battle for Modernism*, 13; Gino Pollini, 'Fabbrica e quartiere a Ivrea', in *La comunità concreta: progetto ed immagine. Il pensiero e le iniziative di Adriano Olivetti nella formazione della cultura urbanistica ed architettonica italiana*, Marcello Fabbri and Antonella Greco (eds), (Rome, Fondazione Adriano Olivetti, 1988), 155–9; Rossano Astarita, *Gli architetti di Olivetti: una storia di committenza industriale* (Milan, Franco Angeli, 2012 [2000]); and Billiani and Pennacchietti, *The Novel and Architecture*, 181–6.

the most incisive of *Quadrante*'s battles, for it captured the regime's use of rationalist architecture to boost its popularity, while preserving the idea of State art as morally sound and supported by a united front of artists and disciplines.

In 1933, Mussolini established the Istituto per la ricostruzione industriale, IRI (Institute for Industrial Reconstruction), in an attempt at linking the efforts of Italian industry to the regime's social modernizing strategies and gain their economic support. Sabaudia was ready in two years (1933–4). The BBPR and Gaetano Ciocca competed for the urban planning of Pavia in 1933 and named it the first 'corporativist city' because it realized the full spectrum of synergies between the CIAM's theories and those of corporativism. Pavia's historical heritage had to be preserved and ingrained within modern infrastructures which could facilitate more salubrious living conditions. In 1933, Bottoni, Lingeri, Terragni and Cattaneo won the competition for the urban planning of Como; and, in 1936, BBPR, Figini and Pollini and Bottoni that for the regional plan for the Valle d'Aosta, commissioned by visionary industrialist Adriano Olivetti. Still in the spirit of the early days of rationalism, the Valle d'Aosta plan was the first attempt at reformulating through urbanism not only the city space but to boost the economy of an entirely underdeveloped and marginal region. This 'regional' plan marked a new era in Italian urbanist studies because it called for a synergy between individuals, collectives, and local realities and their unexplored potentials. If Olivetti's New Deal for the Valle d'Aosta was received with praise (Bardi and the Corrente group for instance), the BBPR did also proceed with the demolition of the ancient sites of the city centre to accommodate an urban vision which coincided with that of the new towns of the regime. The progression of the history of architecture from 1935 to the fall of the regime was mostly about the political value of architecture rather than its aesthetic elaboration, centring increasingly around possible declensions of the official *stile littorio* while a progressively larger slice of the national budget was destined to military expenses.[146]

Broadly speaking, however, these rationalist urban plans tended to move the working classes out of the town centre and group them together in suburban areas, in a way that suited the regime, and strengthen the presence of citizens within the urban fabric. Such neighbourhoods did not have specific spaces for moments of interaction and were often an adaptation of previous districts – as for example, in the Milanese districts of Lorenteggio, Baggio, Bruzzano (1933–8) and Vialba (1937–9). The Quartiere 'Fabio Filzi' (Istituto fascista autonomo per le case popolari in Milan), planned by architects Albini, Camus and Palanti (1935–8) was an exception to the rule.[147] The accommodation was airier than the norm; and homes were not simply stacked together, with just a communal garden. The climax of the debate was reached in the mid-1930s with the new towns, the *dopolavoro* (fascist National Recreational Club) and the so-called African campaign. In an article entitled 'La cooperative Förbundet' in Sweden, Persico wrote:

[146] Bonfanti and Porta, *Il gruppo BBPR*, 2.
[147] Pagano, 'Un'oasi di ordine (Franco Albini – Giancarlo Palanti – Renato Camus)', *Casabella-Costruzioni*, XI/144 (December 1939), 7–21.

One of the most important aspects of new architecture is without a doubt its popular character. [...] The theorisers of rationalism, like Taut, see it as foundational for modern style, [...]. The architecture of New Frankfurt, of Le Corbusier plans, of Gropius 'Hochhäuser', is affirming itself around the world as the face of the same civilisation.[148]

The working classes were offered better living standards that also included leisure time. The debate on urbanism was lively, but construction of homes for the population was regulated by the State through the IACP, and as such, no private initiative was permitted.[149] During the first half of the 1930s, in Milan, the regime announced several competitions to redevelop or build urban areas. According to Grandi and Pracchi: 'Calls for public competitions set at 25, 33, 40 and 50 square meters the dimensions of the dwellings; they set out generic prescriptions about services [...], required a "noble simplicity" in the façades, on top of conformity with the municipal regulations about building and hygiene'; on the one hand the regime encouraged the '*edilizia popolare*'; on the other, it removed caps on rents and thus created an untenable situation for the poorer sectors of society.[150]

In light of such a packed and militant seven years, in a 1934 article in *Casabella*, Pagano was able to draw some conclusions and announce that, after Guidonia, Littoria, Sabaudia and the Florence train station: now 'modern architecture is State art' and now modern architecture is officially invested of major historical responsibility'.[151] In January 1934, *La Città nuova* came back into print, in 1935 Fillìa published *Gli ambienti della nuova architettura* (Turin, Utet). After 1934, the architectural discourse became less inventive and much more centralized, lacking the probing debates of the age of consensus. In the same year, Persico published a long and militant article in *Domus* significantly entitled, 'Punto ed a capo per l'architettura', where he too drew some conclusions about 'modern' and 'rationalist' architecture.[152] He attributed to the rationalist movement the merit of having borrowed from the European tradition, at least at its inception, but he also accused it of having given into nationalist spirits later on. He was averse to both *romanità* and *mediterraneità* (and to rationalist architects' affiliation with the regime for the 'conquista dello Stato'), because both aesthetic dispositions were equally damaging to rationalism in so far as they constrained it within the limits of its national reach and prevented it from evolving further.[153] In a similar

---

[148] '*Uno degli aspetti più importanti dell'architettura nuova è, senza dubbio, il suo carattere popolare [...]. I teorici del razionalismo, come Taut, lo pongono a fondamento dello stile moderno [...]. L'architettura della Nuova Francoforte, dei "piani" di Le Corbusier, della "Hochhäuser" di Gropius, questa architettura nuova che si afferma in tutto il mondo come il volto stesso di una civiltà*', 'Cooperativa Foerbundet', *Casabella*, VIII/92 (August 1935), 8. In 1934 Gropius was in correspondence with Gino Ghiringhelli about possible projects to be developed around modern architecture.

[149] Grandi and Pracchi, *Guida all'architettura moderna*, 197 for details.

[150] Ibid., 126–7, 189.

[151] '*l'architettura moderna è arte di Stato*' and '*gli architetti moderni sono ufficialmente investiti di una grande responsabilità storica*'. As a member of the Scuola di mistica fascista, Pagano wrote, 'Mussolini salva l'architettura italiana', *Casabella*, VII/78 (June 1934), 3.

[152] 'Punto e da capo per l'architettura', *Domus*, 83 (November 1934), 1–7.

[153] Edoardo Persico, 'L'architettura mondiale', *L'Italia letteraria*, (2 July 1933), in Persico, *Destino e modernità. Scritti d'arte (1929–1935)* (Milan, Medusa, 2001), 185.

manner to Piacentini's critique of rationalism's lack of social perspective, Persico's conclusions were predictably unceremonious and trenchant since 'Italian rationalists are anti-historicists', while to his mind they should have rather been in touch with the social fabric of their times in the name of modernity and modernization.[154] From 1935 onwards, Piacentini sat on all important committees and juries, spelling out the end for rationalist architecture, whose experimental drive, as he saw it, had removed it from the social problem which, with the collapse of consensus, the regime needed to tackle.[155]

Despite the decline of rationalist and modern architecture and despite the relentless effort of *Quadrante* and of its members in renewing Italian architectural discourse by engaging in transnational dialogues and new visions, of particular significance are some experiments in urbanism, which remained unrealized.[156] In 1938, Terragni collaborated with Sartoris in planning the Quartiere operaio di Rebbio, designed to be a working-class neighbourhood located in the former municipality of Rebbio, a satellite town of Como which, during the 1930s, was a municipality of around three thousand inhabitants working mainly in the agricultural and textile industries.

Terragni and Sartoris's plan also anticipated the incorporation of two other villages, Breccia and Albate, based on forecast demographic growth in the Como region. In a project inspired by international rationalism, Rebbio was to be a modern, independent and 'ideal' district. Regrettably, it was never built because of budget problems, a demographic decrease and the imminent outbreak of the Second World War.

The debate on urbanism allowed rationalist architects to remain in dialogue with European culture whilst maintaining a sense of usefulness for the nation. According to the principles of the Athens Charter drawn at the IV CIAM congress (1933) and, Como's new urban plan (effective from 1937), and Gropius's 'Diagrams relating building heights, spacing and population density', the aim had been to develop Rebbio as a geometrical residential area of apartment buildings and terraced houses with easy transport connections to the city of Como within a self-contained urban extension.[157] The expansion envisaged by the two architects followed the most modern principles of urban development, largely based on the idea of the *ville radieuse*, and the *zeilenbau* system of linear and parallel blocks. Rebbio was also to have been equipped with every key public and private service: sports facilities and parks, schools and a church. The affordable plots were already connected up with electricity, water and heating services; they would be proportionally parcelled up and occupied by the two types of homes, apartments and terraces. Inside, these homes were conceived as perfect spaces for families with homogeneous environments: furnished with light, spacious and of good build quality. All of the buildings would be surrounded by green space and key community services such as a Casa del fascio, complete with a Torre Littoria and an Arengario (a place for public assemblies), kindergarten, technical schools and a public

[154] 'Punto e da capo per l'architettura', *Domus*, 83 (November 1934), 7.
[155] See Grandi and Pracchi, *Guida all'architettura moderna*, 207–8 for a more nuanced idea of the relationship between new architecture and Piacentini in terms of continuity rather than rupture.
[156] See district Francesco Baracca in San Siro, Milan, ibid., 190–1.
[157] *Quadrante*, 4 (April 1935), 14.

ARCH. A. SARTORIS E G. TERRAGNI - PROGETTO PER UN QUARTIERE SATELLITE A REBBIO - GLI EDIFICI A SEI PIANI

ARCH. A. SARTORIS E G. TERRAGNI - PROGETTO PER UN QUARTIERE SATELLITE A REBBIO - GLI EDIFICI A UN PIANO

Figure 13 Alberto Sartoris with Giuseppe Terragni, Project for the Rebbio Working-Class District (Quartiere operaio di Rebbio). Credits: Photo from *Costruzioni-Casabella* 158 (1941): 36.

market. The extensive use of local materials, in accordance with the fascist economic principle of autarky and the examples of colonial architecture, and cutting-edge construction methods and materials such as reinforced concrete, revealed the modern side of this urban planning in line with the 'democratic' choice to standardize all the elements of the homes.

The architects wished to construct an ideal housing project for a family-based community, but also a district for their leisure and free time, education and politics which reproduced the regime's structure and ideology and contributed to its sacralization. Overall, the Quartiere operaio di Rebbio embodied a utopia of modern rationalist architecture; a working-class city born for a 'practical' purpose with excellent car, tram and train links to the city. As in many of the cases already discussed, the plan for Rebbio was, however, a point of contention between two opposite positions which had defined the aesthetics and politics of the regime for over a decade: on the one hand, the modernity of the buildings, inspired by an international rationalist style and well-served with living, public and service spaces, was consistent with the most innovative studies on urban planning; on the other, a strong conservative tradition placed emphasis on the family unit as the cornerstone of public life, consolidating a paternalistic view of society.[158]

Published in *Casabella*, *Milano verde* (Proposta di piano regolatore per la Zona Sempione Fiera, 1938) was an urban project designed to accommodate some 45,000 people, to be built in the zona Fiera.[159] The Milano verde district was to be a continuation of the central Vincenzo Monti street. Pagano began its design in 1938 with Albini, Gardella, Minoletti, Palanti, Predaval and Romano. The idea was to erect a chessboard-type neighbourhood divided by two horizontal axes and a vertical one, filled with tall, medium and low houses. At its centre would be its services – school, churches, markets, shops, gymnasia – and around this, its sub-neighbourhoods. Everything was to be aligned in perfect symmetry and equilibrium; the streets designed no longer as impromptu meeting places, but simply functional for movement and transport. Pagano's cadre paid attention to green spaces and their relative proportion in the overall urban scheme. The influences were Gropius and Oud in their hierarchical alignment of scale, distribution of services and relationship between green areas and orientation of buildings. Everything remained relatively theoretical, however, and in many ways did not look at the true dynamics of everyday life in Italy.

A year later, Pagano endorsed another utopian project by Irenio Diotallevi and Franco Marescotti, to be built in Milan: the *Città orizzontale*, 'sovrapposto', to be located in Corso Garibaldi and designed to house eight thousand people.[160] The most distinctive feature of the project was its study of the *casa-unità* (the single family unit, or *casa unifamiliare a corte*) to be used as the main dwelling model for residents. The *casa-unità* in this case had an L-shaped plan and a green space in the middle. The kitchen and bathroom were positioned at the corner between the two arms of the L, while the inside walls looked out onto the garden, giving the possibility of extending out through the open windows. The bedrooms too looked over the long corridor which was the space for the dining room, again with views onto the garden. However, the arrangement was a relatively impractical model for living, since it did

---

[158] As the neighbourhood of Rebbio was never built, our reading can only be based on the sketches, typological plans and drawings that remain. It is nevertheless an interesting urban experimentation trying to foresee the configuration of a broad city dealing with a growth of population; see Marcianò, *Giuseppe Terragni*, 8–9.

[159] I progettisti, 'Milano verde: progetto di sistemazione della zona Sempione-Fiera' (Franco Albini, Ignazio Gardella, Giulio Minoletti, Giuseppe Pagano, Giancarlo Palanti, Giangiacomo Predaval, Giovanni Romano), *Casabella-Costruzioni*, X/132 (December 1938), 4–10; R. G., 'Progetto per un nuovo quartiere d'abitazione a Milano (Architetti: Pagano, Bianchetti, Pea)', *Casabella-Costruzioni*, X/127 (July 1938), 10–13. See also 'Un progetto di case in serie per impiegati, a Schio (Diotallevi, F. Marescotti)', *Casabella-Costruzioni*, X/130 (October 1938), 22–3.

[160] Grandi and Pracchi, *Guida all'architettura moderna*, 177.

not guarantee privacy between the bedrooms and the dining area. In principle, the design represented the ideal culmination of the ville and *case razionaliste*: everything calculated in percentages, the number of houses proportionate to the space available and there had to be sanitary regulations. The green space, the separation between zones (day and night) and the highly stylized use of space were developments for the masses of the initial design. This *Città orizzontale* was never to see the light of day: the regime's rapid decline meant there was no funding available. It did, however, function as a positive prototype design just like the houses of the Gruppo 7 for some post-war housing developments.[161]

The problem of internal immigration from the countryside affected Milan to a great extent even before the 1950s and 1960s.[162] A group consisting of Franco Albini, Piero Bottoni, Renato Camus, Franco Fabbri, Maurizio Mazzocchi, Giulio Minoletti, Palanti, Mario Pucci and Aldo Putelli designed a plan for the Costanzo Ciano quarter (Istituto fascista autonomo per le case popolari) as an entirely autonomous and self-sufficient satellite city of Milan in 1939–40.[163] The satellite city model was the last type of urban development planned before the war by Giuseppe Gorla, vice-president of the IFACP. Paolo Nicoloso made a similar point when discussing Mussolini's visits to Milan, concluding that:

> Between 1935 and 1939, 13,700 homes were built, which could host 75,000 people, while to satisfy the country's entire housing needs the Ministry of Public Work had estimated that it would have been necessary to build 320,000 dwellings for over twenty years.[164]

In 1939, the demand was for around 70,000 new homes, but the Istituto managed to assign only 4,900 houses, the declining regime privileging mere celebrative art instead over concrete actions for modernizing the infrastructures supporting the country.[165]

---

[161] Antonino Saggio, *L'opera di Giuseppe Pagano tra politica e architettura* (Bari, Dedalo, 1984), 124–5 for a bibliography on these projects.

[162] Anna Treves, *Le migrazioni interne nell'Italia fascista* (Turin, Einaudi, 1976), 98–9 for a law against immigration to the urban centres and details and figures about internal migrations.

[163] Grandi and Pracchi, *Guida all'architettura moderna*, 201–3.

[164] Nicoloso, *Mussolini architetto*, 22–3.

[165] Grandi and Pracchi, *Guida all'architettura moderna*, 202–3.

Agon 4: Art and Construction: The Avant-gardes

Dissonances: Photodynamism

Anton Giulio Bragaglia's portrayal of a woman is a guiding example of photodynamism: a series of photographs in motion that he and his brother Carlo Ludovico had begun to take in July 1911, eventually collecting sixteen of them in the slim volume *Fotodinamismo futurista* (1913). Bragaglia was interested in capturing the trail left by the moving shot and not in the dynamics of its internal kinetics, thereby problematizing the relationship between line, movement and trajectory through a process of disembodiment. These images in motion are one of the first incarnations of futurist photography, projected as a challenge to conventional and realistic modes of constructing reality, as eloquently set out by its inventor and theorizer Anton Giulio. 'Photodynamism', he wrote, 'can establish results from positive data in the construction of moving reality, just as photography obtains its own positive results in the sphere of static reality.'[1] This, he continues, is because:

> *The picture [...] can be invaded and pervaded by the essence of the subject.* [...] It will be an active thing that imposes its own extremely free essence on the public.[2]

Photodynamism did align itself with futurist research about forms of representation that rejected realism as mimesis, and favoured instead the idea of realism as artificial construction and as vitalism: lines break and transform into dissolving arcs; gravity

---

[1] Bragaglia, *Fotodinamismo futurista* (with essays by Maurizio Calvesi, Maurizio Fagiolo, Filiberto Menna and introduced by Giulio Carlo Argan) (Turin, Einaudi 1970), 31 (26). The publication consisted of a forty-seven-page essay, accompanied by sixteen plates, divided into fifty-five numbered sections. A second edition was published on 30 June 1913. The volume was enlarged by six additional sections, making it to sixty-one in total, and eighteen smaller expansions of the text, typically a single sentence in length. A few months later a third edition was published, unaltered from the second. (The third edition was later reprinted: see Bragaglia, *Fotodinamismo futurista*). The text presented here is taken from the third edition, the most widely accessible; however, in the eight instances where that edition transmits material added in the second edition (and so not contained in the first edition of 1911), these are registered in a list of variants indicated in the text by an alphabetical superscript.

[2] Ibid., 35 (paragraph 29).

is defeated or intensified; objectivity is experienced and enjoyed according to a new aesthetic paradigm that calls for its augmentation and for the multiplication of perspectives.[3]

In its early days, photodynamism was even more controversial than other 'modern' artistic expressions: it was not simply the brainchild of the Bragaglia brothers since it echoed Marinetti's idea of dynamism as expressed in his 1909 *Manifesto*, Boccioni's pictorial theories, Francesco Balilla Pratella's musical dynamism, Étienne-Jules Marey's chromatographs and Eadweard Muybridge's motion studies.[4] Bragaglia's experimentations with photography were also later publicly dismissed in a joint letter from Boccioni, Balla, Carrà, Russolo, Severini and Soffici, published in the Florentine journal *Lacerba* in 1913, that labelled his works not 'true' art in comparison with painting, sculpture and architecture.[5] Boccioni on his part rejected photodynamism because he judged it unable to capture the true essence of reality through its static point of observation.

Initial scepticism aside, futurist photography was to develop further in the 1930s with the *Manifesto della fotografia futurista*, authored in 1930 by Marinetti and aeropainter Tato (aka Guglielmo Sansoni) under an overarching aesthetic theorization of aeropainting, for their common embrace of change in perspectival perception of objective reality. Other subsequent decidedly experimental developments in photography shared a similar aesthetic of non-linearity and anti-representation, including Studio Bertieri and Piero Boccardi's *cinetizzazioni* (kineticisms), Tato and Farfa's *assemblaggi e spaziamenti* (assemblages and spacings), Maggiorino Gramaglia's *sovrimpressioni e sovrapposizioni* (superimpositions and overlays), Giuseppe Guarnieri's *travestimenti di oggetti* (object disguises), Giulio Parisio's *composizioni di carte di accento scenotecnico* (composites of scenography papers; that is, the forerunners of animation cinema), Luigi Pirrone's *fotomontaggio ed effetti ad obiettivo multiplo e anamorfici* (photomontage and effects from multiple and anamorphic objects) and Tato's *visualizzazioni di stati d'animo* (visualizations of states of mind), all photographic artworks presented in Trieste during the Mostra nazionale fotografia futurista (April 1932). Celebrated aeropainters Tullio Crali and Trisno (aka Tristano Pantaloni) were before known for their *aerofotografia*. Regrettably though, experimental, non-mainstream and innovative as they were, they were all similarly taking to the extreme an idea of avant-garde aesthetics that placed

[3]   Claudio Marra, *Fotografia e pittura nel Novecento (e oltre)* (Milan, Bruno Mondadori, 2012), 11.
[4]   Probably an attack against Balla's concept of the lines, ibid., 26–7 (paragraph 19). Giovanni Lista, *Futurism & Photography* (London, Merrell Publishers and Estorick Collection, 2001), 21.
[5]   Lista, *Futurism & Photography*, 24–5, 26 on the exclusion of the Bragaglia brothers. Marra, *Fotografia e pittura*, 4, 18–20 on the real motivation of Boccioni and the involvement of the Gallery-owner Giuseppe Sprovieri, Galleria in Via del Tritone 125, Rome. Balla had been crucial in the development of photodynamism, with his reflections on the '*linee andamentali*' he observed and reproduced in the '*colpo d'ala della rondine*', Linee andamentali + successioni dinamiche (1913). The attack on Bragaglia by Boccioni could also be read as an indirect one to Balla. Shortly afterwards, in 1914, Bragaglia was expelled from the futurist group, but he subsequently went on to set up the legendary Teatro degli Indipendenti in Rome in 1922.

itself firmly within an autonomous sphere of action, a position that, we should like to demonstrate, was no longer maintainable during the dictatorship.[6]

While the early avant-gardes theorized an anti-representational and dynamic aesthetic paradigm for an understanding of reality based on a type of relationship between subjectivity and objectivity which eluded the problem of 'realism' to favour that of 'autonomy', in the 1920s and 1930s futurism in particular, one of the most vocal contenders in the race for hegemony in State art, built its aesthetic economy as one that had to addressed the question of the real with urgency. The abstracticism of the 1930s followed suit when it conceptualized the arts as a form of rationalization of the real expressed through the aesthetic paradigm of minimalism. Therefore, the aesthetic premises of futurism and abstracticism were particularly apt to enter into dialogue with State art because of their flexible theorization of the relationship between art and life; their explicit claims about the close correlation between aesthetics and politics; their articulation of a new relationship between subjectivity and objectivity as a way of reframing the idea of the New Man/Woman; their inclination towards an anti-representational and anti-figurative aesthetic paradigm that encapsulates a rationalized view of the real through the use of the straight line; and finally in view of their public presence in key national and international networks and exhibitions.[7]

In this Agon, we test our hypothesis by analysing a series of aesthetic debates which centre on the political role of the avant-gardes. By retelling the history of futurism and abstracticism from the point of view of their intersecting aesthetic and political agendas alongside that of their public life through exhibitions, we explore such theorizations and intersections in works by Fillìa, Enrico Prampolini, Thayaht, Bruno Munari, and Carlo Belli as exemplary of different aesthetic and political transformations. Therefore we ask: to what extent did the autonomy of the avant-gardes gain through aesthetic claims and performances a political signification in the race for supremacy in State art?

Synthesis I: Autonomy and Heteronomy

In his *Teoria dell'arte d'avanguardia*, Renato Poggioli wrote that 'the futuristic manifestation represents, so to speak, the utopian and prophetic phase, the State, if not of the revolution, of agitation and preparation for the announced revolution'.[8] While in *Aesthetic Theory*, Theodor Adorno claimed that the new is what defines the movements

---

[6] On experimental photography in provincial Italy, Friuli-Venezia Giulia (Udine, Gorizia and Trieste), see Bruno Passamani, 'Dall'alcova futurista d'acciaio al Tank ai Macchi 202. Energie futuriste e costruttiviste tra rivolta, utopia e realtà alla frontiera giulia', in AA.VV., *Frontiere d'avanguardia. Gli anni del Futurismo nella Venezia-Giulia* (Gorizia, Arti grafiche Campestrini, 1985), 18–61.

[7] Carlo Belli, in Giuliano Gori (ed.), *Anni creativi al Milione, 1932–1939* (Cinisello Balsamo, Silvana Editoriale, 1980), 11 on the impossibility of explaining abstract art without adopting an interdisciplinary perspective.

[8] *Teoria dell'avanguardia* (Bologna, il Mulino, 1962), 85. For a history of the term avant-garde reaching back to the Middle Ages throughout the Renaissance and for its parallel development as a political term too, see Günter Berghaus, *Theatre, Performance and the Historical Avant-garde* (Basingstoke, Palgrave, 2005), 35–7. For a complete reconstruction of the history of the movement, see Claudia Salaris, *Storia del futurismo* (Rome, Editori Riuniti, 1985).

of the avant-garde, since '[t]he authority of the new is that of the historically inevitable'; further, by operating '[i]n sharp contrast to traditional art, new art accepts the once hidden element of being something made, something produced'.[9] Culture in this sense is then both behind and in front of the artistic vanguard, as in Walter Benjamin's *Angelus Novus*. Lagging behind it is culture as tradition; leading it is new culture, poised to become traditional in its turn. What was then the position of the avant-gardes in all of this: stranded between old and new – autonomy and heteronomy?

Many scholarly accounts of the relationship between autonomy and heteronomy, including those of Peter Bürger, Richard Murphy and Andrew Webber, in close dialogue with one other, have sought to locate and explain the avant-gardes in terms of the dialectical relationship between superstructure of aesthetic production (autonomy) and the constraints that society necessarily imposes upon artists and upon artworks (heteronomy). Bürger has maintained that the historical avant-garde movements (such as futurism) sought to establish a connection between art and the praxis of life, in opposition to its denial – which instead characterized bourgeois art – as well as a relationship between individual production and reception of artistic products. Bürger attempted to systematize the avant-gardes by developing an encompassing theory that took as its twin points of departure Adorno's notion of the avant-gardes as 'the most advanced stage of art in bourgeois society', and Lukács' theory of realism that reclaims the social function of avant-garde art.[10] If for Adorno the avant-gardes were the fundamental expression of reason within bourgeois society, for Lukács they signified instead decadence. Bürger ultimately perceived that art in itself is always also an institution and should be analysed as such, thereby resolving Lukács and Adorno's dichotomy about the notion of autonomy through arts' historicity.[11] Bürger defined the avant-garde above all in terms of its integration of art into life, and stressed that the theoretical self-consciousness of the avant-gardes embodied in its desire to act politically within the social sphere and not in a simple declaration of autonomy. In this regard, Bürger read the aesthetics as practices of the avant-gardes as opposed to and not as a continuation of those of decadentism.

According to Murphy, Bürger's model main weakness was to be found in 'his fundamental ambiguity with regard to the category of autonomy'.[12] Murphy rejects Bürger's rebuff of avant-garde aesthetic autonomy (art vs life), upholding instead a view of the avant-gardes as 'de-aestheticised autonomous art': namely, a view of life which is not an idealization of the real but a fragmented version of objectivity.[13] Autonomy should still be dismissed because it anaesthetizes the arts from any form of political action, a perilous exercise resulting in the loss of any potential for critical opposition. If contrary to modernism, the avant-gardes, continues Murphy, are always fully aware

---

[9] *Aesthetic Theory*, 29 and 36. For an assessment of Adorno's theory in relation to the notion of autonomy, see Lambert Zuidervaart, 'The Social Significance of Autonomous Art: Adorno and Brüger', *The Journal of Aesthetics and Art Criticism*, 48/1 (Winter 1990), 61–77.

[10] Peter Bürger, *Theory of the Avant-Garde* (Manchester, Manchester UP, 1984), 1

[11] Ibid., 10.

[12] Ibid., 27.

[13] Ibid., 32

of the limitations to form and content imposed by any institutional framework, then Benjamin's position in 'The Author as Producer' is to be revaluated as sustainable in so far as it facilitates dialogical interactions with the external world. Through a heightened perception and an obvious use of technique, the avant-gardes could retain a sense of distance and thus, in Benjamin's words, 'articulate an awareness of the social and historical conditions of art'.[14]

Describing the narratives of the avant-gardes and of modernism, Webber aptly summarizes and elaborates further on such transitions; he wrote: 'A defining feature of the new versions of the epic is the transmutation of the extension of the Realist novel (its developed representation of the social environment) into elaborate forms of intention (in the in-depth, though often uncertain, representation of subjectivity).'[15] Or, to use Benjamin's formulation, the avant-garde fragments the object, whereas realism places it in its context, often historical and material in nature.[16] In sum, Webber's and Benjamin's theoretical claims implicitly state that the critical issue to address is not so much the attempt to draw up boundaries between objectivity and subjectivity (however significant this step may be), or between fragment and totality, context and autonomy, life and art, but to extent their reach to the outer world.[17] Is it vital to view the avant-gardes as a primary example of negotiation of boundaries and of theoretical redefinitions against, we add in our specific case, the working mechanisms of a totalitarian apparatus which acts upon artistic freedom of expression by controlling and shaping artistic institutions and forms of explicitly patronage. In the scholarly assessments we have just discussed the political as historically connotated remains implicit while we bring it to the forefront of our analytical model. By largely neglecting to single out and to contextualize the strong influence exerted by politics per se in outlining the profile and identity of the avant-gardes, the inner aesthetic and political workings are diluted into an overarching theoretical systematization.

Since autonomy is unattainable as a *modus vivendi* for artworks – which are never either fully detached from the social sphere nor a mere reproduction of it – the challenge is rather to determine the potential that can be elicited for social critique through languages and forms on the one hand and modes of production and circulation on the other. And, moreover, from moments of artistic intersections within an understanding of the arts, and of the avant-gardes, as a system.

Having said that, addressing the relationship between autonomy and heteronomy within a dictatorial context as well as the integration of art and life is made harder by constraints spanning ideological prescriptions and the working mechanisms of institutions. Broadly speaking, aesthetic experimentation demands autonomy of execution when pushing boundaries of language and form; whilst any action

---

[14] Ibid.

[15] Andrew Webber, *The European Avant-garde: The European Avant-garde: 1900–1940* (Cambridge, Polity, 2004), 166.

[16] Max Pensky, 'Method and time: Benjamin dialectical images', in David S. Ferris (ed.), *The Cambridge Companion to Walter Benjamin* (Cambridge, Cambridge UP, 2004), 185–8.

[17] On this point, see the discussion in Lucien Goldmann, *Towards a Sociology of the Novel* (London, Tavistock, [1964], 1975), 1–17.

directed towards the ideological and political fields calls for heteronomy, in terms of a connectedness to structures of cultural production. Subsequently, the subjectivity of the avant-gardes as autonomous ought to be reconfigured within the collective, heteronomous, ethos of State art and the regime's collectivist project. In a nutshell, language and forms doubtless obeyed the laws of experimentation and autonomy, but avant-garde modes of production and reception changed historically as a result of the new political subject represented by collectivities, crowds and composite mass audiences, and by the requirements of State art. By the 1930s in Italy, in order to achieve a position of relevance within the system of the arts of the day, the avant-gardes had to come to terms with the demands of mass society and of social modernization, as well as with a dictatorial regime. The total autonomy of the arts – in either its bourgeois or avant-gardist expression – was no longer conceivable, since under a repressive regime there was no notion of a total heteronomy. Conversely, it was imperative for the artists to find a suitable compromise between the two, one that could account for the collective as the new social and political subject. What connects these two stances, once again, is the idea of art as a modern aesthetic expression impacting on the modernization processes occurring within the social sphere, as we see happening in the publication of manifestos, participation to national and international exhibitions, debates and networks, and in the artistic production per se.[18]

Synthesis II: The Relationship between Modernity and Modernization as a Dialectical Project

The second wave of futurism began at the end of the First World War, as Marinetti sought both to rebuild the movement and to elevate it to the status of official State art.[19] In his pioneering 1969 *Il mito della macchina e altri temi del futurismo*, Enrico Crispolti has famously classified the futurism of the 1920s and 1930s as a second incarnation of futurism, characterized by an attention to a massified dimension of the artwork.[20] More recently, Christine Poggi has recognized an analogous hiatus between the first and second waves of futurism in the way the relationship between the past and present was articulated. If the rejection of tradition was *de rigueur* for the 'futurist of the first hour', in the 1920s and 1930s this relationship was more nuanced: staged as continuity rather than rupture.[21] In his book on futurism and politics, Giovanni Lista has identified some states of exception in what is very often perceived as a movement formed like a monolith: that is, between futurism and *Marinettismo*, and between textual expressions which can, according to their political or aesthetic alignments, be classified as 'futurist

---

[18] On the connections between futurist poetics and twentieth-century scientific discoveries, especially in mathematics and physics, see Cioli, *Il fascismo e la 'sua' arte*, 84–95, and Silvia Evangelisti, (ed.), *Fillìa e l'avanguardia futurista negli anni del fascismo* (Milan, Mondadori, 1996), 15–18 to situate the most cosmopolitan fringes of the Italian avant-gardes against contemporary European scientific discoveries.

[19] Crispolti, *Il mito della macchina e altri temi del futurismo* (Trapani, Celebes editore, 1969), 36.

[20] Ibid., 37–9.

[21] Christine Poggi, *Inventing Futurism* (Princeton and Oxford, Princeton UP, 2009), 232.

heterodoxy' or 'orthodoxia'.[22] In *Le due avanguardie*, in the same vein, Maurizio Calvesi has insisted precisely on a plurality within the movement, with both a right- and a left-wing brand of futurism that together constitute a defining feature of the movement.[23] Certainly, continuities and ruptures cannot but occur over more than three decades, but scholarly consensus exists on the movement's identity-defining interest in the overlaps between the artistic and the political spheres. By identifying ruptures within a trajectory of continuity, these scholarly works have argued for the importance of the historical dimension in the understanding of futurism since its true significance only comes to the fore if the movement is taken as a whole and not reduced to self-standing artistic or political moments.

If futurism has been explored from endless different perspectives, we should like to make particular mention here of Günter Berghaus's, Claudia Salaris's and Ernest Ialongo's contributions to the political history of futurism. Taken as a corpus, these publications have facilitated a non-polarized interpretation of the role the avant-gardes played both aesthetically and politically in shaping the 1920s, the 1930s and the first half of the 1940s.[24] Berghaus reconstructs with great detail the relationship between futurism and politics and argues for the need to fine-tune any dichotomy or overlaps between futurism and Fascism. Relying on archival evidence, Berghaus started questioning any assumption about futurism's unidimensional alignment with Fascism, an assumption we fully agree with in this book.[25]

Ialongo's study focuses on Marinetti's politics as the kernel of the movement to ask how the leader of an avant-garde movement became a fervent supporter of a reactionary political regime and thus provide an explanation for the longevity of such a collaboration. To answer this question, Ialongo foregrounds politics over aesthetics, continuity over rupture but, and more importantly, accounts for the historical dimension of Marinetti's political discourse with a detailed analysis of many of the most topical debates involving Marinetti as a futurist. By looking only at one aspect of futurism, scholars have risked falling victim of sectarian views that have encouraged a sometimes partisan interpretation of Marinetti's choices, while, according to Ialongo, and to us, only by looking systemically at *them* it is possible to gain a deeper understanding of futurism's impact upon Italian cultural and political societies from 1909 to Marinetti's death in 1944.[26] Ialongo further specifies the multiple nature of many of Marinetti's large claims on nationalism, anarchism, republicanism, anticlericalism, internationalism and situates them historically. Futurism as a system, thanks to Marinetti's leadership, acted like a chameleon, but not exclusively out of opportunism, since in his predispositions and in the steps he took he mirrored Mussolini, or better still as Ialongo put it: he worked 'towards Mussolini'. If aesthetic

---

[22] Giovanni Lista, *Arte e politica* (Milan, Mudima, 2009), 14.

[23] Maurizio Calvesi, *Le due avanguardie. Dal Futurismo alla Pop Art* (Rome-Bari, Laterza, 2020), 23–4.

[24] Crispolti, *Il mito della macchina*; Salaris, *Storia del futurismo*; Lista, *Arte e politica*; and Poggi, *Inventing Futurism*.

[25] Günter Berghaus, *Futurism and Politics: Between Anarchist Rebellion and Fascist Reaction, 1909–1944* (New York/Oxford, Berghahn, 1996).

[26] Ernest Ialongo, *Filippo Tommaso Marinetti*, 2, 4.

choices alone cannot explain why and how the movement enjoyed such a long duréee, their interconnectedness can helps us move forward, a critical stance Ialongo's study is perhaps less concerned with.

Walter Adamson and Monica Cioli have discussed the issue of the avant-gardes' hegemony within the fascist system of the arts. According to Adamson, the relationship between futurism and Fascism was mutable, eclectic and pluralistic: the futurists, in the guise of 'embattled avant-gardes', were profitably able to 'survive' the regime because of their ability to adapt and reshape themselves in relation to what they saw as a fluid rather than static political doctrine.[27] In this regard, Adamson has fittingly demonstrated how the often-antagonistic relationship between the Novecento and futurism shaped the Italian landscape since it started to grow from the early 1920s and continued throughout the 1930s; and we should like to add that it also showcased the need for an understanding of the arts as working as a system, even when dialectically conceived. Futurism's composite aesthetic practices, read against the international backdrop of the European avant-gardes, helped Marinetti to reinvent both himself and his movement constantly, an attitude that could be extended to many other protagonists of the day to resist aesthetic standardization.[28] Arguably, as we discuss in the last part of this book, with the 1940s war aerofuturism, the futurists climbed towards an hegemonic position within the system of the arts and within State art more overtly than any other movement, by reworking their aesthetic premises to produce artworks that symbolized Italy and the regime nationally and internationally.

Based on an impressive wealth of primary sources, Cioli's main argument is that futurism and Fascism found a common operational ground which suited both agendas. With such mutual understanding, a fascist model of art, or art under the Fascist regime, could come into existence.[29] Over three decades, futurism transformed itself from a putative largely aesthetic revolutionary practice to one of the most significant regimes of the arts under the dictatorship, particularly in respect to popular culture. Within the system of the arts, it is safe to claim that second futurism alone decided to address the large audiences that constituted the leading political subject sustaining the totalitarian project, especially after 1924. It did so by rephrasing, or reformulating, some theoretical statements of wider appeal and influence (e.g. aerofuturism and mechanical art), and also through the continual search for transformation and a reshaping of forms.[30] Following from Cioli's analysis, we could add that futurism is one of the artistic expressions that most clearly exemplifies the contradictions of the system of the arts and the regime's political agenda: on the one hand, futurism is part of that system; on the other, it surpasses it. And it can do so, when challenging the notion of realism as mimetic and representative to put forward instead an idea of realism as

---

[27] Walter Adamson, *Embattled Avant-Gardes*, 3.

[28] Ibid., 227–63 and 'How Avant-Gardes End—and Begin: Italian Futurism in Historical Perspective', *New Literary History*, 41/4 (2010), 871–2.

[29] Cioli, *Il fascismo e la 'sua' arte*, 53–5.

[30] For example, according to Bossaglia, the traditionalist Novecento could only find an international dimension when romanticizing itself as anti-abstract art in the 1920s, 'Milano negli anni Venti', in Paolo Biscottini (ed.), *Arte a Milano 1906–1929* (Milan, Electa, 1995), 177.

artificial construction and vitalism – as we have seen emerging in Bragaglia's early photodynamic experiments.

Still, the problem of the realist aesthetic continually resurfaced as central to the idea of State art: a problem the avant-gardes could not circumvent by reverting to a notion of artistic autonomy. However puzzling this might be, even abstracticism, the quintessentially autonomous art had to comply with the official demand for realism as per State art for it to be in a position to acquire any aesthetic significance, as his most prominent theorizer Carlo Belli admitted in his *Lettera sulla nascita dell'astrattismo in Italia*.[31] The Italian abstracticists theorized their own relationship between subjectivity and objectivity in a way that gained political resonance because of its intersections with architecture, as Belli openly stated.[32] His 1935 manifesto *Kn* stands in parallel to P. M. Bardi's political pamphlet *Rapporto sull'architettura* because it attempts at theorizing and politicizing abstracticism: 'the heresiarch wants a fascist era. In politics it already exists. In architecture, too, even though such manifestations happen outside of Italy: Le Corbusier, Mies van de Rohe, are all fascist architects', Belli claimed in the *Kn*, or, else, the arts can not but have a political function, we ought to conclude.[33] On this occasion, abstracticism could also fulfil its ambitions by calling for the aesthetic realm to function as a mirror of morals in art (another pillar of State art), with Belli's *Kn* performing as a 'Rosmini-like theological demonstration of the existence of art': or as a presupposition that the arts have to be enjoyed through an act of faith. As Caramel puts it: the relationship between Belli and the regime was 'theoretical rather than practical': naturally.[34] The second wave of the avant-gardes spanning futurism and abstracticism can be situated at precisely this juncture between aesthetic experimentation and political normalization, in its stab at finding an autonomous artistic dimension that could at the same time imitate, and be heteronomous to, the politics of the regime when tackling the questions of realism, subjectivity, the New Man/Woman, morality and modernization.

Fusions I: Futurisms and Their Politics

By 1929, Marinetti had been elected academician of Italy, and thus had been totally absorbed into the institutional structure by means of a process of inclusion that had

---

[31] Belli, in Giuliano Gori (ed.), *Anni creativi*, 17.

[32] See for example, Belli's declarations about abstract art as the only art apt to decorate rationalist houses, in *Anni creativi*, 13, 29–30.

[33] '*L'Eresiarca vuole una età fascista. Nella politica ormai esiste. Nell'architettura pure, anche se le manifestazioni sono fuori d'Italia: Le Corbusier, Mies van de Rohe, sono architetti dell'età fascista*', Belli, *Kn* (Macerata, Giometti & Antonello, 2016), 134. On this point, see also Paolo Fossati, *L'immagine sospesa. Pittura e scultura astratta in Italia, 1934–40* (Turin, Einaudi, 1972), 101 and Tempesti, *Arte dell'Italia fascista*, 204–5.

[34] Caramel, 'Carlo Belli e gli astrattisti italiani anni Trenta', in Giuseppe Appella, Gabriella Belli and Mercedes Garberi (eds), *Il mondo di Carlo Belli* (Milan, Electa, 1991), 73; see also Tempesti, *Arte dell'Italia fascista*, 199; Luigi Serravalli, 'Carlo Belli da Rosmini a Kandinsky', in Appella, Belli and Garberi (eds), *Il mondo di Carlo Belli*, 60; Carlo Belli, Giuseppe Appella (ed.), *Gli anni della formazione* (Rome, Edizioni della Cometa, 2001), on morality in art, 64. Letters from Peppino Ghiringhelli to Belli (27 September 1935, R.42/c.172, 17) and (18 May 1936, R.42/c. 172, 24) f. 'Peppino Ghiringhelli', MART.

started as early as 1918, with the putative foundation of the Fasci politici futuristi and the publication of a *Manifesto del partito politico futurista italiano*. This *Manifesto* was first issued in the final edition of the Florentine periodical *L'Italia futurista* in February 1918, before the official end of the First World War, and was later republished in the first issue of the fresh *Roma futurista*, founded in Rome by Marinetti, Mario Carli and Emilio Settimelli, with the aim of disseminating fascist political ideas.[35] From 1918 to the first Congresso nazionale futurista with its national celebrations of Marinetti in 1924, the relationship between the arts and politics became decidedly fluid and predisposed to rapid changes and abrupt transitions, as follows.

In 1918, the *Manifesto del partito politico futurista* was a mixture of often incoherent socio-political propositions about universal suffrage (including women's suffrage), the patriotic education of the proletariat, land reclamation for war veterans, progressive taxation, abolition of the obligatory army in favour of a voluntary one, the freedom to strike and of the press and an eighteen-hour working day. Further, a proposal for the technicalization of Parliament was included, with the recruitment of industrialists, agricultural workers and technical engineers and businessmen to form a rational and practical Parliament, that in turn could be swiftly dismantled if it failed to deliver results. The *Manifesto* also championed 'every passéist State intervention in the arts'.[36] Amongst its signatories were Massimo Bontempelli, Giuseppe Bottai, Mario Carli and the sculptor Ferruccio Vecchi, all on Marinetti's side, together with Piero Bolzon, Auro d'Alba, Ottone Rosai and Enrico Rocca. Not differently from any other artistic or political movement of the roaring 1920s, the *Manifesto*'s ecumenical tones called for a united political front, in a milieu characterized by fragmentation, in order to gain a prominent position and possibly find new allies to move further in a divided milieu. As Ialongo has observed, Marinetti

> allied with the Arditi through Mario Carli in the summer to begin the process. Thereafter he began publishing the FPP's newspaper *Roma futurista*, set up FPP units, or Fasci, throughout Italy, and secured an alliance with Mussolini. These combined forces converged on defending Italy's claims at the Paris Peace Conference and combating a resurgent Socialist Party, and they eventually formalized their union in the Fasci di Combattimento in March 1919.[37]

Differences began to surface nonetheless.[38]

Soon after, in April 1919, via the Rome-based publisher Facchi, Marinetti issued a collection of articles previously published in the journals *Roma futurista* and *L'Ardito*, in the usual form of a highly pitched political pamphlet entitled *Democrazia futurista*.

---

[35] On this point, see Antliff, 'Avant-garde Modernism', 231, and Golomstock, *Totalitarian Art*, 36. F. T. Marinetti, 'Manifesto del partito futurista italiano', *Roma futurista*, I (20 September 1918), 1–2 [reproduced in every issue, from nn. 2 to 11 throughout 1918].

[36] See also Volt, 'Aboliamo il Parlamento', *Roma futurista*, I/11 (30 December 1919), 2, and 'Come sostituire il Senato', *Roma futurista*, II/1-2 (5–12 January 1919), 1.

[37] Ialongo, *Filippo Tommaso Marinetti*, 76.

[38] Salaris, *Storia del futurismo*, 116–28. For a detailed analysis of futurism and politics, see Berghaus, *Futurism and Politics*.

Dinamismo politico. Marinetti called forcefully for a new democratic form, dynamic in spirit and led by a combination of individuals with particular qualities (the self-styled 'geniali' geniuses) reminiscent of his readings of Sorel.[39] At the first congress of the Fascist party in Florence in October 1919, for instance, Marinetti launched the idea of a vanguardist group, '*proletariato dei geniali*' (proletariat of the geniuses), to lead the country, proclaiming the need for the 'de-Vaticanizing' of Italy: an anti-monarchic, anticlerical group, but one that was not entirely democratic or socialist in conception. There was very little of significant novelty in this piece of writing: the notion of the arts as separate from politics was already present and clearly articulated in the 1918 *Manifesto*, as was a critique of the policies of previous governments about the arts. Marinetti's appraisal essentially reduced everything to an assay in soliciting the indiscriminate support of as many groups as possible after the war. Resonant of Mussolini's programme of the early days, everyone that accepted the policies of the plan, Marinetti declared, was welcome in the futurist party, regardless of aesthetic orientation or political preference. As Claudia Salaris has noted, the core of Marinetti's early political programme was deeply irrational, since it rejected class conflict to read instead the class struggle not in terms of hegemonic and subaltern groups of people, rather of violence and *elan vital*; it was nonetheless decidedly strategical and modern in so far as it sought to make the arts part of the political sphere.[40] Crucially, it failed to propose clear measures for change and reform: the most progressive, yet utopian, element of Marinetti's programme concerned reform of the '*tematiche istituzionali e di costume*'.[41] And even more crucially, he naively neglected to speak to collectivities as those political subjects who could persevere in their futurist revolutionary spirit and who would form the core of the regime's cultural and social policies, a grave mistake he will repeatedly make.

After the Impresa di Fiume (12 September 1919–27 December 1920) and the electoral humiliation of (November 1919), Marinetti finally left the Fasci di Combattimento.[42] The main point of disagreement was Mussolini's support of the collaboration between the proletariat and the 'productive bourgeoisie', especially in the provinces which were deemed to be the latest strategic players after the electoral defeat. By the time of the II Congresso nazionale dei Fasci italiani di combattimento in May 1920 in Milan, the relationship between the two movements was already strained and over the next couple of years Marinetti would return to, and remain firmly within, the realm of the aesthetic alone.[43] In the 1920 pamphlet, *Che cos'è il futurismo. Nozioni elementari*, Marinetti, Settimelli and Carli unambiguously stated once more that political and artistic futurisms were two different undertakings that addressed two different social groups.[44] The first was about the masses; the second, the elites: the

[39] Berghaus, *Futurism and Politics*, 28–33.

[40] Ibid., 117.

[41] Angelo D'Orsi, *Il futurismo tra cultura e politica*, 73.

[42] Enrico Rocca, 'Noi futuristi rivoluzionari vogliamo Fiume ad ogni costo! Viva Fiume!', *Roma futurista*, II/24 (15 June 1919), 1. For an analysis of Marinetti's departure from the Fasci di Combattimento and Fiume, see Ialongo, *Filippo Tommaso Marinetti*, 90–3.

[43] For further details about this process, see D'Orsi, *Il futurismo tra cultura e politica*, ch. 5, 111–28 and the section on primary texts, 294, 309.

[44] *Roma futurista*, II/7 (16 February 1919), 4. [reproduced in every issue until October].

futurist political party was the '*interprete immediato dei bisogni urgenti della nuova Italia, scaturita dalla vittoria*'.[45]

Attempting to correct his political lapse, in August 1920, with his thirty-page pamphlet 'Al di là del Comunismo' published in *La Testa di Ferro. Giornale del Fiumanesimo* directed by Mario Carli, Marinetti responded to Mussolini by reviving the movement's pre-war nationalist streak. He elaborated on the idea of old idea of *patria*, which could function as a point of convergence for the bourgeoisie and the proletariat, striving together to make Italy great again.[46] Once more, he wrote in largely palingenetic, nationalism, anticlerical and anti-republican tones, proposing no clear political programme or addressing a clear political constituency but instead hoping for another incarnation of a suitably indefinable 'genio anarchico' (a genius of anarchy) to prevail.[47] Intellectual and artists should be involved, he argued, in the running of the State and against any socialist intervention. This was the text that defined his distancing from Mussolini and from any active political militancy because neither Socialism nor Fascism were viable options for him: the former too close to a proletariat he did not believe in other than in generic terms, the latter too conservative and removed from his more progressive views on Church, armed forces, bureaucracy.[48] Meanwhile, after Fiume, Bottai – who had initially joined the debate with clear anti-socialist positions in two articles entitled 'Futurismo contro socialismo' and 'Insisto: futurismo contro socialismo' – rejected Marinetti's brand of futurism as politically inconclusive. The future Minister of Education reacted especially negatively to 'Al di là del Comunismo', and from then continued to align himself firmly with Mussolini.[49]

In delineating the main strategic moves of the period, Michele Dantini has explained this disagreement and has persuasively underscored the political meaning in Marinetti's *Manifesto del partito politico futurista* (1918), which was later transposed into the *Democrazia futurista. Dinamismo politico* (Milano, Facchi, 1919) and into the *Programma dei fasci di combattimento* (June, 1919) as far as corporativism was concerned. In Dantini's analysis, the wider idea of '*inegualismo*' (inequality) links Marinetti and Bottai because of their common antiparliamentary polemic which is associated to the idea of a technical government and to the slogan about the 'proletariat of the geniuses'.[50] Contrary to Marinetti, however, Bottai firmly trusted the role of the State, while the *Manifesto del partito politico futurista* rejected it as a form of hierarchical control: hence the growing distance between futurism and Fascism on a political level

[45] In D'Orsi, *Il futurismo tra cultura e politica*, 304.
[46] See Berghaus, *Futurism and Politics*, on how Martinetti was able to appeal to the workers, 56–7.
[47] Bottai disagrees from *L'Ardito*, Crali from *La Testa di ferro* approves.
[48] Salaris, *Storia del futurismo*, 131.
[49] Bottai started writing for *Roma futurista*, *L'Ardito*, *Nemici d'Italia*, *La Testa di ferro* in 1919. See D'Orsi's assessment of 'Al di là del Comunismo', as a 'masterpiece of vagaries', 136–7 and Ialongo, *Filippo Tommaso Marinetti*, 97–8. Bottai on 9 November 1919 had written a rather critical article 'Futurismo contro Socialismo', *Roma futurista*, II/46 (9 November 1919), 1–2, in which he declared the two political ideologies as incompatible, *Roma futurista*, II/52 (21 December 1919), 1.
[50] Dantini, *Arte e politica in Italia*, 69–70. See also Marinetti, *Democrazia futurista*, 53. And Marinetti, 'Il proletariato dei geniali', *Dinamo*, I/5 (June 1919), 8–9.

and the movement's reidentification as mainly an aesthetic force working towards the same ideological and political aim.

In his *Modernism and Fascism*, Roger Griffin has argued that, for the regime, the desire for palingenetic rebirth – despite not always working as a force for progress – still represented a constant aspiration towards a far-reaching idea of modernity. Griffin's theorization about modernism as able to 'provide a tool for understanding why fascism could attract the allegiance of some avant-garde artists, namely because a powerful elective affinity could arise between artistic and political revolutionaries who radically rejected the present and longed for the dawning of a new age' comes to life in the many attempts at creating myths to make the Fascist regime visible in public buildings.[51]

In September 1920 at the Congresso dell'Internazionale comunista another possible dialogue was at stake when it came the notorious publication by Anatoly Lunacharsky of *Marinetti rivoluzionario*, a text later more or less spontaneously reworked by Antonio Gramsci and published on 5 January 1921 in *L'Ordine nuovo* as 'Marinetti rivoluzionario?'. According to Gramsci, if structured and organized, futurism and communism working together had the potential to allow Italy to replicate a cultural situation similar to that underway in the Soviet Union. Gramsci recognized the anti-bourgeois power of the futurist conception of a disruptive role for the arts in its attempts to dismantle consolidated institutions. Following on from Gramsci's recognition of the futurists, the Sezione Proletkult Internazionale di Mosca was set up in Turin. Strategic in this climate was the Turinese group Sindacati artistici futuristi led by, amongst others, Tullio Alpinolo Bracci and by Fillìa himself. The group sought closer integration between the arts and the masses, unified in the name of the proletarian 'workforce': theirs was a social programme that facilitated the arts as a force for social transformation and militancy. In this regard, some fringes of the left hoped to galvanize action and agitate more support through Marinetti's stance on culture as fundamental to the very definition of politics as a self-standing set of practices.[52]

Hypothesis I: Linee

In an essay on Ruskin, Rancière discussed a notion of 'lines and ornament', proposing in relation to any distinction between Arts and Crafts, Art Deco, Bauhaus and Esprit Nouveau that: 'behind the battle between the future and the past, the industrial machine and the artisanal tool, rational straightness and the ornamental curve, there lies a far

---

[51] Griffin, *Modernism and Fascism*, 69.

[52] Gramsci, 'Marinetti rivoluzionario?', *L'Ordine nuovo*, (5 January 1921), in David Forgacs and Geoffrey Nowell-Smith (eds), *Antonio Gramsci: Selections from Cultural Writings* (London, Lawrence and Wishart, 1985), 97. If Gramsci had somehow seen in Marinetti the possibility of social renewal and palingenesis through the arts in order to support better education for the working classes, and thus their emancipation, the more conservative Amedeo Bordiga and his followers remained highly sceptical of the futurist leader's precise intentions, his bourgeois thinking, and his lack of sympathy with the proletariat as agent of social change.

more complex play between function and expression'.[53] He further points out that what all these artworks had in common was their attempt to reformulate an association between reality and sign, beginning to move away from an idea of art as representation to an idea of art as a reproduction of the inner mechanisms of an artwork programmed to work as a cogent whole.[54] The straight line was to be read as an aesthetic paradigm that aimed at rendering the conceptual complexity of objects, and thus reformulating the very same idea of the materiality of the artwork. In Rancière's analysis, 'if they rehabilitated the Ruskinian principle of "sincerity", and especially faithfulness to material, they did so in order to reject the swaying and swirling of the organic line by celebrating the beauty of functional lines and the honesty of the machine.'[55] Such was the case with Peter Marx, Peter Behrens and the Werkbund when they decided to convert to functional architecture.

Theorizing such a shift in the understanding of the relation between form, geometry and technique called for a constructive synergy, which ultimately aimed in 1920s and 1930s Italy to produce the total work of art. Style was to be seen not simply as an individual choice; rather it came into existence through a fusion of social ideas and ethical missions. Straight lines could therefore be continuous or fragmented, but from a metatheoretical level the effect had to be one of dissociation from reality, of self-awareness and self-consciousness, of shock and of non-organic movement; all in the name of what Benjamin described as a 'non-organic' or allegorical work of art that rejects the idea of totality for one of fragmentation instead. The second generation of futurists wanted a '*ricostruzione futurista dell'universo*', based on a notion of a plastic universe and geometrical forms, as evoked by the '*astrattisti futuristi*' Balla and Depero in Milan in 1915 with their *Manifesto*; one that could embrace the total work of art, as we have already seen with architecture, one that could make use of multiple materials, and one that could foreground a new understanding of the line as foundational to anti-representational aesthetics.[56] The *Manifesto* reclaimed the role of the machine as a means for connecting subject with object: there was both a spiritual as well as practical function to be performed.[57]

Many of these theoretical statements converged around abstracticism, aeropainting and mechanical art. Nonetheless, they can and should be traced back to Boccioni's early reflections on the relationship between technique, *linee-forza* and new materials as foundational to the re-semanticization of aesthetics, articulated by Boccioni in the *Manifesto tecnico della pittura futurista* in 1914.

> Boccioni: We say lines to mean the directions of the forms-colours.
>
> We need to start from the central nucleus of the object we want to create, to discover its own new laws, that is those new forms which link it invisibly, but mathematically to the **visible plastic infinitum** as well as to the **interior one**.

[53] Rancière, *Aisthesis*, 143.
[54] Ibid.
[55] Ibid., 147.
[56] The four-page Manifesto was printed in Milan at the Stabilimento Tipografia Taveggia – in Via Ospedale 3 on 11 March 1915. On this point, see also Poggi, *Inventing Futurism*, 231–5 and Calvesi, *Le due avanguardie*, 47.
[57] Ada Masoero, *Universo meccanico. Il futurismo attorno a Balla, Depero, Prampolini* (Milan, Mazzotta, 2003), 9.

My spiral-shaped architectonical construction creates instead continuity of forms for the spectators, a continuousness they admit to follow, through the **forms-strength** that derives from the **form-real**, a new closed line which contours the body in its several movements.[58]

Boccioni, then, evoked the necessity of rejecting the idea of the line as a close and continuous entity, to be replaced by the centrifugal *forma-forza* that tended towards a 'physical transcendentalism', a metaphysical state beyond materiality.[59] He consequently led the way towards a redefinition of the very basis of the understanding of the relationship between materiality, objectivity and subjectivity, as it would be developed not only by the second wave of futurism in the visual arts and sculpture but also by architects and muralists.

In a document written in September 1934 entitled 'Sviluppo dei principi boccioniani', Thayaht reflected upon Boccioni's aesthetic ideas and how to develop them further. The main element he considered was the straight line which, according to Boccioni, was the unique means which could lead to the primitive virginity of a new architectural construction of masses'.[60] This belief, for Thayaht, was the cardinal principle that new fascist art should be reprising and developing. He wrote:

The initial experiences of the contemporary primitivism, in which the straight line [...] is the essential element with which hyper-modern subjects are represented, with vigorous simplification which are intelligible to everyone.[61]

Thayaht's *Tuffo* is a majestic sculpture in plaster on a metal base.[62] It is almost 3 metres tall: a streamlined representation of a man diving into water with tremendous levity, creating concentric circles around his point of entry into the water. It was exhibited at Venice's 1932 XVIII Biennale, shortly after its completion but not in Berlin for the 1936 Olimpiade because it was too modern, according to Thayaht:

I am very sorry that my work, so favourably reviewed at the 1932 Biennale, has been excluded from the XI Olimpiade in Berlin, because the novelty of my

---

[58] 'Boccioni: Diciamo linee intendendo con ciò le direzioni delle forme-colore.' 'Noi dobbiamo partire dal nucleo centrale dell'oggetto che si vuol creare, per scoprire le nuove leggi, cioè le nuove forme che lo legano invisibilmente, ma matematicamente all'*infinito plastico apparente* e all'*infinito plastico interiore*.' 'La mia costruzione architettonica a spirale crea invece davanti allo spettatore una continuità di forme che gli permette di seguire, attraverso la **forma-forza** che scaturisce dalla **forma reale**, una nuova linea chiusa che determina il corpo nei suoi moti materiali', Boccioni, 'Linee-forza', in Zeno Birolli (ed.), *Pittura e scultura futuriste* (Milan, Abscondita, 2006), 101–2.

[59] Ibid., 101.

[60] See also '*il solo mezzo che potesse condurre alla verginità primitiva di una nuova costruzione architettonica delle masse*', *Manifesto tecnico della scultura futurista*, 11 April 1912, 1, published in Milan. Available online at this website: http://www.arengario.it/opera/manifesto-tecnico-della-scultura-futurista-4878/ (accessed 13 May 2020).

[61] F. 'Thayaht', Tha. 3.2.2. 13, 'Sviluppo dei principi boccioniani', MART.

[62] On Thayaht's trajectory towards sculpture, via Art Deco decorative patterns, see Fonti, *Thayaht. Un futurista eccentrico*, 21–3. To note how the Art Deco experience allowed Thayaht to develop a sense of the arts as synergically connected and not hierarchically organized, 21. On this point, see also Mauro Pratesi, *Futurismo e bon ton*, 37–8.

presentation and of the athletic gesture caught in its more DINAMIC moment in the race would have certainly been of interest to the international jury.

Perhaps the size is a problem? An alloy of metal would render better the meaning of the human torpedo as it slides into the water.[63]

In 1936, it was shown at the I Mostra nazionale dell'arte sportiva (First National Exhibition of Sport Art) organized by the Comitato Olimpico Nazionale Italiano (C.O.N.I.) and the Confederazione Fascista Professionisti Artisti in Rome together with Prampolini, Dottori, Crali, from where it was selected to be presented at the Olympics in Berlin.[64] After the work was rejected for its exceptional dimensions, Thayaht produced a second, smaller version, in a metallic alloy upon poet Raniero Nicolai's (at the Ufficio Stampa e Propaganda, C.O.N.I) advice which was to be accepted: the sole artwork was sent and exhibited there. In every aspect of life, from sculpture to design to fashion and photography, Thayaht believed in the principle 'simplify to innovate'.[65] In common with the futurists, he perceived a sense of unity in the arts, seeing a necessity for them to function as a concerted whole.[66] In the *Tuffo*, particularly, this principle is embodied, above all, in the use of the straight line applied to the representation of a 'modern subject': the New Man here embodied as a *siluro umano*, a human torpedo, in which grace and strength are fused together because fascist art, he wrote, is defined by rationalized aesthetics.[67]

Tuffo is one of Thayaht's works in which these codes emerge most clearly. The diver can be considered a modern, active subject of contemporary life, and one celebrated by Fascism and fascist art through sport. However, such coeval subject is reduced to its essential forms (a straight line, a square, circles), and stripped off of any ornament or psychological temperaments. Thayaht's theorization implied that this simplification has a 'social' goal: namely, to make art more comprehensible to all, and therefore more

---

[63] '*Sono dispiacente che l'opera mia, così favorevolmente quotata alla Biennale del 1932, sia stata esclusa dalla XI Olimpiade di Berlino, poiché la novità della mia presentazione e del gesto tipicamente sportivo colto nell'attimo più DINAMICO della gara avrebbe certamente interessato la giuria internazionale [...]. Forse la grandezza è una difficoltà? [...] Una fusione in metallo renderebbe ancora meglio il senso di siluro umano proprio del tuffatore di classe che lo infila nell'acqua*' (Florence, 25 April 1936, typewritten, to the On. Segretario of the C.O.N.I., C. Generale G. Vaccaro, Stadio del P.N.F., Via dello Stadio 14, Rome, Tha. 1.2.7, MART), for the whole correspondence see Scappini, *Thayaht*, 326–7, 489 (footnote 172). Carli, Dottori, Gambini, Prampolini are the only futurists artists to be invited to the Berlin Olympics in 1936. In the papers held at the MART there are other important documents which demonstrate Thayaht theoretical interest in the idea of the New Man as geometrically constructed "L'uomo Romano e quadrato. La lettera 'M', 'Problema della rotazione' and 'Il postulato del punto nello spazio e conseguenze' (F. 'Thayaht', Tha. 3.2.2., *c*. 1930, MART).

[64] In 1932, he takes part in the exhibition 'Prampolini et les peintres et sculptures futuristes italiens' at the established Galerie de la Renaissance in Paris in 1932 and at the 'Ausstellung Italienischer Kunst von 1800 bis Zur Gegenwart' in Berlin in 1937.

[65] 'Sintetismo in "versi". Semplificare per rinnovare' (F. 'Thayaht', 13 August 1938, Tha. 6.2, MART, in Scappini, 463–65). On Thayaht's biography, see Scappini, *Thayaht*, 1–27, and for the exhibitions and the Florentine futurist milieu, 16–17. As detailed by Scappini, Thayaht frequented assiduously both the Italian and international artistic circles and he holds exhibitions in Italy and abroad.

[66] Thayaht takes part in the first three Quadriennali, Scappini, *Thayaht*, 17–18.

[67] F. 'Thayaht', 'Arte fascista e la formula della resistenza', Tha. 3.2.2.11, 8 April 1934 (*ottobre* added in the original draft), MART.

popular. The straight line here is not Boccioni's *linea-forza*, but a dynamic line that creates strength across the three-dimensional play of volumes: no mechanical sample, but rather the kernel of the mechanism which organizes volumes through converging planes. In the Florentine artist's own formulation, it was a '*traiettiva*' ('a new word the best expresses this very new form of graphical representation), a form that:

> Studies the object during the time observed from points of view which are different and fixes a series of diverse aspects thinking about and comprehending them in a given space. When an object in movement follows a trajectory above a certain speed, the human eye perceives some unexpected deformation, and these are precisely the deformations that the 'traiettiva' will have to study and classify to produce a sound scientific theory.[68]

Such aesthetic progression from a fluid to a more geometrical line can be observed in, for example, Thayaht's *Violinista*, the *Bautta*, *Il flautista*, the *Direttore d'orchestra*, and was be embodied in his *Dux* in 1929, and in his collaborations with Marinetti. The *Tuffo*, despite this extreme rationalization of its forms through lines, remains alive, dynamic in its downward vertical spiralling and anthropomorphic rendering of the human body.

Hypothesis II: Universo Meccanico

Mark Antliff has implicitly denied any claim to total autonomy by futurism, when he commented that the second wave of futurism presented itself as fragmented not only in aesthetic but also political terms, citing Carrà and Soffici's appeal for a conservative 'return to order'; Bottai's, Mario Carli's and Settimelli's detachment from Marinetti over political affairs in the 1930s; and, crucially, Prampolini's theorization of a brand of futurism that came close to a dada-influenced aesthetic declension through the journal *Noi* that arguably represented the most important attempt to put the Italian avant-gardes on the international map.[69]

Just a handful of non-mainstream exhibitions taking place in Italy and abroad is enough to illuminate further Antliff's assertion and signal not only the development of new avant-garde aesthetics but their practical transgenerational applications in a way that preserved futurism international prestige, or even just consolidated the symbolic

---

[68] '*[i]l nuovo vocabolo che meglio si adatta ad esprimere questa forma nuovissima di rappresentazione grafica*' [...] '*studia l'oggetto nel tempo osservato da punti di vista differenti e ne fissa una serie di aspetti successivi considerandoli e compenetrandoli in un dato spazio. [...] Quando un oggetto in movimento segue una traiettoria oltrepassando una certa velocità, l'occhio umano percepisce delle deformazioni inaspettate, sono appunto queste deformazioni che la traiettiva dovrà studiare e classificare per giungere alla creazione della teoria scientificamente esatta*', Scappini, Thayaht, 35–6. For his sculptures, Thayaht created the taittite, an alloy made of alluminium and silver, precisely made of 91 per cent aluminium, 5 per cent silicon, 2 per cent tin, and 2 per cent nickel.

[69] Tzara signed the first dada manifestos in 1918 and then in 1920. See Berghaus, *Futurism and Politics*, 230 about Settimelli's expulsion from the movement and the PNF, 230.

capital accumulated in the first wave. In October and November 1920, alongside a retrospective of Boccioni, the new futurists were invited to show at the well-known Výstava Moderního Umění Italského k Oslavě Danteově in Prague. Over the next two years, the exhibition travelled to Brno and Košice in 1921, reaching topical locations such as Berlin and Düsseldorf in 1922. Around the same time, the transgenerational contingency made of Balla, Boccioni, Evola and Gerardo Dottori took part in the Exposition internationale d'art moderne in Geneva (running from December 1920 to January 1921), followed by another high-profile show, the Exposition des peintres futuristes italiens et conférence de Marinetti again with Balla and Prampolini, at the en vogue Galerie Reinhart at n. 12 Place Vendôme in Paris in May 1921, marking the return to the international scene of futurism in the company of mechanical art.

Closer to home, the well-received Esposizione futurista internazionale at Turin's Winter Club (27 March–27 April 1922) – organized by Marinetti and by Franco Rampa Rossi and then publicized on the *Ordine nuovo* – showcased several examples of mechanical art, from painting to architectural drawings by Pannaggi, Prampolini and Paladini, marking the birth of mechanical art on Italian soil. On 2 May 1922, the leading Casa d'Arte italiana in Rome hosted the 1 Esposizione della Section d'Or de Parisà with Archipenko, Léger and Prampolini. Prampolini's *senso plastico* (plasticity) diverged from Mondrian's geometries, from van Doesburg's dynamic diagonals, Ozenfant's purism and from Léger's cubism, since its plasticity required a constructive ethos foundational to the theoretical formulations of the Italian system of art as progressively evolving under the regime's State art – a notion that politicized as such was foreign to the European avant-gardes. Significantly, the same pattern was followed at regional level through the I Esposizione futurista in Macerata curated by Pannaggi in June and July 1922, for example, thereby demarcating the three-tier system of circulation of the second wave of futurist art.

The major international event which shaped the art world in both aesthetic and political terms was the Congress of Independent Artists held on 29–31 May in Düsseldorf in 1922. The main outcome of this congress could be identified in the split between the idea of arts as collective construction (Richter and Lissitzky) and that of pure subjective abstraction (van Doesburg and Hausmann).[70] With Ruggero Vasari and Prampolini headlining the Italian delegation to the congress, as Cioli discusses, there seemed to be the beginnings of a shift from a strictly defined machine perspective to a more organic view of a spiritual fusion between Man and the universe, as Prampolini set out in the paper he delivered at the event, 'L' estetica della macchina e l'introspezione meccanica nell'arte'.[71] Prampolini's intervention also called for the State to support the arts, particularly the avant-garde arts, and for promoting more frequent international exchanges.

---

[70] Cioli also discusses Prampolini's *L'estetica della macchina e l'introspezione meccanica nell'arte* published in De Stijl as a '*prodotto dei dibattiti che avevano animato il Congresso degli artisti progressisti*', which took place in Düsseldorf in 1922 (*Anche noi macchine!*, 115) and which marked the leadership of Prampolini; see, Andrea Baffoni, *Contro ogni reazione. Enrico Prampolini teorico e promotore artistico* (Città di Castello, Lantana, 2015), 149.

[71] Godoli, *Guide all'architettura moderna*, 40–1 and Cioli, *Anche noi macchine!*, 117 for the relationship with De Stijl and the aftermath of the Düsseldorf congress.

In a renowned 1922 article on modes of participation and agency of intellectuals within the public sphere, Vinicio Paladini sought to form a coalition between artistic and political vanguards of a Bolshevik orientation, described as the chief attempt at finding a viable compromise between Marinetti's nationalism and the Communist Party's internationalism. Paladini shaped a new type of intellectual regrettably reminiscent of dated Leninist elitism because he did simplistically elevate forms of mental activity above practical ones. In all this, the machine was still to be the engine of the revolution, however permanent the latter might or might not have been.[72]

In June 1922, Pannaggi and Paladini published the *Manifesto dell'arte meccanica futurista* in *La Nuova Lacerba*, with two of their artworks inserted inside: Pannaggi's *Proletario* and Paladini's *Composizione meccanica*.[73] Less than a year later, in May 1923, Prampolini, Pannaggi and Paladini published another manifesto, *L'arte meccanica. Manifesto futurista* in the journal *Noi*, with an additional commentary by Paladini entitled 'Estetica meccanica', on page 2.[74] Pannaggi and Paladini had written the second version of the manifesto in October 1922 and Prampolini, at that time editor-in-chief of the journal, decided to add his signature in the *Noi* version.[75] Silvia Evangelisti has detailed the potential influences on Fillìa of the European avant-gardes, from purism to constructivism, during his formative years in Paris, to show how they impacted on his 'constructive rigour', and has argued for the centrality of *Noi* as a vehicle for disseminating such works in Italy.[76] There are identifiable differences between the two versions of the *Manifesto*: the second one being much longer and placing unambiguous

---

[72] See Paladini, 'La rivolta intellettuale', *Avanguardia: giornale della Federazione italiana giovanile socialista aderente al P.S.I.*, 15 (23 April 1922), in Giovanni Lista, *Arte e politica*, 196–8. Other than Paladini's first article, similar contributions about a new art, socially aware and interdisciplinary in nature, can be found in *Noi, Interplanetario*. Comprehensive studies of futurist left-wing groups across the peninsula, and not only in Rome and Turin, are Carpi, *Bolscevico immaginista* and *L'estrema avanguardia del Novecento* and the detailed study on the relationship between the Italian and Russian avant-gardes by Christina Brungardt, *On the Fringe*.

[73] See Cioli, *Anche noi machine!*, 111–15 and Poggi, *Inventing Futurism*, 240–5 for a discussion of the *Manifesto*. On the precursors of l'arte meccanica and on Prampolini's relationship with Archipenko, see Andrea Baffoni, *Contro ogni reazione*, 106. According to Poggi and Masoero (*Universo meccanico*, 7), the *Manifesto dell'arte meccanica futurista* was first published anonymously in Rome in *La Nuova Lacerba*, 1 (20 June 1922), and then reprinted as a revised version in 1922 in *Noi*, series II, I/2 (May 1923), 1–2. Prampolini added his own signature without Paladini and Pannaggi's permission (Poggi, *Inventing Futurism*, 244) and was later reprinted in *Il Futurismo*, II/8 (1 October 1923), 1–2, a journal with a print run of fifty thousand copies. Cioli attributes to the *Manifesto* published in *La Nuova Lacerba* a clear political meaning since it showed a progressive shift on the left of certain fringes of the movement, before the March on Rome (ibid., 113–14).

[74] I/II, 1–2. According to Masoero, earlier elaborations of similar ideas can be found in Prampolini's 'Estetica della macchina e l'introspezione meccanica nell'arte' (2, 1922, *De Stijl*, with the title 'Fragment de la relation italienne présentée du congrés international de Düsseldorf') and in another text he published in the same year in Prague in *Veraycon*, March–April 1922 (Masoero, *Universo meccanico*, 7). In this text, Prampolini is in favour of State support for the arts.

[75] Poggi, *Inventing Futurism*, 244 on Prampolini 'appropriation'. Poggi ascribes the changes in attitude to Mussolini's raise to power while Cioli claims one should look more carefully at the European aesthetic inclination towards the machine as discussed in the Congresso degli artisti progressisti in May 1922 in Düsseldorf to account for the change (244–5, Cioli, *Anche noi machine!*, 115–90).

[76] Evangelisti (ed.), *Fillìa*, 24–5.

emphasis on the spirituality of the machine, and written in less iconoclastic tones.[77] Of course the machine had been central to futurism since 1909, but upon its return, it was reshaped as an organic form that could contour the relationship between art and life.[78] On this theoretical juncture, predictably, two new elements were added: its spirituality and a widespread necessity for 'construction', perceptible across the many artistic fields converging squarely in State art. In an earlier article '*L'atmosferastruttura*. Basi per un'architettura futurista', Prampolini had made such connections rather explicit; and he wrote that:

> Just like painting is an abstract consequence of sculpture, and sculpture is an abstract consequence of architecture, thus architecture has been an abstract consequence of natural elements which have originated because of intrinsic needs of primitive human life.[79]

Likewise, Fillìa's 'Valori plastici' sought a geometrical structure that could accommodate them by relying either on chromatic plays or a fluidity of lines converging on an end point. For Fillìa, as would too be the case for Prampolini – and differently to how it was for Boccioni and the first wave of futurists – composition was not about bodies in motion, rather about the architecture of the composition. It was a question of technique and materials, just as architecture was a question of new materials, languages and designs, and as politics was a question of fusing different constituencies and agendas together.[80] In terms of reflection on mechanical art, the distinctive contribution of the futurists was the emphasis on the subject and their subjectivity, not as passively guided by the machine, but as an active cog in the machine itself, moved by an analogical and geometrical psycho-chromatism, that was itself imbued by an ethical, religious and mystical spirit (contrary to abstracticism).

Christine Poggi has also written on Pannaggi and Paladini's *Manifesto*, contending that 'attention is focused on the body, its metallisation, standardised anonymity, and fragmentation into distinct though interconnected parts, and the interchangeability of these parts with the mechanical tools they engage'.[81] Poggi insists on the aristocratic nature of the 'new race' that communism would shape; and we might also argue that

---

[77] Of the same years are Prampolini's *Simultaneità architettonica*, 1921, and *Simultaneità di paesaggio*, 1922. On the intertextual references echoing previous *Manifestos* by Marinetti, Severini, Russolo, see Masoero, *Universo meccanico*, 7, Evangelisti (ed.), *Fillìa*, 19, Poggi, *Inventing Futurism*, 241–4.

[78] *Manifesto*, 2.

[79] 'Come la pittura è una conseguenza astratta della scultura, e la scultura è una conseguenza astratta dell'architettura, così l'architettura è stata una conseguenza astratta degli elementi vegetali della natura originati per evoluzione di necessità intrinseche della vita umana primitiva', 'L'"atmosferastruttura" basi per un architettura futurista', *Noi*, II/1-2 (February 1918), 1, to be read alongside Virgilio Marchi, 'Sant'Elia, architetto futurista', *Noi*, series II, I/2 (May 1923), 3 and Antonio Sant'Elia, 'L'architettura futurista', *Noi*, ibid., 4–5. In *Dinamo*, directed by Settimelli, Carli and Remo Chiti, Virgilio Marchi published an article to argue for a connection between futurist architecture and the aesthetics of plasticity which were advocated also by the Novecento movement, 'Architettura futurista', I/5 (June 1919), 5.

[80] Fillìa and Giuseppe Oriani, 'Progetto di chiesa futurista', in Fillìa, *La nuova architettura*, 67.

[81] Poggi, *Inventing Futurism*, 241.

this is perfectly in line with Marinetti's previous statements about his ideal political party.[82] It is problematic not to see many obvious connections with pre-First World War futurism in this 1923 *Manifesto*: speed and movement, revolution and transition, modernity vs tradition are all relentlessly evoked. Nonetheless, it is indisputable that this very same *Manifesto* functioned as a robust nexus between the two moments in the history of the movement, by announcing for the arts a more 'positive' role in shaping the social good. Poggi further observes, in accord with Umberto Carpi, how this *Manifesto* was also a testimony of a shift to the left by the second wave of futurism in an attempt to increase social momentum.[83] In all, however, this *Manifesto* together with the journal *Stile futurista* (Turin, 1934–5) edited by Fillìa and Prampolini was one of the most significant statements about the role of the arts within modern society. In her recent study of the role of machines in futurist aesthetics, Cioli has justifiably concluded that in this later *Manifesto* the machine had the utopian mission of initiate social change by renovating its most imminent environment. In this specific transformative effort, she has located the major difference between the first and second waves of futurism.[84]

Pannaggi's *Treno in corsa* illuminates the first type of aesthetic of the machine: geometrical lines woven together in vorticial movement, with a central, conic and lighter focus point looking at the viewer and diagonally facing a brighter rectangular on the opposite side of the painting. Any figurative shape is thus removed from the work, and yet it preserves a dramatic tone, achieved through geometry.[85] Paladini's *Ritmi meccanici* is another example of this early machine aesthetic, with a conglomeration of industrial-style shapes at the centre which divide the composition into upper and lower parts in dialectical opposition.[86] For the factory is squarely the site of revolt, according to his political beliefs (as he had also argued in his paper 'La rivolta intellettuale').[87] Depero's artistic production of the period moves somehow sideways from the more heterodox expressions of mechanical art. *Ciclisti* (1922), with its '*scadenze salde e volumetriche*', rejected Boccioni's *linee-forza*; *Marinetti temporale patriottico* (1924) presented a synthesized view of the futurist leader with the colours of the Italian flag and a whirl of lines.[88] Depero's wall-hanging *Guerra=festa* (1925) sits at the vortex of two temporalities, marking an aesthetic transition: the pre-futurist war, seen as a cathartic moment, and then its somehow playful, dadaist replica as '*festa*' (party).[89] The colours (the white, red, green of the Italian flag with a border of flags, daggers

---

[82] Ibid., 241; on this point see also Cioli, *Anche noi macchine!*, 113.

[83] Poggi, *Inventing Futurism*, 241.

[84] Cioli, *Anche noi macchine!*, 111–12. See Baffoni, *Contro ogni reazione*, 136–41 about Čapek's play *Rossum's Universal Robots*, 1920, which introduced the new human machines, the robots.

[85] 1922, 120 × 100 cm, Fondazione Carima – Museo Palazzo Ricci, Macerata. See also Poggi's analysis of Depero's *Guerra=festa* and *Treno nato dal sole*, in *Inventing Futurism*, 238–9 and for a similar take on the notions of speed and machine, Ivo Pannaggi *Treno in corsa*, 1922 (oil on canvas, 100 × 120 cm, Fondazione Carima, Palazzo Ricci, Macerata).

[86] (1922), featured in *Noi*, series II, 1/2 (May 1923), 10.

[87] *Avanguardia. Giornale della Federazione italiana giovanile socialista aderente al P.S.I.* 16, 15 (April 23, 1922), 3.

[88] Masoero, *Universo meccanico*, 12.

[89] Wool appliqué on cotton backing, 330 × 243 cm, Galleria Nazionale d'Arte Moderna, Rome.

and mask-like heads) prevail over lines, in an attempt at creating a chaotic atmosphere suspended between reality and imagination and, in all this, a denial of any historically bounded dimension in favour of a somehow primitive notion violence. The *festa* has been mechanized and transformed from rural, purifying celebration following nature to, instead, an historical moment that obeys the rules of politics (with the Blackshirts in the middle).[90] Such theorizations and practices can all be linked more broadly to how the system of the arts will develop in the two decades to follow. The sacralization of politics needed a spiritual declension: the Fascist anthropological and its putative utopian revolution were not about 'deconstruction' but about 'construction'. The dissonant element in this 1920s scenario was the drive towards 'realism', 'morality' and 'representation' imposed by State art, something the futurists will address in the 1930s.

In the same issue of *Noi* that had featured the second version of the *Manifesto dell'arte meccanica* in May 1923, three artworks appeared one after the other in a progressive glorification of the machine: Depero's *Gloria plastica di Marinetti*, Pannaggi's *Donna macchina da cucire* and Prampolini's *Ritmi spaziali meccanizzati*. Even a brief comparison of these early works and Fillìa's own work in his most productive years, such as *Idolo meccanico* (1925) or *Biciclette* (1925), indicates for him the extent to which *materialità* (the material) and the mechanical idols are animated and becomes almost psychologized.[91] The machine must produce new morals and, as Poggi notes, in its stylized geometry Fillìa's *Idolo meccanico* evokes the 'formal character of a Byzantine icon'.[92] His *Nudo meccanico* (1925) is characterized by what Crispolti has termed the 'spiritual alphabet' that accompanied the research into mechanical art. *Nudo meccanico*, which Fillìa went on to use as an illustration for his collection of short stories entitled *La morte della donna* (1925), employed chromatisms to point towards a psychological anguish reflected into the geometrical compositions of mechanical art.[93] For instance, Prampolini's contemporaneous *Architettura femminile* (1925) used parallelepipedal volumes and more vibrant colours: the yellow of the female figure, set against the dark backdrop of the landscape, encourages a robust response in the viewer; while the linearity of the compenetrating volumetric plans is toned down.[94] Contrary to Prampolini who borrowed from his friend Archipenko, as Crispolti observes, Fillìa's strong political left-wing imperative at least until 1926 was coupled with a religious imperative.[95] This combination endorses a view of technology which is not simply an aesthetic moment, but rather a means of communication between theory, practice and social reality, as well as an exploration of the unconscious.[96] Paladini trusted

---

[90] Exhibited for the first time at the XV Biennale in 1926, it enjoyed considerable success and was purchased by the Galleria Nazionale d' Arte Moderna di Roma (where it still is) for forty thousand lire. See Poggi, *Inventing Futurism*, 238.

[91] F. 'Fillìa', 'Spiritualità aerea', 5813/I and II, MART.

[92] 'Manifesto dell'arte sacra', in Poggi, *Inventing Futurism*, 252.

[93] Ink on paper, 22 × 9 cm, Gianni Mattioli collection, Milan.

[94] Tempera and oil on canvas, 70 × 92 cm, private collection, Rome.

[95] Enrico Crispolti, 'L'avventura di Fillìa fra immaginario meccanico e primordio cosmico', in Enrico Crispoliti (ed.), *Fillìa*, 37.

[96] On this point, see also Carpi, *Bolscevico immaginista*, discussing Pannaggi and Paladini's positions, 55–94 and Christina Brungardt, *On the Fringe of Italian Fascism* for a recent assessment of their collaboration, including its discrepancies.

mechanical art to be able to transform itself into proletarian art but – an architect himself – noted nonetheless that such art had very little potential for application in real-life architecture. If any aesthetic practices could be applied to architecture, it was constructivism, where the rational simplification of volumes and lines would better serve the purpose of meeting people's needs.[97]

These three areas were pivotal in the development of futurist aesthetics in the late 1920s and 1930s, signposting the main trends the movement followed, especially in connection with State art.[98] Colour had the primary function in creating the work of art, something which along with fluidity of volumes would define the aesthetic of both decades across the whole spectrum of futurist art. These sets of poetics were the first attempt in linking chromatism with psychological development in what is known as 'psychological analogism': 'creations which fix "an elementary chromatic conception", fitting squarely with the aesthetic of the machine, and in general with postcubist "purism". Yet, with a rigour and creative clarity which recall interwar European concretism'.[99] New lines of aesthetic enquiry were linked in different ways to the main themes that had developed around futurist art: the poetics of mechanical art, from the 1920s onwards; and later the repertoire of aeropainting, from the 1930s until the fall of the regime. Essentially, the *mechanical line* of the 1920s and the *organic line* of the 1930s both pointed towards a reconfiguration of subjectivity within a complex objectivity that exceeded the individual and became collective (albeit still at spiritual and cosmic levels). Mechanical art, the cosmic universe, aeropainting and futurist architecture are all characterized by intense chromatism and flat volumetric constructions immersed in oneiric and aerial dimensions, which call for a transcendent collective identification with a superior reality, may it be that reality the State.

On the opposite side of the peninsula, in the Friuli-Venezia Giulia region, other groups were gathering around a concept of the new age of futurism that functioned similarly as a critical aesthetic response to the various *Marinettismi* through international dialogue that was facilitated by geographical proximity with the Norther and Eastern European countries. The Giuliano style of futurism was led by Sofronio Pocarini (Gorizia), Michele Leskovic (Escodamè, Udine) and Bruno G. Sanzin (Trieste), and then later by the aeropainter Tullio Crali (Gorizia). On his first visit to Gorizia on 4 March 1922, Pocarini interviewed Marinetti, and criticized him for the conservative turn the movement had taken. These young minds included Leskovic, Roberto Clerici and Piero Albrighi, who wrote the manifesto *Svegliatevi studenti d'Italia!*, published by the Direzione del Movimento Futurista in Milan, proposing the renewal of formal education and the inclusion of technical elements. Anchored to the early *Manifestos*, these young fringes were critical of the centralization and normalization that futurism

---

[97] See Paladini, 'Arte d'avanguardia e futurismo' (Rome, 1923) and 'La rivolta intellettuale', *Avanguardia*, in Lista, 194–6, and Godoli, *Guide all'architettura moderna*, 42–4 for a description of his architectural projects.

[98] On previous contributions by Fillìa and Bracci on the debate on the arte meccanica, geometry and chromatism, see Crispolti (ed.), *Fillìa*, 21.

[99] Ibid., 24. The artworks of this period were largely displayed at the 'Sale futuriste' exhibition in Turin in January 1925.

was undergoing in attempting to became State art, having hoped it would take a more experimental role, particularly on the culture front.

In 1923, in an attempt at channelling centrifugal forces and regaining control, Marinetti published in both *Futurismo* and *Noi* his own 'manifesto' for the fascist government, entitled *I diritti artistici propugnati dai futuristi. Manifesto al governo fascista:* a return, as it were, to the contested matter of the role of the arts in the political arena.[100] Marinetti envisaged intellectuals as autonomous figures with no requirement to interfere in the political sphere. Marinetti asked for a long list of benefits for artists and for modern artists in particular, including special credits and favourable conditions for travelling internationally; in return, artists with their art would have supported the regime.[101] This important positional paper signalled the reconciliation between Marinetti and Mussolini in respect of their separate positions held on different grounds and the start of the race for hegemony on reciprocally beneficial political and aesthetic terms: whether or not the political and the aesthetic domains had to be ruled by one Duce at a time, they were nonetheless mutually dependent and existing beyond rigid classifications such as autonomous and heteronomous, especially when viewed as a system which was soon to be functioning under the overarching concept of State art.

Fusions II: The Machine of Exhibitions: 1924–30

In 1924, the socialist MP Giacomo Matteotti was assassinated by fascist squads, and the regime began to silence any form of dissent that could be detrimental to political and artistic unity and a steady process of statalization. On 23 and 24 November, the I Congresso nazionale futurista took place in Milan, with Marinetti and Mino Somenzi again in charge. On 23 November 1924, the first of the granting of Solemn National Honours to F. T. Marinetti premiered at the Teatro dal Verme in Milan, sponsored by a committee chaired by Somenzi, Prampolini and Azari.[102] As a result of the previous skirmishes between the two Duces, this congress was marked by an attitude of depoliticization of the movement and of consolidation of its artistic sphere of influence, which was to demarcate the years to come. Marinetti and his peers (Depero, Dottori, Polidori for theatre, Fillìa, and Azari for aerofuturism) claimed for themselves an artistic position with no direct repercussions for the political scene, and Mussolini agreed with it. In 1294 Marinetti moved to Rome with his wife Benedetta Cappa. Rome rather than Milan would become the main centre for the second wave of futurism, together with a distinctive geographical cluster that included Gorizia, Macerata, Trento, Trieste, Palermo and Udine – to name just a few of the cultural and linguistic realities that illustrated the spread, reach and strength of what we might call

---

[100] *Il Futurismo*, II/5 (1 March 1923), 1–4 and *Noi*, series II, I/1 (April 1923), 1–2.

[101] Ialongo, *Filippo Tommaso Marinetti*, 143.

[102] F. T. Marinetti, 'Primo Congreso Futurista Italiano', *Il Futurismo*, IV/11 (11 February 1925), 2–3 and 'Primo Congresso Futurista. Le solenne onoranze nazionali a F. T. Marinetti', ibid., V/11 (11 January 1926), 1–23.

the building-years of the second wave of futurism.[103] Almost unavoidably, this initial fragmented phase had to come to an end in 1924 when a minimalist programme for futurism was drafted, implicitly seeking its election to the rank of State art, whilst simultaneously rejecting the notion that the arts had any social mission to carry out.[104]

Notwithstanding this volte-face, at the 1924 Venice Biennale, under the patronage of the *grande dame* Margherita Sarfatti, the Novecento Gruppo dei Sei was invited to exhibit nineteen artworks and the futurists were not welcome.[105] In his habitually flamboyant manner, which gave him a degree of artistic gravitas and indirect soft power, Marinetti had a very disruptive response at the opening of the Biennale and again at the Caffè Florian in Piazza San Marco; unfortunately, perhaps, only in front of a limited and somewhat sceptical audience.[106] That same year, in March, in response to Sarfatti's obstructionism, via publisher Campitelli in Foligno, Marinetti circulated his third and last political pamphlet *Futurismo e fascismo,* hinting at a possible reconciliation between the two Duces after a period of marginalization. Marinetti's arguments were predictably far more conciliatory than the ones pushed forwards in the *Diritti artistici dei futuristi*, for he intended to leave the protagonist role to Mussolini, so as in return to assert even more strongly his interest in aesthetics as a potential means of facilitating the effectiveness of the political realms, but not vice versa. Artists, notwithstanding their withdrawal from all things political, should continue to act upon social transformations, regardless of the political sentiments of both parties: for Marinetti the nation was still the supreme entity futurists should have an obligation towards.

At the Convegno per la cultura fascista held in Bologna (29–30 March 1925), Marinetti's intervention repositioned futurism in relation to the regime's political agenda: he spoke of the need for a new national art and proposed the setting up of an Istituto di credito (Credit Institute) for artists; in this way, he unambiguously linked the arts with the State through the question of financial support, in line with Bottai's own vision of precisely the same constitutive relationship (see Agon 1). These events marked the start of a new phase, focused on delivering aesthetic paradigms that could win the race for hegemony and at the same time maximize futurism's national and international aesthetic value and visibility.

In his efforts to win accolades and preserve the cosmopolitanism of the early days of the movement, Marinetti returned to Russia in 1925, where he had last been in 1913. In that first trip, reactions to Italian futurism had been more positive, but in 1925, his relationship with Fascism and his more explicitly bourgeois artistic and

---

[103] From December 1918, the Fasci politici futuristi were established and by 1919 there were about twenty disseminated across Italy.

[104] 'Programma', *Il Futurismo* (single issue) published on 9 March 1924 by the Sindacati Artistici del Movimento Futurista Torinese directed by Tullio Alpinolo Bracci and Fillìa, in Carpi, *L'estrema avanguardia,* 107–8.

[105] On this occasion, Paladini published a book entitled *L'Arte nella Russia dei Soviet* (La bilancia, 1925) in which he discusses Russian artists participation to the Biennale while drawing similarities between the Italian avant-gardes and the Russian ones in terms of constructivism. He also expresses some reservations about Malevich's suprematism (*Manifesto* published in 1924) and laments the absence of constructivism the Venice Biennale in 1924.

[106] See Enrico Prampolini 'L'arte futurista italiana esclusa dalla XIV Biennale veneziana. La protesta di Marinetti alla presenza del Re', special issue *Noi,* series II, II/7–8 (1924), 12.

social leanings triggered grave doubts amongst Russian's intelligentsia first and at home later.[107] In *Literatura in revolucija,* published in Moscow in 1923, Lev Trotsky described futurism as an intrinsically bourgeois movement. Mayakovsky, likewise, had never shown a particularly positive disposition towards futurism, as evidenced in his nine questions to the bourgeois Marinetti.[108] Despite such setbacks for the 'Caffeina d'Europa', futurism's international resonance continued to grow. Notably, Balla, Depero and Prampolini were invited to show at the Exposition internationale des arts décoratifs et industriels modernes in Paris in 1925, introduced by Sarfatti in person. Nationally, too, after futurism's slender presence at the II Biennale romana, that had featured only Dottori, the III Biennale romana. Esposizione internazionale di belle arti (1–30 June 1925) hosted a room that was dedicated entirely to the futurists, with a Mostra futurista of Balla, Depero, De Pistoris, Dottori, Marasco, Prampolini, Tato and a Boccioni retrospective, including a significant fifty artworks. Amongst the exhibits, there were some important, field-defining examples of mechanical art, such as *Architettura femminile, Costruzione spaziale, Ritmi di danza, Costruzione dinamica dello spazio* and *Paesaggio di Capri* by Prampolini; *Splendori meccanici alpestri, Ballerine di cristallo* by Depero; *Idea luminosa, Scienza che spacca* by Balla; and *Plastica dei colori in 4 versioni* by Dottori.[109] In his introduction to the exhibition, Marinetti did not enter political grounds, underlining how the futurist painter '*crea immediatezza*' and '*meccanizza l'opera*', since the machine is a force for life, which can alone bring together theory and creation.

The year 1925 represented yet another turning point in the development of the aesthetic of the machine and in the transformation of the line from geometrical to 'organic'. In Fillìa and Bracci's contribution to the *futur-fascist* journal *L'Impero,* particularly in the article, 'La pittura spirituale' (18 March 1925), they drew an interesting parallel between the three notions of 'plastic construction', 'chromatisms' and 'new architecture', thereby indicating a broader concern of the time. The arts had to cut across innovation and State art to function as system and not as individually defined fields.[110] Fillìa theorized his religious and mystical artistic disposition in the *Manifesto dell'arte sacra meccanica,* written with Calligaris and Curtoni (*L'Antenna,* 1926), and in *L'idolo meccanico* (*L'Impero,* 1925), in which a man-cum-machine hybrid referred to as 'the mechanical idol' still 'dominated its world' and ruled over human manifestations.[111]

---

[107] Armando Zanetti, *Il Giornale d'Italia,* (5 March 1914), in Lista, *Arte e politica,* 135–42.

[108] De Michelis, *L'avanguardia trasversale,* 179. Nikolay Gorlov does not critique futurism as such but that strand of futurism close to Fascism, 191. For details about Marinetti's first trip to Russia in 1913, Salaris, *Storia del futurismo,* 61–2.

[109] *La casa del mago, Ciclista veloce, La rissa* (Depero); *Gatti futuristi* (Balla); *Primavera umbra* (Dottori).

[110] '*Gli oggetti naturali perdono la loro forma primitiva e per compensarsi in una costruzione plastica, divengono un tutto indispensabile e ottengono la nuova architettura. Annullamento perciò dello spazio vuoto, della linea indeterminata, del colore senza importanza*', Fillìa-T. A. Bracci, 'La pittura spirituale', 3. See also the article Fillìa, 'L'idolo meccanico', *L'Impero,* (20 July 1925), 3.

[111] Poggi, *Inventing Futurism,* 251. Under the cosmopolitan headings of 'Art, mechanical and cubist scenography, ballets russes, Russian theatre (Meyerhold, Kamernij), scenography in Latvia and Ceko-Slovakia', *Noi* published works by constructivists, dadaists and the De Stijl (Léger, Picasso, Pitoëff, Marcoussis, Survage, Kiesler, Huszar-Wils, Smaltzigaug, Tschelischef, Vesnin, Exter, Tatlin, Strunke). For the front cover of the journal, see http://www.arengario.it/opera/n-6789-anno-i-ii-serie-numero-speciale-teatro-e-scena-futurista-12172/ (accessed 10 May 2020)

The triple track – national, regional and international – of futurism continued to function and thus give the movement a significant advance in public exposure. However, Marinetti's race for hegemony had to happen in line with the regime's progressive process of centralization of infrastructures and powers. After their controversial exclusion from the 1924 Biennale, the futurists were powerfully in evidence at the 1926 Biennale, showing a total of sixty artworks, and with all major and indeed minor figures of the movement invited for a *sui generis* ceremony of national consecration. Because of the devaluation of their currency, Russia had to cancel its participation in forty international exhibitions in 1925, including the 1926 Biennale. After some negotiations between Maraini, the Politburo and the Russian ambassador to Italy Kerzenec, just ten days before the opening, it was decided that the Pavilion should have been used to exhibiting Italian artists, and the futurists were, possibly and largely by implication only, the most modern amongst Italian artists.[112] They were hosted in the USSR Pavilion with their mechanical art on full display and, also on display, aerofuturist Azari's debut exhibit, *Prospettive di volo.*[113] Prampolini led the way, as he would do for the whole 1930s, and offered a substantial amount of works forming in themselves a system: five mechanical and synthetic artworks (*Architettura femminile, Danza meccanica, Mussolini (sintesi plastica), Marinetti (sintesi plastica)* and *Il convegno degli dei*), five tapestries and carpets, two bas-reliefs and two stage sets for Marinetti's play *Il Vulcano*. Established and on-the-rise artists alike, Lionello Balestrieri, Russolo, Pannaggi, Benedetta (with her much celebrated *Velocità di motoscafo*), Corona, Tato, Depero (with the famous *La rissa* and seven tapestries, including the equally well-known *Guerra=festa, Velocità, Fascismo*), Balla, Boccioni (with his seminal *Volumi orizzontali*), Angelo Caviglioni, Vittorio Corona, Dottori, Fedora Alma, Fillìa, Angelo Maino and Paladini, were also in attendance. To note: Pannaggi featured with seven mechanical and constructivist 'European-inflected' paintings (*Funzione architettonica H03, 3U, PM, A, E, K*, and *Il Costruttore*) and two sculptures, and so did Pippo Rizzo with a 'celebratory' one, *Futurismo e fascismo*. Russian avant-garde has been made visible by Paladini's book *L'arte nella Russia dei Soviet* published in 1925 as a résumé of works exhibited by Soviet artists during the 1924 Biennale. The first official participation of the futurists to a national exhibition was political in tone since many of the artworks paid homage to the regime and, if Marinetti had hoped for a connection between futurism and the Russian avant-gardes, that was not drawn by the press who largely ignored any iconoclastic ferment in Marinetti's ranks.

More criticism towards Marinetti's freshly found conformism was to come from the Giuliani's contact with Slovenia, the former Yugoslavia, Austria and Germany. Published in what was then Czechoslovakia, *Il fronte 1926. Almanacco moderno* issued an enquiry by Vladimir Prusa into modern art. Le Corbusier, Walter Gropius, Adolf Loos and Pocarini were invited to express their opinion. In his reply, Pocarini explicitly suggested the formation of an 'internazionale degli artisti geniali' as a way forward, as a means for advocating modernity in the arts in a fashion not dissimilar to Marinetti's

---

[112] Matteo Bertelé, *Arte sovietica alla Biennale di Venezia (1924–1962)* (Udine, Mimesis, 2020), ch. 2 of the online version.
[113] Azari, 'Vogliamo la libertà del cielo', *Roma futurista*, II/19 (11 May 1919), 1.

idea of the leadership of the 'geniali' in politics. In 1927, Escodamè was amongst the founders of the Società per la protezione delle macchine (along with Fedele Azari, Marinetti, Depero, Casavola, Catrizzi, Gerbino and Russolo), lending his support on this occasion to the aesthetics of the machine that was spreading internationally and arguing against the establishment and promoting the matching as a conceptual framework to emancipate people and improve their living condition by facilitating a classless society.[114]

In a series of fast-paced moves, Marinetti sidelined the provinces and attained a somewhat leading position through an action-reaction strategy within its own movement. In 1926, Balla, Depero and Prampolini all took part in the Exhibition of Modern Italian Art at the Grand Central Gallery in New York, initially, and then went on a tour of the USA that took them to Chicago, Washington and Boston.[115] In response to Milan's 1926 I Mostra del Novecento, in 1927 he set up the Mostra di trentaquattro pittori futuristi at the Galleria Pesaro, which had become populated by emerging Milan-based futurists, Andreoni, Bruno Munari, Ricas, Bot, Regina and Bracchi, thereby assuring aerofuturism a prestigious and visible place as it refocused its paradigm in between the mechanical of Prampolini and the lyrical cosmology of Fillìa, as can be seen in Benedetta's aforementioned *Velocità di motoscafo*.

Marinetti's escalation was not to end any time soon: at the 1928 Esposizione internazionale in Turin, Prampolini built the Futurism Pavilion in celebration of the aesthetics of mechanical art, youth and futurist architecture (including interior design, in pursuit of the total work of art).[116] That same year, in collaboration with Prampolini and Fillìa, Gerardo Dottori decorated the seaplane base in Ostia with a fresco (now destroyed).[117] At the 1928 Biennale, only eighteen paintings by twelve futurists were admitted because the selection was stricter: although the group was also in stark numerical contrast to the 248 artworks presented by traditionalist Ojetti in the Mostra della pittura italiana dell'800, it was nonetheless singled out as existing in its own right with an individual entry in the 'Elenco degli artisti ammessi dalla giuria' as like-minded artists.[118] Amongst the futurists, not only leading artists were welcomed but also those from the provinces: for instance, the likes of Ugo Brescia, Vittorio Corona, M. G. Dal Monte, Luigi Fattorello, Fillìa, Alfredo Gaudenzi, Antonio Marasco, Aligi Sassu and Giovanni Varvaro alongside the more established Diulgheroff and Rizzo, to emphasize

---

[114] See the *Manifesto*, http://www.arengario.it/opera/per-una-societa-di-protezione-delle-macchine-manifesto-futurista-11686/ (accessed 13 May 2020).

[115] Worth remembering also the *International Exhibition of Modern Art arranged by the Société Anonyme for the Brooklyn Museum*, New York (1926, extended to January 1927) with works by Severini, Dottori, Paladini, Pannaggi and *Mostra futurista*, Turin, Sindacato della stampa subalpina (19 May 1926) with Prampolini and Dottori on show.

[116] Benito Mussolini, 'Mussolini a Marinetti', *I Lupi*, I/3 (29 February 1928), 1 and F. T. Marinetti, 'Sensibilità dinamica creativa', ibid., 2. The full set of pavilions can be visualized here: https://issuu.com/newdist/docs/aaa_2017 (accessed 23 April 2020).

[117] A landmark in the history of aeropainting, according to Marinetti, Massimo Duranti (ed.), *Gerardo Dottori. Pittura totale* (Bologna, Edizioni Galleria Marescalchi, 1993), 21.

[118] On balance and contrary to other years, the 1928 Biennale's contribution by artists from the USSR was noteworthy, totalling 259 artworks not of great quality and often indulged in old-fashion realist aesthetics.

the far-reaching geographical spread of the movement. This Biennale was not political in tone largely because of the notable absences of Prampolini, Depero and Balla, who were perhaps too established and therefore unwilling to be subject to a selection.

In the year of the Concordat and the collapse of Wall Street, once elevated to the high ranks of the regime, Marinetti turned the wheel again towards his last 'revolution', the aero one with a string of manifestos. Along with Balla, Benedetta, Depero, Dottori, Fillìa, Prampolini, Somenzi and Tato, he signed the *Manifesto dell'aeropittura futurista*, and later he published the Monreale edition of the *Primo dizionario aereo*, with Azari, thereby saluting aerofuturism for the years to come. Several aeropainting manifestos followed over the next decade, especially with regional settings, connotating the range of the movement but with little theoretical innovation, and doubling as propaganda advertisements for war in its race for hegemony.[119] In the same year, the Mostra di trentatré artisti futuristi present at the Galleria Pesaro championed even more strongly aerofuturism as the future, and mechanical art as something that was slowing coming to an end, with a room reserved to cosmopolitan, chromoconstructivist architect and painter Diulgheroff. At the same time, Sarfatti's movement began to suffer unfriendly fire from the conservative fringes of the regime, when A. F. Della Porta of the *Giornale degli artisti* initiated a movement for a Risorgimento Artistico Italiano supported by Farinacci, and accused the novecentists of excessive internationalism, instead of embracing a healthier attitude of promotion of the national tradition – a rhetorical strategy that will be appositely deployed for anyone to be sidelined. Novecento was similarly at the peak of its international success in the early 1930s, because of the numerous exhibitions abroad, from Argentina to Germany and Switzerland, which conferred to Sarfatti a high degree of visibility and sway.[120] Sarfatti replied via the *Popolo d'Italia* on 10 July 1929, calling for a '*ripulisti in arte a suon di manganellate*' (a clean-up in the arts with batons), attracting in response a violent campaign of negative press, orchestrated by Della Porta, and by association endorsed by politically prominent intellectuals Maraini, Soffici and others for its excessive cosmopolitanism.[121]

At the 1930 conference at the Galleria Pesaro, Napoleone-like Marinetti started his campaigns. He reacted to allegations from the Novecento by accusing the national grand dame of excessive cosmopolitanism (something of which he, of course, was not guilty) and of traditionalism, via yet another of his routine publication entitled *Futurismo e novecentismo* (Milan, Edizioni Galleria Pesaro, 1930). At the 1930 Biennale, Marinetti secured a room for the futurists and, as was his wont, put distance between his movement and the internationalist and cosmopolitan French avant-gardes by leaping ahead with the *estetica della macchina* and *simultaneità*.[122]

---

[119] For a detailed account of Marinetti's manipulations in order to shape futurist architecture as State art see Godoli, *Guide all'architettura moderna*, 68–73 and Evangelisti (ed.), *Fillìa*, 115–20 for the introduction.

[120] Salaris, *Storia del futurismo*, 190.

[121] The same pattern can be identified in the internationalization process and appeal of the two movements: Peintres futuristes italiens a Paris, Galerie 23, 1929–30, Salaris, *Artecrazia*, 95.

[122] '*per estetica della macchina noi intendiamo lo splendore giometrico [sic] e numerico fatto di sintesi*', Marinetti, 'La nuova pittura futurista', *Catalogo XVII Esposizione Biennale Internazionale d'Arte*, 1930, 141.

Naturally, then, Prampolini could but not dominate the event with some twenty-four important works (including *Maternità*, *Il palombaro delle nuvole*, *Mussolini*, *Elementi costruttivi*). The older generation had also to feature – Balla's prestige signified through three of his works; but a focus on that regional futurism that had been fuelling the most innovative expressions of futurist art had been particularly carefully planned, covering Milan (Munari, Carlo Duse, Andreoni, Gino Soggetti, Aldo Fiozzi), Turin (Fillìa, Mino Rosso with *Architettura femminile* and *Piani architettonici di una testa*, Diulgheroff, Ugo Pozzo, Pippo Oriani), Emilia (Tato, Bot, Angelo Caviglioni), Rome (Benedetta, Ballelica, Domenico Belli), Naples (Luigi Pepe Diaz, Carlo Cocchia, Gildo Derosa, Guglielmo Peirce, Mario Lepore), Sicily (Vittorio Corona), Gorizia-Trieste (Pocarini), Florence (Thayaht with *Bautta*, *Violinista*, *Timoniere*), Veneto (Carlo Maria Dormal) and Switzerland (Paolo Alcide Saladin).[123] Serendipitously perhaps, despite Marinetti's much heartfelt anti-cosmopolitan declarations, in the same Biennale, the New Objectivity of Otto Dix, Ernst Max, George Grosz, together with abstracticist Klee and Kandinsky, was on show in the German Pavilion, alongside purists Ozenfant, Léger and Arp. Fusing political necessity and artstic myopia, in his role as director of the State Gallery of Dresden, Hans Posse praised German art for being in close contact with reality, the primary source of artistic inspiration, even to the extent of maintaining that Klee was more connected to the real than Kandinsky was.[124] Realism, presentism and geographical reach had artificially become the three pillars of the politics of aesthetics of the 1930s alongside the impeding demands of State art and across a variety of artistic expressions and movements. A direction which futurism will follow.

Theatre of Objects: *Analogie Cosmiche*

Fillìa died very young, in 1936. His most productive years artistically were 1927 and 1928, when he elaborated his *primordio cosmico*: a theory and a practice that placed strong emphasis on the constructive element to be included within the boundaries of the composition. Contrary to the approaches of post-cubism, constructivism and De Stijl, Fillìa's understanding of mechanical art did include a subjective, oneiric, mystical and psychological element; one which effectively distinguished the Italian brand of second futurism.

Of particular interest for how they fuse mysticism and geometry are the mechanical portrayals of femininity of *Donna seduta* (1927), *Femminilità* (1928) and *Gli amanti* (1928), this latter being exhibited at the I Mostra sindacale piemontese in Turin in June and July 1929, and then at the Pesaro in October of that year, in a room dedicated

[123] There was also sculpture by Mario Zucco; Severini supplied war-themed artworks, *Sintesi plastica della guerra*, *Cannoni in azione* (*parole in libertà e forma*).

[124] Posse, Introduction to 'Padiglione della Germania', *Catalogo XVII Esposizione Biennale Internazionale d'Arte*, 1930, 225. See also De Sabbata, *Tra diplomazia e arte*, 235–53. It is worth remembering that the abstracticist Cercle & Carré group had taken part in the 1930 Biennale.

to Fillìa alone. During this short period, Fillìa pawed the way by renouncing clearly delineated geometrical patterns in favour of a distinctively mystical and mysterious rendering of objectivity. In *Gli amanti*, the rhythm of the objects, with their soft, curving, interweaving lines sliding through intersecting planes, stands in sharp contrast to the geometry of the background. The muted colours (from beige to brown) are less vivid than in *Ritmi di forme* (1929), as they melt into an almost pastel palette of coordinated shades and the clear symmetry of volumes signalled a move towards a more anthropomorphic representation. The clearly demarcated lines and bright contrasting colours in *Ritmi di forme*, though, foreground the volume of the objects, so the work exudes an aura of mechanical composition different to the spirituality of *Plasticità d'oggetti*.[125] Rather, it is reminiscent of Braque and of early cubism in its cleanliness of lines and the fully representational assemblage of overlapping objects and compenetrating volumes, realized in harmoniously fused shades of toning colours. In Fillìa's work, rhythm and matter began progressively to embrace subjective, spiritual and mystical elements in the representation of the machine: still individual, still isolated from any landscape and still dominant over human agency, still to be made collective in any way; but absolutely functioning as a nucleus for future developments including mural paintings.[126]

As early as the mid-1920s, after moving to Paris, Prampolini was in close contact with the European avant-gardes, since he understood that 'the only successful strategy was that of productive collaboration […] to build a new culture'.[127] Prampolini had changed his mechanical aesthetic direction towards a more spiritual dimension following the Exposition Internationale des Arts Décoratifs et Industriels Modernes in 1925. This aesthetic outlook was particularly prevalent around the Studio Mondrian, Abstraction-Création, František Kupka, Pierre Antoine Gallien, Friedrich Vordemberge-Gildewart, Georges Fouquet and before then around the Cercle & Carré group. It became evident, for example, in Prampolini's artworks *Intervista con la materia*, *Itinerario plastico* and *Intervista con lo spirito* (1930), all of which he showed at the Cercle & Carré exhibition on 18 April 1930 at *à la page* Galerie 23 in Rue de la Boetie.[128] The new fluidity of lines in these works married abstracticism and polymateric art into a form of *surrealismo organico* (Arp, Ernst, Mirò), and evoked metaphysical subtexts contouring the mystery of the universe, mixed up in paint, cork, sponge, mother-of-pearl or pearlescent paint and embossed hammered metal foil. Volumes were created not only with colour but also by the organization of materials, precisely as Prampolini's reflections on a '*cosmos*

---

[125] 1928, oil on canvas, 63 × 57.5 cm, Civica Galleria d'Arte Moderna, Turin.

[126] See also *Elementi geometrici*, *c.* 1927, tempera on paper, lost. *Plasticità d'oggetti*, *c.* 1928, oil on canvas, 63 × 57.5 cm, Civica Galleria d'Arte Moderna, Turin.

[127] Lista, *Prampolini*, 13.

[128] Details on the numerous Parisian exhibitions Prampolini took part in, Lista 'Prampolini e i gruppi dell'"arte astratta" in Francia', in Crispolti (ed.), *Prampolini dal futurismo all'informale*, 303. For more details on the first issue of Cercle & Carré at the Galerie 23 in Paris and Fillìa, Prampolini, and Sartoris's inclusion, see Enrico Crispolti (ed.), *Nuovi archivi del futurismo* (Rome, De Luca editori d'arte, 2010), 360–2.

architéctonique', and Sartoris's '*système animateur des éléments lyriques et constructifs*', had anticipated in the first issue of the *Cercle & Carré* journal.[129]

During the first half of the 1930s, Prampolini entered his cosmic phase, culminating in works such as *Analogie cosmiche (Apparizione cosmica)* and *Metamorfosi cosmica* in 1935.[130] Much has been written about these well-known artworks: materiality transfixed into an extra-terrestrial dimension; basic forms assuming profoundly symbolic meaning through emotional associations. The ubiquitous symbolism of the sphere, according to Lista, is a reference to Cicero's idea of the perfect shape as image of impenetrable divine intelligence; and, before then, to the allegorical image of the cosmos as unknowledgeable entity, as in, for example, *Il palombaro delle nuvole* or *Maternità cosmica* (1930).[131] More significantly, Prampolini's consideration originated in his French acquaintances with surrealism and manifested itself in a reflection on the ineffability of knowledge which might, however tangentially, refer to a regime that was adopting ever more autocratic attitudes, and whose process of sacralization intensified after 1935. The relationship between Man and Nature could not be articulated along the lines of rational thought; it needed instead to develop according to emotional patterns which grasped the notion of a universe organized by a superior force, often assuming non-anthropomorphic, or stylized, connotations. The recognizable human shapes of *Venere meccanizzata* (1930), *L'automa quotidiano* (1930) and *Apparizione magica* (*Visione magica*) (1931) had been superseded by floating malleable volumes governed by fluid lines of varying dimensions and materials in a semi-coherent whole – which nonetheless remained suspended in the air, and inaccessible. The multi-materiality, which serves a political purpose too, is an assemblage of substrates offering diverse tactile sensations (sand, metallized cortex ['*corteccia metallizzata*']), sandpaper that reflects a physical, non-mental relationship with life and with cosmology. In this respect, *arte polimaterica* would be useful within the discourse of State art.

With respect to our line of argument here, Munari's *Macchina inutile* angular sculpture series of the 1930s merits particular mention: made of light materials, either freestanding or suspended from the ceiling on thin wires which floated over and around the viewer, they challenged the gaze in multiple directions and simulated an aerial perspective, generative units of multiple visions. Munari takes a step further in the *universo meccanico* by developing that anthropomorphic element already present in Fillìa brand of rationality; and moves the dimension of the sequence into a surrealist scenario in which neither reason nor mysticism can be merged in any coherent totality. The dialectic subjectivity-objectivity in Munari's *Macchine inutili* is not resolved

---

[129] There are several versions of the same artwork: 1930, oil, enamel, cork, sponge on wood, Museo Civico Galleria d'Arte Moderna, Turin; *Intervista con la materia*, 1930; Galleria Nazionale d'Arte Moderna, Rome and *Intervista con la materia*, 1930 (collage with mixed techniques on cardboard), Galleria Narciso, Turin. Relevant to the discussion is also Boccioni's essay on the use of colours, their relationship to individuality and their patterns, such as those defined by complementary colours, see 'Complementarismo dinamico', in Birolli, *Pittura e scultura futuriste*, 115–19.

[130] Lista, *Prampolini*, 244.

[131] Ibid., 214.

through synthesis; it remains suspended between rational and practical explanation and idle playfulness, rebuffing any superior order.[132] Munari's later *Macchina inutile* (1934, private collection, Novara) is another case in point: it problematized the complexity and plurality of Italy's artistic milieu in so far as it went beyond mechanics and spirituality, in an imaginary-like space that welcomed abstraction and surrealism and proposes an alternative to normative views of the machine. By contrast, Munari's kinetic sculptures, *Macchine*, are strangely physical in their floating geometry and different to the simpler aerial nature of Fillìa's mystical figurations. Indeed, it is their figurative geometrical dimension that questions even more radically the truth of objectivity while placing a surreal and ethereal subjectivity at its centre.[133] As Ara H. Merjian notes, '[w]hat does it mean for an artist – for any artist – to have engaged with Rationalism and Surrealism to the same degree during the 1930s?'.[134] Probably, an attempt to became an example of artistic intersections beyond the limitations imposed by State art. Eclectic as he was in his influences, Munari traversed futurism, dadaism and surrealism whilst dialoguing with Prampolini, Fillìa, Sartoris and the Milione group in an ideal system of the arts in full swing by the mid-930s.[135]

Fusions III: The Machine of Exhibitions: 1932–3

The 1930 Biennale's 109 futurist works towered over the forty-nine chosen for the I Quadriennale, thereby acting as a sort of pre-Quadriennale of national art. The futurists' participation at the Biennale was of significance not because of its numbers, rather because of the artistic trends it brought together during one event which acted as the flagship of national art, a sui generis Quadriennale for the futurist ranks. Benedetta with *Il Grande X*, Balla, Cocchia, Corona, Pepe Diaz, Dottori with *La famiglia Marinetti*; there was Duse, Lepore, Marasco (*Lirismo stereomeccanico*), Munari (*Velocità* and *Dinamismo di corpo femminile*), Oriani, Tato (*Lavoro, Giovinezza, Sport*, triptych), while Fontana exhibited his own *Vittoria fascista* (1929, bronze). There was, too, Depero (*Dinamismi futuristi I, II, III*), Rosso, Fillìa (*Tre donne, Paesaggio italiano, Aeroplano*); fifty drawings by pioneer architect Sant'Elia and eight of Prampolini's works which marked the start of his cosmic period.[136] Not unexpectedly, the contribution of futurists to the I Quadriennale mapped onto the 1930 Biennale in terms of similar artistic presences, but with fewer than half the number of artworks.

---

[132] On Munari's understanding of useless machines, see his article 'Che cosa sono le macchine inutili e perché', *La Lettura*, 37/7 (1937).

[133] See for example, *Ritratto di Luigi Russolo*, 1927, or the lithograph illustration *Il Cantastorie Campari*, 1932, cited in Pierpaolo Antonello, Matilde Nardelli and Margherita Zanoletti (eds), *Bruno Munari: The Lightness of Art* (Oxford Bern, Peter Lang, 2017), 34, 37.

[134] '"On the Verge of the Absurd": Munari, Dada, and Surrealism in Interwar Italy', in Antonello and Nardelli and Zanoletti (eds), *Bruno Munari*, 28.

[135] Ibid., 33–48.

[136] *La metamorfosi degli idoli, L'automa quotidiano, Venere meccanizzata, La rivelazione dello spazio, Il seduttore della velocità, Apparizione magica, Analogie cosmiche* and *Immagini futuriste*.

Still their presence was strategic both because of the profile of the artists and the trends they presented. Thayaht's *Vittoria dell'aria*, a topical a rework of the *Nike of Samothrace* once so passionately vilified by Marinetti, now placed at the centre of the rotunda, was a forceful example of rationalization of lines assembled through architecturally linear construction; one that celebrated the regime by re-semanticizing classical themes for modern times and the modernization of the social sphere.[137]

The 1932 and 1934 Biennali saw an even clearer shift in direction towards aeropainting as State art and a pattern of acquisitions headed by the State and by public institutions rather than private buyers; a shift that was less obvious again by the 1936 Biennale, and then was barely perceptible in the 1938, 1940 and 1942 Biennali. Notable political exclusions from the 1930s Biennali were potential competitions such as the abstracticists and the muralists: each group well connected with either the most progressive theorization of State art, such as those by Massimo Bontempelli and Pietro Maria Bardi's *Quadrante*, or with the V Triennale in 1933, at least until Sarfatti could exercise some influence. Marinetti hosted room 50 of the Mostra dell'aeropittura e della pittura dei futuristi italiani to expound how aeropainting changed the notion of perspective: the connection between viewer and artist, and that between subject and object, seen as detached and acting independently. Therefore, the perceptive modern subject could be in control of objectivity as dictated by a socially useful, or else at the service of modernization, understanding of the artistic expression. The solo exhibitions were by Depero (works included *New-York-Città bassa*, *Elasticità di gatti*, *Nitrito in velocità*, *Prismi lunari*, *Ciclista veloce*) and by Prampolini (*Maternità cosmica*, *Analogie cosmiche*, *La magia della stratosfera* (quadro polimaterico), *Introspezione aerodinamica*). These two artists alone were responsible for thirty-six and twenty-five artworks respectively out of the ninety-nine on show. Other notable artists invited to uphold aerofuturism were Benedetta with eight works (including *Laghi salati algerini*, *Lirismo di volo*), Dottori also with eight (including *Ritratto aereo del futurista Mario Carli*, *Architettura aerea*), Fillìa with five (including *Simultaneità*, *Spiritualità aerea*, *L'idolo del cielo*), Tato, who had six (including *Spiralata*, *Coppa Schneider*), and Thayaht, who showed two (including *Tuffo*).[138] On the whole, critical reactions

---

[137] The *Vittoria* was exhibited on various importante occasions: 1931, I Quadriennale in Rome, Galleria la Camerata degli artisti at the Prima mostra di aeropittura in Rome, Mostra futurista. Piuttura–scultura–aeropittura in Florence, Mostra futurista di aeropittura e scenografia in Milan. In 1932 it was placed at the entry hall of the central pavilion of the II Mostra mercato nazionale dell'artigianato, Camera di commercio, Florence, and in 1933 at the Mostra d'arte sacra futurista, Palazzo Spini Ferroni, Florence. Salaris, *aero ... futurismo e mito del volo* (Rome, Le parole gelate, 1985), 54–9 for a full list of projects. Because of their inter-artistic and interdisciplinary nature, of particular note are: Teatro aereo with the *Manifesto Il Teatro Futurista Aeroradiotelevisivo* (the first experiments with TV are from the 1930s); Aeroscultura with the *Manifesto tecnico dell'aeroplastica futurista, aeropoesia e letteratura aerea, aeroceramica, aeromusica, aerodanza, aeropranzo e anticravatta*; and F. T. Marinetti, 'La danza futurista. Danza dell'aviatore. Danza dello Shrapnel. Danza della mitragliatrice. Manifesto', *Roma futurista*, III/73 (7 March 1920), 1.

[138] Other younger, or less mainstream, artists were also presented, including Ambrosi, Andreoni, Caviglioni, Diulgheroff, Marasco, Munari, Oriani and Rosso, each staging one or two artworks, and still populating the Marinetti contingency.

noted that the works presented at the Biennale covered similar themes as before, which seemed to be subdued in comparison with the international avant-gardes and, whilst critics appreciated Thayaht's experimental flair still blooming, they commented sceptically on how Depero started to gravitate towards realism and Tato towards 'cartellonism'. Advertising was indeed one of the 1930s most vivid forms of realism because of its popular appeal but was most welcomed outside official, elite circles such as the Biennale. The 1930s saw Depero occupying a relatively marginal position during State-run events and together with several other talented futurist (Munari, Seneca for example) dedicating himself preferebly to the art of advertisement.

If in 1932 the presence of futurist art at the Mostra della rivoluzione was not of utmost significance, the 1931 exhibition at the Galleria Pesaro, the 1932 III Mostra del sindacato fascista delle belle arti del Lazio (March–April) together with the Mostra Aeropittura, Arte sacra Futurista at the Casa d'Arte at La Spezia (November–December 1932), foregrounded aeropainting with Fillìa, Mino Rosso and Pippo Oriani as a leading cultural movement. At this event, while reiterating the demarcation of the spheres of action of politics and creativity, Marinetti also underlined a separation between arts and politics but to favour a socially present art, capable of social transformation at a popular and not just elite level.

At the iconic V Triennale in 1933, the futurist Pavilion kept flying the flag for State art with Prampolini's *Stazione per aeroporto civile* (produced in collaboration with Marinetti, Andreoni, Depero, Dottori, Duse, Fillìa, Oriani, Ricas, Rosso, Thayaht and Munari) as an example of a total-environmental creation, with the aeroplane at its centre, surrounded by works of aerosculpture, aeropainting and futurist architecture in an example of a non-permanent total work of art that brought together different artists in a meaningful synthesis.[139] As customary in Marinetti's tactics, other journals appeared embracing the same strategically totalizing ambition of futurism at the centre of the system of the arts: in October 1933, *Sant'Elia* (Somenzi with Mazzoni) and *Artecrazia* (to be shut down in 1939) engaged in topical debates on arts and politics, with a focus on architecture as the new force towards State art, along with a clear interest in popular culture and the professed '*arti minori*' as functioning together.[140] Shortly after, the I Mostra nazionale d'arte futurista was inaugurated on 29 October 1933 at the Palazzo degli ingegneri in Rome, opposite Marinetti's home. The largest ever display of futurist art across disciplines was finally realized, sacralizing the movement and its – according to Marinetti's personal calculations – five hundred adherents at last embodying the cherished total work of art.

[139] Prampolini designed the Italian Pavilion at the Chicago Exhibition in 1932. Giancarlo Palanti, 'Stazione per aeroporto', *Edilizia Moderna*, XI–XII/10–11 (August–December 1933), 56–7 praised for its use of new materials.

[140] Millefiorini, *Tra avangardia e accademia*, 73. In Milan *Nuovo futurismo* (1934) initiated a critique to *Futurismo* for its support of Marinetti's conservative politics. 'Agonia di un movimento', *Nuovo futurismo*, I/2 (15 June 1934), 1; Lino Cappuccio Treskovsky, 'Punti di vista', ibid., I/3 (30 June 1934), 1, 'Futuristi vecchi e nuovi', ibid., I/6 (15 October 1934), 1.

Fusions IV: Abstracticism

In parallel with the futurist's trajectory in those years of maximal consensus and visibility, we might also trace the history of abstracticism, unfolding largely but not exclusively around the Milan-based Galleria Il Milione and *Quadrante*, since around 1933. Il Milione was essentially a bookshop with some annexed exhibition spaces, similarly to the Bottega di Poesia in Via Monte Napoleone, and La Libreria della Fiera Letteraria in Piazza San Carlo; moreover, it customarily published its own bulletin (*Bollettino del Milione* with a distribution of about 1,200 copies of which 300 were in Milan and 150 abroad).[141] The brainchild of Persico (director until February 1931) and of brothers Gino and Peppino Ghiringhelli it opened on 30 November 1930 in the gallery spaces previously owned by Bardi before his move to Rome. It housed a library with subscriptions to international art journals, including *Cahiers d'Art*, Michel Seuphor and Joaquín Torres's *Cercle & Carré*, van Doesburg's *Art Concret* featuring Jean Hélion, Auguste Herbin, Georges Vantongerloo, and Étienne Béothys and Abstraction-Création (1932–6), which published volumes such as the Bauhaus book designed by Moholy-Nagy, *Bauhausbücher*, and Kandinsky's *Point and Line to Plane* (1926). Albeit lacking the capillary organization of futurism, and producing far fewer programmatic declarations, abstracticism nonetheless rooted itself in certain locations and important networks: at Il Milione, in Turin at the 1935 I Mostra dell'astrattismo sponsored by Casorati with the Gruppo dei Sei and Paolucci, and in Como, with a group of rationalist architects that included Terragni, Pietro Lingeri and Cesare Cattaneo and the Quadrante group of P. M. Bardi, Sartoris, Bontempelli, Figini, Pollini and Belli. Il Milione, however, and the Ghiringhelli brothers, always looked with suspicion at Rome, perceived as too traditionalist artistically, and, lamenting the sporadic political support they received from the friend Bardi, turned their gaze further afield.

Not differently from what futurism had done before, Il Milone arguably created a considerable network nationally and internationally and such connections were indispensable for its survival.[142] As reported in one communication from the A.L.A. (Agenzia letteraria internazionale) on 14 January 1932, during a period of economic crisis, international art dealers looked with interest at purchasing Italian art.[143] Indeed, the exchange could be reciprocated, since the first three issues of the *Cahier abstraction-création: art non-figuratif*, in 1932, 1933 and 1934, celebrated Prampolini's cosmic futurism and authoritatively consecrated him as a leading figure of non-figurative and abstract art. Momentously, over the course of less than a 'troubled' decade, Il Milione gallery staged several major exhibitions that opened their doors to Europe: Léger, Lurçat, Marcoussis and Ernst and the Cubists (1932), including works by Pascin and

---

[141] As noted by Pontiggia, the Milione gallery organized two exhibitions per month, dedicated a lot of space to music and had an up-to-date collection of international arts and literary magazines. It functioned as an interdisciplinary hub, *Il Milione e l'Astrattismo, 1932–1938. La galleria, Licini e i suoi amici* (Milan, Electa, 1988), 13.

[142] Letters from Peppino Ghiringhelli to Carlo Belli (10 April 1932, R. 42/172, 1) and Gino Ghiringhelli to Carlo Belli (21 February 1933, R. 42/169, 1), MART.

[143] F. 'Bardi', document number 427.

Bertolini (a total of fifteen pieces), Kandinsky's first solo show in Italy featuring forty-five watercolours and thirty drawings, together with examples of the geometrical phases of the Bauhaus (1922–34), thanks to Alberto Sartoris's mediation with Kandinsky on holiday in Forte dei Marmi in 1936. A year before, in 1935, other prominent members of the Bauhaus, concretist Josef Albers and Frederick Vordemberge-Gildewart, had visited the Milone. In 1936 architect Belgioisoso of the BBPR spent time at the new Academy of Fine Arts Ozenfant had just opened in London in May of that year.

In this cosmopolitan milieu, its first director, Persico, set out an agenda that leaned towards *i primitivi* (Ottone Rosai, Ubaldo Oppi, Tullio Garbari, Francesco Di Terlizzi, Lino Enea Spilimbergo), endorsing an anti-Sarfatti, novecentist idea of classicism, and as expected such an heterodox directorship was not to last very long. Persico resigned his directorship in 1931 on the grounds of aesthetic divergences with the Ghiringhelli brothers; and was succeeded by Gege Bottinelli, the soon-to-be wife of Luigi Figini. The link between the Gruppo 7 and rationalist architecture was established as early as 1931, and validated by P. M. Bardi's *Rapporto sull'architettura*. Bardi was never in complete agreement with Il Milone because of his dislike for abstract painting but they always maintained a mutually supportive relationship, especially around the problem of rationalist architecture, and the culture wars of the 1930s between Sironi, Maraini, Oppo and the entourage of the Ministero delle corporazioni. In 1933, Carlo Belli published the first chapter of his *Kn* (written in 1930) in the n. 2 of *Quadrante* and in 1932 Il Milone exhibited Sartoris's axonometries. Meanwhile, up-and-coming abstract artists, such as Mauro Reggiani, Veronesi, Melotti, Fontana, Soldati, Oreste Bogliardi and Virginio Ghiringhelli were gravitating around the gallery.[144] As Rifkind noted, Belli took advantage of Bardi's momentary neglect of the gallery to focus on the preparation of the South-American exhibition of contemporary Italian architecture in October 1933.[145] Close connections with architecture were made explicit by Peppino Ghiringhelli in a letter to Belli on 7 October 1935: the 'theoretical ambition' of the abstract movement were reinforced by its collaboration with modern architects (Figini and Pollini, BBPR and Lingeri) and of course with Bardi.[146] Equally explicit was the disagreement with part of the establishment and of some key players in the definition of State art: Oppo, Maraini above all, together with Pagano and scepticism towards Carrà.[147]

---

[144] For a detailed picture of the Milanese artistic scene of the 1930s, see *Il Milione e l'Astrattismo*, ibid., 11–37. About the significance and meaning of the publication of *Kn* as a vector for enhancing the visibility and the appeal of the gallery, see a letter from Gino Ghiringhelli to Carlo Belli (19 January 1935, R. 42/169, 15, MART). Similarly, in a non-dated letter but probably around October–November 1935 (the first page is missing), Peppino Ghiringhelli told Belli that he did not see the point in sending a copy of the *Kn* to the Florentine *Bargello* because of Giovacchino Conti, and to Sarfatti and to Alberto Rossi at the *Gazzetta del popolo* because they were not very responsive readers. He also wondered if Le Corbusier would read it, in case they could send him a copy (R. 42/169, 34, MART).

[145] Rifkind, *The Battle for Modernism*, 70.

[146] Peppino Ghiringhelli to Belli (Letter, R. 42/c 172, 18, MART).

[147] Peppino Ghiringhelli to Belli, described Pippo Rizzo as an artist at the service of Oppo's political plans. In a later letter, 26 June 1936, to Belli he reiterated his dislike for Maraini and Oppo while reporting that Alessandro Pavolini had visited the gallery (Letters, R. 42/c 172, 3 and R. 42/c 172, 26, MART).

In 1933, Anton Atanasio Soldati's show, often considered the first unofficial abstracticism exhibition, opened at the Milione to mixed reviews. Belli wrote the introduction of the former architecture student, delivering an anti-art establishment subtext – calling out Piacentini, Maraini and Ojetti – that he later toned down when it was published a few months later in *Quadrante*. Soldati was a keen supporter of Belli's *Kn* in its rejection of figuration and narrative. The following year, 1934, an exhibition of Bigliardi, Ghiringhelli and Reggiani marked the birth of the Italian abstracticist movement on these very same grounds. The I Mostra dell'astrattismo italiano – with a *Dichiarazione degli espositori* that functioned as a manifesto – rejected mechanical art for a 'Mediterranean order' and any form of art as mimesis to create a *rivoluzione dell'ordine* that elevated abstract beauty to typify the ultimate ambition of creativity.[148] From 1933 to 1938, the gallery hosted several events, but it was not until 1935 that Licini, Melotti, Soldati, Veronesi and Fontana had solo exhibitions, against the low sales of abstract art in Italy in the mid-1930s. On 4 March 1935 in Turin, in the *atelier* Casorati and Paolucci, a group consisting of Bogliardi, Ghiringhelli, Licini, Melotti, Fontana, Reggiani, Soldati, Veronesi and D'Errico exported abstract art to Turin in the same ideal line that had connected the architects of Turin and Milan just a few years earlier.

Carlo Belli's *Kn* was finally published for the first time in 1935 by Edizioni della Galleria Il Milione in Milan, after having circulated underground for a couple of years.[149] *Kn* was a manifesto that solidified the presence of abstract art in Italy whilst historicizing earlier artistic movements, often in a somewhat uncompromising way.[150] The 'K' of the title refers to the constitutive elements of painting, colour and form; the 'n' is the number of unlimited combinations these can assume. Kandinsky notoriously labelled *Kn* as the 'gospel of abstract art'. Abstracticism wanted to reach an absolute through objects reduced to their most minimal geometrical forms: reality rationalized, in order to arrive at its most universal meanings. Art is an autonomous form, determines *Kn*'s author, representing his conclusion through a circular diagram locating abstract art at the arrival destination of every aesthetic mission.[151] This is a destination arrived at by Paul Klee and Wassily Kandinsky, Le Corbusier, Mies van der Rohe, Giuseppe Terragni, by late cubism, concretism, and musicians such as J. S. Bach – but one that according to Belli the futurists totally missed, affected as they were by 'psychologism'.[152]

Kn is a book about pathways and deferred arrivals set in an Empyrean realm where psychologism is not welcomed. Despite Belli's support of Fascism, *Kn*'s rejection of

[148] 'Dichiarazione degli espositori', *Bollettino del Milione*, 1934, and Caramel, 'Carlo Belli e gli astrattisti italiani anni Trenta', Appella and Belli and Garberi (eds), *Il mondo di Carlo Belli*, 75. See also Fossati, *L'immagine sospesa*, 73 and Tempesti, *Arte dell'Italia fascista*, 201.

[149] On the genesis of the *Kn*, see Lorenza Trucchi, 'Da "Kn" a "Interlogo"', in Giuseppe Appella and Maria Grazia Tolomeo (eds), *Carlo Belli e Roma* (Rome, Viviani arte, 1998), 37.

[150] Trucchi, 'Da "Kn" a "Interlogo"', 38 on influences on the genesis of the *Kn*.

[151] Belli, *Gli anni della formazione*, 47 for the author's point of view on his anti-Wagnerian, anti-impressionist influences (Cocteau and for the new classics Picasso and Stravinsky), which coincided with those of the Gruppo 7 in architecture.

[152] On the relationship between Belli and Kandinsky, see Serravalli, 'Carlo Belli da Rosmini a Kandinsky', 55 and passim. See Carlo Belli, *Kn* for Kandinsky's letters to Belli about the *Kn*, 145–7.

Man as a psychologically declined being was difficult to justify in a cultural milieu that favoured precisely the construction of new forms of subjectivity within the public sphere. This rather apodictic vision and dismissal of automorphism meant that *Kn* initially caused some controversy, and it polarized its readers, which counted, amongst many others, intellectual figures such as Bontempelli, Anceschi, Giuseppe Marchiori and Bragaglia. Belli's programme was to reject Croce, embrace Bergson and thus shape an abstract aesthetic model that could assist in creating interdisciplinary links with other arts, mostly notably architecture, where classicism and a locally inflected *mediterraneità* acted as focal points.[153] Pontiggia, indicating a somewhat heretical line of the abstract movement in the mid-1930s, proposed that: 'These artists were moving away from the neoromantic convictions of the period, by denying in toto both the relationship between art and life and a notion of art as representation of Man, of his psychology, of his passions. Painting without the I am Belli's dream.'[154] Pontiggia has also specified how the close relationship with classical art and culture was an essential factor in the development of Italian abstracticism.[155]

In his self-presentation of 1935, Fausto Melotti declared that '*noi crediamo all'ordine della Grecia*' (we believe in the order of Greece) as a means of refuting accusations of psychologism, and of connecting internal order with social order and modernization.[156] Tempesti commented that 'naturally *Kn* is also a parallel book and emulator of P. M. Bardi *Rapporto sull'Architettura* because, once it demonstrated the excellence of art – in this case abstract art –, the *Kn* moves on to the corollary that this is the only possible art for a similarly new, inventive, creative regime'.[157] For his part, Fossati has identified it in the rejection of the 'taste' and 'aesthetic of the machine', or of any practical application of the arts, the core of Italian abstracticism.[158] Admittedly, the Milanese abstract sculptures of Fontana and Melotti sought to achieve a balance between full and empty volume, giving an aerial quality to their works.[159] Their lines and rhythms – whether Fontana's *Linee contro l'aria* in his *Tavolette* or Melotti's rhythmical formal parallelisms in *Scultura 11* to *25* (1935) – are well described by Paolo Fossati when he wrote that: 'Melotti's effort is therefore that of generating a crisis […]: and in this Fontana, Melotti as far as plasticity is concerned, and Licini more in general agree. But Melotti understand this process in a different sense: that is, by thinning down the plastic walls.'[160] In terms of lines and rhythms, and in what could be an abstract rendering of artistic intersections as matrixes for infinite reproductions, we

[153] Belli, *Gli anni formativi*, 54.
[154] Pontiggia, *Il Milione e l'Astrattismo*, 32.
[155] Elena Pontiggia, 'Tra la Grecia e l'Europa. Carlo Belli teorico dell'astrattismo', in Appella and Belli and Garberi (eds), *Il mondo di Carlo Belli*, 99–116.
[156] Fausto Melotti, 'Autopresentazione', *Bollettino della Galleria del Milione* (4 May 1935).
[157] Tempesti, *Arte dell'Italia fascista*, 205.
[158] Fossati, *L'immagine sospesa*, 73.
[159] Belli, *Lettera sull'astrattismo*, in *Anni creativi*, 24, 33. Carrà wrote a positive review of Licini's first solo exhibition at the Milione and mentioned Melotti's works, often neglected by critics, 'Mostre d'arte', *L'Ambrosiano*, (16 May 1936).
[160] Fossati, *L'immagine sospesa*, 182.

can also see how Luigi Veronesi was concerned with the rhythms of colours and music, and with the variations and assonances of linear rhythm and sound rhythms. Closer to Cézanne and the novecentists, Reggiani maintained a sense of solidity and construction in his compositional syntax. While Bogliardi's use of curvilinear patterns produced a sense of suspension and almost magical hesitation in the viewer, consistent also perhaps with Soldati's sense of the playfulness of creation. Gino Ghiringhelli embraced the most essential sobriety with no concession to any type of figuration. Further, in Osvaldo Licini's *Archipitture* (1936), inspired by Sophie Taeuber-Arp as well as Klee and Kandinsky, the visible structure became a visual representation of both a universal rhythm as well as a constructive pattern reduced to its minimal assembling mechanism.[161]

By 1935 the political centre of art scene was in Rome. On 3 January 1935, the 'great' II Quadriennale had opened its doors to celebrate Italian art and futurism within State art. Novecento was virtually absent and the futurist contribution covered one main theme: '*plastica dell'aria e della vita fascista*'.[162] Forty-three artists took part in the event with forty-three works in total, and twenty-five of Prampolini's cosmic geometries and aerodynamism were celebrated on a grand scale. In room IX, Oreste Bogliardi, Cristoforo De Amicis, Virginio Ghiringhelli, Osvaldo Licini, Mauro Reggiani, Atanasio Soldati and Alberto Magnelli (working in Paris) championed the same abstracticism they had displayed the previous year in Milan. Up-and-coming Milanese abstract artists close to Bardi and Bontempelli were invited at the official debut of the Milione group; but without the deeply geometrical more radical abstracticism practiced by Fausto Melotti, Luigi Veronesi, Manlio Rho and Mario Radice. As Elena Pontiggia has noted there were other telling absences: Depero and Funi, previously virtually omnipresent; and, from the new generation, highly talented and promising artists such as Renato Birolli, Aligi Sassu, Giacomo Manzù and Munari.[163] Abstracticism soon became a point of contention: not because it was too experimental, but rather because it was too derivative, an accusation critics had already moved to aerofuturism at the Biennali. Marinetti's ever-strategic introduction could not help but find a link between a 'more figurative and realist' abstracticism and *plastica murale*, the newest addition to the State art plan following its official consecration at the 1934 show in Genoa, in an attempt at grouping together all the avant-gardes as a system under the wing of futurism as State art and to further his hegemonic cause.[164]

---

[161] Other similar works are Licini, *Archipittura*, 1933, private collection; *Composizione, linee nere e blu*, 1935, Collection Hellstrom Riccitelli, Ascoli Piceno; *Archipittura*, 1937, private collection; and *Aeropittura*, 1934, Galleria d'Arte Moderna di Roma, exhibited at the III Quadriennale.

[162] On the reception of futurism at the II Quadriennale, see Carli and Pontiggia (eds), *La grande Quadriennale 1935*, 133–5.

[163] Solo exhibitions by Severini, Luigi Bartolini, De Pisis, Mario Mafai, Enrico Paolucci, Fausto Pirandello, Prampolini, Giuseppe Capogrossi – all artists were between thirty and forty years old; there were group exhibitions for Cagli, Carrà, Arturo Tosi, Ottone Rosai, Martini, Gianni Vagnetti, Socrate and Felice Casorati.

[164] On the lack of interest for the artists and the critique about poor originality, Carli and Pontiggia (eds), *La grande Quadriennale 1935*, 58–9.

1935 marked a turning point with Melotti's solo exhibition opening at the Milione gallery. On the one hand, Melotti's show brought together the various disciplines of the art world and consecrated the avant-gardes within the paradigm of State art; but, on the other, it also began to witness their disintegration. Despite its perhaps derivative nature, Italian abstracticism was the most theoretically viable avant-garde alternative to futurism because it proposed a conceptual model of aesthetics of politics, and vice versa, which had the potential of becoming a system of the arts functional to the totalitarian project. Abstracticism deployed anti-figurative, anti-representational and geometrical forms and patterns to voice a political message in line with State art, while seeking to remain anchored to the rock of the real, however abstract and rationalized the latter might have become, and while designing a matrix allowing intersections over estrangements. In place of the fracture indicated by Belli in his *Kn* between futurism and abstracticism, and according to our understanding of the position of arts within a working system, Caramel has also identified some points of convergence in the system of the arts in the 1930s: a continuity between the 1909 futurist *Manifesto*, mechanical art, Balla and Depero's *Manifesto* of 1915, De Chirico, Evola's *Arte astratta* (1920), Prampolini's *Noi* and his collaborations with the group Abstraction-Création, and the later developments of abstracticism in Italy in 1934 and 1938. Moreover, Caramel has also detected continuity between Marinetti's late exhibition in 1938 at the Milione gallery of futurist aeropainters – most of whom were, by then, leaning back towards representational codes and were fully integrated in the regime's plans for the arts – and their later presence at the Biennali as a group.[165]

Straight alliances over wars of position were de rigour towards the end of the regime as a matter of survival for all involved, and the avant-gardes were no exception as autonomy was not a worthwhile practice. From 1938 onwards, the abstract movements had been clustering around the journal *Valori primordiali*, founded by Franco Ciliberti and published by Augustea (Rome-Milan). After the III Quadriennale in 1939, futurists, abstracticists and important Como-based architects formed the Gruppo primordiale i futuristi Sant'Elia, branding themselves as the last bastion of the avant-gardes fighting for the survival of Italian art under the regime, as Marinetti himself admitted in his even more bombastic than usual presentation. A tempered anti-bourgeois spirit could still be detected, diluted by an amalgamation of directions which lacked incisiveness and focus. Their *Manifesto del gruppo futuristi primordiali – primordialità futurista* was signed by Ciliberti, Badiali, Magnaghi, Nizzoli, Munari, Radice, Rho, Soldati, Benedetta, Licini and Prampolini, architects Sartoris, Terragni, Cattaneo, Lingeri, Marinetti, and was published in *L'Ambrosiano* on 15 October 1941. In the same year, the group staged an exhibition at the Galleria Mascioni in Milan and returned to a simplified idea of art which existed in an autonomous space and was

---

[165] On the importance of the galleries within the State art project, see Salvagnini's comprehensive analysis, *Il sistema delle arti*, 173–314. Notable galleries in Milan were Galleria Milano, Le Tre Arti, Dedalo, Annunciata (for the Chiarista movement); for more details on the working mechanisms of art galleries, see AA.VV., *Abstracta, Germania, Austria, Italia, 1919–1939* (Milan, Electa, 1997), 135–9.

detached from the political one, but admittedly there was a real and not putative war to be dealing with.[166]

Abstract art did not at any time claim an ascendency to the status of State art, other than by proximity with its supporters, but it nonetheless epitomized the degree of rationalization that Italian art as a whole was seeking at a theoretical level. Moreover, it did function as an important theoretical sounding board, since it hypothesized more than any other movement the process of rationalization through lines and rhythms. Its lack of any explicit social or political commitment could not but be regrettable in the 1930s, reducing it to a lesser artistic movement in terms of topicality.

---

[166] Ludovico Biaggi, 'Dove va l'atrattismo', *Perseo*, IX/111 (June 1938), 1, reduced abstracticism to a meaningless bizzaria.

Agon 5: Aerofuturism: Journeys and Explorations

Aeropainting has been widely researched, and widely discussed in criticism and scholarship as one of the key distinctive features of the second wave of futurism since it pervaded, in theoretical terms, and united, in practical terms, all the artistic strands we have so far discussed here.[1] Aerofuturism has a synthetic role to play in our understanding of both the system of the arts and of State art for two main reasons. Firstly, it brings together all the aesthetic trends identified in this monograph, from the representational to the non-representational. Secondly, it responds to the ideological propositions articulated by the regime, particularly in the 1930s, through the creation of new myths to foster forms of mass consensus, especially during the Second World War. Aeropainting and aerosculpture make manifest precisely the relationship between aesthetics and politics that our argument has sought to outline thus far. Amongst the many expressions of aeropainting, our particular interest here are those that bring to the fore such poles in an explicit fashion: that is, the State-supported exhibitions discussed, and the aesthetics of powered flight.

Prepare for Take-off

The debate on aerofuturism began as early as 1919, when former war pilot Fedele Azari flew over Milan dropping leaflets for the *Teatro aereo futurista*. His coup de théâtre marked the start of the use of flight as a new means of rendering futurism spectacular.

---

[1] Amongst the many scholarly contributions on aeropainting, it is worth mentioning those by Federico Caprotti, 'Profitability, practicality and ideology Fascist civil aviation and the short life of Ala Littoria, 1934–1943', *The Journal of Transport History*, 32/1 (2012), 17–38; 'Overcoming Distance and Space through Technology: Record Aviation Linking Fascist Italy with South America', *Space and Culture*, 14(3) (2011), 330–48; and 'Technology and geographical imaginations: representing aviation in 1930s Italy', *Journal of Cultural Geography*, 25/2 (2008), 181–205; Roberto Esposito, *Fascism, Aviation and Mythical Modernity*; Eric Lehmann, *Le ali del potere. La propaganda aeronautica nell'Italia fascista* (Turin, Utet, 2010); Christine Poggi, 'The Return of the Repressed: Tradition as Myth in Futurist Fascism', in Claudia Lazzaro and Roger Crum (eds), *Donatello among the Blackshirts: History and Modernity in the Visual Culture of Fascist Italy* (Ithaca, NY, Cornell UP, 2005), 203–22; Claudio Rebeschini (ed.), *Aeropittura. La seduzione del volo* (Milan, Skira, 2017); Claudia Salaris, *aero … futurismo e mito del volo*; and Elisa Sai, *Aeropittura, Futurism and Space in the 1930s: Continuity, Innovation and Reception* (Bristol PhD thesis, University of Bristol, 2010). All these scholarly works situate the discussion within the broader historical context of the day.

The aviator-hero was not yet the New Man, but an individual and isolated heroic figure: neither the Man of the mechanical revolution, nor the collective subject shaped by the Fascist anthropological revolution.[2] After the pioneering days of Francesco Baracca and the First World War, aviation progressively assumed a much more prominent position, both in its civic and military manifestations. Azari's highly performative flight over Milan was quickly followed by a number of other spectacular moments in the history of aviation. In 1921, Arturo Ferrarin made the first flight from Rome to Tokyo; in 1925, Francesco de Pinedo rose to fame with his Ansaldo SVA-9 aeroplane flight from Rome to Melbourne, Tokyo, then back to Rome; and in 1927, he piloted a Savoia Marchetti seaplane from Rome to Brazil via the African continent. In 1928, Ferrarin and Carlo Del Prete set the world distance record over a closed circuit for a flight from Rome to New York, and in 1928, Italo Balbo's first passenger flight from May 25 to June 2 flew from Orbetello to the Balearics, then along the Spanish and French coasts and back to Italy, and was hailed as a triumph of Italian aviation.

The Ministero dell'aeronautica (previously the Commissariato dell'aeronautica, established in 1923) was officially inaugurated in 1927; the same year that the Coppa Schneider, hosted in Venice, was won not by England as anticipated but by the underdogs, Italy. The regime had invested significantly in this event, as is evident in, for instance, an Umberto di Lazzaro's advertisement celebrating the technological triumph of the orange-red seaplane, the Macchi M. 52, in flight across a deep blue sky over a sparkling sea, with a white horse rearing up from the water, and in general of Italian aviation.[3] The vivid colours of the advertisement invite a clear and positive response from the viewer: fascist modernity is to be set against the beauty and mythologies of the past, projecting a repertoire of fresh myths to signify a new era and the political and aesthetic sphere proceed in parallel as we have seen in many of the analyses thus far.

Flying was a force of nature and was indicative of technological prowess, a symbol of Man dominating nature itself, but needed to be visualized as Public art. To paraphrase Fillìa, it was a lyrically engineered, mechanical idol (see Agon 4). In 1929, Balbo led a crossing of the Western Mediterranean (a three-leg route covering Orbetello–Athens–Istanbul–Odessa) by 40 planes and 130 crew members; on landing in the Soviet Union, he was given an enthusiastic reception.[4] In the same year, Marinetti's secretary Luigi Scrivo set up the press agency L'ALA (Agenzia Letterario–Artistica) to disseminate topical news about literary and artistic matters, particularly in relation to aerofuturism. Between December 1930 and January 1931, the former *quadrumvir* Balbo completed his first transatlantic flight, from Orbetello to Rio de Janeiro, deploying fourteen planes and reaching the extraordinary speed of 162 km per hour on the flight. This achievement is beautifully illustrated by Umberto di Lazzaro in his poster *Il volo in massa Italia–Brasile* (1931, 100 × 70 cm), which featured all the great pilots who had taken part in so modern an exploit. The poster uses bright colours expressionistically: the Brazilian sky is yellow rather than blue; the sea is green; the planes are painted in

---

[2]   Esposito, *Fascism, Aviation and Mythical Modernity*, 229–30, 357–61.
[3]   Lehmann, *Le ali del potere*, 233–4.
[4]   Ibid., about other similar press releases, 170.

blue and light orange to suggest their proximity to the sun, and indeed to the new sun of Brazil. Only eleven planes actually arrived in Rio on 15 January 1931 to see this new sun, but such details were quickly forgotten.

The Crociera Aerea Italiana Roma–Chicago–New York–Roma del Decennale, held from 1 July to 12 August 1933, was the aviation sector's public contribution to the celebration of the sacralization of the dictatorship, and it was a great public success, featuring twenty-five SIAI-Marchetti SM.55 planes and fifty-two pilots, a chief engineer and sixty-two highly qualified non-commissioned officers.[5] The Mayor of Chicago, Edward J. Kelly, on 21 July 1933, sent his best regards to the Mayor of Milan and congratulated the Italian government for the 'gesture of good will made by dispatching Balbo to the United States'.[6] In his study of aviation in Italy, Eric Lehmann has defined Balbo's exploits between 1929 and 1933 as a 'Balbo system' because of how he used cinematography and advertisement for self-publicity and self-fashioning.[7] Balbo, we might suggest in line with what we have already discussed in this book, had single-handedly transformed the individual aristocratic hero of the early days of aviation into a collective and mass phenomenon. Aeropainting was also highly functional for the other main ambition of both the second wave of futurism and of futurism as State art: it turned autonomous aesthetic practices into practices of the everyday. At the V Triennale, the Stazione per aeroporto civile aeropainters used 'plastica murale' in their frescoes. In 1936, the newly founded MinCulPop (Ministry for Popular Culture) supported the organization of the Prima mostra nazionale del cartellone e della grafica pubblicitaria held at the Palazzo delle Esposizioni in Rome. Advertising was a testimony to this shift to the quotidian, with its ability to circulate images that became myths of the everyday; that is, myths that could contribute to the sacralization of the regime, whilst maintaining an aesthetic attractiveness, contrary to the monumentality and severity of Public art. Mario Gros's *Cioccolato ali d'Italia Talmone* (1937), for example, introduced the myth of the military aviator and the aeroplane into the popular imagination, tying it on the one hand to chocolate and on the other to Christopher Columbus's explorations and conquests of new worlds. Marcello Dudovich's *Crociera aerea del decennale* (1933) also sacralized Balbo as a national hero, and elevated aviation to the ranks of national glory, as a result of his ambition and bravery in discovering new worlds that could be introduced to fascist civilization.[8]

This handful of examples illustrates just how pervasive was the use of flying-related propaganda amongst youth organizations, during military and civic events, and for promotional purposes at the Opera nazionale dopolavoro, one of the chief State apparatuses for creating consent. The aeroplane was the machine that could render spectacular and could mythologize the regime in every aspect of people's private and

---

[5] See, for example, Ivanhoe Gambini, *L'ala di Balbo verso i grattacieli*, 1932. For a timely résumé of the successes and axes of Italian aviation, see Luigi Contini, 'Le tappe fondamentali dell'aviazione nazionale', *Emporium*, LXXVII/465 (September 1933), 161–79.

[6] Letter found in the Rivolta folder, AGR. Similar letters were sent from Milan to the Mayors of Montreal, New York and of Chicago on 29 May 1933 on the occasion of the Crociera del Decennale.

[7] Lehmann, *Le ali del potere*, 169–70.

[8] On Munari's borrowings from North American culture, see Schnapp, 'The Little Theatre of the Page', in Antonello-Nardelli-Zanoletti (eds), *Bruno Munari*, 120.

public lives, as we have seen in the decoration of post offices. Some of the publicity posters displayed quotidian or tourist activities, frequently using Art Deco figurative codes, as for example in *Tutti a volare. Partenze dall'aeroporto civile di Taliedo* (1931, anonymous), or in Umberto di Lazzaro's *Giro aereo d'Europa* (7–20 August 1929) which showed planes flying over Milan's Duomo, the Lion of Venice and the Mole Antonelliana in Turin.[9] Flying, we are invited to believe, is a modern myth and an elegant activity. Two further interesting examples of the aesthetics of flight because of their experimental flare, pervasive as it were of State art itself, are Bruno Munari and Lucio Fontana's advertising design *Lloyd Triestino* (1936), and Fontana's *Expressdienst Nach Allen Erdteilen, Italia-Cosulich-Lloyd Triestino-Adria* (1935). Through the use of rationalized forms, the modern myth of transport as a modernizing fact in peoples' everyday lives is shaped. In the case of Fontana's poster, the ship is the symbol not only of a new aesthetics but also of a new type of elegance that can offer freedom of movement to larger groups. Flying and transport were no longer therefore to be seen simply as the preserve and sport of the elite, but instead could be packaged for mass consumption, mass tourism or indeed for political and social propaganda.

In his analysis of the propaganda films used to encourage young Italians to join the ranks of the aviation forces, Lehmann points out how technological advancements in aviation were also used as a persuasive tool for recruitment.[10] It was not only military pilots that were used to publicize aviation; so too were civil pilots, as for example in the Giro d'Italia aereo per veivoli da turismo (August–September 1930).[11] In military aviation, under the regime's support, the Palazzo dell'aeronautica was inaugurated in 1931, designed by the architect Roberto Marino and commissioned by Italo Balbo.[12] The new Scuola di guerra aerea in Florence was built later, in 1937–8, designed by Raffaello Fagoni.

Suspended in the Air

The artistic production of aeropainting is vast if somewhat erratic in quality, and highly diverse in execution. This notwithstanding, we can observe a gradual change from the lyrical and mystical nature of Fillìa's artworks to later exempla that emphasize the technical advantages of the machine, those of the aviator, and those of the artist which, in concert, could make Italy great. The same year the *Manifesto dell'aeropittura futurista* was published in the *Gazzetta del popolo* (22 September, 'Prospettive di volo') and signed by Marinetti, Balla, Depero, Prampolini, Dottori, Benedetta, Fillìa, Tato, Somenzi, on his part Fillìa completed his *Spiritualità dell'aviatore* (1929), an artwork that epitomized the mystical aspect of aeropainting and continues what he had started

---

[9] Sonia Pellegrini (ed.), *L'officina del volo: futurismo, pubblicità e design 1908–1938* (Cinisello Balsamo, Silvana Editoriale, 2009), 68, 80.

[10] Lehmann, *Le ali del potere*, 179.

[11] Ibid., 181.

[12] For the poster marking the occasion, see Pellegrini, *L'officina del volo*, 65.

with *Sensibilità futuriste* in 1926.[13] The centre of the composition is a simplified and rationalized image of an aviator criss-crossed by trails of colours over his head and heart. Colours prevail over any form of realistic representation: the pilot is a red figure framed by two splashes of yellow around his eyes and heart, and by a blue and white contrail. Aeropainting, as interpreted by Fillìa, is quite simply an exploration of an impossible journey and an interrogation of anything that can surpass the material. Any transcendent reality must be connected with its mundane objectivity, and in this dialectics between subjectivity and objectivity we find a clear link with future developments of aeropainting and State art as we have discussed thus far.[14] Stylistically, lines are no longer rendered according to rigid geometries but instead seem to envelop a form of subjectivity that is becoming one with the form of cosmic idealism: materiality and cosmos fused together through 'synthesis', 'colour', 'fluid shapes' and 'analogies'.[15] Indeed, in 1932, Fillìa – who signed, alongside Marinetti, the *Manifesto dell'arte sacra futurista* in 1931 – organized a solo exhibition at the Casa d' Arte Bragaglia of fifteen paintings that could be developed into larger sizes. This pointed towards what would soon become *arte murale* featuring aeropainting and sacred art in an indirect parallelism, as would be the case at the larger exhibition, Aeropittura – Arte sacra futurista, at the Casa d'Arte in La Spezia with Fillìa, Oriani and Rosso.

The first aeropainting show in Rome – the Prima mostra di aeropittura dei futuristi Balla, Ballelica, Benedetta, Diulgheroff, Dottori, Fillìa, Oriani, Prampolini, Bruna Somenzi, Tato, Thayaht – was held at the Camerata degli artisti and then subsequently at Rome's Aeroclub, in February 1931, and was later followed by shows in Trieste, Paris and Milan's Galleria Pesaro, featuring forty-one aeropaintings. At that first show in Rome, Balla presented his *Celeste metallico italiano* (*Balbo e i trasvolatori italiani*): a celebration of Balbo's feats and a statement about futurism and State art in more palingenetic and political terms.[16] In this representation, Balbo is a New Man and a new heroic figure upholding a propagandistic role of the arts. Other examples help to bridge this gap. Osvaldo Peruzzi was an engineer by training but under Fillìa's influence began to experiment with aeropainting in 1932, producing aerial 'landscapes' filled with '*splendori geometrici aeroterrestri, spiritualità aerea*' (geometrical splendours, aereoterrestrial spirituality). In 1933, he made his *Trasvolata atlantica o Squadriglia sui grattacieli* an artwork that combined the architecture of skyscrapers with a still-lyrical yet geometrical portrayal of the aircraft.[17] This is revealed to the viewer along

---

[13] Oil on canvas, 100 × 70 cm, On. Pietro Campilli private collection, Rome. The work was realized around the same time as those at the Palazzo delle Poste in La Spezia to critical acclaim.

[14] Poggi, *Inventing Futurism*, 254–5.

[15] *Spiritualità aerea*, *c*. 1931, oil on cardboard, 65 × 50 cm, Germana Colombo private collection, Turin. This notion was rather important to aeropainting aesthetics, especially to Fillìa. He discussed it twice in his theoretical writings which outline the principles of aeropainting: namely, 'Spiritualità aerea' (*Oggi e domani*, 4 November 1930) and 'Spiritualità futurista' (*Oggi e domani*, 26 October 1931).

[16] Oil on canvas, 52.5 × 68 cm, currently at the Stato Maggiore dell'Aeronautica Italiana in Rome.

[17] Tempera on paper, 60 × 45 cm, Eredi Peruzzi collection. Exhibited at Mostra nazionale futurista, Rome 1933, Hamburg 1934, Berlin 1934, Sindacale Livornese, Livorno 1934–5, Biennale Venezia 1938, Futuristi aeropittori di guerra, Ferrara 1941.

dynamic diagonal lines that contour the landscapes in a composition that stands in a precarious equilibrium between Sant'Elia, the universe of mechanical art and the later 'cosmic lyricism' of Prampolini. The *Trasvolata atlantica* simultaneously conveyed fascist rigour and order, the utopianism of Balbo's conquest of the skies and the lyrical ambition of the art of flight, a conflation we have also seen in advertising. *Volo sui grattacieli* was also inspired by Balbo's *Crociera aerea del Decennale*, but realized instead in a deep pallet of hues that embraced the expressionist tones of Benedetta's earlier blues and greens in her *Velocità di motoscafo* or *Laghi salati algerini*. Peruzzi continued to use geometrical abstraction in conjunction with an expressionistic use of colours, often tones of blue, but the overall composition is more geometrical and architecturally structured than earlier, dedicated to Balbo's transatlantic flight.[18]

Another thought-provoking example of war aeropainting as an expression of how the art transverses the dictatorship is the *Battaglia aeronavale* (1939), which combined soft curvilinear forms demarcating a distinguishable aircraft, a ship and a biomorphic shape again reminiscent of Benedetta's pioneering *Velocità di motoscafo*.[19] The war-like atmosphere is rendered in surrealist tones: a landscape no longer recognizable in a naturalistic way, as in the case of the *Trasvolata atlantica o Squadriglia sui grattacieli*.[20] In 1939, at the opening of his exhibition in Cagliari, futurist Corrado Forlin noted that 'an object does not end where another one starts, but continues its dynamic action'.[21] Dynamism between objects, then, erased boundaries, creating thereby a simultaneous effect of compenetrating spaces and units of time, as well as compenetrations between objects themselves. Forlin continued his presentation at the *vernissage* by emphasizing how Cagliari's *federale*, Gaetano Pattarozzi, agreed with this idea of dynamism since it encapsulated strength and vigour in motion – which differed from the static reproduction of reality practiced by traditional artists. Forlin associated an aesthetic problem with a political one, and in so doing shifted the terms of the comparison between aesthetic and politics in preparation for the last phase of futurist aesthetics in general and of aerofuturism in particular. In 1941, the Savarè group organized the ninth Mostra di aeropittura di guerra, in honour of the prematurely deceased great hero Italo Balbo in Ferrara. If we compare the exhibits to earlier works, we can see a decline into more didactic visual codes, reducing aeropainting to a means of publicizing nationalistic and propagandist – often belligerent – messages.[22]

---

[18] Oil on paper, 65 × 50 cm, Eredi Peruzzi collection. Exhibited at the Padiglione italiano at the Paris Expo, 1937.

[19] Exhibited at the III Quadriennale, oil on card, 93 × 70 cm, Frati collection, Livorno.

[20] Other similar works are Barbara, *La città che ruota*, 1935, and *Battaglia aerea*, 1942.

[21] '*un oggetto non finisce dove comincia un altro oggetto, ma continua, prosegue e sviluppa la sua azione dinamica*', F. For. 1.1.6, Mostra di aeropittura Cagliari, January 1939, MART.

[22] This type of initiative continued throughout the war years, including solo exhibitions of Tato (Ministero dell'Aeronautica, 1941) and Crali (Mostra personale, Biennale, 1941) or in 1942 publications on Caviglioni (*L'aeropittore futurista A. Caviglioni e il Futurismo Bolognese*, Edizioni del Gruppo futurista Guglielmo Marconi, Bologna) in an attempt at historicizing and sacralizing futurism.

Prepare for Landing

Before this decline, though, in 1933 Depero himself drew some conclusions about aerofuturism and, indirectly, about 1930s futurist art, in his comments on the work of certain futurist artists. For example:

Prampolini

Palombaro nello spazio

A terraqueous globe which sails across the clouds, appears at the entrance of a tunnel of sidereal shades. The action of forces in play is expressed with deep thought, with few but sufficient realistic reference and with evanescent tones of significance, and take the viewer to the intuitive expressive centre of the artwork itself.

Dottori

A true aeropainting not only because of its subject matter, but mostly because of the mechanical atmosphere, polygonal, machine-made-noise that live in it. A synchronization between the terrestrial vision and the agitate, vertiginous, wrestling space.

Caviglioni

Esploratore dello spazio

It is a real cloud of abstract, fabricated humanity, a palpable nudity of light and space.

Munari

Costruire

Pyramids made of arches, trunks, tubes, pylons, compenetrating and piled up in a kind of glass mountain.[23]

In his assessment of aeropainting, Depero elucidated and summarized some essential points: Prampolini could fuse abstraction and realism in such a way as to create mystery and the longing for universal absolution; he could put human and

---

[23] Prampolini *Un globo terraqueo naviga fra le nubi, appare all'imbocco di un tunnel di ombre siderali. L'azione delle forze in gioco espressa con profondo pensiero, con pochi ma sufficienti richiami realistici con evanescenza di toni e forte rilievo, portano l'osservatore al fulcro intuitivo ed espressivo dell'opera stessa.* Dottori *Creazione aeropittorica non solo per il soggetto che tratta, ma soprattutto per l'atmosfera meccanica, poligonale, motorumoristica che in essa si vive. Sincronizzazione fra la visione terrestre e lo spazio agitato, vertiginoso e arrovellato.* Caviglioni *È un'autentica nube di astratta umanità inventata, una palpabile nudità di luce e spazio.* Munari *Piramide di archi, di portici, di tronchi, di tubi, di tralicci, compenetrati e accatastati in una specie di montagna vitrea.* F. 'Depero', Dep. 4.1.69, ms 7276, f. 'Commento alle opera di pittori futuristi [di F. Depero [1933]', MART.

supernatural synthesis, universal freedom and the anxiety of the everyday all on the same level. Dottori, meanwhile, was able to synchronize the terrestrial with the aerial through shared rhythms and lines and, on his part, the political ambition of conquering the skies. Angelo Caviglioni's *Esploratore dello spazio* is futurist abstraction fused with dynamism that reflects human nature in its compositions of light and space. Finally, Munari constructs: but he is not simply assembling parts; rather, he multiplies the parts of an infinite machine that can be observed and operated from a hundred different perspectives, constituting a new non-figurative realism.

After 1938, aeropainting became a form of war propaganda. One of the most iconic of the artists involved was Tullio Crali. Crali's *plastica spaziale* continued along the same lines as Prampolini's work.[24] *Incuneandosi nell'abitato (in tuffo sulla città)* is one of the most famous futurist aeropaintings because of how it reconfigures the relationship between subjectivity and objectivity, and elevates the heroic New Man/Woman to conqueror not only of the absolute zone of the skies but also of a modern city full of skyscrapers and tall buildings.[25] If we compare it with Mino Delle Site's *Viaggi interplanetari* of 1937, we can see how the atmosphere has changed: the evocative power and mysteries of flying have been replaced by a more aggressive and figurative language, one that strives to assert a supremacy of one over the other, rather than a quest for knowledge.[26]

Crali's point of observation is from above, set just behind the pilot, and the sense it invites in the viewer is a desire for supremacy. We can see the pilot's head and shoulders from inside a cockpit that is open not only at the front but also the sides and even the top. The urban environment is organized according to principles of rationalist architecture: the buildings are cubes; some have lines of square units – windows – on their façades. This type of pictorial organization emphasizes the sense of imminent danger, of a potential crash; but also invokes the control of the pilot over technology. The New Man/Woman can triumph not only over nature but also over new civilizations, in guise of a modernizing hero and coording to the voice of fascist, as well as futurist, rhetoric. War aeropainting reworked some earlier themes to adapt them to a new political situation. *Incuneandosi nell'abitato* is far more realistic than *Spiritualità dell'aviatore*, and is closer to new aesthetic paradigms such as those put forward by Corrente. The journey is no longer an exploration of mystery, but a form of conquest of a new space in order to construct a new, modernized civilization. Fascist rhetoric and futurist rhetoric are both explicit in stating and illustrating a putative victory that, in the final analysis, actually signified defeat.

Despite the somewhat poor results of such artistic exploits, there remained, right until the fall of the dictatorship, this focus on the importance of the new relationship between aesthetics and politics, subjectivity and objectivity, individuality and

---

[24] In order to be able to glorify the war, Tullio Crali and other artists were dispensed from '*ogni servizio e godranno della massima libertà e ospitalità ai campi e ai reparti presso i quali saranno accreditati*' to produce aeropaintings to be exhibted at the Biennale (F. 'Crali 2. 212/52', 12 July 1941, f. 'Ministero dell' Aeronautica to Tullio Crali', MART).

[25] 1939, oil on cardboard, 130 × 155 cm, MART.

[26] Oil on canvas, 40 × 50 cm, private collection.

collectivity, on the New/Man and woman, on technology and modernization of the public sphere, on the reconfiguration of realist and figurative representations into non-mimetic forms.

Towards an Aesthetic of War, 1934–44

On 1 February 1934, in *Sant'Elia*, Marinetti, Somenzi and Mazzoni published the *Manifesto dell'architettura aerea*, with its illustration of the *aerocity*, a theme of Le Corbusier's repertoire, which was to feature prominently in aeropainting only a few months later. Shortly after, with a similar-sized contingent of ninety-five artworks, the futurists arrived at the 1934 Biennale. Marinetti's presentation was shorter but more pointed than ever; the variety of artists was greater; and there were no solo exhibitions. In his propagandistic summative introduction, Marinetti could easily historicize and sacralize aerofuturism, by listing in full all the exhibitions of aerofuturism which had preceded the Venice Biennale.[27] The key proponents of aeropainting were still Dottori, Fillìa, Munari, Oriani, Prampolini and Tato, Rosso and Thayaht for sculpture, together with new arrival Tullio Crali. Women artists also starred: Benedetta, Fides Testi, Regina, Marisa Mori; and there were new male artists too, including Roberto Baldessari, Alessandro Bruschetti, Ivanhoe Gambini and Beppe Santomaso, and the most appreciated work was Tato's *Splendore meccanico* because of its 'realism', or a document of an action. According to Marinetti's introduction, who was trying to negotiate a position of compromise with Mussolini, aeropainting was a purer form of avant-garde art contaminated neither by Judaism or Marxism. As a result, it was a distinctive brand of Italian art that worked better than others in support of fascist aviation.

The Mostra dell'aeronautica italiana opened on 16 June 1934 at the Palazzo dell'Arte in Milan and was quintessentially instrumentalized art, with the façade decorated by Erberto Carboni with a stylized *fascio littorio* towering over a group of fighter planes effectively politicizing aeropainting in a similar fashion to the other arts we have discussed.[28] A stylized portrayal of Mussolini, the New Man, similar to that on the Casa del fascio, was placed, propaganda-style, at the entrance. It would later gain prominence as an emblem of Italy that functioned as a trigger to artistic experimentation. In his inaugural speech the podestà Visconti di Modrone, himself a man of the air, made

---

[27] I Mostra di aeropittura, February 1931 at the Camerata degli artisti in Rome; Mostra futurista. Pittura–scultura–arti decorative–architettura, organized by the Gruppo futurista toscano in February 1931; the Mostra at the Galleria Pesaro in October 1930; the Pittura aeropittura futurista exhibition in Trieste (6–20 March 1931) at the Sala Bianca del Circolo Artistico di via del Coroneo with Prampolini, Tato, Dottori, Fillìa, Benedetta, Pozzo, Oriani and Diulgheroff showing a total of seventy-three artworks. Internationally, aerofuturism had also been exhibited in Paris (March 1931 at Sala de l'Effort, at the prestigious Galerie de la Renaissance with Marinetti's presentation), in Brussels (at the Palais des Beaux Arts, April–May 1931), and in Athens (April 1931).

[28] Fernando Esposito, 'In "the shadow of the winged machine … ": The Esposizione dell' Aeronautica Italiana and the Ascension of Myth in the Slipstream of Modernity', *modernism/modernity*, 19/1 (2012), 139–52.

three important points: glory of Italy aside, the Mostra contributed to the economy of the aesthetics, since it was a way of showcasing Italian industrial production and indeed a source of income for the city. The speech moved between a propagandistic tone quoting the feats of Balbo and Gabriele D'Annunzio and a local one, which complimented the 'building companies and private citizens' contributing to staging of the event.[29] The exhibition was not meant to show merely the technical prowess of Italian aviation but its social usefulness for the citizens, including hints at commercial and touristic exploitations of flight. The Duce authorized the event but the working party included the Ministero dell' Aeronautica, the Fondazione Bernocchi for the staging (with a budget of 750,000 lire) in Milan and the city municipality. The selection of pieces to be exhibited was to be approved by a committee chaired by the podestà Visconti di Modrone and comprising of important Milanese citizens, industrialists, high-ranked military officers and experts.

Furthermore and once more, the Mostra did not stop in Milan. Thanks to Marinetti's several tours he embarked on during the 1930s who took him to South America as well as around Europe, the international resonance of aerofuturism reached Hamburg, with the Luft und Flugmalerei show that Vasari curated, which opened on 24 February with Göring, Goebbels and Rust (Minister of Education) in attendance. Marinetti insisted on placing Thayaht's *Dux* at the entrance as a telling example of State art. At the dinner that followed the *vernissage*, Gottfried Benn praised the relationship between art and State that Italian futurism had been able to develop, singling out aerofuturism as a particularly powerful example of such collaboration for its ability to invite consensus across the masses. Just one month later, on 25 March 1934, Berlin's *vernissage* had been deserted by these authorities after Marinetti was accused by Alfred Rosenberg, in a circular signed by his spokesman the leading art critic Robert Scholz, of anarchic sympathies.[30]

The year 1936 unfolded with some significant changes. Marinetti left for Ethiopia with the Division 28, Lino Pesaro died and Carrà stopped writing for *L'Ambrosiano*. Sarfatti made her last public appearance with Mussolini, at the ceremony for the proclamation of the Italian empire; and the 1939 Triennale was postponed to 1940.

At the 1936 Biennale, 112 futurists exhibited, hosted once again in the Russian Pavilion after Moscow had granted its authorization and deserted the Venice show.[31] On this occasion, Marinetti praised the artists that had fought, as he had, in the African campaign: that is, Menin, Belli, Baldessari. For the futurist leader little had changed: since the war was still something exhilarating and to be seen as a source of aesthetic inspiration, for three reasons, he said: namely, in order to:

---

[29] F. 'Rivolta', f. 62 'Inaugurazione della Mostra dell'Aeronautica' (16 June 1934), and f. 'L'Esposizione dell'Aeronautica italiana a Milano', AGR.

[30] Salaris, *Artecrazia*, 189 discusses the negative reactions to the exhibition and the progressive German ostracism towards the avant-gardes classed as 'degenerate art'. The *Dux* was selected for a prize at the Prima adunta nazionale professionisti e artisti, 1929. Jonathan Petropoulos, *Artists under Hitler: Collaboration and Survival in Nazi Germany* (New Heaven, Yale UP, 2014), 339.

[31] Matteo Bertelé, *Arte sovietica alla Biennale di Venezia* (Udine, Mimesis, 2020).

1. Express the constructive dynamism of fighting
2. Guess and fix the plastic form of the different sounds
3. Express the exciting simultaneity which characterizes the battle of Africa.[32]

The African campaign was predictably reworked into an artistic expression that re-semanticized previous statements in attempting to gain even more prominence within the regime as, for example, in celebrated Mario Menin's representations of the war he fought with Marinetti (according to Marinetti). Together with praise there was also criticism towards aeropainting because of its repetitive nature and scarcity of innovation. But, on this occasion, State acquisitions of aeropaintings were even higher than those in 1934 because of the propagandistic tone of these works.

The Mostra di aeropittura futurista at the Ministry of Aviation in 1937 privileged artworks with a more accessible didactic and nationalist message for its audience to grasp, with sizeable space devoted to Tato and Ambrosi, setting a trend for all the national exhibitions until the fall of the regime.[33] In 1937, A. F. Della Porta, of *Perseo* and *Il Popolo d'Italia*, launched a campaign against Marinetti (labelled 'the Italian from Egypt'), Somenzi and futurism. Farinacci's *Il Regime Fascista* followed suit together with more moderate interventions by Maraini in *Il Popolo d'Italia* and Ojetti in column at the *Corriere della Sera* in August. In 1938, the polemic between Marinetti and Interlandi in the *Tevere* was one of avant-garde art being accused of being Bolshevik and Jewish. The defence of modern art was on the grounds of its fidelity to *italianità*; but it was difficult to ignore a cosmopolitan disposition amongst the avant-gardes. Bottai's mediations in 1938 calmed matters somewhat when he separated the sphere of action of the State from that of the arts. However, in 1939 (after at least two seizures), *Artecrazia* had to be closed down.[34]

In 1938, naturally, futurism had to defend its position more vigorously. The sixty-three artworks on display at the 1938 Biennale explored similar themes to the 1936 Biennale, but on this occasion, Marinetti included the Spanish civil war in his routine presentation, this time entitled 'Futuristi aeropittori d'Africa e di Spagna'. As an introduction to the exhibition, it was longer and more detailed than that of 1936 for a grand total of twelve pages, and set out thoughts he would later put forward again at the III Quadriennale. Relentlessly until the very end, he kept on historicizing the movement, claiming a long lineage of relationship with the regime at all junctures of its history. His principal argument was relatively sharp and to the point: aeropainting and aerosculpture were the most suitable aesthetic paradigms for representing and now for documenting almost figuratively the current glory of the Italian empire, and not just that of the nation. More women were enrolled into the futurist movement; Olga

---

[32] 1) *Esprimere il dinamismo costruttivo del combattimento; 2) Intuire e fissare le forme plastiche dei diversi fragori; 3) Esprimere l'eccitante simultaneità gonfia di lirismo che caratterizza una battaglia d'Africa*, Catalogo della XX Esposizione Internazionale d'Arte della Citta di Venezia, 1930, 180.

[33] In this press release, exactly the same point is made, F. 'Rivolta', f. 'Note per la cronaca, 25 May 1940. Comune di Milano', AGR.

[34] Salaris, *Artecrazia*, 198 and passim. For a detailed account of the accusations towards Marinetti and of his responses, see Ialongo, *Filippo Tommaso Marinetti*, 259–71.

Biglieri Scurto, aka Barbara (*aviatrice-pilota*) and Leandra Angelucci; representations of Mussolini and other prominent figure as pilots became abundant. Portraiture now functioned as trivializing Public art and as unrefined propaganda art. These counted, amongst others, those by much praised Alfredo Gauro Ambrosi's *Aeroritratto di Benito Mussolini aviatore*, *Aeroritratto di S. E. Galeazzo Ciano*, *Aeroritratto di Marinetti aeropoeta* and *Aeroritratto di Gianni Caproni pioniere dell'aviazione italiana*; Corrado Forlin's *Ritratto sintetico di Benito Mussolini*; Sante Monachesi's *Mussolini aviatore*; and Leonida Zen's *Mussolini in volo*, in an attempt at reviving both the cult of the Duce and its modernity more vividly and accessibly.[35] Other themes for works depicted aerial fights (Cesare Andreoni, Angelo Caviglioni, Chetofi, Mino Rosso), and bombing (Alessandro Bruschetti, Tullio Crali, Italo Fasullo) as a collective endeavour and not the feat of some grandee à la Balbo. A notable presence from the provinces in this Biennale was 'rising star' Tullio Crali, with his landmark *Incuneandosi nell'abitato*. Another was Osvaldo Peruzzi, with *Trasvolata atlantica* and *L'uomo aereo*. Such themes were at the same time autarchic, able to reach out across the entire nation, and not 'esterofile', or xenophilic – a clarification designed to divert attacks from Interlandi and Farinacci.

At the Mostra futurista di aeropittori e aeroscultori (a hundred artworks comprising paintings and sculptures and, *de rigueur*, Prampolini's show), during the III Quadriennale, 1939, Marinetti divided aeropainting into four categories featuring rather extravagant titles: Dottori and Benedetta's work as *trasfiguratrice lirica*, Prampolini's as *stratosferica cosmica bionica*, Fillìa's as *essenziale mistica ascensionale pittorica* and Tato and Ambrosi's as *sintetica documentaria dinamica di paesaggi e urbanismi visti dall'alto e in velocità*.[36] What's more, on this occasion, Marinetti honoured Thayaht as the prime representative of *aerocultura polimaterica, astratta, simbolica, cosmica* (multi-material, abstract, symbolic, cosmic aerosculpture), thereby bringing to a synthesis the entire debate of the 1930s on the total work of art and on the phenomenology of aeropainting. Notwithstanding the usual dominance of Prampolini and his peers, in fact other anti-Novecento movements began to grow in visibility and to articulate alternative aesthetic and theoretical prepositions spanning established, non-conformist and up-and-coming artists such as Fontana, Guttuso, Manzù, Pirandello, Paolucci, Mirko and Frazzini.

During the first of the war Biennali, in 1940, the futurists arrived as a coherent group, and forcibly as the only avant-garde movement still existing on its own terms, bringing a total of sixty-two artworks.[37] It is worth mentioning that in 1938 and 1940 the value of artworks sold raised again over one million lire, almost reaching the levels of the pre-statalization levels of the 1920s (1,225,456 and 1,183,012 lire, respectively). If the 1930s governmental or local institutions purchased most of the artworks, while

---

[35] Marinetti, 'Gli aeroritratti del Duce', *Meridiano di Roma*, (19 May 1940).

[36] Marinetti had already presented *Aeropittura aerocultura arte sacra futuriste e mostra postuma di Fillìa* at the retrospective dedicated to Fillìa, held at the Salone della *Gazzetta del Popolo* in Turin in 1938. Similar remarks were also present in the introduction to the 'Futuristi aeropittori d'Africa e Spagna' at the Biennale in 1938.

[37] See Salaris, *Artecrazia*, 220 on State subsidies for the futurists in the war period.

private citizens or foreign representatives very few, this trend was reversed during the 1940s with industrialists starting to purchase more art, especially futurist art.

By then a celebrated star, Tullio Crali took centre stage with a solo exhibition of fourteen works which turned aeropainting into more or less lyrical war painting and sold extremely well (notably, *Seduttore di nuvole, Decollo, Sopra vuoti d'aria, Sfiorando la città, In tuffo sulla città, Volo danzato sul nemico, Prima che si apra il paracadute, Calando nel golfo*), but that offered no new themes or stylistic innovations. For instance, even Mino Rosso's *L'Aeroscultura in bronzo del Paese degli aviatori, Aeroscultura in bronzo della gran volta* and *Bozzetto in bronzo per aeroscultura monumentale* lacked the dynamism and tensions of his earlier work. Regina's representations of war, violence and women (*Aeroferro di donne abissine, Aeroferro di stratosfera*) struck a new chord, but that was again silenced in propagandistic and derivative rendering of the Duce by Zen (*Duce simultaneo – N. 1 and N. 2, Autoritratto – N. 3, and N. 5*) and by equally unimpressive ones by Frolin (*Aeroritratto del futurista Mario Massai, Aeroritratto del creatore di Carbonia, Palombari e donne sottomarine, Nudità di donne e motori* and *Marcia su Roma*). Needless to say that the futurists were also later present in droves at the apex of war State art: that is, the ultra-nationalist Premio Cremona, which showcased Forlin, Zen and Dottori.[38]

Abstracticists Radice and Rho joined in with futurist aeropainters and participated with a triple *Aeroritratto segreto, Doppio Aeroritratto segreto* and *Aeroritratto di uno stato d'animo – N. 81, N. 95, N. 67* – renouncing more explicit abstract motives for celebratory ones, but still preserving the notion of numeric progression, *Kn*, as trademark of avant-garde art. In 1940, Mussolini could still be portrayed according to a non-figurative aesthetic paradigm; one that inscribed within itself '*i diversi dinamismi condensandoli*' (the diverse chromatism fusing them together), rather than accepting simplistic propagandist art.[39]

On the whole the war Biennali were somewhat conservative in nature, since 'we are presented with nineteenth-century selections […], which consecrate artists which are total strangers to twentieth-century art' and the critical debate was less antagonistic.[40] The attendance of the futurists at these later Biennali was less distinctive, and in some way subdued, Prampolini maintained his symbolic capital: other artists were progressively taking centre stage. Abstracticists and futurists joined forces at the 1942 Biennale with war-focused aeropainting presented by groups that included all the geographical spectrum of the movement: Savarè, Boccioni, Sant'Elia, Fillia-

---

[38] Salaris, *Storia del futurismo*, 144–71. On 3 June 1940, Corrado Forlin, on behalf of the gruppo Savarè in Monselice, wrote the *Manifesto dell'ardentismo nell'aeropittura futurista*, published in the *Resto del Carlino*; on this little-known group, see Alberto Cibin, *Corrado Forlin e il Gruppo futurista Savarè* (Trento, Scripta edizioni, 2012). In 1941, Renato di Bosso published the *Manifesto dell'aerosilografia*, http://futurismo.accademiadellacrusca.org/immagine.asp?idscheda=202&file_seq=1 (accessed 12 May 2020), and Dottori his *Manifesto umbro dell'aerofuturismo*.

[39] Marinetti, *Catalogo della XXII Esposizione Internazionale d'Arte della Città di Venezia* (1940), 180–1.

[40] See Giuliana Tomasella, *Biennali di guerra. Arte e propaganda negli anni del conflitto (1939–1944)* (Padova, Il Poligrafico, 2001) about the themes selected for the six competitions, all perfectly in line with the State's main social and cultural programmes, such as 'Squadrismo', 'Marcia su Roma', 'Le nuove città', 37, 42.

Platone, Marras-Pandolfi, Adoratori della Patria, Aria Madre, Marconi, Mediterraneo Futurista, Azari and Gondar.[41] At the 1942 Biennale, the solo exhibitions showed both futurist and abstractists: Prampolini, Radice and Rho, Radiali and Bianchi manifesting 'abstract dynamisms geared towards an absolute devotion to Art, the Future, Synthesis', as Marinetti put it, alongside Tato and Dottori, Antonio Marasco and Bruno Tato.[42] Marinetti saluted, with anticipation, the alliance futurists and the Como-based architects in his catalogue's even more chaotic contribution, entitled 'Aeropitture di guerra cosmiche biochimiche sacre documentarie meccaniche espressioni trasfiguratrici dell'infinitamente grande e dell'infinitamente piccolo in velocità voli micidiali mari in guerra matite di fuoco e dinamismi astratti'; since, he wrote, 'every contact with existing reality is to be excluded', because 'painting remains lyrical, mechanical, spiritual, plastic and geometrical transfiguration'.[43] Just like he had done in 1918, Marinetti was engaged in a desperate attempt to create a united avant-garde front, in order to be able to face inevitable defeat and to be ready for the post-war era.[44] And, not surprisingly therefore, the 1942 Biennale saw a record number of exhibits, with 235 artworks, including even more works by filo-futurists women, such as Leandra Angelucci, Carla Badiali, Barbara, Cordelia Cattaneo, Maria Ferrero Gussari, Magda Falchetto Korompay and Carla Prina and plain critical appreciation.

At the 1943 national IV Quadriennale, in the shared room of the returning fleet of the avant-gardes 'Aeropittori di guerra – aeropittori cosmici e astrattisti-futuristi', the theme, of course, could only be the war, realistic and collective as per State art. In 1943, remarkably, Prampolini had a solo exhibition once more with his mythopoeias connected with recent history (*Trasfigurazione del pilota – aeroritratto di Italo Balbo*). Other presences included a toned down Gruppo comasco: Radice and his tutor Eligio Torno, Rho, Prina, Badiali, Virgilio Bianchi. Abstracticism and the Scuola romana (Soldati and Cagli in particular) were being singled out by Interlandi as Jewish outcasts, indicating the beginning of the final decline, while sales did not decline sharply but indicated a change in favour of private investment.[45]

Sartoris portrayed this lost generation neatly when he wrote that even when fighting these artists (for example Terragni on the Russian front) think about their art and their science and in this way show their heroism.[46] Soon after Terragni died at home traumatized. The war years erased the dialectics between autonomy and heteronomy

[41] In his 1942 presentation Marinetti lists all different types of aeropittura: '*sintetica documentaria dinamica*', '*trasfiguratrice lirica spaziale*', '*essenziale mistica*', '*stratosferica cosmica biochimica*', '*aeroscultura*', '*sintentica trasfiguratrice*', '*polimaterica astratta simbolica cosmica*' and the '*astrazioni plastiche dei futuristi astratti*' of the Como-based artists, Alessandro Sagramora (ed.), *I futuristi e le Quadriennali* (Milan, Electa, 2008), 35.

[42] '*dinamismi astratti improntati ad una devozione assoluta all'Arte al Futuro alla Sintesi*', ibid., 232.

[43] '*[o]gni contatto con la realtà contingente è escluso*' '*[l]a pittura rimane trasfigurazione lirica, meccanica, spirituale, plastica e geometrica*', ibid., 223.

[44] Ibid., 30–1. As specified by Tomasella: '*gli aeropittori, che già affollano numerosi e con numerose opere l'ex padiglione belga, dominano incontrastati anche nel padiglione della Regia Aeronautica dedicato al concorso della guerra*', Biennali di guerra, 93.

[45] Salaris, *Artecrazia*, 213.

[46] Sartoris, 'Artisti, poeti e student in guerra', *Il Popolo d'Italia*, (19 June 1943).

which had characterized the file of the avant-gardes under the regime. Such a dialectical relationship had guaranteed innovation within the contains of a repressive political apparatus. Once the equation lost its balance, the result was a diluted avant-garde which tried to survive by adopting almost randomly aesthetic paradigms unable to voice the contradictions and complexities of the era they lived under, able merely to portray them with a diminished figurative realism which had lost topicality.

Exodus

The system of the arts during the dictatorship was naturally a complex one: autonomous and heteronomous at the same time in relation to State art, modern as well as traditional and organized around varying declensions of the aesthetic paradigm of realism and 'construction'. In other words, it was functional, rationalized, pluralistic and eccentric. Still, only if we take a synoptic and synergistic view of the art world, can we see just how many of these forms of artistic expressions intersected with one another into a system held together by the overarching concept of State art. The arts contributed to the totalitarian project in so far as they helped shape the imaginary that the dictatorship wanted to provide to, and for, the people. Sometimes, this was achieved through Public art or propaganda art in the most explicit terms; at other times, by deploying subtler and refined artistic statements, the arts retained a degree of autonomy that allowed for experimentation. Sometimes, all of this was theorized; sometimes it was politically orchestrated; and, at other times, it was a spontaneous response to the spontaneous desire for innovation. Architecture, too, was part of this system in a somewhat erratic manner. The aspiration towards a new architecture was realized through public buildings and personal homes. The houses were at the same time affordable, experimental or even upper class, but all of them nonetheless retained the ambition of creating new spaces for the citizen both as an individual and as a collectivity. New towns were one of the regime's flagships but new neighbourhoods did contribute to the reconfiguration of the Italian social fabric within large and small cities.

In all this, the elite and the popular cannot be taken as separate categories as Gramsci has notoriously stated about Italian culture, since the guiding principles for understanding the relationship between the arts and politics cut across forms of interlinked subjectivity and objectivity, rites for the sacralization of the New Man/ Woman and schemes for the modernization of the public space. The arts were asked to contribute to such endeavours, which were foundational to the totalitarian project. The arts subsidized the totalitarian project when they were functional to the advancement and transformation of the public sphere where politics was also operating.

Not very differently, modernity and modernization navigated the political and the artistic landscapes at both elite and popular levels. As mere abstract, overarching concepts, these notions can become devoid of meaning; but if punctually historicized, they can prove to be forces for a probing scrutiny of complex phenomena. In enacting social modernity, the arts could retain a degree of autonomy and of freedom in innovation. The pluralistic, vague and eclectic attitude of the regime moved in parallel with the degree of autonomy the arts could allow themselves: the more the regime lost consensus and momentum, the more the arts lost autonomy and became heteronomous to the dictatorship. Yet such an equivalence was never fully realized, not even in war aeropainting. The *longue durée* of the experimental 1920s and the early 1930s had made it impossible for the arts to be simply the mirror of a dictatorship. The arts lived under, and with, the dictatorship; but more importantly, the arts endured through their pursuit of meaning, however precarious such an exploit can be.

The regime finally fell in 1943, but the artistic repertoire that had flourished over two decades did not fall with it. Mussolini's regime had not silenced the avant-gardes, nor had it silenced the arts en masse: rather, it had brought them together as a resorceful, resilient and, alas, chameleon-like system in the name of its own State art.

Bibliography

Abbreviations

f. file
F. folder
u. unity

Archives

Archivio Centrale dello Stato, Rome (ACS)
    Archivio Fondazione Piero Portaluppi, Milan
    Archivio Storico, Triennale, Milan
    Fondo Anceschi, Biblioteca dell'Archiginnasio, Bologna
    Fondo Bardi, held at the Archivio Storico Civico (ASC), Milan
    Fondo Giuseppe Rivolta (AGR), held at the Archivio Storico Civico (ASC), Milan
    L' Archivio del '900 (MART), held at the Museo d'Arte Moderna e Contemporanea di Rovereto e Trento, Rovereto

Secondary Sources

AA.VV., *Annitrenta, arte e cultura in Italia* (Milan, Mazzotta, 1982).
AA.VV., *Frontiere d'avanguardia. Gli anni del Futurismo nella Venezia-Giulia* (Gorizia, Arti grafiche Campestrini, 1985).
AA.VV., *Novecento. Catalogo dell'arte italiana dal futurismo a Corrente, n. 4* (Milan, Editoriale Giorgio Mondadori, 1994).
AA.VV., *Abstracta, Germania, Austria, Italia, 1919–1939* (Milan, Electa, 1997).
AA.VV., *Futurismi, Aeropittura. Aeropoesia, Architettura nel golfo della Spezia* (La Spezia, Cassa di risparmio della Spezia, 2007).
Adamson, Walter L., *Avant-garde Florence: From Modernism to Fascism* (Cambridge, MA, Harvard University Press, 1993).
Adamson, Walter L., 'The Culture of Italian Fascism and the Fascist Crisis of Modernity: The Case of *Il Selvaggio*', *Journal of Contemporary History*, 30/4 (1995), 555–75.
Adamson, Walter L., 'Avant-garde Modernism and Italian Fascism: Cultural Politics in the Era of Mussolini', *Journal of Modern Italian Studies*, 6/2 (2001), 230–48.
Adamson, Walter L., *Embattled Avant-Gardes: Modernism's Resistance to Commodity Culture in Europe* (Berkeley, University of California Press, 2009).
Adamson, Walter L., 'How Avant-Gardes End—and Begin: Italian Futurism in Historical Perspective', *New Literary History*, 41/4 (2010), 855–87.
Adorno, Theodor W., *Aesthetic Theory*, Robert Hullot-Kentor (ed.) (London, Continuum, 2002).

Adorno, Theodor W., and Max Horkheimer, *Dialectic of Enlightenment: Philosophical Fragments* (Stanford, Stanford University Press, 2002).

Adorno, Theodor W., Walter Benjamin, Ernest Bloch, Bertolt Brecht and Georg Lukács, *Aesthetics and Politics* (London, Verso, 2007).

Affron, Matthew, and Mark Antliff (eds), *Fascist Visions: Art and Ideology in France and Italy* (Princeton, NJ, Princeton University Press, 1997).

Alberti, Sandro, *Mino Rosso. Scultore e pittore 1904–1963* (Turin, Editris, 1993).

Alfieri, Dino, and Luigi Freddi, *Partito Nazionale Fascista. Mostra della Rivoluzione Fascista* (Milan, Industrie Grafiche Italiane, 1982).

Altara, Edoardo, *Compendio storico-tecnico delle ferrovie italiane*, vol. 1 (Cortona, Galosci, 2012).

Alvaro, Corrado, *Gente in Aspromonte* (Florence, Le Monnier, 1931).

Andreazza, Fabio, 'Prima della specializzazione. La traiettoria di Umberto Barbaro dalla letteratura al cinema', in Raffaele De Berti and Massimo Locatelli (eds), *Figure della modernità nel cinema italiano (1900–1940)* (Pisa, ETS, 2008), 315–31.

Andreotti, Libero, 'Architecture as Media Event: Mario Sironi and the Exhibition of the Fascist Revolution', *Built Environment*, 31/1 (2005), 9–20.

Andreotti, Libero, 'The Techno-aesthetics of Shock: Mario Sironi and Italian Fascism', *Grey Room*, 38 (2010), 38–61.

Antliff, Mark, 'Fascism, Modernism, and Modernity', *The Art Bulletin*, 84/1 (2002), 148–69.

Antonello, Pierpaolo, Matilde Nardelli and Margherita Zanoletti (eds), *Bruno Munari: The Lightness of Art* (Oxford Bern, Peter Lang, 2017).

Antonio Gramsci, *Pensare la democrazia* (Einaudi, Turin, 1997).

Appella, Giuseppe (ed.), *Carlo Belli 1920–1930. Gli anni della formazione* (Rome, Edizioni della Cometa, 2001).

Appella, Giuseppe, and Fabrizio D'Amico (eds), *Roma 1934* (Modena, Panini Edizioni, 1986).

Appella, Giuseppe, Gabriella Belli and Mercedes Garberi (eds), *Il mondo di Carlo Belli* (Milan, Electa, 1991).

Appella, Giuseppe, Laura Novati, Carlo Bertelli and Mauri Paolo (eds), *Vanni Scheiwiller e l'arte da Wildt a Melotti* (Cinisello Balsamo, Silvana Editoriale, 2019).

Astarita, Rossano, *Gli architetti di Olivetti: una storia di committenza industriale* (Milan, Franco Angeli, 2012 [2000]).

Avon, Annalisa, '"La casa all'italiana": modernità, ragione e tradizione nell'organizzazione dello spazio domestico dal 1927 al 1930', in Giulio Ernesti (ed.), *La costruzione dell'utopia. Architetti e urbanisti nell'Italia fascista* (Rome, Edizioni Lavoro, 1991), 47–66.

Azzoni, Giuseppe (ed.), *Fascismo a Cremona e nella sua provincia: 1922–1945* (Cremona A.N.P. I., 2013).

Baffoni, Andrea, *Contro ogni reazione. Enrico Prampolini teorico e promotore artistico* (Città di Castello, Lantana, 2015).

Bardi, Pietro Maria, *Rapporto sull'architettura (per Mussolini)* (Rome, Critica fascista, 1931).

Baxandall, Michael, *Painting & Experience in Fifteenth-Century Italy* (Oxford, Oxford University Press, 1988).

Belli, Carlo (with a note by Manuel Orazi), *Kn* (Macerata, Giometti & Antonello, 2016).

Ben-Ghiat, Ruth, 'The Realist Aesthetic in Italy, 1930–1950', *The Journal of Modern History*, 67/3 (1995), 627–65.

Ben-Ghiat, Ruth, *Fascist Modernities: Italy, 1922–1945* (Berkeley, University of California Press, 2001).

Benzi, Fabio (ed.), *Mario Sironi, 1885–1961* (Milan, Mondadori Electa, 1993).

Benzi, Fabio (ed.), *Corrado Cagli e il suo magistero. Mezzo secolo di arte italiana dalla Scuola Romana all'astrattismo* (Milan, Skira, 2010).

Benzi, Fabio, 'Arte di Stato durante il una storia di fallimenti nel segno dei maccanismi del "consenso"', *pianob. Arti e culture visive*, 3/1 (2018), 162–85.

Benzi, Fabio (ed.), *Dal Futurismo al Classicismo 1913–1924* (Cinisello Balsamo, Silvana Editoriale, 2018).

Berezin, Mabel, *Making the Fascist Self: The Political Culture of Interwar Italy* (Ithaca, NY, Cornell University Press, 1997).

Berghaus, Günter, *Futurism and Politics: Between Anarchist Rebellion and Fascist Reaction, 1909–1944* (New York/Oxford, Berghahn, 1996).

Berghaus, Günter, *Theatre, Performance and the Historical Avant-garde* (Basingstoke, Palgrave, 2005).

Bernardi, Michele, Alessia Cadetti et al. (eds), *'Il grano* di Pietro Gaudenzi. Stato di conservazione e problematiche di intervento'. *IV Congresso Nazionale IGIIC–Lo Stato dell'Arte* (L'Aquila, Accademia Di Belle Arti di L'Aquila, 2016).

Bertelé, Matteo, *Arte sovietica alla Biennale di Venezia (1924–1962)* (Udine, Mimesis, 2020).

Biasin, Gian-Paolo, 'Il rosso o il nero: testo e ideologia in *Rubè*', *Italica*, 56/2 (1979), 172–97.

Bignami, Silvia, and Antonello Negri (eds), *Anni '30: arti in Italia oltre il fascismo* (Florence, Giunti, Fondazione Palazzo Strozzi, 2012).

Billiani, Francesca, *Culture nazionali e narrazioni straniere: Italia 1903–1943* (Florence, Le Lettere, 2007).

Billiani, Francesca, 'Return to Order as Return to Realism in Two Italian Elite Literary Magazines of the 1920s and the 1930s: *La ronda* and *Orpheus*', *The Modern Language Review*, 108/3 (2013), 839–62.

Billiani, Francesca, 'Documenting the Real across Modernity in the 1930s: Political and Aesthetic Debates around and about the Novel in Fascist Italy', *Italian Studies*, 71/4 (2016), 477–95.

Billiani, Francesca, and Laura Pennacchietti, *Architecture and the Novel under the Italian Fascist Regime* (Basingstoke, Palgrave, 2019).

Biondi, Marino, and Alessandro Borsotti (eds), *Cultura e fascismo. Letteratura e spettacolo di un Ventennio* (Florence, Ponte delle Grazie, 1996).

Birolli, Zeno (ed.), *Pittura e scultura futuriste* (Milan, Abscondita, 2006).

Biscossa, Franco, '"Quadrante": il dibattito e la polemica', in Giulio Ernesti (ed.), *La costruzione dell'utopia. Architetti e urbanisti nell'Italia fascista* (Rome, Edizioni Lavoro, 1991), 67–89.

Biscottini, Paolo (ed.), *Arte a Milano 1906–1929* (Milan, Electa, 1995).

Bona, Rodolfo. *Il Premio Cremona (1939–1941) Opere e protagonisti* (Piacenza, Edizioni Scritture, 2016).

Bonfanti, Ezio, and Marco Porta, *Il gruppo BBPR nella cultura architettonica italiana 1932–1970* (Milan, Hoepli, 2009).

Bonino, Guido Davico [1985], 'Nota', in *Mario Soldati* (Palermo, Sellerio, 2003).

Borgese, Giuseppe Antonio, *Rubè* (Milan, Treves, 1921).

Borgese, Giuseppe Antonio, *Tempo di edificare* (Milan, Fratelli Treves, 1923).

Bossaglia, Rossana, *Il Novecento italiano* (Milan, Charta, 1995).

Bossaglia, Rossana, and Howard Rodger MacLean, 'The Iconography of the Italian Novecento in the European Context/L'iconografia del Novecento italiano nel contesto europeo', *The Journal of Decorative and Propaganda Arts*, 3 (1987), 52–65.

Bottai, Giuseppe, *Fronte dell'arte* (Florence, Vallecchi, 1943).

Bottai, Giuseppe, *La politica delle arti. Scritti 1918–1943*, Alessandro Masi (ed.) (Rome, Editalia, 1992).

Bragaglia, Anton Giulio, *Fotodinamismo futurista* (with essays by Maurizio Calvesi, Maurizio Fagiolo, Filiberto Menna and introduced by Giulio Carlo Argan) (Turin, Einaudi, 1970).

Braun, Emily, *Mario Sironi and Italian Modernism: Arts and Politics under Fascism* (Cambridge, Cambridge University Press, 2000).

Breuer, Stefan, 'The Truth of Modern Society? Critical Theory and Fascism', *New German Critique*, 131/44, no. 2 (August 2017), 75–103.

Briganti, Alessandra, 'Umberto Barbaro dall'avanguardia al neorealismo', *Letteratura italiana contemporanea*, 5/11 (1984), 187–209.

Briganti, Alessandra, '*Occidente* e la capitale delle avanguardie', *Letteratura italiana contemporanea*, 9/25 (1988), 1–24.

Brungardt, Christina, *On the Fringe of Italian Fascism: An Examination of the Relationship between Vinicio Paladini and the Soviet Avant-Garde*, PhD thesis (CUNY, New York University, 2015).

Buchignani, Paolo, 'Avanguardie durante il fascismo: Umberto Barbaro, il realismo, l'immaginismo', *il Mulino*, 36/313 (1987), 724–49.

Buonanno, Enrico, 'Il Novecento immaginario di Massimo Bontempelli', *Studi Novecenteschi*, 30/66 (2003), 239–62.

Bürger, Peter, *Theory of the Avant-Garde* (Manchester, Manchester University Press, 1984).

Buscaroli, Beatrice, Roberto Fabbri Floreani and Anna Possamai Vita (eds), *Scultura futurista 1909–1944. Omaggio a Mino Rosso* (Cinisello Balsamo, Silvana Editoriale, 2009).

Calvesi, Maurizio, *Le due avanguardie. Dal Futurismo alla Pop Art* (Rome-Bari, Laterza, 2020).

Campbell, Timothy C., '*Infinite Remoteness*: Marinetti, Bontempelli, and the Emergence of Modern Italian Visual Culture', *MLN*, 120/1 (2005), 111–36.

Cannistraro, Philip V., 'Mussolini's Cultural Revolution: Fascist or Nationalist?', *Journal of Contemporary History*, 7/3–4 (1972), 115–39.

Caprotti, Federico, 'Technology and geographical imaginations: representing aviation in 1930s Italy', *Journal of Cultural Geography*, 25/2 (2008), 181–205.

Caprotti, Federico 'Overcoming Distance and Space through Technology: Record Aviation Linking Fascist Italy with South America', *Space and Culture*, 147/3 (2011), 330–48.

Caprotti, Federico 'Profitability, practicality and ideology Fascist civil aviation and the short life of Ala Littoria, 1934–1943', *The Journal of Transport History*, 32/1 (2012), 17–38.

Caramel, Luciano (ed.), *Mario Radice. Catalogo generale* (Milan, Electa, 2002).

Caramel, Luciano, 'Carlo Belli e gli astrattisti italiani anni Trenta', in Gabriella Giuseppe Appella and Mercedes Garberi Belli (eds), *Il mondo di Carlo Belli* (Milan, Electa 1991), 69–98.

Carli, Carlo F., and Elena Pontiggia(eds), *La grande Quadriennale 1935. La grande arte italiana* (Milan, Electa, 2006).

Carpi, Umberto, *Bolscevico immaginista: comunismo e avanguardie artistiche nell'Italia degli anni venti* (Naples, Liguori, 1981).

Carpi, Umberto, 'Gli indifferenti rimossi', *Belfagor*, 36/6 (30 November 1981), 696–709.

Carpi, Umberto, *L'estrema avanguardia del Novecento* (Rome, Editori Riuniti, 1985).

Casero, Cristina, 'La Casa del Fascio di Como e la sue "decorazioni". Uno strumento di comunicazione del potere', *Ricerche di S/Confine*, I/1 (2010), 118–34.

Casetti, Giuseppe (ed.), *Movimento Immaginista a Roma nel V anno del R. F.* (Rome, Edizioni Stampa Alternativa, 1990).

Castellana, Riccardo, 'Realismo modernista. Un'idea del romanzo italiano (1915–1925)', *Italianistica: Rivista di letteratura italiana*, 39/1 (2010), 23–45.

Cazzato, Vincenzo (ed.), *Istituzioni politiche e culturali in Italia negli anni Trenta*, vol. 1 (Rome, Istituto poligrafico e zecca dello Stato, 2001).

Celant, Germano (ed.), *Post Zang Tumb Tuuum. Art Life Politics: Italia 1918–1943* (Milan, Fondazione Prada, 2018).

Celant, Germano, and Hulten Pontus (eds), *Arte italiana. Presenze 1900–1945* (Milan, Bompiani, 1989).

Cennamo, Michele, *Materiali per l'analisi dell'architettura moderna* (Naples, Fausto Fiorentino editore, 1973).

Ceserani, Remo, 'Italy and Modernity: Particularities and Contradictions', in Mario Moroni and Luca Somigli (eds), *Italian Modernism: Italian Culture between Decadentism and Avant-garde* (Toronto, Toronto University Press, 2004), 35–62.

Chioma, Gabriella, 'La sfida di Marinetti a tutti i poeti d'Italia e "L'Aeropoema parolibero del golfo della Spezia": Precedenti e cronaca analitica', in AA.VV., *Futurismi, Aeropittura. Aeropoesia, Architettura nel golfo della Spezia* (La Spezia, Cassa di risparmio della Spezia, 2007), 165–80.

Cibin, Alberto, *Corrado Forlin e il Gruppo futurista Savarè* (Trento, Scripta edizioni, 2012).

Cioli, Monica, *Il fascismo e la 'sua' arte. Dottrina e istituzioni tra futurismo e Novecento* (Florence, L. S. Olschki, 2011).

Cioli, Monica, *Anche noi macchine! Avanguardie artistiche e politica europea (1900–1930)* (Rome, Carocci, 2018).

Cioli, Monica, Maurizio Ricciardi and Pierangelo Schiera (eds), *Traces of Modernity: Art and Politics from the First War to Totalitarianism* (Frankfurt/New York, Campus Verlag, 2019).

Ciucci, Giorgio, 'L' autorappresentazione del fascismo. La mostra del decennale della marcia su Roma', *Rassegna*, 4/10 (1982), 48–55.

Ciucci, Giorgio, 'Lo stile di Libera', in Giorgio Mascherpa (ed.), *Adalberto Libera. Opera completa* (Milan, Electa, 1989), 62–90.

Ciucci, Giorgio, *Giuseppe Terragni. Opera completa* (Milan, Electa, 1996).

Ciucci, Giorgio, *Gli architetti e il fascismo: architettura e città 1922–1944* (Turin, Einaudi, 2002 [1989]).

Colombo, Katia, *Il 'foglio in rossetto e bistro'. 'Corrente' tra fascismo e antifascismo* (Udine, Mimesis, 2020).

Colombo, Nicoletta (ed.), '"Pittori di muraglie". Voci e vicende della pittura murale negli anni Venti e Trenta', in AA.VV. (eds), *Novecento. Arte e vita in Italia tra le due guerre* (Cinisello Balsamo, Silvana Editoriale, 2013), 59–67.

Colombo, Nicoletta, and Elena Pontiggia (eds), *Milano anni trenta. L'arte e la città* (Milan, Mazzotta, 2005).

Conforti, Claudia, Roberto Dulio and Marzia Marandola, '"La stazione di Firenze è bellissima"', in Claudia Conforti, Roberto Dulio, Marzia Marandola, Nadia Musumeci and Paola Ricco (eds), *La stazione di Firenze di Giovanni Michelucci e del Gruppo Toscano, 1932–1935* (Milan, Electa Architettura, 2016), 11–41.

Cresti, Carlo *Architetti e architetture dell' 'Era Fascista'* (Florence, Angelo Pontecorboli Editore, 2015).

Crispolti, Enrico, *Il mito della macchina e altri temi del futurismo* (Trapani, Celebes editore, 1969).

Crispolti, Enrico, 'Il Cagli "romano": traccia per una ricostruzione', in Enrico Crispolti (ed.), *Cagli e la 'Scuola di Roma' 1927-1938* (Milan, Electa, 1985), 12-40.

Crispolti, Enrico (ed.), *Fillìa. Fra immaginario meccanico e primordio cosmico* (Milan, Mazzotta, 1988).

Crispolti, Enrico (ed.), *Prampolini: dal futurismo all'informale* (Rome, Edizioni Carte Segrete, 1992).

Crispolti, Enrico (ed.), *Arte e Stato. Le esposizioni Sindacali nelle Tre Venezie (1927-1944)* (Milan, Skira, 1997).

Crispolti, Enrico (ed.), *Nuovi archivi del futurismo* (Rome, De Luca editori d'arte, 2010).

Dal Falco, Federica, *Stili del razionalismo: anatomia di quattordici opere di architettura* (Rome, Gangemi, 2002).

Danesi, Silvia, and Luciano Patetta (eds), *Il razionalismo e l'architettura in Italia durante il fascismo* (Milan, Electa, 1988 [1976]).

Dantini, Michele, *Arte e politica in Italia. Tra fascismo e Repubblica* (Rome, Donzelli, 2018).

De Angelis, Daniela, *Il Sindacato Belle Arti. Una ricerca sui documenti dell'Archivio delle Stato dell'E.U.R. a Roma* (Nettuno, Gruppo 88, 1999).

de Grassi, Marino (ed.), *Crali e il futurismo. Avanguardia culturale* (Gorizia, Edizioni della laguna, 2019).

De Maria, Luciano, *La nascita dell'avanguardia. Saggi sul futurismo italiano* (Venice, Marsilio, 1986).

De Micheli, Mario, *Le circostanze dell'arte* (Genoa, Marietti, 1987).

De Micheli, Mario *L'arte sotto le dittature* (Milan, Feltrinelli, 2009).

De Micheli, Mario *Le avanguardie artistiche del Novecento* (Milan, Feltrinelli, 2018 [1986]).

De Michelis, Cesare G., *L'avanguardia trasversale. Il futurismo tra Italia e Russia* (Venice, Marsilio, 2009).

De Sabbata, Massimo, *Tra diplomazia e arte. Le Biennali di Antonio Maraini (1928-1942)* (Udine, Forum, 2006).

De Sabbata, Massimo, *Mostre d'arte a Milano negli anni Venti: dalle origini del Novecento alle prime mostre sindacali, 1920-1929* (Turin, Allemandi, 2012).

de Seta, Cesare, 'Cultura e architettura in Italia fra le due guerre: continuità e discontinuità', in Silvia Danesi and Luciano Patetta (eds), *Il razionalismo e l'architettura in Italia durante il fascismo* (Milan, Electa [1976] 1988), 7-11.

de Seta, Cesare, *La cultura architettonica in Italia tra le due guerre* (Naples, Electa Napoli, 1998).

de Seta, Cesare, *Architetti italiani del novecento* (Milan, Electa, 2006).

Del Puppo, Alessandro, 'Da Soffici a Bottai. Una introduzione alla politica fascista delle arti in Italia', *Revista de Història da Arte e Arqueologia*, 2 (1995-6), 192-204.

Del Puppo, Alessandro, 'Il "realismo magico" e la fortuna dei primitivi nella pittura italiana dei primi anni Venti', in Mario Sartor (ed.), *Realismo magico fantastico e iperrealismo nell'arte e nella letteratura latinoamericane* (Udine, Forum, 2005), 46-61.

Del Puppo, Alessandro, *Egemonia e consenso: Ideologie visive nell'arte italiana del Novecento* (Macerata, Quodlibet, 2019).

Di Giovanna, Maria, *Teatro e narrativa di Umberto Barbaro* (Rome, Bulzoni, 1992).

Doordan, Denis, *Building Modern Italy: Italian Architecture, 1914-1936* (Princeton, NJ, Princeton Architectural Press, 1988).

D' Orsi, Angelo, *Il futurismo tra cultura e politica. Reazione o rivoluzione?* (Rome, Salerno editrice, 2009).

Durante, Lea, 'Avanguardia e realismo in *Luce fredda* di Umberto Barbaro', *Critica letteraria*, 28/1 (2000), 111–27.

Duranti, Massimo (ed.), *Gerardo Dottori. Pittura totale* (Bologna, Edizioni Galleria Marescalchi, 1993).

Eisenmann, Peter, 'Giuseppe Terragni e l'idea di testo critico', in Giorgio Ciucci (ed.), *Giuseppe Terragni* (Milan, Electa, 1996), 139–48.

Emanuelli, Enrico, *Radiografia di una notte* (Milan, Ceschina, 1932).

Esposito, Roberto, *Il sistema dell'indifferenza. Moravia e il fascismo* (Bari, Dedalo, 1978).

Esposito, Fernando, 'In "the shadow of the winged machine … ": The Esposizione dell' Aeronautica Italiana and the Ascension of Myth in the Slipstream of Modernity', *modernism/modernity*, 19/1 (2012), 139–152.

Esposito, Fernando, *Fascism, Aviation and Mythical Modernity* (Basingstoke, Palgrave, 2015).

Etlin, Richard, 'Italian Rationalism', *Progressive Architecture*, (July 1983), 86–94.

Etlin, Richard, *Modernism in Italian Architecture, 1890–1940* (Cambridge, MA, MIT Press, 1991).

Evangelisti, Silvia, and Jeffrey Schnapp (eds), *Universo Futurista* (San Lazzaro Savena, Fondazione Cirulli, 2019).

Evangelisti, Silvia (ed.), *Fillìa e l'avanguardia futurista negli anni del fascismo* (Milan, Mondadori, 1996).

Fabbri, Fabiano, *I due Novecento. Gli anni Venti fra arte e letteratura: Bontempelli versus Sarfatti* (Lecce, Manni, 2003).

Fagiolo dell'Arco, Maurizio, *Classicismo pittorico. Metafisica, Valori Plastici, Realismo Magico e '900'* (Genova, Costa e Nolan, 1991).

Fagone, Vittorio, 'Arte, politica e propaganda', in *Annitrenta: arte e cultura in Italia* (Milan, Mazzotta, 1982), 43–52.

Fagone, Vittorio, *L'arte all'ordine del giorno. Figure e idee in Italia da Carrà a Birolli* (Milan, Feltrinelli, 2001).

Falasca-Zamponi, Simonetta, *Fascist Spectacle: The Aesthetics of Power in Mussolini's Italy* (Berkeley, University of California Press, 2000).

Fergonzi, Flavio, 'Dalla monumentalità alla scultura arte monumentale', in Flavio Fergonzi and Maria Teresa Roberto (eds), *La scultura monumentale negli anni del fascismo. Arturo Martini e il Monumento al Duca d'Aosta* (Turin, Umberto Allemandi, 1982), 135–211.

Ferme, Vittorio, 'Redefining the Aesthetics of Fascism: the Battle between the Ancients and the Moderns Revisited', *Symposium: A Quarterly Journal in Modern Literatures*, 52/2 (1998), 67–84.

Ferrari, Daniela (ed.), *Margherita Sarfatti, Il Novecento italiano nel mondo* (Milan, Electa, 2018).

Ferrari, Gian Claudia, *Sironi. Opere 1919–1959* (Milan, Charta, 2002).

Fillìa, *La nuova architettura* (Turin, Utet, 1931).

Fioravanti, Gigliola, *Inventario. Partito Nazionale Fascista. Mostra della Rivoluzione Fascista* (Rome, Archivio Centrale dello Stato, 1980).

Fonti, Daniela (ed.) *Thayaht. Un futurista eccentrico* (Rome, Manfredi edizioni, 2017).

Forgacs, David, and Geoffrey Nowell-Smith(eds), *Antonio Gramsci: Selections from Cultural Writings* (London, Lawrence and Wishart, 1985).

Fossati, Paolo, *L'immagine sospesa. Pittura e scultura astratte in Italia, 1934–40* (Turin, Einaudi, 1972).

Gagliardi, Alessio, *Il corporativismo fascista* (Rome-Bari, Laterza, 2010).

Gazzotti, Melania, and Anna Villari (eds), *Futurismo e Dada. Da Marinetti a Tzara. Mantova e l'Europa nel segno dell'Avanguardia* (Cinisello Balsamo, Silvana Editoriale, 2010).

Gentile, Emilio, *Il mito dello stato nuovo dall'antigiolittismo al fascismo* (Rome-Bari, Laterza, 1982).

Gentile, Emilio, 'Fascism as Political Religion', *Journal of Contemporary History*, 25 (1990), 229–51.

Gentile, Emilio, *The Struggle for Modernity: Nationalism, Futurism and Fascism* (Westport, Praeger, 2003).

Gentile, Emilio, *Fascismo di pietra* (Rome-Bari, Laterza, 2007).

Gentile, Emilio, *Il culto del Littorio. La sacralizzazione della politica nell'Italia fascista* (Rome-Bari, Laterza, 2009).

Ghirardo, Diane Y., 'Politics of a Masterpiece: The Vicenda of the Decoration of the Façade of the Casa del Fascio, Como, 1936–39', *The Art Bulletin*, 62/3 (1980), 466–78.

Ghirardo, Diane Y., 'Architects, Exhibitions, and the Politics of Culture in Fascist Italy', *Journal of Architectural Education*, 45/2 (1992), 67–75.

Ghirardo, Diane Y., 'Città Fascista: Surveillance and Spectacle', *Journal of Contemporary History*, 31/2 (1996), 347–72.

Ghirardo, Diane Y., *Italy: Modern Architectures in History* (London, Reaktion Books, 2013).

Ginex, Giovanna, Tulliola Sparagni and Vittorio Fagone (eds), *Muri ai pittori. Pittura murale e decorazione in Italia 1930-1950* (Milan, Mazzotta, 1999).

Gino Pollini, 'Fabbrica e quartiere a Ivrea', in Marcello Fabbri and Antonella Greco (eds), *La comunit. concreta: progetto ed immagine. Il pensiero e le iniziative di Adriano Olivetti nella formazione della cultura urbanistica ed architettonica italiana* (Rome, Fondazione Adriano Olivetti, 1988), 155–9.

Giuntini, Andrea, 'Management e progetto nelle ferrovie italiane tra le due guerre', in Mauro Cozzi, Ezio Godoli and Paola Pettenella (eds), *Angiolo Mazzoni (1894-1979): architetto ingegnere del Ministero delle Comunicazioni* (Milan, Skira, 2003), 99–110.

Godoli, Ezio, *Guide all'architettura moderna: Il Futurismo* (Rome-Bari, Laterza, 1983).

Goldmann, Lucien, *Towards a Sociology of the Novel* (London, Tavistock, [1964], 1975).

Golomstock, Igor, *Totalitarian Art: In the Soviet Union, the Third Reich, Fascist Italy and The People's Republic of China* (London, Collins Harvill, 1990).

Gori, Giuliano (ed.), *Anni creativi al Milione 1932-1939* (Cinisello Balsamo, Silvana Editoriale, 1980).

Gramigna, Giuliana, and Sergio Mazza, *Milano* (Milan, Hoepli, 2005).

Gramsci, Antonio, *Pensare la democrazia* (Einaudi, Turin, 1997).

Grandi, Maurizio, and Attilio Pracchi, *Guida all'architettura moderna* (Milan, Libraccio, 2008).

Greene, Vivien (ed.), *Italian Futurism 1909-1944: Reconstructing the Universe* (New York, The Solomon R. Guggenheim Museum, 2014).

Gregotti, Vittorio, and Giovanni Marzari (eds), *Luigi Figini, Gino Pollini: opera completa: [1927-1991]* (Milan, Electa, 1997).

Gregotti, Vittorio, 'Milano e la cultura architettonica tra le due guerre', in Silvia Danesi and Luciano Patetta (eds), *Il razionalismo e l'architettura in Italia durante il fascismo* (Milan, Electa, 1988 [1976]), 16–31.

Griffin, Roger, *Modernism and Fascism: The Sense of a Beginning under Mussolini and Hitler: The Sense of a New Beginning under Mussolini and Hitler* (Basingstoke, Palgrave, 2007).

Grillandi, Massimo, *Mario Soldati* (Florence, La Nuova Italia, 1979).

Gropius, Walter, *The New Architecture and the Bauhaus* (London, Faber & Faber, 1968).

Groys, Boris, *The Total Art of Stalinism: Avant-Garde, Aesthetic Dictatorship and Beyond* (London, Verso, 2011).

Güntert, Georges, 'Né dannunziano né verista: Corrado Alvaro e i racconti di *Gente in Aspromonte*', *Esperienze Letterarie*, 29/3 (2004), 19–42.

Herf, Jeffrey, 'Dialectic of Enlightenment Reconsidered', *New German Critique*, 117/39, no. 3 (Fall 2012), 81–9.

Ialongo, Ernest, *Filippo Tommaso Marinetti: The Artist and his Politics* (Madison-Teaneck, Fairleigh Dickinson University Press, 2015).

Iannacone, Giuseppe, *Il fascismo sintetico* (Milan, Greco & Greco, 1999).

Irace, Fulvio, *Giovanni Muzio 1893–1982: opere* (Milan, Electa, 1984).

Isastia, Alessandro, and Orsina Simona Pierini (eds), *Case milanesi 1923–1973. Cinquant'anni di architettura residenziale a Milano* (Milan, Hoepli, 2017).

Isnenghi, Mario, 'Per la storia delle istituzioni cultural fasciste', *Belfagor*, 30/3 (1975), 249–75.

Isnenghi, Mario, *Intellettuali militanti e intellettuali funzionari* (Turin, Einaudi, 1979).

Jansen, Monica, and Luca Somigli, 'The "necessary modernization" of Sacred Art: A "double vision" on Modernism and Modernity', in MDRN (eds), *Time and Temporality in Literary Modernism* (1900–1950) (Leuven/Paris/Bristol, Peeters, 2016), 125–36.

Jeffrey Herf, 'Dialectic of Enlightenment Reconsidered', *New German Critique*, 117/39, no. 3 (Fall 2012), 81–9.

Jewell, Keala, 'Magic Realism and Real Politics: Massimo Bontempelli's Literary Compromise', *modernism/modernity*, 15/4 (2008), 725–44.

Kallis, Aristotle, *The Third Rome, 1922–43: The Making of the Fascist Capital* (Basingstoke, Palgrave, 2014).

Kirk Rossi, Terry, *The Architecture of Modern Italy/Visions of Utopia, 1900–Present*, vol. 2 (New York, Princeton Architectural Press, 2005).

Lacagnina, Davide, 'Politica, ideologia, militanza. Pippo Rizzo, critico d'arte e uomo delle istituzioni', in Davide Lacagnina (ed.), *Immagini e forme del potere. Arte, critica e istituzioni in Italia fra le due guerre* (Edizioni di Passaggio, Palermo 2011), 97–122.

Laclau, Ernesto, *On Populist Reason* (London, Verso, 2005).

Lazarus, Neil, 'Modernism and Modernity: T. W. Adorno and White South African Literature', *Cultural Critique*, 5 (Winter 1986–7), 131–55.

Lazzari, Marino, *L'azione per l'arte*, with a preface by Giuseppe Bottai (Florence, Le Monnier, 1940).

Le Corbusier, *Towards a New Architecture* (Hawthorne, CA, BN publishing, 2013).

Lehmann, Eric, *Le ali del potere. La propaganda aeronautica nell'Italia fascista* (Turin, Utet, 2010).

Lewis, Pericles, *Modernism, Nationalism, and the Novel* (Cambridge, Cambridge University Press, 2000).

Lima, Antonietta Iolanda, 'Il palazzo delle Poste di Palermo', in Mauro Cozzoli, Ezio Godoli and Paola Pettenella (eds), *Angiolo Mazzoni (1894–1979): architetto, ingegnere del Ministero delle Comunicazioni* (Milan, Skira, 2003), 243–54.

Lista, Giovanni, *Dal Futurismo all'Immaginismo. Vinicio Paladini* (Bologna, Edizioni del Cavaliere Azzurro, 1988).

Lista, Giovanni, *Futurism & Photography* (London, Merrell Publishers and Estorick Collection, 2001).

Lista, Giovanni, *Arte e politica. Il futurismo di sinistra in Italia* (Milan, Mudima, 2009).

Lista, Giovanni, *Enrico Prampolini futurista europeo* (Rome, Carocci, 2013).

Lista, Giovanni, and Ada Masoero (eds), *Futurismo, 1909-2009. Velocità+Arte+Azione* (Milan, Skira, 2009).

Longari, Elisabetta, *Sironi e la V Triennale di Milano* (Nuoro, Ilisso, 2007).

Lukács, Georg, 'The Theory of the Novel', in Vassiliki Kolocotroni, Jane Goldman and Olga Taxidou (eds), *Handbook of Modernism* (Edinburgh, Edinburgh University Press, 1999), 225-9.

Luperini, Romano, and Massimiliano Tortora (eds), *Sul modernismo italiano* (Naples, Liguori, 2012).

Luti, Giorgio, *La letteratura nel ventennio fascista. Cronache letterarie tra le due guerre: 1920-1940* (Florence, La Nuova Italia, 1972).

Malvano, Laura, *Fascismo e politica dell'immagine* (Turin, Boringhieri, 1988).

Mangoni, Luisa, *L'interventismo della cultura: intellettuali e riviste del fascismo* (Rome-Bari, Laterza, 1974).

Mantero, Enrico, *Giuseppe Terragni e la città del razionalismo italiano* (Bari, Dedalo, 1993).

Marcianò, Ada Francesca, *Giuseppe Terragni. Opera completa 1925-1943* (Rome, Officina edizioni, 2008).

Mariani, Riccardo, *Razionalismo e architettura moderna: storia di una polemica* (Milan, Edizioni di Comunità, 1989).

Marra, Claudio, *Fotografia e pittura nel Novecento (e oltre)* (Milan, Bruno Mondadori, 2012).

Martinelli, Alberto, *Global Modernization: Rethinking the Process of Modernity* (London, Sage, 2005).

Masi, Alessandro, *Un'arte per lo stato. Dalla nascita della Metafisica alla Legge del 2%* (Naples, Marotta & Marotta, 1991).

Masoero, Ada, *Universo meccanico. Il futurismo attorno a Balla, Depero, Prampolini* (Milan, Mazzotta, 2003).

Masoero, Ada (ed.), *Futurismo* (Pisa, Fondazione Palazzo Blu, 2020).

Mauro, Walter, *Invito alla lettura di Corrado Alvaro* (Milan, Mursia, 1973).

Mazower, Mark, *Dark Continent: Europe's Twentieth Century* (London, The Penguin Press, 1998).

Mazzoni, Guido, *Teoria del romanzo* (Bologna, il Mulino, 2011).

Mele, Angelo, 'Corrado Alvaro. La Calabria favolosa e lirica e la civiltà tecnologica dell'Europa borghese, l'idillio paesano e la babele urbana, fra mito poetico e saggio utopico', in Giovanni Grana (ed.), *Novecento. Gli scrittori e la cultura letteraria nella società italiana*, vol. 6 (Milan, Marzorati, 1983), 5305-25.

Merjian, Ara, H., '"On the Verge of the Absurd": Munari, Dada, and Surrealism in Interwar Italy', in Pierpaolo Antonello, Matilde Nardelli and Margherita Zanoletti (eds), *Bruno Munari. The Lightness of Art* (Oxford Bern, Peter Lang, 2017), 27-63.

Millefiorini, Federica, *Tra avanguardia e accademia. La pubblicistica futurista nei primi anni Trenta* (Pisa, Giardini editori e stampatori, 2006).

Mitchell, W. J. T., *What Do Pictures Want? The Lives and Loves of Images* (Chicago, The University of Chicago Press, 2005).

Mondello, Elisabetta, Roma futurista: *I periodici e i luoghi dell'avanguardia nella Roma degli anni Venti* (Milan, Franco Angeli, 1990).

Mondini, Marco, 'The Construction of a Masculine Warrior Ideal in the Italian Narratives of the First World War, 1915-68', *Contemporary European History*, 23/3 (2014), 307-27.

Moravia, Alberto, *Gli indifferenti* (Milan, Bompiani, 1949).

Morelli, Romana Francesca (ed.), *Cipriano Efisio Oppo. Un legislatore per l'arte* (Rome, Edizioni De Luca, 2000).

Moroni, Mario, and Luca Somigli (eds), *Italian Modernism: Italian Culture between Decadentism and Avant-garde* (Toronto, Toronto University Press, 2004).

Murphy, Richard, *Theorizing the Avant-Garde: Modernism, Expressionism, and the Problem of Postmodernity* (Cambridge, Cambridge University Press, 1999).

Muthesius, Hermann [1975], 'Propositions', in Charlotte Bentono (ed.), *Documents: A Collection of Source Material on the Modern Movement* (Milton Keynes, Open University Press, 1979).

Negri, Antonello, Silvia Bignami, Paolo Rusconi, Giorgio Zanchetti and Susanna Ragionieri (eds), *Anni Trenta. Arti in Italia oltre il fascismo* (Florence, Giunti Editore, 2012).

Neri, Maria Luisa, *Enrico Del Debbio* (Milan, Idea Books, 2006).

Neudecker, Edith, *Gli edifici postali in Italia durante il fascismo (1922–1944)* (Latina, Casa dell'architettura edizioni, 2007).

Nicoloso, Paolo, *Gli architetti di Mussolini* (Milan, Franco Angeli, 1999).

Nicoloso, Paolo, *Mussolini architetto: propaganda e paesaggio urbano nell'Italia fascista* (Turin, Einaudi, 2008).

Orr, John, *Tragic Realism & Modern Society: The Passionate Political in the Modern Novel* (London, Macmillan, 1989).

Pagano, Giuseppe, *Architettura e città durante il fascismo*, in Cesare de Seta (ed.) (Milan, Jaca Book, 2008 [1976]).

Parkinson, John R., *Democracy & Public Space: The Physical Sites of Democratic Performance* (Oxford, Oxford University Press, 2012).

Parlato, Giuseppe, *La sinistra fascista. Storia di un progetto mancato* (Bologna, il Mulino, 2000).

Passamani, Bruno, 'Dall'alcova futurista d'acciaio al Tank ai Macchi 202. Energie futuriste e costruttiviste tra rivolta, utopia e realtà alla frontiera giulia', in AA.VV., *Frontiere d'avanguardia. Gli anni del Futurismo nella Venezia-Giulia* (Gorizia, Arti grafiche Campestrini, 1985), 18–61.

Patetta, Luciano, *L'architettura in Italia 1919–1943. Le polemiche* (Milan, Clup, 1972).

Paul, Catherine E., and Barbara Zaczek, 'Margherita Sarfatti & Italian Cultural Nationalism', *modernism/modernity*, 13/1 (2006), 889–916.

Pederson, Sanna, 'From Gesamtkunstwerk to Drama Music', in David Imhoof, Margaret Eleanor Menninger and Anthony J. Steinhoff (eds), *The Total Work of Art: Foundations, Articulations, Inspirations* (New York/Oxford, Berghahn, 2016), 39–55.

Pellegrini, Sonia (ed.), *L'officina del volo: futurismo, pubblicità e design 1908–1938* (Cinisello Balsamo, Silvana Editoriale, 2009).

Pensky, Max, 'Method and time: Benjamin dialectical images', in David S. Ferris (ed.), *The Cambridge Companion to Walter Benjamin* (Cambridge, Cambridge University Press, 2004), 185–8.

Persico, Edoardo, *Destino e modernità. Scritti d'arte (1929–1935)* (Milan, Medusa, 2001).

Petropoulos, Jonathan, *Artists under Hitler: Collaboration and Survival in Nazi Germany*, (New Haven, CT, Yale University Press, 2014).

Piacentini, Marcello, *Architettura moderna*, Mario Pisani (ed.) (Venice, Marsilio, 1996).

Pinottini, Marzio, *Diulgheroff Futurista. Collages polimaterici 1927-1977* (Milan, All'insegna del pesce d'oro, Scheiwiller, 1977).

Poggi, Christine, 'The Return of the Repressed: Tradition as Myth in Futurist Fascism', in Claudia Lazzaro and Roger J. Crum (eds), *Donatello among the Blackshirts: History and Modernity in the Visual Culture of Fascist Italy* (Ithaca, NY, Cornell University Press, 2005), 203–22.

Poggi, Christine, *Inventing Futurism* (Princeton and Oxford, NJ, Princeton University Press, 2009).

Poggioli, Renato, *Teoria dell'avanguardia* (Bologna, il Mulino, 1962).

Ponti Licitra, Lisa, *Giò Ponti: The Complete Works 1923–1978* (London, Thames & Hudson, 1990).

Pontiggia, Elena (ed.), *Il Milione e l'Astrattismo, 1932–1938. La galleria, Licini e i suoi amici* (Milan, Electa, 1988).

Pontiggia, Elena (ed.), *Sironi: Il mito dell'architettura* (Milan, Mazzotta, 1990).

Pontiggia, Elena, 'Tra la Grecia e l'Europa. Carlo Belli teorico dell'astrattismo', in Giuseppe Appella, Gabriella Belli and Mercedes Garberi (eds), *Il mondo di Carlo Belli* (Milan, Electa, 1991), 99–116.

Pontiggia, Elena (ed.), *Da Boccioni a Sironi. Il mondo di Margherita Sarfatti* (Milan, Skira, 1997).

Pontiggia, Elena, *Il Novecento italiano* (Milan, Abscondita, 2002).

Pontiggia, Elena, *Modernità e classicità. Il Ritorno all'ordine in Europa, dal primo dopoguerra agli anni Trenta* (Milan, Bruno Mondadori, 2008).

Pontiggia, Elena (ed.), *Il movimento di* Corrente (Milan, Abscondita, 2012).

Prampolini, Enrico, *Arte polimaterica (Verso un'arte collettiva?)* (Rome, Edizioni del secolo, 1944).

Pratesi, Mauro (ed.), *Futurismo e bon ton. I fratelli Thayaht e Ram* (Milan, Leo S. Olschki editore, 2005).

Rancière, Jacques, *Aisthesis: Scenes from the Aesthetic Regime of Art* (London, Verso, 2013).

Rancière, Jacques, *The Politics of Aesthetics: The Distribution of the Sensible* (London, Bloomsbury, 2013).

Rasmussen, Mikkel Bolt, and Jacob Wamberg (eds), *Totalitarian Art and Modernity* (Aarhus, Aarhus University Press, 2010).

Ratti, Marzia, 'Il palazzo delle Poste della Spezia e i mosaici futuristi di Prampolini e Fillìa', in Mauro Cozzoli, Ezio Godoli and Paola Pettenella (eds), *Angiolo Mazzoni (1874–1979): architetto, ingegnere del Ministero delle Comunicazioni* (Milan, Skira, 2003), 283–94.

Rebeschini, Claudio (ed.), *Aeropittura. La seduzione del volo* (Milan, Skira, 2017).

Rifkind, David, 'Furnishing the Fascist Interior: Giuseppe Terragni, Mario Radice and the Casa del Fascio', *History*, 10/2 (2006), 157–70.

Rifkind, David, *The Battle for Modernism: Quadrante and the Politicization of Architectural Discourse in Fascist Italy* (Vicenza, Centro internazionale di studi di architettura Andrea Palladio; Venice, Marsilio, 2012).

Roberts, David D., *The Total Work of Art in European Modernism* (Ithaca, NY, Cornell University Press, 2011).

Rundle, Christopher, *Il vizio dell'esterofilia. Editoria e traduzioni nell'Italia fascista* (Rome, Carocci, 2019).

Russoli, Franco, and Raffaele De Grada (eds), *Cagli* (Milan, SEDA, 1964).

Saggio, Antonino, *L'opera di Giuseppe Pagano tra politica e architettura* (Bari, Dedalo, 1984).

Sagramora, Alessandro (ed.), *I futuristi e le Quadriennali* (Milan, Electa, 2008).

Sai, Elisa, *Aeropittura, Futurism and Space in the 1930s: Continuity, Innovation and Reception* (PhD thesis, University of Bristol, 2010).

Salaris, Claudia, *aero ... futurismo e mito del volo* (Rome, Le parole gelate, 1985).

Salaris, Claudia, *Storia del futurismo* (Roma, Editori Riuniti, 1985).

Salaris, Claudia, *Artecrazia. L'avanguardia futurista negli anni del fascismo* (Florence, La Nuova Italia, 1992).

Salaris, Claudia, *La Roma delle avanguardie* (Rome, Editori Riuniti, 1999).

Salaris, Claudia, *Futurismi nel mondo* (Pistoia, Gli Ori, 2015).

Salvagnini, Sileno, *Il teorico, l'artista, l'artigiano del Novecento. Bontempelli, Terragni, Sironi* (Verona, Bertani editore, 1986).

Salvagnini, Sileno, *Il sistema delle arti in Italia, 1919–1943* (Bologna, Minerva soluzioni editoriali, 2000).

Salvati, Mariuccia, *L'inutile salotto. L'abitazione piccolo-borghese nell'Italia fascista* (Turin, Bollati e Boringhieri, 1992).

Santomassimo, Gianpasquale, *La terza via fascista: il mito del corporativismo* (Rome, Carocci, 2006).

Santoro, Marco, *Storia del libro italiano. Libro e società in Italia dal Quattrocento al nuovo millennio* (Milan, Editrice bibliografica, 2006).

Sartoris, Alberto, *Gli elementi dell'architettura funzionale. Sintesi panoramica dell'architettura moderna* (Milan, Hoepli, 1932 [1941]).

Savorra, Massimiliano, *Enrico Agostino Griffini: la casa, il monumento, la città* (Naples, Electa, 2000).

Scappini, Alessandra (ed.), *Thayaht. Vita, scritti, carteggi* (Milan, Mart-Skira, 2005).

Scaramuzza, Gabriele, 'Antonio Banfi tra "arte vivente" e "crisi dell'arte", in Sileno Salvagnini (ed.), *Banfi e l'arte contemporanea* (Naples, Liguori, 2012), 57–77.

Schnapp, Jeffrey, '18 BL: Fascist Mass Spectacle', *Representations*, 43 (1993), 89–125.

Schnapp, Jeffrey, *Anno X: la Mostra della rivoluzione fascista del 1932* (Pisa, Istituti editoriali e poligrafici internazionali, 2003).

Schnapp, Jeffrey, *Building Fascism, Communism, Liberal Democracy* (Stanford, Stanford University Press, 2004).

Schnapp, Jeffrey, 'The People's Glass House', *South Central Review*, 25/3 (2008), 45–56.

Schnapp, Jeffrey, 'Piero Portaluppi's Errant Line', in Francesca Santovetti (ed.), *Modernitalia* (Bern, Peter Lang, 2012), 53–75.

Schumacher, Thomas L., *Surface & Symbol: Giuseppe Terragni and the Architecture of Italian Rationalism* (Princeton, NJ, Princeton Architectural Press, 1991).

Scott, James, *Seeing Like a State: How Certain Schemes to Improve the Human Condition Have Failed* (New Haven, CT, Yale University Press, 1999).

Sechi, Mario, '"Critica Fascista" 1929–1932. Idealismo politico e fermenti di cultura nuova alla svolta del regime', *Lavoro critico*, 19 (1980), 271–322.

Sechi, Mario, *Il mito della nuova cultura: giovani, realismo e politica negli anni trenta* (Bari, Lacaita, 1984).

Sedita, Giovanni, *Gli intellettuali di Mussolini. La cultura finanziata dal fascismo* (Florence, Le Lettere, 2010).

Selvafolta, Ornella, 'Introduzione', in Luigi Figini, *L'elemento verde e l'abitazione* (Milan, Libraccio editore, 2012), x–xvi.

Settimelli, Emilio, *Il codice della vita energica. Ostrica d'Arno. Pensieri di arte e di vita*, Mario Verdone (ed.), *Scritti inediti* (Cosenza, Pellegrino, 2003).

Serravalli, Luigi, 'Carlo Belli da Rosmini a Kandinsky', in Giuseppe Apparella, Gabriella Belli and Mercedes Garberi (eds), *Il mondo di Carlo Belli* (Milan, Electa, 1991), 55–68.

Sironi, Andrea (ed.), *La grande decorazione* (Milan, Mondadori Electa, 2004).

Sironi, Mario, *Scritti editi ed inediti*, Ettore Camesasca (ed.) (Milan, Feltrinelli, 1980).

Soldati, Mario, *24 ore in uno studio cinematografico* (Palermo, Sellerio, 2003).

Somigli, Luca, 'Modernismo italiano e modernismo globale. Appunti per un dibattito in progress', *Narrativa*, 35/36 (2013/14), 65–75.

Stone, Marla S., *The Patron State: Culture and Politics in Fascist Italy* (Princeton, NJ, Princeton University Press, 1998).

Storchi, Simona, '*Il fascismo è una casa di vetro*: Giuseppe Terragni and the Politics of Space in Fascist Italy', *Italian Studies*, 62/2 (2007), 231–45.

Tafuri, Manfredo, 'Il soggetto e la maschera', *Lotus International*, 20 (1978), 4–13.

Talamona, Mariaida, 'Primi passi verso l'Europa (1927–1933), in Vittorio Gregotti and Giovanni Marzari (eds), *Luigi Figini, Gino Pollini: opera completa: [1927–1991]* (Milan, Electa, 1997), 55–81.

Tarquini, Alessandra, *Storia della cultura fascista* (Bologna, il Mulino, 2011).

Tempesti, Fernando, *Arte dell'Italia fascista* (Milan, Feltrinelli, 1976).

Tentori, Francesco, *P. M. Bardi: con le cronache artistiche de 'L'Ambrosiano' 1930–33* (Milan, Mazzotta, 1990).

Terraroli, Valerio (ed.), *Realismo magico. Origini, ragioni e sviluppi di una stagione della pittura italiana negli anni Venti e Trenta* (Milan, Electa, 2018).

Terrile, Maria Cristina, 'La narrazione dell'inettitudine in *Rubè* di Giuseppe Antonio Borgese', *Italica*, 72/1 (1995), 40–53.

Tomasella, Giuliana, *Biennali di guerra. Arte e propaganda negli anni del conflitto (1939–1944)* (Padova, Il Poligrafico, 2001).

Tortora, Massimiliano (ed.), *Il modernismo italiano* (Rome, Carocci, 2018).

Touraine, Alain, *Critique de la modernité* (Paris, Fayard, 1992).

Tranfaglia, Nicola, and Albertina Vittoria, *Storia degli editori italiani. Dall'Unità alla fine degli anni Sessanta* (Rome-Bari, Laterza, 2000).

Treves, Anna, *Le migrazioni interne nell'Italia fascista* (Turin, Einaudi, 1976).

Trivellin, Eleonora, *1933, la villa razionalista: BBPR, Terragni, Figini e Pollini* (Florence, Alinea, 1996).

Trucchi, Lorenza, 'Da "Kn" a "Interlogo"', in Giuseppe Appella and Maria Grazia Tolomeo (eds), *Carlo Belli e Roma* (Rome, Viviani arte, 1998), 37–40.

Troisi, Sergio, *Pippo Rizzo* (Sellerio, Palermo, 1989).

Urso, Simona, *Margherita Sarfatti: dal mito del Dux al mito americano* (Venice, Marsilio, 2013).

Veronesi, Giulia (ed.), *Edoardo Persico. Tutte le opere (1923–1935), primo volume: politica, letteratura, pittura, scultura, teatro, fotografia, grafica, varie* (Milan, Edizioni di Comunità, 1964).

Veronesi, Giulia, *Difficoltà politiche dell'architettura in Italia, 1920–1940* (Milan, Christian Marinotti edizioni, 2008).

Vittoria, Albertina, 'Le riviste di regime: "Gerarchia", "Civiltà fascista", "Critica fascista"', *Studi romani*, 28/3 (1980), 312–34.

Vittoria, Albertina, 'Totalitarismo e intellettuali: L'Istituto nazionale fascista di cultura dal 1925 al 1937', *Studi storici*, 23/4 (1982), 897–918.

Vittoria, Albertina, *Le riviste del duce* (Turin, Guanda, 1983).

Vivarelli, Pia, 'La politica delle arti figurative negli anni del Premio Bergamo', in AA.VV., *Gli anni del premio Bergamo. Arte in Italia intorno agli anni Trenta* (Milan, Electa, 1993), 24–38.

Voza, Pasquale, 'Il problema del realismo negli anni Trenta: *Il Saggiatore, Il Cantiere*', *Lavoro critico*, 21/22 (1981), 65–105.

Webber, Andrew J., *The European Avant-garde: 1900–1940* (Cambridge, Polity, 2004).

Wollaeger, Mark, with Matt Eatough (ed.), *Global Modernisms* (Oxford, Oxford University Press, 2012).

Zagarrio, Vito, *Primato. Arte, cultura, cinema del fascismo attraverso una rivista esemplare* (Rome, Edizioni di storia e letteratura, 2007).

Zevi, Bruno, 'Terragni cospiratore modenista', in Bruno Zevi (ed.), *Giuseppe Terragni*, (Bologna, Zanichelli, 1980), 9–17.

Zhdanov, Andrey, Maxim Gorky, Karl Radek, Nikolai Bukharin et al. (eds), *Soviet Writers' Congress 1934: The Debate on Socialist Realism and Modernism in the Soviet Union* (London, Lawrence and Wishart, 1977).

Zuidervaart, Lambert, 'The Social Significance of Autonomous Art: Adorno and Brüger', *The Journal of Aesthetics and Art Criticism*, 48/1 (Winter 1990), 61–77.

Zunino, Pier Giorgio, *L'ideologia del fascismo* (Bologna: il Mulino, 1985).

Index